China and Transboundary Water Politics in Asia

Water-related conflicts have a long history and will continue to be a global and regional problem. Asia, with 1.5 billion of its people living in shared river basins, and with very few transboundary rivers governed by treaties, is especially prone to such conflicts. The key to mitigating transboundary water conflicts and advancing cooperation in Asia is largely in the hands of China, the upstream country for most of Asia's major transboundary rivers. To avert the looming water crisis, apart from spending billions of dollars on domestic water transfer projects such as the South–North Water Diversion Megaproject, as well as on water conservancy and pollution abatement, China has sought to utilize the water resources of the major rivers that run across borders with neighbouring countries. On these transboundary rivers, China has built or plans to build large dams for hydroelectricity and major water diversion facilities, which has triggered anxiety and complaints from downstream countries and criticism from the international society.

This book aims to systematically examine the complex reality of water contestations between China and its neighbouring countries. It provides a discussion on transboundary hydropolitics beyond the state-centric geopolitical perspective to dig into various political, institutional, legal, historical, geographical, and demographic factors that affect China's policies and practices towards transboundary water issues. This book also provides a collection of comparative case studies on China's water resources management on the Mekong River with other five riparian states in the Lower Mekong region: the Salween River with Myanmar, the Brahmaputra River with India, the Amur River with Russia and Mongolia, the Ili and Irtysh Rivers with Kazakhstan, and the Yalu and Tumen Rivers with North Korea. Furthermore, this book sheds light on China's future role in global water governance.

Hongzhou Zhang is a Research Fellow in the China Programme at the S. Rajaratnam School of International Studies (RSIS) at Nanyang Technological University, Singapore.

Mingjiang Li is an Associate Professor and Coordinator of the China Programme at the S. Rajaratnam School of International Studies (RSIS) at Nanyang Technological University, Singapore.

Politics in Asia series

www.routledge.com/Politics-in-Asia/book-series/PIA

Negotiating the U.S.-Japan Alliance
Japan Confidential
Yukinori Komine

Chinese Foreign Policy Under Xi
Edited by Hoo Tiang Boon

A History of Human Rights Society in Singapore
1965–2015
Edited by Jiyoung Song

Japan's Security and Economic Dependence on China and the United states
Cool Politics, Lukewarm Economics
Keisuke Iida

Japan and the shaping of post-Vietnam War Southeast Asia
Japanese diplomacy and the Cambodian conflict, 1978–1993
Andrea Pressello

Japan's International Democracy Assistance as Soft Power
Neoclassical Realist Analysis
Maiko Ichihara

Reimagining Nation and Nationalism in Multicultural East Asia
Edited by Sungmoon Kim and Hsin-wen Lee

New Media Political Engagement and Participation in Malaysia
Sara Chinnasamy

China and Transboundary Water Politics in Asia
Edited by Hongzhou Zhang and Mingjiang Li

China and Transboundary Water Politics in Asia

Edited by
Hongzhou Zhang and Mingjiang Li

Routledge
Taylor & Francis Group
LONDON AND NEW YORK

First published 2018 by Routledge

2 Park Square, Milton Park, Abingdon, Oxfordshire OX14 4RN
52 Vanderbilt AVenue, New York, NY 10017

Routledge is an imprint of the Taylor & Francis Group, an informa business

First issued in paperback 2019

British Library Cataloguing-in-Publication Data
A catalogue record for this book is available from the British Library

Library of Congress Cataloging-in-Publication Data
Names: Zhang, Hongzhou, editor. | Li, Mingjiang, editor. | Container of (work): Moore, Scott, 1985– Assessing China's domestic hydropolitics.
Title: China and transboundary water politics in Asia/edited by Hongzhou Zhang and Mingjiang Li.
Description: New York: Routledge, 2018. | Series: Politics in Asia series | Includes bibliographical references and index.
Identifiers: LCCN 2017041169 | ISBN 9781138060654 (hardback) | ISBN 9781315162973 (ebook)
Subjects: LCSH: Water resources development—Political aspects—China. | Water resources development—Political aspects—Asia. | Water-supply—China—International cooperation. | Water-supply—Asia—International cooperation. | Water rights—China. | Water rights—Asia. | China—Foreign relations—Asia. | Asia—Foreign relations—China.
Classification: LCC HD1698.C5 C47 2018 | DDC 333.9100951—dc23
LC record available at https://lccn.loc.gov/2017041169

ISBN: 978-1-138-06065-4 (hbk)
ISBN: 978-0-367-37559-1 (pbk)

Typeset in Galliard
by codeMantra

Contents

Contributors

Anamika Barua, Department of Humanities and Social Sciences at the Indian Institute of Technology-Guwahati, India.

Arundhati Deka, the South Asia Consortium for Interdisciplinary Water Resources Studies (SaciWATERs), Hyderabad, India.

Eugene Egidarev, Pacific Geographical Institute, Far East Branch, Russian Academy of Sciences / Amur Branch of the World Wildlife Fund (WWF–Russia), Vladivostok, Russian Federation.

Safa Fanian, the South Asia Consortium for Interdisciplinary Water Resources Studies (SaciWATERs), Hyderabad, India.

R. Edward Grumbine, The Grand Canyon Trust, Arizona, USA; World Agroforestry Center (ICRAF) East and Central Asia, Kunming, Yunnan; and Kunming Institute of Botany, China Academy of Sciences, Kunming, Yunnan, China.

Vishaka Gulati, the South Asia Consortium for Interdisciplinary Water Resources Studies (SaciWATERs), Hyderabad, India.

Yanjun Guo, the Institute of Asian Studies at China Foreign Affairs University and Research Fellow at the Collaborative Innovation Center for Territorial Sovereignty and Maritime Rights.

Julian Kirchherr, Copernicus Institute of Sustainable Development, Faculty of Geosciences, Utrecht University, the Netherlands.

Mingjiang Li, S. Rajaratnam School of International Studies (RSIS), Nanyang Technological University, Singapore.

Zhifei Li, the National Institute of International Strategy, Chinese Academy of Social Science, China.

Scott Moore, the World Bank Group, Water Global Practice.

Johan Nordensvard, Department of Sociology, Social Policy, and Criminology, University of Southampton, Southampton, UK.

Giuseppina Siciliano, Center for Development, Environment, and Policy (CeDEP), School of Oriental and African Studies (SOAS), University of London, London, UK.

Eugene Simonov, International Coalition Rivers without Boundaries / Daursky Biosphere Reserve, Nizhny Tsasuchei, Zabaikalsky Kray, Russian Federation.

Frauke Urban, Center for Development, Environment and Policy (CeDEP), School of Oriental and African Studies (SOAS), University of London, London, UK.

Sumit Vij, Public Administration and Policy group, Wageningen University, the Netherlands.

Ruolin Wang, Sunshine Law Firm, Hangzhou, China.

Hongzhou Zhang, S. Rajaratnam School of International Studies (RSIS), Nanyang Technological University, Singapore.

Zhanggui Zhou, International Institute for Water Resources, Center for Non-Traditional Security & Peaceful Development Studies (NTS-PD), Zhejiang University, China.

Acknowledgements

The majority of the chapters published in this volume are based on the conference papers presented at the workshop "Hydropolitics and Conflict Management in Transboundary River Basins: China and its Neighbors", which was held at the Nanyang Executive Centre, Nanyang Technological University (NTU) in Singapore, on 22 July 2016. The workshop was funded by the China Programme, Institute of Defense and Strategic Studies, RSIS, NTU.

Acknowledgements should first be given to all the paper presenters and discussants at the workshop for their intellectual contribution: Aidar Amrebayev, Anamika Barua, Asit K. Biswas, Gang Chen, Ed Grumbine, Selina Ho, Julian Kirchherr, Scott Moore, Jiwei Qian, Dajun Shen, Evgeny Simonov, Otto Spijkers, Frauke Urban, Huijuan Wu, Mu Yang, Daojiong Zha, Jun Zhang, Zhanggui Zhou (listed according to surnames in alphabetical order).

All colleagues of the China Programme including Fengshi Wu, Irene Chan, James Char, Tiang Boon Hoo, Xue Gong, and RSIS staff Sharlene Ee, Farik Bin Mohd Hussain, and Scott Lai provided essential support at different stages of the project, without whom the workshop nor the book would have come to fruit.

We would like to take this opportunity to thank Cecilia Tortajada, Editor-in-Chief of the *International Journal of Water Resources Development*, for allowing us to use the revised versions of the papers published in a special issue with the Journal. Last, but not least, we would like to thank Chan Boh Yee for her editing support.

Acknowledgements

The majority of the chapters published in this volume are based on the conference papers presented at the workshop "Hydropolitics and Conflict Management in Transboundary River Basins: China and its Neighbors", which was held at the Nanyang Executive Centre, Nanyang Technological University (NTU) in Singapore, on 22 July 2016. The workshop was funded by the China Programme, Institute of Defense and Strategic Studies, RSIS, NTU.

Acknowledgements should first be given to all the paper presenters and discussants at the workshop for their intellectual contribution: Aidar Amrebayev, Anamika Barua, Asit K. Biswas, Gang Chen, Ed Grumbine, Selina Ho, Julian Kirchherr, Scott Moore, Jiwei Qian, Dajun Shen, Evgeny Simonov, Otto Spijkers, Frauke Urban, Huijuan Wu, Mu Yang, Daojiong Zha, Jun Zhang, Zhanggui Zhou (listed according to surnames in alphabetical order).

All colleagues of the China Programme including Fengshi Wu, Irene Chan, James Char, Tiang Boon Hoo, Xue Gong, and RSIS staff Sharlene Ee, Farik Bin Mohd Hussain, and Scott Lai provided essential support at different stages of the project, without whom the workshop nor the book would have come to fruit.

We would like to take this opportunity to thank Cecilia Tortajada, Editor-in-Chief of the *International Journal of Water Resources Development*, for allowing us to use the revised versions of the papers published in a special issue with the Journal. Last, but not least, we would like to thank Chan Boh Yee for her editing support.

Part I

Key factors shaping China's transboundary water policies and practices

1 Thirsty China and its transboundary waters

Hongzhou Zhang and Mingjiang Li

Introduction

At the Security Council meeting on "Maintenance of International Peace and Security: Preventive Diplomacy and Transboundary Water" held on 6 June 2017, Bolivian president Evo Morales noted that since 1947, some 37 conflicts have taken place between countries related to water. He added: "If current patterns of consumption continue unabated, two-thirds of the world's population will be facing water shortages as a daily reality by 2025" (Lederer, 2017). Growing water shortages could aggravate water conflicts among countries at the transboundary river basins. Asia, with 1.5 billion of its people living in shared river basins but very few transboundary rivers governed by treaties, is arguably most prone to water conflicts. While the risk of shared waters is widely recognized as a source of conflict (or conflict multiplier), the key to advancing transboundary water cooperation in Asia is largely in the hands of China, the upstream country for most of Asia's major transboundary rivers.

Despite having 19 per cent of the world's population (1.38 billion people), China has only 6 per cent of the world's freshwater supplies. Although China is one of the top 5 countries with the largest freshwater resources, its per capita water supply is only one-fourth of the global average, making it one of the most water-scarce nations in the world. China's water challenge is further compounded by a highly uneven spatial distribution. North China, with 65 per cent of the land area and 45 per cent of the country's total population, has only 17 per cent of China's total freshwater resources, whereas South China has 83 per cent of China's freshwater resources (Li & Wu, 2016). Owing to very low precipitation, North China relies heavily on groundwater supply. At the national level, groundwater supply only makes up 18.3 per cent of China's total freshwater supply; however, in some of the northern provinces such as Henan and Hebei, the figure can reach 50 per cent (Ministry of Water Resources, P.R. China, 2017). Worse still, water pollution has emerged as one of the most critical environmental challenges for China. A Greenpeace report in 2017 indicated extremely high water pollution levels in China's major cities. For instance, in Beijing, nearly 40 per cent of water bodies were too polluted for any use. In Tianjin, over 95 per cent of the water supply is unfit for human consumption. Local governments throughout the country have been digging deeper wells to find clean water, yet this has become harder to come by because 80 per cent of groundwater from major river basins is "unsuitable for human contact" (Greenpeace, 2017).

To avert the looming water crisis, apart from spending billions of dollars on domestic water transfer projects such as the South–North Water Diversion Megaproject, as well as on water conservancy and pollution abatement, China has sought to utilize the water resources of the major rivers that run across Chinese borders (He, et al., 2014; Yong, 2006). As complaints from its neighbouring states increase, China faces mounting pressures to improve its management of shared transboundary watercourses, because contention over transboundary water resources could potentially undermine the stability and cooperation needed for China's Belt and Road Initiative (BRI) to succeed.

Although the stakes are very high, current research on China's transboundary policies and practices still proves inadequate. In particular, many academic and journalistic articles outside China follow the realist approach to examine China's transboundary practices. In many articles, China is portrayed as a malevolent hydro-hegemon, whose unilateral actions to use shared water resources could spark "water wars". The popular "water wars" narrative has contributed to the securitization of transboundary waters.

This edited volume aims to adopt a multidisciplinary approach to systematically examine the complex reality of water interactions between China and its neighbouring countries. It provides a discussion on transboundary hydropolitics beyond the state-centric geopolitical arena to dig into political, institutional, legal, historical, geographical, and demographic factors that affect China's policies and practices towards transboundary water issues. This edited volume also provides a collection of comparative case studies on China's water resources management on the Mekong River with five riparian states in the Lower Mekong region: the Salween River with Myanmar, the Brahmaputra River with India, the Amur River with Russia and Mongolia, the Ili and Irtysh Rivers with Kazakhstan, and the Yalu and Tumen Rivers with North Korea. Furthermore, this edited volume aims to shed light on China's future role in global water governance.

China's transboundary waters

China as the water tower in Asia

"Transboundary water" does not only refer to transboundary rivers, but also includes lakes, inland waters, and aquifers (Han, 2015). China is one of the countries with the largest number of transboundary rivers on the planet, ranking third together with Chile and second to Russia and Argentina. As "Asia's water tower", China's transboundary policies inevitably affect many downstream countries and communities. Table 1.1 provides a summary of China's major transboundary rivers.

China's large dam projects for hydroelectricity and impressive water diversion facilities on these transboundary rivers have infuriated downstream countries

Table 1.1 Major transboundary rivers in China

River	*Basin area (10^3 Km^2)*		*River length (Km)*		*Origin*	*Countries*
	Total	*China*	*Total*	*China*		
Amur River	1843	887	3474	2854	China, Mongolia (Kherlen River)	China, Russia, Mongolia
Yalu River	63.8	32	795	795	China	China, Russia
Tumen River	33.2	22.9	505.4	490	China	China, Russia North Korea
Suifen River	17.3	10	443	258	China	China, Russia
Irrawaddy River	431	43.3	2150	178.6	China	China, Burma
Salween River	325	124.8	3673	2013	China	China, Burma, Thailand
Mekong River	800	164.8	4880	2129	China	China, Burma, Laos, Thailand, Cambodia, Vietnam
Pearl River	453.7	453.7	2214	2214	China	China, Vietnam
Brahmaputra River	622	330	3100	2070	China	China, Bhutan, India, Bangladesh
Ganges River	1073	2.3	2700	49	China	China, Nepal, India, Bangladesh
Indus River	1166	24.9	2880	419	China	China, India, Pakistan, Afghanistan
Red River	113	74	1280	677	China	China, Vietnam, Laos
Irtysh–Ob River	1640	53.7	4248	633	China	China, Kazakhstan, Russia, Mongolia
Ili River	151.2	56	1236	442	Kazakhstan	Kazakhstan, China

Source: (Li & Wu, 2016).

and triggered international criticism. For instance, China's hydro-projects on the Upper Mekong River have become one of the major sources of conflicts between China and Southeast Asian countries (see Chapters 4 and 7). Some scholars and diplomats view the Mekong River as "the next South China Sea" to derail Sino- Association of Southeast Asian Nations (ASEAN) relations. In 2012, Vietnamese President Truong Tan Sang said at the APEC meeting:

> We cannot deny the fact that tensions over water resources are threatening economic growth in many countries and representing a source of

> conflict, especially at a time when countries are accelerating their economic development. Dam construction and stream adjustments by some countries in upstream rivers constitute a growing concern for many countries and implicitly impinge on relations between relevant countries.
>
> (Yeophantong, 2013)

Similarly, China's plans to harness the waters of the Brahmaputra River have set off ripples of unease in the two lower riparian states, particularly India (see Chapter 9). Many Indian and international security experts have warned the world of future "water wars" between the two countries. In the case of the Ili and Irtysh Rivers, while China has shown more willingness to cooperate with Kazakhstan on transboundary river issues, soaring water demand in Xinjiang has resulted in the significant diversion of water flows from the Ili and Irtysh Rivers for China's internal use (see Chapter 10).

Water resources scarcity and conflicts

The majority of critics outside of China have followed the realist approach to examine China's transboundary practices (Baxter, 2014; Liebman, 2005; Menniken, 2007; Sinha, 2012; Svensson, 2012). Many articles have been written to describe China as a malevolent hydro-hegemon and warn that China's unilateral actions to utilize the shared water resources could lead to "water wars" (Chellaney, 2011, 2013; Christopher, 2013; Economy, 2008; French, 2014; Hussain, 2014; Padmanabhan, 2014; Nickum, 2008).

Nevertheless, some scholars take a different theoretical approach which focuses on China's overall hydropolitical approach to its shared rivers and downstream neighbours. Varis et al. (2014) focus on assessing the socioeconomic-environmental vulnerability of different river basins in China. They found that the low vulnerability level of the Chinese sections of the transboundary basins could (to a certain extent) explain China's "thin" transboundary water policies. Kattelus, Kummu, Keskinen, Salmivaara and Varis (2015) conclude that the lack of salience of international river basins in China's decision-making can be partially explained by geography: most border areas are relatively unpopulated and inhabited by minorities that lack economic or political clout. Biba (2014) believes that China has not acted in a manner consistent with the strictly uncooperative upstream hegemon as suggested by the theory of hegemonic stability. Instead, Biba reasons that China has repeatedly sought to reconcile its hydropolitics with its own broader policy objectives and those of its neighbours. Ho (2014) maintains that China manages its transboundary water as a subset of its broader relations with other riparian states, and this results in discernible differences in China's approaches to its international river systems. In another study, Ho (2016) compares case studies of the Mekong and the Ganges to understand China's and India's hydro-hegemonic behaviour. Ho points out that the regional context and domestic politics of hydro-hegemons constrain their behaviour and determine whether they have a positive or negative leadership style.

While the existing research has greatly contributed to the understanding of transboundary water issues, both in general and in the Chinese context, certain major issues need further study to shed light on China's transboundary policies and practices.

Unique characteristics of each river basin

Most studies on China's approaches to transboundary water issues tend to neglect the unique characteristics of each river (or river basin). This could potentially lead to faulty conclusions in comparative studies. For instance, the absence of a water-sharing treaty between China and other riparian states (or states on a river basin) could simply be due to the absence of conflict over shared water, particularly the quantity of water in that river basin. To better understand the key factors that influence China's responses to different basins, it is crucial to start with mapping the unique characteristics of each river (or river basin).

Different river basins have different physical and environmental characteristics: political, institutional, and legal frameworks; water demand and use patterns, and water-use efficiencies; and economic and management capacities. Figure 1.1 shows that transboundary rivers can be broadly divided into three major types: (1) transborder rivers, (2) border rivers, and (3) mixed rivers (i.e. a major river with many tributaries and multiple crossings at the border). This distinction has crucial implications. Countries with rivers running across the boundary might face resource-scarcity conflict, whereas countries where the river forms the border might face conflict caused by fluid and fuzzy borderlines (Gleditsch, Furlong, Hegre, Lacina, & Owen, 2006). In addition, empirical evidence suggests

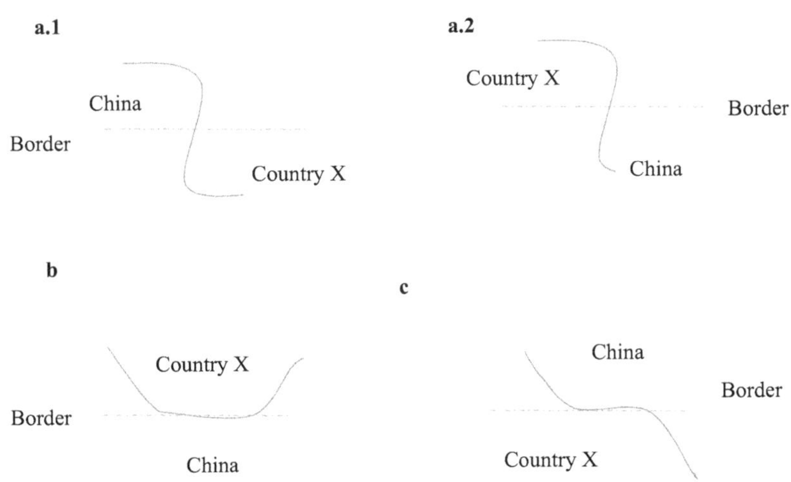

Figure 1.1 Different types of transboundary rivers.
Source: Own construction.

that water scarcity is positively related to conflict between countries that share a transborder river rather than border river (Gleditsch et al. 2006; Voza, Vuković, Carlson, & Djordjević, 2012), though some scholars argue that even upstream-downstream asymmetries appear to have a very small or no significant effect on international water cooperation and conflict (Beck, Bernauer, Siegfried, & Bohmelt, 2014). Nonetheless, a major river could consist of multiple tributaries. Some might be border rivers. Others might be transborder rivers with China either upstream or downstream. The rest could be mixed rivers.

Next, China certainly enjoys upstream advantages in most of the major transboundary rivers (such as the Brahmaputra, Mekong, Irrawaddy, and Salween) that pass through its territories. But in several cases, China occupies the downstream part of a transborder river or a tributary. Upper and lower riparian status could lead to very different approach by a state towards the shared water resources. While downstream states are in certainly in a disadvantaged position when it comes to non-navigational use of water, their negotiation power can be significantly enhanced with the control of the estuary of the river, which could be an important navigation channel, as in the case of the Amur (see Chapter 5), the Yalu (see Chapter 6), and to a lesser extent, the Mekong (Dore, Lebel, & Molle, 2012), given the desperate need of China's landlocked provinces to gain access to seas (Li Z., 2014).

Lastly, even under the most common upstream-downstream asymmetries, with China upstream, certain criteria must be met for transboundary rivers to become a source of interstate conflicts. According to Isaac and Shuval (1994), the likelihood of conflict can be determined by four key factors: (1) the degree of water scarcity, (2) the extent to which water supply is shared by more than one region or state, (3) the relative power of the basin states, and (4) the ease of access to alternative freshwater resources. The concept of the degree of water scarcity should go beyond water quantity to include water quality and other important aspects of rivers: fishing, navigation, and hydropower generation (Brochmann & Gleditsch, 2012).

Still, water could be a source of conflict multiplier, as in the case of China-India border disputes. Both India's and China's hydropower projects and potential water diversion plans are carried out in problematic areas where cooperation on transboundary water issues and regional economic development is undermined by ongoing territorial disputes (Feng, He, & Wang, 2015; Kattelus et al., 2015). When water issues intertwine with border disputes, more severe conflicts can be induced than the issues of water quantity.

Role of subnational actors

Even though the central government has the crucial role of defining formal governance structures and even informal interaction in transboundary water issues, an overemphasis of its role is inefficient for two major reasons. First, decision-making processes in transboundary water governance are highly dynamic due to different actors operating at multiple governance levels. How water is controlled and managed within each of the countries involved can shape the hydropolitical dynamics at particular transboundary river basins quite differently (Beach et al., 2000). Second, the state-centric approach does not explain how a particular national policy or approach to a transboundary water issue develops nor how it influences international power dynamics because the scalar relationships and interactions between regional, national, subnational actors are overlooked (Dore et al., 2012; Fox & Sneddon, 2007; Hirsch, 2016; Sneddon & Fox, 2006; Suhardiman & Giordano, 2012; Warner, 2012; Zawahri & Hensengerth, 2012). Yeophantong (2017) and Moore (2017a,b) noted that water policy does not always occur as a top-down, linear process when conflicts of interest and contending mandates occur between rival agencies, even in authoritarian and semi-authoritarian regimes. Instead, subnational units (i.e. provinces and cities) play an important role in water resource management, and their interests often vary considerably from those of their parent nation states (see Chapter 2).

China is often regarded as a unitary, centralized state, or even as an authoritarian state with formal authority residing at the central government. The relations between the central government and local governments, however, are far more complex than the concept of a unitary state might suggest (Young et al., 2015). The responsibilities and duties of transboundary water governance among the relevant ministries and official departments are separately assigned by the Chinese central government. As a result, there is not a single leading agency in China to coordinate different ministries' and departments' actions related to transboundary water issues. Worse still, there are too few intergovernmental coordinating mechanisms for expanding transboundary water cooperation. In fact, at the national scale, central ministries are mostly issue-oriented and do not have the power to settle trans-jurisdictional water disputes (Huang & Xu, 2017). Limited communication on transboundary water issues between the relevant departments and ministries inevitably causes delayed responses and compromised decision-making. The highly-fragmented water management system leaves room for local governments (particularly the provincial governments) and non-state actors (i.e. non-governmental organizations [NGOs] and energy enterprises) to intervene in transboundary water governance.

Local governments could be as important as central bureaucracies, particularly in the field of water resources management and overall interaction with neighbouring countries (Ho, 2014; Li, Beresford, & Song, 2011; Moore, 2014; Shen & Wu, 2016). Moore (2014) points out that it is quite possible for local governments to pursue competing, individual jurisdictional preferences and interests, even within a centralized political system that is explicitly designed to put constraints on them in the field of water resources management (see Chapter 2).

Furthermore, local governments are important actors in shaping the development of China's relations with neighbouring countries (Li, 2014, 2016). The development of China's relations with Southeast Asia is partially attributed to the local provincial governments in China, primarily Yunnan and Guangxi, in collaboration with their counterparts in the neighbouring countries. In many cases, local governments also take a lot of initiative. They make major proposals and actively lobby the central government for consent and support (Freeman, 2017; Ho, 2016; Räsänen et al., 2017).

Apart from national and provincial governments, the role of other players should not be neglected. Warner (2012) highlights the crucial role of international NGOs in shaping basin politics through their influential anti-dam discourse. Zawahri and Hensengerth (2012) point out that environmental activists can achieve what years of international negotiations between riparian states fail to accomplish. Media and civil-society groups have occasionally succeeded in halting the pollution of waterways by local enterprises. Scholars, NGOs, and the media in China have also powerfully advocated the suspension of the proposed hydro-projects (Guo, 2014; Magee, 2006; Mertha, 2009; Yeophantong, 2017).

From conflict–cooperation spectrum to water interaction

Previous studies on China's approach to transboundary water issues were often framed within the conflict–cooperation spectrum, which highlighted the central government's willingness and practices regarding the formulation of an international agreement or treaty (Li, 2015; Li & Wu, 2016; Ho, 2014; He, 2015; Biba, 2014; Ho, 2017). In particular, the water event intensity scale (BAR Scale) has been widely adopted (Wolf, Yoffe, & Giordano, 2003; Yoffe & Larson, 2001). The BAR scale defines water-related events from "–7", the most conflictive (war), through "0" (neutral events), and up to "+7", the most cooperative (voluntary merging of countries). Although the BAR scale could be a very useful tool in the quantitative analysis of China's policies and practices in different basins, the separation of conflicts on the one end of the spectrum and cooperation on the other end implies that "the less ugly faces of conflict and less pretty faces of cooperation are overlooked, and the political aspects of the interaction are routinely ignored" (Zeitoun & Mirumachi, 2008).

In addition, the existence of an international water agreement is also a poor indicator of the status of cooperation between two countries over shared water resources. As rightly pointed out by Warner and Zawahri (2012), even when international water agreements are signed, it does not mean that contracting states are actually cooperating, and the lack of agreement does not mean that riparian states are fighting. In other words, the presence of a treaty does not automatically translate into behaviour-altering cooperation. Worse still, treaties that lack the flexibility to accommodate changes may hinder cooperation, force countries to deviate from an agreement after it is in place, and constitute an immediate risk to international conflicts (Bruyne & Fischhendler, 2013). Furthermore, while water treaties, hydrological data-sharing arrangements, technical exchanges, and establishment of basin organizations may indicate some degree of concord at the interstate level, this does not necessarily imply a lack of discord at other levels of governance. Cooperation in the form of water agreements and treaties may amount to symbolic gestures aimed more at mollifying an irate public (Yeophantong, 2017).

Many consider China's reluctance to enter water-sharing agreements to share hydro-data with its neighbours as a clear indicator of China's uncooperative stance towards transboundary water issues. This could largely be due to several reasons. First, with the exception of the Ili and Irtysh Rivers with Kazakhstan, water shortage is not a major issue. Despite media hypes, China's actual utilization of transboundary waters upstream in the Mekong, Brahmaputra, Indus, and Amur is very low. Therefore, water-sharing is not a high priority in many basins' transboundary water negotiation. Second, highly-fragmented water governance also means that water-sharing agreement is very difficult to achieve. As Li et al. (2011) highlight, water-sharing among different provinces has been very problematic because local governments in China do not disclose scientific information regarding existing water resources and the annual amount of abstraction licensees approved by local authorities. Similarly, under the Indian Constitution, Indian states have exclusive power to regulate water supplies (Ching & Mukherjee, 2015). Inevitably, a serious conflict of interest exists between two main Brahmaputra-bearing states: Arunachal Pradesh (Southern Tibet) and Assam (Moore, 2016; Samaranayake, Limaye, & Wuthnow, 2016).

Therefore, a more robust and nuanced understanding of the multifaceted reality of transboundary water conflict and cooperation in China is required for further analysis and for better policymaking. Instead of a conflict–cooperation spectrum, the authors employ Zeitoun and Mirumachi's (2008) transboundary "water interaction" concept. Transboundary water interaction can be defined as the relations of coexisting cooperation and conflicts among communities, groups, or states over international or subnational waters, with a focus on interstate interaction (Zeitoun & Mirumachi, 2008).

A process-based framework to study transboundary water issues in China

With the above research goal in mind, this introductory chapter presents a process-based framework (see Figure 1.2) that is inspired by previous studies on the process-focused approach (Molle, Philippus, & Hirsch, 2010; Suhardiman & Giordano, 2012). This process-based framework essentially consists of three major steps.

Step 1 - river types, vulnerability, and conflict assessment

In China, transboundary rivers can be broadly divided into two groups: (1) transborder rivers with China upstream such as the Nujiang-Salween River, the Yarlung Zangbo-Brahmaputra River, the Yuanjiang-Red River Ganges River, the Indus River, the Lancangjiang-Mekong River, and the Irtysh River; and (2) border rivers, or transborder rivers with China downstream, and mixed rivers. Most of the transboundary rivers in the Northeast region are either border rivers or mixed rivers, including most notably the Amur, the Yalu, and the Tumen River. Although China is located upstream in most cases, there are a

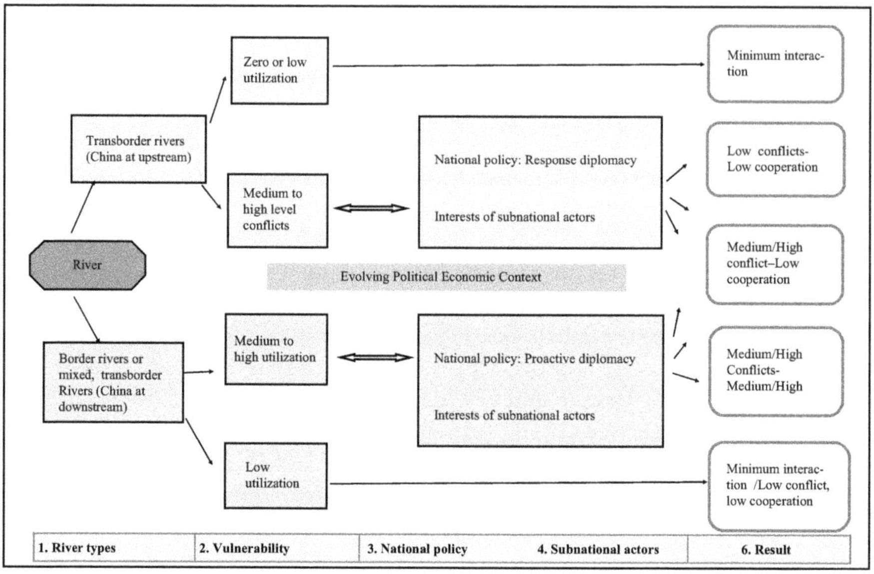

Figure 1.2 A process-based framework.
Source: Own construction.

few rivers where China is downstream. For instance, China is downstream from the Kherlen River that originates from Mongolia. The Ili River is a much more complicated case. The biggest source of Ili River-Tekesi River originates from Kazakhstan, and another important tributary of Ili River is Khorgos River that serves as the 150 km border between China and Kazakhstan.

The above categorization of China's transboundary rivers is helpful for analysing the degree of vulnerability from China's perspective and for predicting the likelihood of conflicts between China and neighbouring countries over a shared river. China feels more vulnerable when the country is located downstream of a particular transboundary river and over a border river. This is not only due to water-related issues, but also due to the impact of changes in the river course on national sovereignty.

In contrast, where China is upstream, China is at an advantage. This implies fewer incentives for China to enter into negotiations on transboundary water issues with neighbouring countries. The likelihood of conflicts between China and neighbouring countries is determined by four key factors: (1) the degree of water scarcity (including other important aspects of water), (2) the extent to which water supply is shared by more than one region or state, (3) the relative power of the basin states, and (4) the ease of access to alternative freshwater resources. For instance, only less than 6.7 per cent of transboundary water resources are utilized in water-abundant Northeast China and Russia's Far East. While water quantity is not a critical problem, severe pollution emitted by China's intensive industrial activities has made water *quality* the main source of transboundary river conflicts. Over 130 organic contaminants have been detected in Songhua waters (He et al., 2014). The difference between China's approaches to the Mekong River and the Brahmaputra River could be due to the higher likelihood of conflicts between China and Southeast Asian countries in the Mekong Basin compared to that of China and India in the Brahmaputra River Basin. The Mekong River is of great importance to downstream countries: China's utilization rate of hydraulic resources in Yunnan province reached 50 per cent

As the upstream big country in almost all the major river basins, China's role is very influential. It is far less vulnerable than its downstream neighbours because of the smaller Chinese population in these areas (see Table 1.2). The differences in terms of basin areas under China's control and size of Chinese population in the river basin could at least partially explain the variances of some of the key dynamics in each river basin. For instance, while both the Indus and the Brahmaputra Rivers originate from China and are both critically important to India, India is far less concerned with upstream China's activities on the Indus than on the Brahmaputra. With only a very small Chinese population and a tiny portion of river basin under Chinese control in the Indus River Basin (see Table 1.2), China is less likely to embark on mega hydro-projects and even if it does, the impact on the downstream country will be very limited.

In comparison, despite the pervasive "water wars" narratives, it is very unlikely that water resources from the Brahmaputra River could directly trigger severe conflicts between China and India. While 50 per cent of the river basin of the Brahmaputra is in Chinese territory, China only contributes 14–30 per cent to the total basin discharge, depending on different estimates or seasonal variations. According to Indian officials, precipitation in China contributes only 7 per cent to the flow of three tributaries of the Brahmaputra—Subansiri, Siang, and Lohit—which originate from China. The water utilization rate in the Brahmaputra River is very low. The current utilizable water of the Brahmaputra system is estimated to be a mere 4 per cent of the total discharge (Zhang, 2015).

Table 1.2 Major transboundary rivers, areas, and population

		Areas in China	*Areas in other countries*	*Population in China*	*Population in other countries*
1	Amur	895.2	1201.9	64.4	4.1
2	Red	84	73.5	11.7	18.1
3	Mekong	168.3	647.4	6.7	64.1
4	Salween	139.8	124.1	3.6	4.4
5	Irrawaddy	21.5	392.9	1.9	34.3
6	Brahmaputra	316.9	1320.3	1.7	645.6
7	Indus	86.1	1058.9	0.04	240.7
8	Irtysh	50.4	2960.6	0.4	28.2
9	Ili	57.7	364.3	2.2	2.9
10	Tarim, Junggar	1411.3	45.1	17	0.07

Source: Varis, et al., 2014.

Nonetheless, as an upstream state on most of its transboundary watercourses, China's great challenge lies in balancing its need for transboundary water with the needs of its downstream neighbours (Wouters & Chen, 2013).

Step 2 - national policies and overall bilateral ties

The degree of vulnerability and the likelihood of conflict will determine the central government's policies on transboundary water issues with neighbouring countries, and China's policies towards transboundary water issues will also be shaped by its overall relations with the neighbouring countries (see Table 1.3). In the absence of a comprehensive transboundary water policy, China manages its shared water issues as a subset of its bilateral relationship with neighbouring countries, or through a one-river, one-country approach (Ho, 2014; Li, 2015; Wouters & Chen, 2013). This, to a certain extent, explains China's most notable success in the use of the Yalu River water, which is shared with its only military ally, North Korea (Chan et al., 2009). Similarly, despite the ups and downs over the management and use of transboundary water resources, positive Sino-Russian political relations have enhanced water-related cooperation in the last few years (Vinogradov & Wouters, 2013).

Furthermore, a good bilateral relationship usually implies the presence of intensive interactions that makes issue linkage possible. China sees a strong partnership with Kazakhstan on a range of issues as critical to its interests: domestic stability issues involving the Uighur minorities in Xinjiang, bilateral Sino-Kazakh economic and energy cooperation, and regional competition for influence and power in Central Asia between Russia, China, and the United States. In addition, in line with its good-neighbourliness policy, China wants to avoid coming across as a bully in its dealings with Kazakhstan. During the China-Kazakhstan negotiation over water issues, Kazakhstan deliberately linked transboundary water issues with energy, economic ties, and security issues

Table 1.3 China's bilateral relationship with other riparian states

Military alliance (The Treaty of Friendship, Cooperation, and Mutual Assistance 1961)	North Korea
Comprehensive strategic partnership of coordination	Russia
All-weather strategic partnership	Pakistan
Comprehensive strategic partnership	Kazakhstan, Cambodia, Laos, Vietnam, Myanmar, Thailand, Mongolia
Strategic partnership	Kyrgyzstan, Bangladesh
Strategic and cooperative partnership for peace and prosperity (border disputes)	India
Comprehensive partnership	Nepal
No official diplomatic relations	Bhutan

Source: Ministry of Foreign Affairs, P.R. China, 2017.

(Deng, 2012; Ho, 2017). China has agreed to share hydrological data regarding the Brahmaputra River with India and Bangladesh. India needs to pay RMB 850,000 or roughly USD 134,000 every April for maintaining three hydrological centres on the Chinese side whereas the same data is provided to Bangladesh for free (Samaranayake et al., 2016). To a certain extent, closer relations between China and Bangladesh could be a factor behind this differential treatment. The absence of a basin-wide water management mechanism in the Brahmaputra River Basin could also be partially attributed to the fact that China has not yet established formal diplomatic ties with Bhutan. Bhutan forms an integral part of the Brahmaputra River Basin, even though it does not come in the path of the river.

Next, low utilization of shared water resources could mean lower risks of conflict between China and its neighbouring countries due to very limited water interactions. In fact, most of the transboundary rivers belong to this category. For 97 out of the 112 transboundary rivers in China, transboundary water interaction between China and neighbouring countries is highly limited due to the insignificance of these rivers as well as the very low degree of utilization by the riparian states. With an upstream status on major transborder rivers, China adopts a *reactive* diplomatic approach because its advantageous position yields a relatively high likelihood of conflict. Many of China's water agreements are negotiated and concluded in response to requests from its downstream neighbours, quite often after an incident. For instance, in June 2000, when a natural dam on a tributary of the Brahmaputra in Tibet broke, 3–4 billion cubic meters of water poured into Arunachal Pradesh and Assam. The flood eventually killed 30 Indians and left 50,000 homeless. In response to India's concerns, China established a series of agreements with India to share hydrological data. (Samaranayake et al., 2016).

In contrast, regarding the major border rivers and transborder rivers which China is located at downstream and the mixed rivers, China largely employs a proactive diplomacy since the degree of vulnerability for China is higher. This means that China will be more willing to sign water agreements, especially when bilateral ties between China and the particular neighbouring country or countries are close. And this proactive diplomacy is to a large extent related to China's efforts to settle the land borders since the late 1970s. It is against this backdrop that most of the 110 treaties that govern matters related to international watercourses concern borders. Moreover, four bilateral agreements specifically touch on transboundary water issues. The 1994 China-Mongolia water agreement covers two border rivers, a border lake, and a transborder river with China at the downstream. The China-Russia and China-North Korea water agreements are related to border rivers. It is the similar case for China and Kazakhstan. In April 2011, the two countries launched the China-Kazakhstan Friendship Joint Water Diversion Project on the Khorgos River, a tributary of the Ili River and a border river between both countries.

Given the fact that some river basins include both border river tributaries and transborder tributaries, China's approach to transboundary water issues could contain both proactive and reactive components. For example, severe pollution accompanying rapid economic development in Northeast Asia has already put a strain on available water resources. It is reported that over 60 per cent of the rivers are polluted. Over 130 organic contaminants including 44 toxins can be detected in Songhua waters (He et al., 2014). On 13 November 2005, an explosion occurred in a petrochemical factory in Jilin City, resulting in hundreds of tonnes of benzene leaking from a factory into the Songhua River and causing severe transboundary pollution downstream (as the Songhua drains into the Amur River separating Russia and China). In 2008, China signed the Agreement on Reasonable Utilization and Protection of Transboundary Waters between China and Russia (see Chapter 5).

Step 3 - the role of the subnational actors

The subnational actors (i.e. the local governments, NGOs, and state-owned enterprises) (see Chapters 3 and 8), can influence the country's transboundary water management practices in three major aspects: (1) the degree of utilization of transboundary rivers, (2) China's overall relationship with neighbouring countries, and (3) the implementation of central government's policy. On the utilization of transboundary water resources, particularly in the realm of dam-building and water diversion projects, the central government's policy can be seen as the result of competition between coalitions of different interests group. In 2003, the Yunnan provincial government signed an agreement to develop hydroelectric stations on the Nu River with the Huadian Corporation to support local heavy industries. Shortly, NGOs, media, and scholars, with support from the National Environmental Protection Bureau, launched a high-profile campaign against the proposed dams, which eventually led to the suspension of the proposed hydro-project (He, 2015; Magee, 2006; Mertha, 2009; Yeophantong, 2017).

In Tibet, the role of the Tibetan military should not be overlooked. The Tibet Military Command, which is directly under the People's Liberation Party (PLA), is one level higher than its counterpart provincial-level military command (Krishnan, 2016). In the case of the utilization of Brahmaputra River, while the Tibetan government is interested in utilizing the hydropower potentials of the Brahmaputra River to solve Tibet's electricity shortage problem, the PLA is one of the strongest supporters of the Grand Western Water Diversion proposal, which intends to divert waters from the Brahmaputra to the country's dry north (Ho, 2014; Zhang, 2015). In 2006, the Grand Western Water Diversion Proposal was endorsed by 118 generals, including 16 three-star generals and 17 lieutenant generals (Fu & Liu, 2006).

In Xinjiang, the Xinjiang Production and Construction Corps (XPCC) is a unique economic and paramilitary government organization that enjoys the same rank as the Xinjiang Uygur Autonomous Region Government; thus, it has administrative authority over several medium-sized cities, settlements, and farms in Xinjiang. As its administrate areas are mostly in the extremely arid areas and its economy is predominantly agriculture-based, the XPCC has become the major driving force behind the water diversion projects along the Ili and Irtysh

Rivers (Wang, 2016; XPCC, 2017). In fact, in 1969, XPCC even engaged in a small-scale armed clash with the soldiers of the former Soviet Union due to disputes over shared Akequeke River, which resulted in five people from XPCC being captured (XPCC, 2015).

More importantly, subnational actors, particularly the provincial governments, are playing an increasingly important role in shaping China's overall relations with neighbouring countries. As discussed in the previous section, the border provincial governments have been pushing for transnational collaboration and cooperation in the economic, social, cultural, and non-traditional security arenas, within the possible national foreign policy parameters. In recent years, landlocked peripheral provinces, including Yunnan, Xinjiang, Heilongjiang, and Jilin provinces, have been highly active in strengthening economic and trade relations with their border countries. More significantly, transboundary rivers provide Heilongjiang, Jilin, and (to a certain extent) Yunan with crucial navigation channels that meet their desperate need for access to seas (Li, 2014).

Consequently, China has been most cooperative in the area of navigation. As Ho (2014) notes, every other multilateral Chinese initiative towards the river involves improving navigation to facilitate trade, and the Yunnan provincial government is also in charge of promoting border trade with the Mekong riparian states and developing infrastructure to link the Mekong countries, as well as attracting foreign investment for hydropower projects. Furthermore, China's participation in the Greater Mekong Subregion (GMS) and Mekong River Commission (MRC) is largely driven by the needs of Yunnan province (Li, 2014). Consequently, more free trade zones, joint development areas, and friendship projects are established along the transboundary rivers. In April 2011, China and Kazakhstan launched the long-awaited China-Kazakhstan Friendship Joint Water Diversion Project on the Khorgos River, a 150 km-long tributary of the Ili River and a border river between both countries. Under the agreement, each side was allocated 50 per cent of the water diverted, and the goal of the project was to improve irrigation, secure water supply for the ecosystem, and mitigate flood damage, especially in Khorgos Port and in the China-Kazakhstan Trade Cooperation Zone.

Conversely, owing to prolonged border disputes and very limited opportunities for expanding bilateral economic ties, the Tibetan government has had a marginal role in shaping the overall Sino-Indian relations. This partially explains the limited cooperation between the two countries along the shared rivers. Although bilateral water agreements are signed at the state level, implementation is carried out by the local governments. This provides more opportunities for local governments to influence the actual outcome of water agreements. Furthermore, local leaders usually propose their own initiatives to engage with neighbouring countries. Take the Sino-Indian Memorandum of Understanding (MoU) on hydraulic data-sharing for example. The problems related to data accuracy and frequency could be partially attributed to the incompetency and lack of motivation from the Tibetan government. On the contrary, Heilongjiang, Inner Mongolia, and Yunnan went beyond what was officially agreed at the state

Table 1.4 China's policies and practices towards two selected river basins

River basin	*River type*	*Vulnerability, conflict*	*Proactive/ Reactive*	*Overall relations*	*Sub-national actors*	*Outcome*
Brahmaputra River	Transborder, China upstream	Low, medium	Reactive	India: strategic rivalry with border disputes	Tibet, dam builders, military	Medium conflicts, low cooperation
Tumen River	Border river	Medium, low	Proactive/ Reactive	North Korea and Russia: very close ties	Jilin	Joint development

Source: Own construction.

level. For instance, the Heilongjiang government initiated the program of inter-regional cooperation to enhance collaboration with the Amur Oblast (Region). It also implemented a nature conservation project on joint monitoring of the quality of surface waters and aquatic living resources (known as the Integrated Management of the Amur [Heilongjiang] Basin between Khabarovsky Krai and Heilongjiang province). Similarly, Inner Mongolia cooperates with Zabaikalsky Krai to protect the water resources and biodiversity of the Argun Basin.

Table 1.4 provides a summary of China's policies and practices related to the two river basins. The Brahmaputra River is a transborder river with China upstream. Owing to abundant water resources, very low population density, and low economic activity, China's basin vulnerability is very low. As China intends to harness the huge hydropower potential of the Brahmaputra River, domestic discussion on the possible water diversion projects and water issues of the Brahmaputra River have emerged as a major source of conflict between India and China (see Chapter 9). In response to India's concern, China adopted a *reactive* diplomatic approach. The lingering border disputes and Sino-Indian strategic competitions on many fronts resulted in an unfavourable diplomatic "atmosphere" for closer bilateral transboundary water cooperation. Besides, subnational actors including the Tibet Autonomous Region Government, the dam builders, and the military are more interested in the economic and strategic benefits of carrying out more hydro-projects. Consequently, in the Brahmaputra River Basin, China's interaction with India can be categorized as "medium conflicts with low level of cooperation".

In comparison, the Tumen River is a border river between China and North Korea that also serves as border river between North Korea and Russia for about 15 km downstream. As a border river, the Tumen is vulnerable to the erosion of river banks and changes of river flow that affect China's territorial integrity (see Chapter 4). Hence, a *proactive* policy was adopted, and on 3 November 1998, the Agreement on the Demarcation Line of National Water Boundaries regarding Tumen River was signed by China, North Korea, and Russia. In fact, since the early 1990s, these three riparian states, together with Mongolia and South Korea, had already engaged in economic cooperation in the Tumen River Basin under the Greater Tumen Initiative. Past decades of rapid industrialization resulted in wastewater discharge from Chinese factories in the Yanbian Korean Autonomous Prefecture in Jilin. Serious water pollution in the Tumen River destroyed fish stocks across the region and contaminated the coastal waters of North Korea and Russia. To alleviate the concerns of North Korea and Russia, China made a sustained effort to reduce water pollution (Byun, 2008). In November 2009, the Chinese government officially approved the "Outline for the Tumen River Area Joint Development Plan" and since then, China has been leading the way to promote joint cross-border development projects with North Korea and Russia. What should be noted is that Jilin province has been the key player in fostering Tumen cooperation among regional countries. In fact, the idea of Tumen cooperation first unfolded in Jilin in the 1980s (Byun, 2008). As only the Tumen River has the estuary in North China to access the Sea of Japan, Jilin province's interest in the restoration of sea access and in the navigation rights through the Tumen River is an important factor behind its development of Tumen River Cooperation projects with North Korea and Russia (Nickum, 2008). Therefore, China's water interaction with North Korea and Russia can be regarded as "joint development".

Conclusion

China's transboundary river policies and practices are not static but constantly evolving with the changing dynamics of the political economy. China's overall ties with neighbouring countries have also shifted over time. Before the 1980s, China's closed-door policy led to very limited interaction with neighbouring countries. Besides, during that time, most parts of the border land remained uninhabited or vacant. Since the 1980s, China has implemented the grand reform by opening up its borders and normalizing relations with neighbouring countries. Great effort was made to build settlements along the land borders, and this led to many agreements related to the border rivers and lakes.

In recent years, under Xi Jinping's leadership, China has attached even higher importance to diplomacy with its neighbouring countries, raising important issues and guiding policy, opening up a sound environment, and laying the foundation for diplomatic work (Freeman, 2017). In late 2013, China launched the high-profile Belt and Road Initiative (BRI) to expand trade and investment and create a new pattern of regional economic integration. Under BRI, both the central government and border provinces such as Yunnan, Xinjiang, Heilongjiang, and Inner Mongolia have been actively working towards full-scale cooperation with neighbouring countries. Following this, China launched the Lancang-Mekong River Dialogue and Cooperation Mechanism, which includes the management of water resources as one of the five priority areas (see Chapters 4 and 11).

Economic development in China could be both a cause for worry and a source of hope in the realm of transboundary water management. On the one hand, rapid urbanization, industrialization, and agricultural development will further exacerbate the water scarcity situations in China, particularly in the country's arid north. As water becomes scarcer, China might utilize more of the transboundary water resources by diverting waters from the relatively underutilized transboundary rivers within its border. China's ambition to reduce carbon emission through developing clean energies will lead to more dam construction projects along the transboundary rivers, albeit at the expense of downstream countries. On the other hand, as pointed out by Gleditsch et al. (2006) and Mirumachi and Allan (2007), wealthier countries can afford to compensate for scarcities by technological substitution or innovation, or they may have different priorities or challenges. A country with a high level of economic diversity and strength will have the option to combine factors of production and in turn find resource alternatives such as water desalination and waste water recycling, water saving, better irrigation efficiencies, water price reform, virtual water trade, and agricultural crop structural shifts (see Chapter 11).

References

Baxter, M. H. (2014). The run of the river: Water, politics, and Asia. *Asian Survey, 54*(4), 611–620.

Beck, L., Bernauer, T., Siegfried, T., & Bohmelt, T. (2014). Implications of hydro-political dependency for international watercooperation and conflict: Insights from new data. *Political Geography, 42*, 23–33.

Biba, S. (2014). Desecuritization in China's behavior towards its transboundary rivers: The Mekong river, the Brahmaputra river, and the Irtysh and Ili rivers. *Journal of Contemporary China, 23*(85), 21–43.

Brochmann, M., & Gleditsch, N. P. (2012). Shared rivers and conflict: A reconsideration. *Political Geography, 31*, 519–527.

Bruyne, C. D., & Fischhendler, I. (2013). Negotiating conflict resolution mechanmism for transobundary water treaties: A transaction cost approach. *Global Environmental Change, 23*, 1841–1851.

Byun, S.-W. (2008). *Provincial impacts of multilateral cooperation: The greater Tumen initiative and environmental protection in Jilin*. Washington, DC: Woodrow Wilson International Center for Scholars.

Chan, M., Lall, U., Narula, N., Pachauri, R. K., Turner, J. L., & Virijasakultorn, V. (2009). *Asia's next challenge: Securing the region's water future*. Washington, DC: Asia Society.

Chellaney, B. (2011). *Water: Asia's new battleground*. Washington, DC: Georgetown University Press.

Chellaney, B. (2013). *Water, peace, and war: Confronting the global water crisis*. New York, NY: Rowman & Littlefield.

Ching, L., & Mukherjee, M. (2015). Managing the social-ecology of very large rivers: Collective choice rules in IWRM narrative. *Global Environmental Change, 34*, 172–184.

Christopher, M. (2013). *Water wars: The Brahmaputra river and Sino-Indian relations.* Newport, RI: US Naval War College.

Deng, M. (2012). International cooperation problems on the transboundary rivers in Kazakhstan. *Arid Land Geography, 35*(3), 365–376.

Dore, J., Lebel, L., & Molle, F. (2012). A framework for analysing transboudnary water governance complexes, illustrated in the Mekong Region. *Journal of Hydrology, 466–477*, 23–36.

Economy, E. (2008). Asia's water security crisis: China, India and the United States. In M. K. Ashley & J. Tellis (Eds.), *Strategic Asia 2008–2009: Challenges and choices* (pp. 365–390). Seattle, WA: National Bureau of Asian Research.

Feng, Y., He, D., & Wang, W. (2015). Identifying China's transboundary water risks and vulnerabilities – A multidisciplinary analysis using hydrological data and legal/institutional settings. *Water International, 40*(2), 328–341.

Fox, C. A., & Sneddon, C. (2007). Transboundary river basin agreements in the Mekong transboundary river basin agreements in the Mekongor securitizing the environment? *International Environmental Agreements, 7*, 237–261.

Freeman, C. P. (2017). Dam diplomacy? China's new neighbourhood policy and Chinese dam-building companies. *Water Interantional, 44*(2), 187–206.

French, M. (2014). Water wars in the middle kingdom. *The International Affairs Review, 22*(2), 6–30.

Fu, J., & Liu, Y. (2006, July 27). 西藏大调水方案引发巨大争议 百余老将军支持 *[Grand western water diversion proposal trigers huge controvasials, supported by over 100 generals].* Retrieved May 23, 2017, from http://finance.people.com.cn/GB/8215/4637090.html.

Gleditsch, N. P., Furlong, K., Hegre, H., Lacina, B., & Owen, T. (2006). Conflicts over shared rivers: Resource scarcity or fuzzy boundaries? *Political Geography, 25*, 361–382.

Greenpeace.(2017). "十二五" 期间中国各省(自治区、直辖市)地表水环境质量改善情况评估 *[12th five year period: China's provinces (including autonomous region and municipality) ground water quality improvement reports].* Beijing, People's Republic of China: Greenpeace.

Guo, Y. (2014). Power diffusion and benefit sharing: A new trend of mekong river hydro-power development and China's response. *World Economics and Politics, 10*, 117–136.

Han, X. (2015). Approaches to investment in Chinese transboundary waters. *Water International, 40*(1), 71–86.

He, D., Wu, R., Feng, Y., Li, Y., Ding, C., & Wenling Wang, D. W. (2014). China's transboundary waters: New paradigms for water and ecological security through applied ecology. *Journal of Applied Ecology, 51*, 1159–1168.

He, Y. (2015). China's practice on the non-navigational uses of. *Water International, 40*(2), 312–327.

Hirsch, P. (2016). The shifting regional geopolitics of Mekong dams. *Political Geography, 51*, 63–74.

Ho, S. (2014). River politics: China's policies in the Mekong and the Brahmaputra in comparative perspective. *Journal of Contemporary Chin, 23*(85), 1–20.

Ho, S. (2016). 'Big brother, little brothers': Comparing China's and India's transboundary river policies. *Water Policy*. doi:10.2166/wp.2016.103.

Ho, S. (2017). China's transboundary river policies towards Kazakhstan: Issue-linkages and incentives for Cooperation. *Water International, 44*(2), 142–162.

Huang, Q., & Xu, J. (2017). Scales of power in water governance in China: Examples from the Yangtze river basin. *Society & Natural Resources, 30*(4), 421–435.

Hussain, W. (2014, December 1). *India-China: Securitising water*. Retrieved June 2, 2015, from Institute of Peace and Conflict Studies www.ipcs.org/article/india/india-china-securitising-water-4760.html.

Isaac, J., & Shuval, H. (1994). *Water and peace in the middle east*. Amsterdam, Netherlands: Elsevier Science.

Kattelus, M., Kummu, M., Keskinen, M., Salmivaara, A., & Varis, O. (2015). China's southbound transboundary river basins: A case of asymmetry. *Water International, 40*(1), 113–138.

Krishnan, A. (2016). *Eye on India, China raises Tibet military command rank to expand its combat role*. Retrieved May 23, 2017, from http://indiatoday.intoday.in/story/eye-on-india-china-raises-tibet-military-command-rank/1/667092.html.

Lederer, E. M. (2017, June). *UN chief warns of serious clean water shortages by 2050*. Retrieved June 6, 2017, from www.businessinsider.com/ap-un-chief-warns-of-serious-clean-water-shortages-by-2050-2017-6/?IR=T/.

Li, M. (2014). Local liberalism: China's provincial approaches to relations with Southeast Asia. *Journal of Contemporary China, 23*(86), 275–293.

Li, M. (2016). From look-west to act-west: Xinjiang's role in China–central Asian relations. *Journal of Contemporary China*, *25*(100), 1–14.

Li, W., Beresford, M., & Song, G. (2011). Market failure or governmental failure? A study of China's water abstraction policy. *The China Quarterly, 208*, 951–969.

Li, Z. (2014). 国际河流河口：地缘政治与中国权益思考 *[International river estuary: Thoughts on geopolitics and China's interest]* (1st ed.). Beijing, People's Republic of China: Ocean Publishing House.

Li, Z. (2015). *Water and China's neighborhood relationship*. Beijing, People's Republic of China: Shishi She.

Li, Z., & Wu, F. (2016). China and shared water resources: Geopolitics, domestic institutions and global governance. In F. Wu & H. Zhang (Eds.), *China's global quest for resources: Energy, food and water* (pp. 59–78). London, UK and New York, NY: Routledge.

Liebman, A. (2005). Trickle-down hegemony? China's "peaceful rise" and dam building on the Mekong. *Contemporary Southeast Asia, 27*(2), 281–304.

Magee, D. (2006). Powershed politics: Yunnan hydropower under great western development. *The China Quarterly, 185*, 24–41.

Menniken, T. (2007). China's performance in international resource politics: Lessons from the Mekong. *Contemporary Southeast Asia, 29*(1), 97–118.

Mertha, A. (2009). "Fragmented authoritarianism 2.0": Political pluralization in the chinese policy process. *The China Quarterly, 200*, 995–1012.

Ministry of Foreign Affairs, P.R. China. (2017). *Asia*. Retrieved May 23, 2017, from www.fmprc.gov.cn/chn//gxh/cgb/zcgmzysx/yz/.

Ministry of Water Resources, P.R. China. (2017). *2015 China water resources report*. Beijing, People's Republic of China: Ministry of Water Resources, P.R. China.

Mirumachi, N., & Allan, J. (2007). Revisiting transboundary water governance: Power, conflicts, cooperation and the political economy. *International Conference on Adaptive and Integrative Water Management CAIWA*, pp. 1–21, Basel, Switzerland.

Molle, F., Wester, P., & Hirsch, P. (2010). River basin closure: Processes, implications and responses. *Agricultural Water Management, 97*, 569–577.

Moore, S. (2014). Hydropolitics and inter-jurisdictional relationships in China: The pursuit of localized preferences in a centralized system. *The China Quarterly, 214*, 760–780.

Moore, S. (2016, May 29). *India's water politics: When drought leads to discord*. Retrieved June 7, 2016, from Foreign Affairs, www.foreignaffairs.com/articles/india/2016-05-29/indias-water-politics.

Moore, S. (2017a). The dilemma of autonomy: Decentralization and water politics at the subnational level. *Water International, 42*(2), 222–239.

Moore, S. (2017b). China's domestic hydropolitics: An assessment and implications for international transboundary dynamics. *International Journal of Water Resources Development*. doi: doi.org/10.1080/07900627.2017.1313157.

Nickum, J. (2008). The upstream superpower: China's international rivers. In O. Varis, C. Tortajada, & A. K. Biswas, *Management of transboundary rivers and lakes* (pp. 227–244). Berlin, Germany: Springer.

Padmanabhan, S. (2014). *Next China-India war: World's first water War – 2029*. New Delhi, India: Manas Publications.

Räsänen, T. A., Someth, P., Lauri, H., Koponen, J., Sarkkula, J., & Kummu, M. (2017). Observed river discharges due to hydropower operations in the upper Mekong basin. *Journal of Hydrology, 545*, 28–41.

Samaranayake, N., Limaye, S., & Wuthnow, J. (2016). *Water resources competition in the Brahmaputra river basin*. Washington, DC: CNA.

Shen, D., & Wu, J. (2016). State of the art review: Water pricing reform in China. *International Journal of Water Resources Development*, 1–36. doi:10.1080/07900627.2016.1171743.

Sinha, U. K. (2012). Examining China's hydro-behaviour: Peaceful or assertive. *Strategic Analysis, 36*(1), 41–56.

Sneddon, C., & Fox, C. (2006). Rethinking transboundary waters: A critical hydropolitics of the Mekong basin. *Political Geography, 25*, 181–202.

Suhardiman, D., & Giordano, M. (2012). Process-focused analysis in transboundary water governance research. *International Enviromental Agreements, 12*, 299–308.

Svensson, J. (2012). *Managing the rise of a hydro-hegemon in Asia: China's strategic interests in the Yarlung-Tsangpo river*. New Delhi, India: IDSA.

Varis, O., Kummu, M., Lehr, C., & Shen, D. (2014). China's stressed waters: Societal and environmental vulnerability in China's internal and transboundary river systems. *Applied Geography, 53*, 105–116.

Vinogradov, S., & Wouters, P. (2013). *Russian transboundary waters: A legal perspective on*. Stockholm, Sweden: The Institute for Security and Development Policy.

Voza, D., Vuković, M., Carlson, L., & Djordjević, D. B. (2012). International water conflict and cooperation: The role of power relations among riparians. *International Journal of Humanities and Social Science, 2*(11), 56–66.

Wang, L. (2016). 新疆额尔齐斯河第十师北屯灌区三干渠引水枢纽拦河建筑物方案比选 [Xinjiang Irytsh river tenth division, north irrigation zone and third cannal water diversion project proposals comparison]. *China Water Transport, 16*(2), 185–187.

Warner, J. (2012). The struggle over Turkey's Ilısu dam: Domestic and international security linkages. *International Environmental Agreements, 12*, 231–250.

Warner, J., & Zawahri, N. (2012). Hegemony and asymmetary: Mutiple-chessboard games on transboundary rivers. *Int Environ Agreements, 12*, 215–229.

Wolf, A. T., Yoffe, S. B., & Giordano, M. (2003). International waters: Identifying basins at risk. *Water Policy, 5*, 29–60.

Wouters, P., & Chen, H. (2013). China's 'Soft-path' to transboundary water cooperation examined in the light of two UN global water conventions – Exploring the 'Chinese Way'. *22 Water Law, 22*(6), 229–247.

XPCC. (2015). "铜墙铁壁"的中国军垦长城 *[An iron bastion: China's military farm great wall]*. Retrieved May 23, 2017, from www.xjbt.gov.cn/c/2015-06-08/2032387.shtml.

XPCC.(2017).七十三团伊犁河龙口引水改造工程顺利通水 确保农业灌溉引水 *[73regiment Ili river Longkou water diversion project completed: Safegarding irrigation water use]*. Retrieved May 23, 2017, from www.xjbt.gov.cn/c/2017-04-13/3576480.shtml.

Yeophantong, P. (2013). *China and the politics of hydropower development: Governing water and contesting responsibilities in the Mekong River Basin*. Oxford, UK: University of Oxford.

Yeophantong, P. (2017). River activism, policy entrepreneurship and transboundary water disputes in Asia. *Water International, 42*(2), 163–186.

Yoffe, S., & Larson, K. (2001). *Chapter 2 basins at risk: Water event database methodology*. Corvallis: Oregon State University.

Yong, J. (2006, January 25). 关于水利发展"十五"计划执行情况和"十一五"规划要点 *[On the implentation details of the 10th five year plan of hydro development and main points of the 11th five year plan]*. Retrieved May 23, 2017, from Ministry of Water Resources, P.R. China, www.mwr.gov.cn/slzx/slyw/200601/t20060126_149512.html.

Young, O. R., Guttman, D., Qi, Y., Bachus, K., Belis, D., Cheng, H., … Zhu, X. (2015). Institutionalized governance processes: Comparing environmental problem solving in China and the United States. *Global Environmental Change, 31*, 163–173.

Zawahri, N. A., & Hensengerth, O. (2012). Domestic environmental activists and the governance of the Ganges and Mekong Rivers in India and China. *International Environmental Agreements, 12*, 269–298.

Zeitoun, M., & Mirumachi, N. (2008). Transboundary water interaction I: Reconsidering conflict and cooperation. *International Enviromental Agreements, 8*, 297–316.

Zhang, H. (2015). Sino-Indian water disputes: The coming water wars? *WIREs Water, 3*(2), 155–166.

2 Assessing China's domestic hydropolitics

Scott Moore

Introduction: domestic versus international hydropolitics

China's unique geographical position at the headwaters of several of Asia's major rivers has spawned something of a cottage industry concerned with its alleged propensity to engage in water-related conflict with its neighbours. In a widely-cited 2013 editorial, Indian strategist Brahma Chellaney wrote that "by building megadams and reservoirs in its borderlands, China is working to re-engineer the flows of major rivers that are the lifeline of lower riparian states" (Chellaney, 2013). However, such claims of China's "hydro-hegemony" are better supported by geopolitical theory than hydrological reality. In the case of the Brahmaputra River, often alleged to be a site of future conflict between China and India, less than one-third of the river's total flow originates from within Chinese territory, limiting Beijing's ability to threaten its downstream neighbours by withholding water, even if it were so inclined (UNFAO, 2011). Indeed, more importantly, the Chinese government would seem to have few incentives to engage in such behaviour. For China, like most countries, the costs of conflict are likely to far outweigh those of cooperation for the foreseeable future (Delli Priscoli & Wolf, 2009; Susskind & Islam, 2012; Uitto & Duda, 2002). However, recent scholarship suggests that China's internal politics may create certain challenges for institutionalized cooperation in transboundary river basins (Li & Wu, 2016). Accordingly, this chapter explores the domestic politics of water resources in China, with the objective of better understanding the dynamics of conflict and cooperation for Asia's major transboundary water resources.

The key message of this chapter is that scholars and policymakers concerned with China's role in transboundary rivers need to pay attention to domestic, as well as international, hydropolitics. While there is yet little evidence that directly links China's domestic and international hydropolitical arenas, it is striking that so much attention has been devoted to the prospect of conflict between China and its downstream neighbours when so little has been given to the far more numerous inter-jurisdictional water conflicts that occur between provinces and municipalities within China. Accordingly, the focus of this chapter is on these inter-jurisdictional disputes and what they signify for China as an actor in regional hydropolitics. The chapter proceeds in three major sections. The first of these details the institutional landscape for water resources management in China, emphasizing the countervailing influences of political centralization and fiscal-economic decentralization. The second section provides a more detailed description of inter-jurisdictional water conflicts in China, particularly the large number of water pollution disputes, as well as a new description of recent policy reforms to attempt to address them. The concluding section builds on the preceding analysis to sketch a research agenda to better understand the potential linkages between China's domestic and international hydropolitical arenas. While the evidentiary basis for such an analysis is currently lacking, answering such questions should be a priority for scholars concerned with hydropolitics in China. The remainder of this introduction, meanwhile, sets the stage for this analysis by defining the concept of hydropolitics and its application to China.

The concept of hydropolitics is useful for describing China's relations with its riparian neighbours as well as the dynamics of conflict and cooperation between subnational administrative units within China. Given the potential for intractable conflicts to arise, the study of hydropolitics has historically been concerned primarily with the prospect of violent conflict on international transboundary rivers, and has therefore been concerned primarily with the actions of nation states (Elhance, 1999; Waterbury, 1979). Subsequent work has generally sought to broaden the scope of concern to a wider range of economic issues and political actors, including subnational jurisdictions (Bagis, 1997; Li, He, & Feng, 2011; Turton & Ashton, 2008). Even more significant for the case of China is the existence of a number of studies that explicitly conclude that domestic water politics influence nation state positions with respect to international transboundary river basins. Using event data, for example, three prominent researchers find that domestic political events directly shaped hydropolitical dynamics in the Middle East and South Asia, for example (Giordano, Giordano, & Wolf, 2002). A second account likewise emphasizes the influence of domestic water use inefficiencies and water resources management failures in generally undermining institutionalized collective action in South Asia's transboundary river basins (Wirsing, 2007). A subset of the much larger literature on the influence of non-governmental organizations (NGOs) and social groups in transboundary cooperation also stresses the extent to which domestic activism can cause governments to adopt less confrontational positions with respect to transboundary waters (Bobekova, 2015; Zawahri & Hensengerth, 2012).

These accounts raise the question of to what extent internal water politics influence transboundary conflict and cooperation dynamics. As the next section describes, this question is especially relevant in the case of China, where, because of its unique form of decentralization, the behaviour of subnational jurisdictions bears some resemblance to that of nation states in shared river basins. However, before proceeding, some important clarifications are in order. China's subnational jurisdictions do have some freedom to play with hydropolitics, but primarily when they do not bear strongly on national-level policy objectives. Beijing holds trump cards, and when it chooses to exercise its authority, as in the case of projects of national strategic importance like the Three Gorges Dam or the South–North Water Transfer Project, it is quite capable of preventing and resolving inter-jurisdictional conflicts, and ensuring the implementation of centrally-formulated decisions (Moore, 2014a). Moreover, it is important to be clear that inter-jurisdictional hydropolitics do not always undermine transboundary cooperation. It is clear that in some cases, provincial governments develop cooperative relationships with neighbouring countries in pursuit of enhanced trade and investment. There is, in short, nothing deterministic about China's subnational hydropolitics. Instead, the key point is that they are deserving of far more attention from scholars and policymakers concerned with strengthening cooperation on Asia's transboundary rivers.

Inter-jurisdictional relations in China: competition, hierarchy, and control

From a comparative perspective, the People's Republic of China represents perhaps the world's most distinctive combination of political centralization and fiscal and administrative decentralization. The basic unity of the state, referred to as *Dayitong* (大一统), has long been seen as the organizing principle of governance in mainland China, and underpins the modern system whereby decision-making is tightly concentrated at the central government level (Wang, 2009). At the same time, however, the practical challenges of governing a large and diverse territory have historically led Chinese officials to delegate substantial administrative powers to subnational levels of government. Moreover, in economic terms China is one of the most decentralized countries in the world, with revenue and expenditure powers largely in the hands of local officials (Dziobek, Mangas, & Kufa, 2011). Chinese officials are thus caught in institutional matrix known as *tiao-kuai* (条-块), in which they are responsible both to line control by functional bureaucracies, such as the various central government ministries, as well as to territorial government leaders, including mayors and provincial governors, and to equivalent officials within the corresponding Chinese Communist Party (CCP) structure (Mertha, 2008). This matrix is intended to ensure that subnational officials pursue priorities set by the central government, but also to provide them with the flexibility to implement these policies according to individual local circumstances. In practical terms, this flexibility results in different applications of specific policies, including those concerning water resources. As economic growth has rapidly increased water demand from multiple sectors, this flexibility has created a divergence in the priorities of central and subnational officials concerning shared water resources, stoking water-related conflict in many parts of China.

The dual nature of the Chinese system as both politically centralized and economically decentralized is reflected in its institutional arrangements for water resources management. Article 9 of the 1982 Constitution provides that water is the property of the Chinese state, and major water policy decisions, such as the construction of large infrastructure projects like the South–North Water Transfer, must be approved by central-level decision-making structures, especially the State Council (*Guowuyuan* 国务院), which is analogous to a cabinet, and the National Development and Reform Commission (NDRC; *Fagaiwei* 发改委), which sets policy on issues of fundamental importance to the economy (National People's Congress, 2004). The largest, most important, and most contentious water resources issues, including construction of the Three Gorges and South–North Water Transfer Projects, are also ratified by the CCP Politburo or its Standing Committee (*Zhongguo gongchandang zhongyang zhengzhi ju* 中国共产党中央政治), each of which is composed of the most senior Party leaders. These bodies set policy objectives and make all important decisions, which are then handed down in hierarchical fashion both to central government bureaucracies and to subnational officials responsible for policy implementation. As a result, Beijing can effectively control water resources policy, and the actions of subnational jurisdictions, on issues of strategic importance. On less important matters, however, subnational actors have much greater autonomy.

Central government ministries are represented at both provincial and local levels, where they coincide with separate territorial administrations at provincial, prefecture/county, and municipal levels. In China's administrative hierarchy, province-level territorial governments possess the same status as central ministries like the Ministry of Water Resources (MWR), creating considerable confusion regarding authority. Every province-level government has an entity, usually called a Water Affairs Bureau, whose functions correspond to those of the central MWR, and most county-level governments also possess a branch whose responsibilities typically encompass water resources conservation and protection, flood control, irrigation, and water supply (Liu & Speed, 2010). In addition to these general-purpose institutions, various special-purpose entities also exist, including dike maintenance committees, irrigation and reservoir district committees, and water user associations (Hubei Sheng Huanggang Diqu Shuili Dianli Ju [Huanggang Prefecture, Hubei Bureau of Water Conservancy and Electric Power], 1977). Lines of responsibility among these institutions are frequently unclear, at times creating conflicting loyalties among local officials. The complex matrix of authority at the subnational level creates tension between the interests of individual localities and the nation at large, despite China's centralized political system. When asked whether he supported the central government, for instance, one Ningxia delegate to the National People's Congress (NPC) declared himself to be "duty-bound to help advance Ningxia's socioeconomic development" (Ningxia Ribao [Ningxia Daily], 2010).

The primary response to the divergence of central and local interests in water resources management has been a combination of administrative and legal institutional reform intended to bolster the Water Conservancy Commissions (WCCs). In 1950, the State Council created China's first such regional institution, the Yellow River Conservancy Commission (YRCC; *Huanghe shuili weiyuanhui* 黄河水利委员会), and placed it directly under the central government out of a desire that it "be free of entanglements and squabbles between provincial governments" (Greer, 1979, p. 41). Similar WCCs were subsequently established in China's other major river basins, as well as in the Lake Tai Basin. Recent legislation, particularly the 1997 Flood Control Law and the 2002 Water Law, has enhanced the authority of the WCCs to develop basin-wide water resources development and water allocation plans, and given the commission's explicit power over other bureaucratic units in certain areas, especially water pollution control (Zhonghua Renmin Gongheguo Zhongyang Renmin Zhengfu [Central People's Government of the PRC], 2006).

However, these institutional reforms have been outstripped by the emergence of divergent interests among the subnational actors they are supposed to control. The central government's reluctance to delegate decision-making power means that although the WCCs are intended to coordinate regional-scale policymaking, they do not include subnational officials or representatives, and they act more as instruments of control than cooperative governance (Shen, 2009). In place of formal institutions for inter-jurisdictional coordination and dispute resolution, conflicts in river basin governance have traditionally been handled informally between elites (Gustafsson, 1984, p. 153). This *ad hoc*, bureaucratic approach decision-making has never been entirely satisfactory, but it has proven increasingly inadequate in the face of dramatic growth in the number of water user groups, as well as the growing role of non-state interests. During the past decade, water pollution and dam construction have emerged as significant social issues, and media and civil-society groups have occasionally been successful in influencing policy decisions regarding these two particular issues (Mertha, 2008; Mertha & Lowry, 2006). In large urban areas, meanwhile, the private sector increasingly constitutes an important source of investment in the water sector, and in some cases, it has become directly responsible for the operations of water supply and treatment systems (Qi, 2011). Amidst this growing pluralization of water users and uses, China's largely centralized approach to water resources management has proven increasingly incapable of containing and preventing conflict over shared water resources. Indeed, water resources issues are perhaps the best example of the centre's incomplete control over local officials (Moore, 2014a,b).

To be sure, the central government has made several attempts to strengthen regional governance institutions in order to address such challenges, especially those related to pollution. Joint water quality bureaus have been created within the river basin commissions in order to more effectively supervise provincial-level authorities within river basins (Shen, 2009). In addition, the 2008 Water Pollution Law mandated water resources planning on a regional rather than jurisdiction-by-jurisdiction basis, in an effort to promote compliance (Shen, 2009; Wouters, Hu, Zhang, Andrew-Speed, & Tarlock, 2004). Finally, recent attempts to develop interprovincial pollution compensation mechanisms reinforce the central government's attempts to improve inter-jurisdictional collective action in shared river basins (Xinhua, 2012). Nevertheless, environmental outcomes remain extremely poor; less than half of the river water can be treated to the point where it is safe for drinking, and a quarter of surface waters are so polluted that they are unfit even for industrial use (Stanway, 2012b). Within this institutional vacuum, conflict persists between levels of government, individual jurisdictions, and water user groups. In large part, this conflict reflects the fact that fiscal independence is not matched by political authority.

China's economic reform strategy since 1978 has relied heavily on economic decentralization, and revenue and expenditure powers have been progressively transferred to subnational levels of government. Local governments have been granted a wide berth with respect to enterprises in their own jurisdictions, creating new sources of finance and fostering inter-jurisdictional relationships outside the central-local state hierarchy (Oi, 1995; Oksenberg & Tong, 1991; Yang, 2004). This process has created a deep symbiosis between local government officials and the enterprises within their jurisdictions, particularly those that are state-owned. Subnational officials, therefore, tend to be deferential to the interests of major economic constituencies within their respective jurisdictions, often to the detriment of resource management and environmental protection objectives. A recent news report on pollution in a large town in Anhui Province, for example, describes a situation in which regulation is lax because "the government and the town's largest employer are all but indistinguishable" (Stanway, 2012a). At the same time, local officials are often fiercely protectionist when it comes to securing natural resources for their respective jurisdictions (Wei, 2000). Thus, despite the existence of potent control mechanisms binding subnational officials to central policy objectives, subnational officials frequently attempt to "cheat" these directives in order to promote economic interests in their areas of responsibility. These sectional tensions are perhaps most evident in increasing accounts of inter-jurisdictional water disputes (***kua xingzheng quyu de shuishi jiufen*** 跨行政区域的水事纠纷) concerning both water quality and quantity issues, which the following section details.

Compelled cooperation: inter-jurisdictional water conflicts in China

Although there are no reliable data on the number of inter-jurisdictional water disputes in China, their number has, by most accounts, been continually increasing since 1978 (Li, Liu, & Huang, 2010). Such disputes fall into several categories, including the maintenance of flood control infrastructure, hydropower utilization, water withdrawals, and effluent flows (Zhang, Zhuang, Lai, & Qiang, 2010). Among these, however, industrial point source pollution is by far the most common cause of inter-jurisdictional water disputes in China, and consequently, this section focuses on water quality disputes. The growing number of such disputes stems from both the incentive structure for subnational officials, which favours prioritizing economic growth in individual jurisdictions over cooperation with neighbouring units, as well as the lack of robust institutional mechanisms to facilitate such cooperation. The weakness of these provisions means that local authorities rarely engage in inter-jurisdictional cooperation, instead adopting a practice known as "shoveling only their own snow" [*zisaomen-qianxue* 自扫门前雪] (Peng, 2009, p. 37).

This tendency toward promoting local economic growth at the expense of pollution control has led to a string of dramatic inter-jurisdictional water-quality incidents. These include a 2001 Jiangsu-Zhejiang incident in which residents of a city in Zhejiang province, tired of receiving heavily-polluted water from an upstream neighbour in Jiangsu, sank old boats in the two cities' shared river, forming a dam that backed up the polluted water into Jiangsu province; the 2005 Songhua River spill, in which 100 tons of highly toxic petrochemicals were released; a 2007 incident when pollution from Shandong Province disrupted water supplies to a city of 200,000 in downstream Jiangsu province for some 40 hours; a 2013 incident between Shanxi and Hebei regarding the release of the chemical amine; and incidents in both 2011 and 2014 between Guangdong and Guangxi (Green, 2009; Li, Kenan, & Long, 2015). The extent to which inter-jurisdictional pollution affects water quality in downstream jurisdictions is illustrated by a government investigation into pollution on the Zhangweixin River, which flows though Henan, Shanxi, and Hebei before emptying into the Bohai Gulf in Shandong province. 82 per cent of the pollutants found in the Zhangweixin in Shandong were found to originate from outside the province (Li, Kenan, & Long, 2015).

Many Chinese commentators blame such disputes on the combination of "local protectionism" (*difang baohuzhuyi* 地方保护主义) and the underlying incentive structure of China's peculiar system of fiscal decentralization, referred to as "cooking on separate stoves" (*fenzao chifan* 分灶吃饭) (Li, Kenan, & Long, 2015). This system fosters, in the eyes of one observer, "a close relationship to local economies and local-benefit thinking on the part of some local governments [*bendi liyi de kaolu* 本地利益的考虑]" (Zhang, 2009). Local governments, which typically bear responsibility for water pollution control and water resources allocation, are generally reluctant to enforce environmental regulations strictly since industrial enterprises typically compromise the majority of the local government revenue base (Jahiel, 1997). Accordingly, they often fail to implement water abstraction limits or pollution-control technology, instead betraying a "tendency towards transferring pollution costs to lower reaches" (Wang, 2007, p. 402). Such inter-jurisdictional conflict also undermines the construction of large infrastructure projects: even the massive Three Gorges Dam was nearly derailed by a combination of factional-bureaucratic infighting and opposition from upstream provinces such as Sichuan (Lieberthal, 1993).

To the extent that scholars have attempted to explain China's internal hydropolitics, such factional-bureaucratic explanations have historically been favoured (Lieberthal, 1992). However, a second, institutional factor is arguably even more important in driving inter-jurisdictional water disputes; namely, the weakness of formal mechanisms for inter-jurisdictional cooperation, communication, and bargaining within the Chinese political system (Moore, 2014a). In general, this system is structured to bind local officials to central decision-makers at the expense of encouraging horizontal cooperation (Lieberthal & Oksenberg, 1988). The consensus view among both Chinese and foreign observers is that the legal foundations for inter-provincial coordination are weak, and insufficient to meet China's current water resources quality and quantity challenges (Liu & An, 2007; Xu & Guo, 2007; Zhao, 2007). China's principal water resources legislation articulates only general principles for addressing inter-governmental disputes, stating only that they should be resolved through "negotiation and consultation" (RMIT International, 2003, pp. 51–52). The National People's Congress, meanwhile, reinforced this informal, *ad hoc* approach by developing instructions on dealing with trans-jurisdictional water-pollution disputes that explicitly direct local officials to handle disputes themselves before seeking the involvement of higher levels of government (Guojia Renda [National People's Congress], 2002).

Indeed, despite its formal power over subnational jurisdictions, in practice the central government's control mechanisms over local officials possess significant institutional deficiencies. Because of their extensive fiscal decentralization, local governments must often finance implementation of centrally-formulated policies, unsurprisingly creating a "lack of enthusiasm" (Fan & Zhang, 2013). Inter-jurisdictional management authorities, such as the various river basin commissions, lack the legal standing or bureaucratic clout to compel action by upstream or downstream jurisdictions. Indeed, under China's hierarchical administrative system, the leaders of province- and municipal-level jurisdictions often outrank their counterparts in central government ministries, meaning that only the highest levels of government can resolve disputes. Under the current system, disputes are handled by the next-highest institution, so that disputes between municipalities are handled by provincial authorities, and disputes between provinces are handled by the State Council (Li, Kenan, & Long, 2015).

This hierarchical system also constrains the ability of the judiciary to address inter-jurisdictional and transboundary disputes in at least three major respects. First, environmental protection departments and law enforcement agencies have little capacity to work across administrative boundaries, often severely hampering the collection of evidence to prosecute cases. Second, there are few precedents for mounting environmental litigation cases across administrative boundaries, and both public authorities and law firms are largely unequipped to take on such cases. Third and finally, courts rarely have jurisdiction across administrative boundaries, which makes it difficult for the legal system to provide remedies to parties harmed by inter-jurisdictional pollution incidents (Li, Kenan, & Long, 2015). As a result of this institutional capability gap, no less an authority than the Chief Justice of China's Supreme Court has said that China's current administrative arrangements are insufficient to meet the challenges of governing transboundary ecosystems (Li, Kenan, & Long, 2015).

The Chinese government has, in recent years, invested considerable effort in redressing these deficiencies through a number of well-intentioned reform efforts. However, these attempts mostly serve to underline the basic point that the Chinese political system provides insufficient incentives for subnational officials to cooperate with their neighbours over shared water resources. In the Huai River Basin, a Water Resources Protection Leading Group has been established to investigate, monitor, and propose solutions to pending pollution disputes (Li, Kenan, & Long, 2015). In China's largest and most important river basins, considerable steps have already been taken to address interprovincial disputes. In 1990, the Comprehensive Utilization Plan of the Yangtze River Basin established a water management mechanism for the provinces of the Yangtze, though this mechanism was primarily for the purpose of building the Three Gorges Dam. In 2011, a similar mechanism was established in the Yellow River Basin, which brought together the departments of Environmental Protection and Water Resources from the nine riparian provinces under the auspices of the YRCC. The mechanism, referred to as the "Yellow River Basin Emergency Pollution Incident Communication, Coordination, and Cooperation Mechanism", includes provisions related to pollution monitoring (Zhongguo minzhu tongmeng Guangdongsheng weiyuanhui [China Democratic Alliance Guangdong Provincial Committee], 2016). Some similar reform attempts have also been made at sub-provincial levels. In 2006, Guangdong province issued regulations that required local governments to more carefully monitor pollution sources near administrative boundaries, establish administrative mechanisms for handling disputes, and required local officials to take responsibility for resolving disputes (Li, Kenan, & Long, 2015).

To some degree, the increasing pace of regional reforms reflects greater central government attention to the problem of inter-jurisdictional water conflict. In 2008, the Ministry of Environmental Protection (MEP) issued instructions intended to prevent interprovincial water pollution disputes. The instructions stipulated that provinces strictly control point source emissions from enterprises located near provincial boundaries and incorporate trans-provincial impacts into Environmental Impact Assessments, which are approved by MEP. The instructions also stress the importance of information-sharing, joint pollution monitoring by different provincial environment departments, "strengthening communication and coordination", and provided that if provinces could "genuinely not coordinate", the MEP would establish coordination mechanisms. In addition, the instructions stipulate that in the event of disputes occurring, provinces must attempt to resolve them through mutual consultation. The central government will only become involved upon application from the two disputing parties. If, with MEP assistance, the two parties still cannot reach agreement, the MEP will submit opinions on the dispute to the State Council for decision and approval. The instructions clearly emphasize the link between pollution disputes and social stability, stating that "environmental protection departments at all levels should attach great importance to environmental problems in trans-provincial basins…and safeguard environmental security and social stability" (Ministry of Environmental Protection, 2008).

These instructions appear to have created a rush of activity at the provincial level. In 2008, Yunnan, Guizhou, Sichuan, and Congqing signed a "Southwest Regional Water Pollution Dispute" MoU to establish a regional coordination mechanism. Also in 2008, Hangzhou, Huzhou, Jiaxing, and Shaoxing cities' Environmental Protection Bureaus set up a joint Office of Enforcement to conduct joint pollution-monitoring and enforcement. By 2012, the joint effort had reportedly reviewed some 300 enterprises and responded to 10 inter-jurisdictional pollution incidents (Li, Kenan, & Long, 2015). In 2009, Guizhou's Zunyi City similarly established an interprovincial cooperation mechanism with Gulin County in the neighbouring Sichuan province to handle disputes. At the signing ceremony, the city's Party Secretary pledged to "strengthen inter-provincial cooperation, enhance friendship between the people of the two provinces, and promote exchanges" (Zhao & Wang, 2009).

Multi-provincial cooperation is most advanced in the Pearl River Basin, which spans the wealthy province of Guangdong and its poorer neighbours. The Pearl River Water Resources Commission began paying attention to water dispute issues in 1998, when it began preparing the "Pear River Basin Inter-Provincial Waters Agreement". After several years of negotiations with provincial governments, it was finally signed in 2007 (Huang, 2007). As part of the agreement, in response to sand and gravel dredging and other construction projects, the Pearl River Water Resources Commission, which spans Yunnan, Guizhou, Guangdong, Hunan, Jiangxi, Fujian, and Guangxi, established a "consultation mechanism" to resolve interprovincial disputes. Under this mechanism, a task force was established between the provinces to encourage integrated planning and consultation for water infrastructure projects, all of which must be reviewed by the Commission. The mechanism also provides for the establishment of joint investigation teams (Li & Zhou, 2016).

However, these reform efforts do not appear to have had a significant effect in reducing the incidence of inter-jurisdictional disputes, and the issue has continually been raised as a concern by provincial officials. Interprovincial pollution disputes became a significant issue during the 2013 sessions of the NPC and Chinese People's Political Consultative Conference (CPPCC). As a news report of the two recorded, "topics related to water pollution sparked heated debate in the two sessions", and the delegation from Anhui called for the urgent establishment of an inter-jurisdictional water pollution prevention and compensation mechanism that would be led jointly by the Ministries of Environmental Protection and Water Resources (Jiang, 2013). Matters have scarcely improved; a 2015 news article reported that sub-provincial inter-jurisdictional pollution disputes are "spreading like wildfire" (*cengchu buqiong* 层出不穷) and that the issue was continuing to cause concern among members of the NPC and CPPCC (Li, Kenan, & Long, 2015). A 2016 article posted by the Guangdong China Democratic League of the CPPCC likewise warned that "pollution at provincial boundaries are increasingly severe, and transboundary water pollution incidents have occurred". In order to meet the demands of future economic development in the region, the article argued, there is an urgent need to establish an inter-provincial coordinating body chaired by provincial governors (Zhongguo minzhu tongmeng Guangdongsheng weiyuanhui [China Democratic Alliance Guangdong Provincial Committee], 2016).

While legal and institutional mechanisms to prevent transboundary water conflict remain weak, more recently efforts have been made to encourage eco-compensation and water rights trading mechanisms as a solution to inter-jurisdictional water disputes, particularly those related to pollution. The design of these systems typically constructs a fiscal transfer contract between upstream and downstream municipalities, under which the downstream jurisdiction pays a set amount to the upstream entity to protect a source water region. The transfers are intended to compensate upstream jurisdictions for the foregone benefit of developing these source water regions, as well as to undertake measures such as erosion control that improve downstream water quality. Eco-compensation mechanisms were first mentioned in a 2005 State Council regulation concerning environmental protection, and have since been included in several Five-Year Plans and work reports. However, eco-compensation lacks a firm legal basis in China, and efforts to develop an Eco-Compensation Ordinance appear to have stalled (Zhang & Bennett, 2011). Some accounts have even warned that these difficulties risk endangering social stability by providing insufficient compensation to upstream actors forced to refrain from pollution-intensive industrial development (Zhonghao, Zhou, & Yaru, 2016).

Against this backdrop, current eco-compensation initiatives in China have achieved modest successes but appear so far to be incapable of satisfactorily containing inter-jurisdictional conflict. Eco-compensation systems have been concluded between a number of jurisdictions, including Beijing and Hebei, Guangdong and Hong Kong, and several cities within Zhejiang province. Several of these agreements have been in operation for over a decade (China Committee for International Cooperation on Environment and Development, 2006). The Beijing-Hebei mechanism is perhaps the most well-known and involves the transfer of USD 60 million annually from downstream Beijing to individual counties in upstream Hebei to fund land conversion from rice irrigation to rain-fed agriculture, afforestation, and other efforts to improve water quality. Sixty per cent of the payments are distributed to forest owners, and 40 per cent designated as incentive payments for forest management and landscape restoration (Zhang & Bennett, 2011).

In 2012, Anhui and Zhejiang provinces inaugurated a more robust trial mechanism whereby upstream Anhui agreed to pay downstream Zhejiang a certain amount if water quality in the Xin'an River were to fall short of proscribed limits; if, however, the quality were to be higher, downstream Zhejiang agreed to pay Anhui, providing a set incentive to improve water quality. However, this example also illustrates the limitations of eco-compensation mechanisms in China: in the news article announcing the establishment of the mechanism, a provincial official complained that Zhejiang's payments only compensated Anhui for pollution treatment and did not include the opportunity cost of denying permits to heavily-polluting industries to operate along the river (Wang, 2012). Other pilot efforts have encountered similar challenges. One eco-compensation mechanism set up between Beijing, Tianjin, and Chengde City in Hebei, for example, envisioned a 32 billion Renminbi (RMB) investment to improve water quality to the downstream cities, but Chengde failed to recoup its investments through transfers from Beijing and Tianjin, largely due to differences between the local governments regarding payment amounts (Zhonghao, Zhou, & Yaru, 2016).

In sum, eco-compensation mechanisms have up to now failed to prevent and contain transboundary water disputes in China, largely because of weaknesses in their design and implementation. While eco-compensation mechanisms often provide benefits directly to resource managers, such as farmers, to adopt certain practices or to refrain from certain activities in order to improve water quality, in China these mechanisms often involve inter-jurisdictional agreements, effectively positioning administrative jurisdictions as middlemen. Under this arrangement, the link between beneficiaries is severed, and the economic value of eco-compensation is reduced (China Committee for International Cooperation on Environment and Development, 2006). As a result, although by 2012 eight provinces had adopted regulations providing for eco-compensation, no trans-provincial mechanisms were in operation (Wang, 2012). The modest success of China's central government in containing inter-jurisdictional water disputes is therefore clearly not for lack of effort. As such, it demonstrates the challenges of encouraging cooperation between subnational jurisdictions, even in a centralized, authoritarian political system that may be expected to feature less factional subnational hydropolitics than a more centralized system. The next, concluding section accordingly delves into greater detail regarding the international implications of these contentious domestic hydropolitics.

International implications of China's domestic hydropolitics

The focus of this chapter has been on highlighting the salience of domestic, as opposed to international, hydropolitics for China. But ultimately, as noted in the introduction, the most interesting question to arise from this fact is whether and to what extent domestic and international hydropolitical arenas are linked. To some extent, the answer seems certain to be yes; the considerable literature on transboundary water governance suggests that most basins feature a network of political actors at both national and subnational levels (Norman & Bakker, 2009; Sneddon & Fox, 2006). At the same time, transboundary rivers like the Nu are a focal point for non-governmental activism, especially opposition to dam-building, and there is some evidence that such activism has played a role in shaping key policy decisions, particularly decisions to abandon dam construction (Tilt, 2014). However, the nature of China's authoritarian political system raises the question of whether this interaction between domestic and international hydropolitical arenas might be more muted than in the case of other countries. Accordingly, the first question to be answered by future research is whether and how China's contentious domestic hydropolitics influences its international relations.

The evidentiary basis for answering this question is surprisingly weak. Nonetheless, existing scholarship on related issues suggests that answering this question is ripe for detailed study. Even as this chapter has highlighted the strength of subnational actors in domestic hydropolitics, the capacity of national-level actors to shape transboundary political dynamics is surprisingly weak. The Ministry of Foreign Affairs, in particular, is typically a secondary player in infrastructure developments that may impact relations with China's neighbours. According to a United Nations Environment Programme report, for example, "few diplomats are familiar with hydrology, water management, or resource development strategies for river basins, and therefore they rely on the expertise of internal water bureaucracies" (Feng & Magee, 2009, pp. 89–110). Detailed case-study analysis that aims to understand decision-making processes with respect to transboundary river basins would do much to help scholars understand the extent to which China's contentious domestic hydropolitics complicates relations with its transboundary riparian neighbours.

Such research could also usefully gauge the degree to which the priorities of national and subnational hydropolitical actors in China stand at odds. As noted in the introduction, China is distinctive in combining political centralization and fiscal-economic decentralization. While again the evidence is primarily anecdotal, there are some suggestions that economic rather than political factors drive inter-jurisdictional water disputes in China, and may also contribute to a more conflictual stance in its international transboundary relations. Province-level governments in particular seem to possess an economic incentive to maximize the construction of water infrastructure irrespective of the implications for China's relations with its transboundary neighbours. One study concluded, for example, that jurisdictions that host dams experience a 16 per cent increase in revenue as a result of multiplier effects associated with dam construction, while their downstream neighbours suffer revenue decreases of similar magnitude (Bao, 2014). It seems likely that, at least in some cases, provincial-level decisions are made without considering central government priorities: determined lobbying by Yunnan officials enabled construction of the Nuozhadu Dam, one of the largest dams in Asia and a key "prestige project" for the province, on a tributary of the Mekong River, even before it had been formally approved by the State Council (Habich, 2016).

The priority for scholars interested in such questions must be to strengthen the evidentiary basis for understanding the factors that drive subnational decision-making over shared water resources, and possible linkages between subnational and international hydropolitics. The prevalence and complexity of China's domestic hydropolitics cry out for greater attention from scholars and policymakers concerned with international transboundary dynamics as well. The pervasiveness of inter-jurisdictional water disputes, particularly over water pollution, provides a clear illustration of the extent to which water resources management within China remains marked by debate rather than consensus on how to tackle fundamental issues including water use allocation and the further development of the country's rivers. It would be unsurprising if this contention to some degree influences China's relations with neighbouring riparian countries. Accordingly, scholars and policymakers concerned with reducing the risk of conflict and promoting prospects for cooperation on Asia's major transboundary rivers would be wise to pay close attention to China's domestic hydropolitics and on preventing conflicts within countries as well as between them.

References

Bagis, A. I. (1997). Turkey's hydropolitics of the Euphrates-Tigris Basin. *International Journal of Water Resources Development, 13*(4), 567–582.

Bao, X. (2014, March). *Dams and intergovernmental transfer: Balancing local interests in China.* Retrieved July 8, 2016, from EconPapers, http://econpapers.repec.org/paper/wyiwpaper/002234.htm.

Bobekova, E. (2015). Third party conflict management of transboundary river disptues. *International Journal of Conflict Management, 26*(4), 402–426.

Chellaney, B. (2013, February 8). *China's Hydro-Hegemony.* Retrieved from The New York Times, www.nytimes.com/2013/02/08/opinion/global/chinas-hydro-hegemony.html.

China Committee for International Cooperation on Environment and Development. (2006, October 31). *Eco-compensation mechanisms and policies in China.* Retrieved July 5, 2016, from China Academy of Environmental Protection, www.caep.org.cn/english/paper/CCICED-TF-Summary-Report-on-Eco-compensation-Policy-in-China.pdf.

Delli Priscoli, J., & Wolf, A. T. (2009). *Managing and transforming water conflicts.* New York, NY: Cambridge University Press.

Dziobek, C., Mangas, C. G., & Kufa, P. (2011). *Measuring fiscal decentralization – Exploring the IMF's databases.* Washington, DC: International Monetary Fund.

Elhance, A. (1999). *Hydropolitics in the third world: Conflict and cooperation in international river basins.* Washington, DC: United States Institute of Peace.

Fan, J., & Zhang, H. (2013, January 9). *Hebei Handan: zhengzai kaolv pinggu Zhanghe wuran zaocheng sunshi [Hebei Handan: Absorbing the costs of water pollution on the Zhang River].* Retrieved October 28, 2016, from Zhongguo Qingnian bao [China Youth Daily].

Feng, Y., & Magee, D. (2009). Hydropolitical vulnerability and resilience in international river basins in China. In United Nations Environment Programme, *Hydropolitical vulnerabilitity and resilience along international waters: Asia* (pp. 89–110). Nairobi, Kenya: United Nations Environment Programme.

Giordano, M., Giordano, M., & Wolf, A. (2002, December). The geography of water conflict and cooperation: Internal pressures and international manifestations. *The Geographical Journal, 168*(4), 293–312.

Green, N. (2009, March). *Positive spillover? Impact of the Songhua River Benzene incident on China's environmental policy.* Retrieved from China Environment Forum, www.wilsoncenter.org/publication/positive-spillover-impact-the-songhua-river-benzene-incident-china-s-environmental.

Greer, C. (1979). *Water management in the Yellow River Basin of China.* Austin: University of Texas Press.

Guojia Renda [National People's Congress]. (2002, April 17). *Kuaxingzhengquyu de shuiwuran jiufen yingdang ruhe chuli? [How should intrans-jurisdictional water pollution disputes be handled?].* Retrieved April 7, 2012, from Zhongguo Renda Wang [China National People's Congress Net], www.yellowriver.gov.cn/xwzx/sszl/201202/t20120213_113788.html.

Gustafsson, J.-E. (1984). *Water resources development in the People's Republic of China.* Stockholm, Sweden: Royal Institute of Technology.

Habich, S. (2016). *Dams, migration and authoritarianism in China: The local state in Yunnan.* New York, NY: Routledge.

Huang, X. (2007, November 6). *Tansuo shuiwuran liangdajizhi jiejue Zhujiang shuiwenti [A look at two mechanisms for resolving Pearl River water issues].* Retrieved from Xinhua, http://info.water.hc360.com/2007/11/06105893684.shtml.

Hubei Sheng Huanggang Diqu Shuili Dianli Ju [Huanggang Prefecture, Hubei Bureau of Water Conservancy and Electric Power]. (1977). Management of the Meichuan Reservoir Irrigation Project. In J. Nickum (Ed.), *Water management organization in the People's Republic of China* (pp. 77–102). Armonk, NY: ME Sharpe.

Jahiel, A. (1997). The contradictory impact of reform on environmental protection in China. *The China Quarterly, 149,* 81–103.

Jiang, H. (2013, March 5). *Anhui daibiaotuan: jinkuai jianli lianfang liankong jizhi, zhili kuajie shuiwuran [Anhui delegation: Establish joint prevention and control mechanisms to manage transboundary water pollution].* Retrieved from Phoneix News, http://news.ifeng.com/mainland/special/2013lianghui/detail_2013_03/05/22769706_0.shtml.

Li, C., Kenan, T., & Long, X. (2015, March 12). *Kuajie shuiwuran jiufen weihe duonian nanjue? [Why are transboundary water pollution disputes intractable?].* Retrieved from Zhongguo huanjing bao [China Environmental Report], www.chinanews.com/ny/2015/03-12/7122747.shtml.

Li, H., Liu, T., & Huang, W. (2010). Kuajie shuiziyuan chongtu dongyin yu xietiao moshi yanjiu [Research on the drivers and resolution modes of transbounday water resource disputes]. *Ziran Ziyuan Xuebao [Journal of Natural Resources], 25*(5). Retrieved from http://d.wanfangdata.com.cn/periodical_zrzyxb201005001.aspx.

Li, Z., He, D., & Feng, Y. (2011). Regional hydropolitics of the transboundary impacts of the Lancang cascade dams. *Water International, 3,* 328–339.

Li, Z., & Wu, F. (2016). China and shared water resources: Geopolitics, domestic institutions and global governance. In F. Wu, & H. Zhang, *China's quest for global resources* (pp. 59–78). London, UK: Routledge.

Li, Z., & Zhou, F. (2016, June 2). *Zhujiang liuyu jianli xieshang jizhi jiejue kuasheng shuishi jiufen [Pear River Delta established consultation mechanism to resolve inter-provincial water disputes].* Retrieved from Shenzhen Jingming Club, http://yy.855bunr.com/pdjcbs/677.html.

Lieberthal, K. (1992). Introduction: The 'fragmented authoritarianism' model and its limitations. In K. Lieberthal, & D. Lampton, *Bureaucracy, politics, and decision-making in post-Mao China* (pp. 1–30). Berkeley: University of California Press.

Lieberthal, K. (1993). China: The Three Gorges Project. In G. O. Fuare, & J. Zubin, *Culture and negotiation: The resolution of water disputes* (pp. 176–195). London, UK: SAGE.

Lieberthal, K., & Oksenberg, M. (1988). *Policy making in China: Leaders, structures, and processes.* Princeton, NJ: Princeton University Press.

Liu, B., & Speed, R. (2010). Water resources management in the People's Republic of China. In X. Sun, R. Speed, & D. Shen, *Water resources management in the People's Republic of China* (pp. 5–20). New York, NY: Routledge.

Liu, H., & An, P. (2007). Jiji xietiao shengji shuishi jiufen, cujin Jing-Jin-Ji dushiquan hexie fazhan [Actively resolve inter-provincial water disputes, encourage harmonious development in the Beijing-Tianjin-Hebei capital region]. *Haihe shuili [Water Resources], 2,* 14–16.

Mertha, A. (2008, December). *China's water warriors: Citizen action and policy change.* Ithaca, NY: Cornell University Press.

Mertha, A., & Lowry, W. (2006). Unbuilt dams: Seminal events and policy change in China, Australia, and the United States. *Comparative Politics, 39,* 1–20.

Ministry of Environmental Protection. (2008, July 7). *Guidance on prevention and disposal of water pollution disputes across provincial boders.* Retrieved from Environmental Management Information for Industry, www.mep.gov.cn/gkml/hbb/bwj/200910/t20091022_174603.htm.

Moore, S. (2014a, September). Hydropolitics and inter-jurisdictional relationships in China: The pursuit of localized preferences in a centralized system. *The China Quarterly, 219*, 760–780.

Moore, S. (2014b). Modernisation, authoritarianism, and the environment: The politics of China's South-North Water Transfer Project. *Environmental Politics, 23*(6), 947–964.

National People's Congress. (2004). *Constitution of the People's Republic of China.* Retrieved February 15, 2017, from www.npc.gov.cn/englishnpc/Constitution/node_2825.htm.

Ningxia Ribao [Ningxia Daily]. (2010, October 3). *Quanguo rendachangweihui guanxin Ningxia zhongdian duban jianyi yishi [NPC Standing Committee gives an on-the-spot report on key supervision work in Ningxia].* Retrieved November 8, 2012, from Quanguo Renmin Daibiao Dahui [National People's Congress], www.npc.gov.cn/npc/xinwen/2010-10/08/content_1597926.htm.

Norman, E., & Bakker, K. (2009). Transgressing scales: Water governance across the Canada-U.S. Borderland. *Annals of the Association of American Geographers, 99*, 99–117.

Oi, J. (1995). The role of the local state in China's transitional economy. *The China Quarterly, 144*, 1132–1149.

Oksenberg, M., & Tong, J. (1991). The evolution of central-provincial fiscal relations in China, 1971–1984: The formal system. *The China Quarterly, 125*, 9–10.

Peng, H. (2009). Kuaxingzhengqu liuyu shuiwuran zhili [Control of trans-jurisdictional river basin water pollution]. *Zhongguo Chengshi Yanjiu (Dianzi qikan) [E-Journal of China Urban Studies], 4*(1), 36–40.

Qi, G. (2011). *Lun Zhongguo de dazhengfu yu qiangzhengfu.* Beijing, People's Republic of China: Shehui Kexue Wenxian Chubanshe [Social Sciences Academic Press].

RMIT International. (2003). *Local legislation to support transjurisdictional water pollution management.* Asian Development Bank. Melbourne, Australia: RMIT International.

Shen, D. (2009, December). River basin water resources management in China: A legal and institutional assessment. *Water International, 34*(4), 484–496.

Sneddon, C., & Fox, C. (2006). Rethinking transboundary waters: A critical hydropolitics of the Mekong Basin. *Political Geography, 25*, 181–202.

Stanway, D. (2012a, November 22). *In beautiful China, local polluters still hold sway.* Retrieved December 5, 2012, from Reuters, www.reuters.com/article/2012/11/22/uk-china-congress-environment-idUSLNE8AL00T20121122.

Stanway, D. (2012b, July 26). *Pollution makes quarter of China water unusuable: Ministry.* Retrieved October 28, 2012, from Reuters, www.reuters.com/article/2010/07/26/us-china-environment-water-idUSTRE66P39H20100726.

Susskind, L., & Islam, S. (2012, September). Water Diplomacy: Creating value and building trust in transboundary water negotiations. *Science & Diplomacy, 1*(3).

Tilt, B. (2014). *Dams and development in China: The moral economy of water and power.* New York, NY: Columbia University Press.

Turton, A., & Ashton, P. (2008). Basin closure and issues of scale: The Southern African hydropolitical complex. *International Journal of Water Resources Development, 24*(2), 305–318.

Uitto, J., & Duda, A. (2002, December). Management of transboundary water resources: Lessons from international cooperation for conflict prevention. *The Geographical Journal, 168*(4), 365–378.

UNFAO. (2011). *Ganges-Brahmaputra-Meghna Basin*. Retrieved from Food and Agriculture Organization of the United Nations, www.fao.org/nr/water/aquastat/basins/gbm/index.stm.

Wang, Y. (2007). Diagnosis and recommendations for transjurisdictional water pollution management in China. *Frontiers of Environmental Science and Engineering in China, 1*(4), 401–417.

Wang, Y. (2009). Water governance and state governance: A transaction cost perspective of China's unitarianism. *Workshop in political theory and policy analysis*. Bloomington: Indiana University.

Wang, Y. (2012, January 30). *Trans-provincial compensation mechanism: A new path for China's water environment protection*. Retrieved from Xinhuanet, http://news.xinhuanet.com/english/china/2012-01/30/c_131382753.htm.

Waterbury, J. (1979). *Hydropolitics of the Nile Valley*. New York, NY: Syracuse University Press.

Wei, Y. (2000). *Regional development in China: States, globalization and inequality*. London, UK: Routledge.

Wirsing, R. (2007). Hydro-politics in South Asia: The domestic roots of interstate river rivalry. *Asian Affairs: An American Review, 34*(1), 3–22.

Wouters, P., Hu, D., Zhang, J., Andrew-Speed, P., & Tarlock, D. (2004). The new development of water law in China. *University of Denver Law Review, 7*(2), 243–308.

Xinhua. (2012, January 30). *Trans-provincial compensation mechanism: A new path for China's water environment protection*. Retrieved November 2, 2012, from Xinhuanet, http://news.xinhuanet.com/english/china/2012-01/30/c_131382753.htm.

Xu, G., & Guo, S. (2007). Changjiang liuyu shengji heliuzhong shuishi jiufen chongtu yu duice cuoshi [Inter-provincial water disputes and conflicts in the Yangtze River Basin and potential countermeasures]. *Shuiziyuan Baohu [Water Resources Protection], 2*, 54–56.

Yang, D. (2004). *Remaking the Chinese Leviathan: Market transition and the politics of governance in China*. Stanford, CA: Stanford University Press.

Zawahri, N., & Hensengerth, O. (2012, September). Domestic environmental activists and the governance of the Ganges and Mekong Rivers in India and China. *International Environmental Agreements, 12*(3), 269–298.

Zhang, B. (2009, November 5). *Kuaxingzheng quyu shuiwuran jiufen jiejue jizhi yanjiu [Trans-jurisdictional water pollution dispute resolution mechanism research]*. Retrieved April 7, 2012, from Wuhan Daxue Huanjingfa Yanjiusuo [Wuhan University Environmental Law Research Institute], www.riel.whu.edu.cn/article.asp?id=30420.

Zhang, J., Zhuang, J., Lai, W., & Qiang, Z. (2010). Zhujiang liuyu kuasheng heliu shuishi maodun ji chuli cuoshi chutan [Initial research on transboundary water disputes in the Pearl River Basin and measures for handling them]. *Renmin Zhujiang [People's Pearl River], 1*, 7–9.

Zhang, Q., & Bennett, M. (2011). *Eco-compensation for watershed services in the People's Republic of China*. Manila, Philippines: Asian Development Bank.

Zhao, J., & Wang, J. (2009, April 21). *Zunyishi, Xishuixian Cifaju jianli maodun jiufen kuasheng diaochu hezuo jizhi [Zunyi City and Xizhui County Courts establish an inter-provincial cooperation mechanism]*. Retrieved from Guizhousheng Renmin Zhengfu Fazhi Bangongshi [Guizhou Provincial People's Government Legal Affairs Office], www.gzfzb.gov.cn/html/zunyi/667/.

Zhao, L. (2007). *Woguo liuyu kuajie shuiwuran jiufen xiediao jizhi yanjiu: yi Weihe liuyu weili [Research on coordination mechanisms for transboundary river basin pollution disputes in China: An example from the Wei River Basin]*. Shanghai, People's Republic of China: Fudan University Press.

Zhongguo minzhu tongmeng Guangdongsheng weiyuanhui [China Democratic Alliance Guangdong Provincial Committee]. (2016, February 4). *Guanyu jiakuai tuijin Zhujiang liuyu kuasheng (qu) shuiziyuan baohu yu shuiwuran fangzhi xiezuo jizhi jianshe de jianyi [Recommendations on speeding up establishment of an inter-provincial water pollution prevention and cooperation mechanism]*. Retrieved from Zhongguo minzhu tongmeng Guangdongsheng weiyuanhui [China Democratic Alliance Guangdong Provincial Committee], www.gdmm.org.cn/UserData/DocHtml/2016/2/4/458205956035.html.

Zhonghao, W., Zhou, N., & Yaru, G. (2016, April 6). *Shuiquan zhidu gaige mianlin "Sanzhongmen" [Water rights system reform faces "Three Gates"]*. Retrieved from Neimongu shuiwen xinxi wang [Inner Mongolia Hydrology Information Network], http://nmgswj.com/2016/monographic_04/457.shtml.

Zhonghua Renmin Gongheguo Zhongyang Renmin Zhengfu [Central People's Government of the PRC]. (2006, January 8). *Jiedu: "Guojia tufa gonggong shijian zongti yingji yuan" [Understanding "National critical public incident coordinated emergency planning"]*. Retrieved November 8, 2012, from Central People's Government, www.gov.cn/zwhd/2006-01/08/content_151018.htm.

3 Transboundary river management in Southeast Asia

The role of Chinese dam-builders

Frauke Urban, Giuseppina Siciliano, and Johan Nordensvard

Introduction

Large dams have been the subject of controversy and debate for several decades as a result of their far-reaching and often irreversible social and environmental impacts (WCD, 2000). In the pursuit of renewable, low-carbon energy and climate change mitigation, hydropower is experiencing a new renaissance in many parts of the world, despite its vulnerability to climate change (IPCC, 2011). At the forefront of the renaissance of large hydropower dams is China, the world's largest dam builder. Internationally, China's engagement in the hydropower sector is reported to be primarily through Chinese state-owned enterprises (SOEs) such as Sinohydro (also known as PowerChina/PowerChina Resources Limited), a firm leading the global hydropower sector in terms of the number and size of dams built, investment sums, and global coverage.

While China has a long history of domestic dam-building, recent developments have led to Chinese overseas dam-building, particularly in low- and middle-income countries in Asia and Africa (Bosshard, 2009; International Rivers, 2012; McDonald, Bosshard, & Brewer, 2009). In recent years, Chinese dam-builders and investors have been particularly active in neighbouring countries along transboundary rivers, such as in the Mekong region with increased Chinese investments and dam-building especially in Myanmar, Laos, and Cambodia.

China's rapid economic growth means the large dams sector is nearly saturated in China, meaning that many big rivers have already been dammed in China, hence the domestic market is very limited. The Chinese government's "Going Out Strategy" (Mohan & Power 2008) and its recent Belt and Road Initiative (BRI) (Xinhua Finance Agency, 2015) therefore encourages overseas investments to access overseas markets for Chinese goods and services, especially infrastructure, and partly also to access natural resources such as minerals, water, and energy (Mohan & Power 2008). It is estimated that there are currently close to 350 Chinese-funded and Chinese-built overseas hydropower projects listed as either completed, under construction, at the Memorandum of Understanding (MoU) stage, or suspended, most of them in Southeast Asia (38 per cent) and Africa (26 per cent) (International Rivers, 2016). These data have to be treated with caution though, as they do not mean that all of these dams will be constructed in the future. For Southeast Asia, about 30 dams were completed by 2016 where Chinese dam-builders or financiers were involved, in comparison to more than 120 dams that were proposed, under construction, suspended, or reported as completed (International Rivers, 2016). Data limitations, however, exist, as the non-governmental organization (NGO) International Rivers is currently the only organization tracking Chinese-built and Chinese-funded dams at the global level, while other databases are regional and hence fractional.

The large majority of these dams are large dams with a capacity over 50 MW. Many were built after 2000, at a time when other dam-building nations and organizations, particularly those from the Organisation for Economic Co-operation and Development (OECD), scaled down their operations.

As China has internationalized its dam-building industry, there have been questions over the motives and mechanisms of Chinese banks and SOEs. Chinese dam-builders are seen as different and distinct actors for a range of reasons, forming part of a wider logic of "encompassing accumulation" that combines state and capital agendas as opposed to being strictly profit-oriented (Lee, 2014). Some argue that their bundling of aid, trade, and investments is a unique financing model. For example, SOEs like Sinohydro benefit from abundant state funding, especially through preferential loans from China ExIm Bank. Finally, the Chinese banks' and firms' pragmatic approach to regional politics and political alliances and an associated tendency not to apply conditionality in their lending may result in ignoring poor governance in recipient countries. Playing into this is a perception that China is "all powerful" and drives these agendas whereas recent work has argued that the agency of the recipient states is key in shaping how and in whose interests these investments play out (Carmody & Kragelund, 2016; Mohan & Lampert, 2013; Urban et al., 2015a; b). Yet, there may be other reasons: Kirchherr, Charles and Walton (2016a), and Kirchherr, Disselhoff and Charles (2016b) suggest that Chinese dam-builders are far cheaper and more effective in constructing dams than their competitors, with far fewer cost overruns and construction time overruns. Hensengerth (2013) found that the role of Chinese dam-builders is often strongly influenced by local host government settings, that their social and environmental performance is improving and that essentially, Chinese dam-builders do not differ that much from their competitors.

At the same time, Chinese dam-builders play a major role in China's transboundary river management, most importantly along the Mekong River. The Mekong River has become the "Battery of Asia", eventually generating hydroelectricity for the region and being a target for Chinese dam-builders a well as other dam builders from Thailand, Vietnam, and elsewhere. China's neighbours along the Mekong River are in a difficult situation: on one side, they welcome Chinese investments in the energy and water sectors and hope to gain prosperity from these investments, such as in Cambodia and Laos, while others fear for their water security and the irreversible impacts of China's dam-building activities upstream, such as in Vietnam.

This chapter investigates China's role as the world's largest builder of and investor in large dams, focussing on the Greater Mekong Subregion (GMS) in Southeast Asia. It addresses the role Chinese actors play in large dam-building as well as the environmental, social, economic and political implications of this by drawing on two selected case studies from Cambodia and Vietnam. The chapter consists of the following sections: the next section elaborates the conceptual framework and the methodology of the research. Afterwards, we present the findings, and finally discuss the findings and conclude the chapter with recommendations.

Conceptual framework and methodology

Conceptual framework: the political ecology of the Asian drivers

The impacts of large hydropower dams are well-known (e.g. Adams, 2000; Biswas, 1982; Tilt, Braun, & He, 2009; Tortajada, Altinbilek, & Biswas, 2012; Scudder, 2012). There is also abundant research on large dams in China (e.g. Chang, Liu, & Zhou, 2009; Dore & Yu, 2004; Hayashi, Murakami, Xu, & Watanabe, 2008; Hwang, Xi, Cao, Feng, & Qiao, 2007; Magee, 2006). A few studies were looking at China and its hydropower role overseas (Bosshard, 2009; Goh, 2004; McDonald, Bosshard, & Brewer, 2009; Yu, 2003). Yet empirical research on China as a large dam-builder overseas is still in its infancy, as until a few years ago, much of the research on China's environmental and social impact overseas was theoretical or conceptual rather than based on empirical evidence (compare Urban et al., 2013a,b,c). This is slowly changing with high quality, empirical work carried out by Hensengerth (2013, 2016), Kirchherr et al. (2016a,b), Matthews and Motta (2013), Lamb and Dao (2015), Chen and Landry (2016), Urban et al. (2015a), Urban, Nordensvard, Siciliano and Li (2015b), Siciliano, Urban, Kim and Lonn (2015), Tan-Mullins, Mang and Urban (forthcoming), and several others in the last few years. However, the transboundary perspective has largely been omitted so far. This chapter is therefore one of the few studies that provides empirical evidence for this important topic.

This research uses a conceptual framework we term the "Political Ecology of the Asian Drivers" (Siciliano & Urban, 2017; Siciliano, Urban, Tan-Mullins, Lonn, & Kim, 2016), which combines the theories and approaches of the "Political Ecology" with those of the "Asian Drivers." The "Political Ecology of the Asian Drivers" framework (Siciliano and Urban, 2017; Siciliano et al., 2016) is a hybrid approach that seeks to elucidate our three broad research aims – analyzing the actors driving the internationalization of dam-building, the channels through which they engage, and the environmental, social, economic, and political impacts on the ground. We use this framework to overcome some of the current gaps in knowledge and understanding in relation to China's rise and its environmental implications. The majority of early work on China's engagement with low- and middle-income countries (LMICs) has been speculative (Mohan & Power, 2008), economistic (Jacques, 2009), and Africa-focused (Alden et al.,

2008; Brautigam, 2009). Crucially, these studies largely ignored the environmental consequences of China's internationalization (Shinn, 2016). The Political Ecology focuses on environmental and ecological implications of power relations that relate to natural resource management, and this approach is therefore useful for understanding China's impacts in overseas dam-building and related water management. Understanding a complex set of international actors, interdependencies, and ecological impacts necessitates a broad theoretical framework (Urban et al., 2013b; Urban et al., 2015) such as the "Political Ecology of the Asian Drivers."

We combine the distinctive approach of the "Asian Drivers" (Humphrey & Messner, 2005) and their impacts with aspects of the "Political Ecology" approach to address China's role in overseas dam-building. The Asian Drivers framework was developed to help understand the rise of Asian "tiger economies" such as Korea, Singapore, Taiwan, and later China. The Asian Drivers framework developed by Schmitz (2006) and Kaplinsky and Messner (2008) assesses China's and other East Asian countries' direct and indirect impacts as a Rising Power and its channels of interaction with LMICs. The Asian Drivers framework focussed on impacts of economic channels of interaction, such as trade, aid, and investments, as well as non-economic channels such as global governance, individuals, and the environment (Kaplinsky and Messner, 2008). It also assessed direct and indirect impacts as well as competitive and complementary dimensions of these impacts for the Asian "tiger economies". The competitive and complementary aspect responded mainly to issues around international economic competitiveness. The framework was aimed at assessing the impacts of these emerging economies and their impacts on other countries, including developed and developing countries. In each of these channels – aid, trade, investment, global governance, individuals (including migrants from China and other East Asian countries), and environment – there will be a mixture of complementary and competitive economic impacts and positive and negative impacts in relation to society and the environment (Kaplinsky & Messner 2008). Urban et al. (2013a,b) and Urban, Nordensvärd, Wang, Khatri and Mohan (2011) advanced the Asian Drivers framework further by addressing motives, actors, and beneficiaries in addition to impacts to analyse in more depth how, why, and with which impacts Chinese actors engage in LMICs. The authors of this chapter amended the channel of interaction entitled "individuals" into "society", as this describes more adequately the dynamics of interaction and who benefits or loses from large dam projects.

However, the Asian Drivers framework is somewhat static and, while it focuses on actors and motives, it does not explicitly address questions of power, nor does it analyse political economy drivers and ecological processes as entwined. To address these issues, we use ideas from Political Ecology (Greenberg & Park, 1994; Perreault et al., 2015; Wolf, 1972). The concepts of the Political Ecology are essentially about human-environment relations (Perreault et al., 2015). They help to analyse the bargaining between actors involved in dam construction, as well as the conflicts caused by the varied forms of control over access to natural resources such as water, energy, land, and forests (Blaikie, 1985; Bryant & Bailey, 1998; Peet & Watts, 2004). Power relations between different actors are at the heart of the Political Ecology framework (Tan-Mullins, 2007), and assessing the unequal power relations between actors allows us to explain the uneven distribution of access and control of environmental resources. Bryant and Bailey (1997) developed three fundamental assumptions in practicing political ecology in developing countries. First, costs and benefits associated with environmental change are distributed unequally. Second, this unequal distribution inevitably reinforces or reduces existing social and economic inequalities. Third, the unequal distribution of costs and benefits and the reinforcing or reducing of preexisting inequalities holds political implications in terms of the altered power relationships that result (Bryant & Bailey, 1997).

Power is related to the differential ability to control and/or access the economic benefits from resource exploitation (Bryant, 1996, 1997; Dauvergne, 1994; Peluso, 1992). Crucially, we examine power across actors and scales in relation to natural resource access (Dittgen, 2015). As we noted, it is often assumed that "the Chinese" hold the power, whereas the agency of host governments as well as wider social actors is important. In terms of SOEs entering LMIC markets, we focus on the brokerage between state elites on both the Chinese and LMIC sides (see Carmody et al., 2012) in which infrastructure deals are often negotiated behind closed doors and bypass domestic channels of accountability.

The "Political Ecology of the Asian Drivers" framework enables us to address the role and impacts of Chinese dam-builders in LMICs, assess issues of power, and deal with the environmental and social implications for global hydropower development. The chapter also focuses on the views and motives of Cambodian and Vietnamese actors towards Chinese hydropower investment and transboundary river management.

We therefore focus on the following channels of interaction in this combined conceptual approach: trade, investment, aid, innovation, politics (addressing issues of power), environment, and society. We also analyse the motives, actors, beneficiaries, and impacts from both the Chinese side and the LMIC side.

Methodology

The empirical research was conducted between 2012 and 2016 with interviews and focus group discussions in Cambodia, China, and to a limited extent, Vietnam. Cambodia and Vietnam have been selected because they both have seen an increase in Chinese investments in the dam sector; however, with different dynamics. Cambodia has been selected as it is one of the countries that Chinese actors heavily invest in, including in the hydropower sector. The political, economic, and cultural relations between China and Cambodia are closely knit and both countries welcome bilateral trade and investment opportunities between their countries. Vietnam has been selected as a contrasting case study as Chinese investment is less heavy and more indirect, for example Chinese actors investing in parts of the value chain or in joint ventures rather than large

Chinese hydropower firms leading large dam projects like in Cambodia. The political, economic, and cultural relations between China and Cambodia are also rather complicated and ambivalent, which in turn creates a different relationship in terms of trade and investments, including in the hydropower sector. Both countries are also located at different places along the Mekong River (Vietnam: very much downstream, close to the sea; Cambodia: also downstream but upstream from Vietnam, meaning that Chinese-built dams will have an impact on Vietnam's water issues). We started by conducting a multi-level stakeholder mapping (Schiffer, 2010) to identify key stakeholders engaged in Chinese overseas hydropower projects and in China itself.

We held 62 interviews and 10 focus group discussions (FGDs) in China, Cambodia, and Vietnam: 20 key informant interviews with institutional actors who were involved in/had expertise about dam construction; 18 interviews with Chinese dam-builders and financiers; 24 interviews with affected community members and their chiefs; and 10 FGDs with local community members. For the institutional interviews, we conducted semi-structured interviews with hydropower firms, policymakers, financiers, NGOs, and academics. These actors were interviewed about their perceptions of the socio-economic and environmental impacts of dams, and governance issues and political implications, as well as the role of Chinese dam-builders. On the Chinese side, semi-structured interviews were held with dam-builders and financiers such as Sinohydro, Export Import Bank, and government officials from authorities like the Ministry for Water Resources and the Ministry of Finance and Commerce. This enabled us to investigate dam contract issues, governance arrangements, and economic and political implications, as well as their understanding of the social and environmental impacts of the dam. For the community fieldwork, we carried out 2 FGDs in 5 affected villages around the Kamchay dam site in Cambodia, hence conducting 10 FGDs in total. In addition, we conducted 22 individual semi-structured interviews with community members and with the village chiefs. See also Siciliano et al. (2016) for parts of the fieldwork.

For the data analysis, we analysed the transcribed, qualitative data by categorizing and coding the fieldwork sources as a means of comparing and contrasting interpretations of events (Wolcott, 1990). The interviews and FGDs were coded according to themes and sub-themes. The broad themes were divided in social, environmental, economic, political, and technological perspectives (see also Siciliano et al., 2016).

Findings: a comparative study of China's dam-building in Southeast Asia

The role of Chinese actors in global dam-building

As the Asian Drivers approach highlights, analyzing the channels of interaction between China and the dam host countries (such as aid, trade, and investment) is crucial for understanding the complementary and competitive economic impacts, motives, actors, and beneficiaries. This paragraph shows how Chinese investment strategies in large hydropower dams are managed vis-à-vis LMICs.

There are numerous Chinese dam-builders, and the companies registered and operating in China can vary from those subsidiaries specifically set up for overseas operation. These actors are usually the ones with the most power to inscribe change on the environment, and subsequently on livelihood options and power relations between the stakeholders at the local level. The main players in overseas hydropower dam building are: China Datang Overseas Investment Company (subsidiary of Datang International Power Generation Company), Gezhouba International, China Huadian Corporation, China Huaneng Group, Power-China Resources Limited (which is an international subsidiary of Sinohydro), Sinohydro Corporation (also known as PowerChina), and China Three Gorges Corporation. There are other small players in the industry, such as suppliers and grid operators, which includes Hydro China, Dongfang, China Southern Grid, and China State Grid. There are several Chinese dam financiers such as China Export-Import Bank (ExIm Bank), Chinese Development Bank (CDB), Sinosure, and to a lesser extent commercial/or non-policy banks, Industrial and Commercial Bank of China (ICBC), and the Bank of China (BoC) (Tan-Mullins et al., forthcoming).

The Chinese government is actively encouraging firms to invest overseas through its "Going Out Policy" (Mohan & Power, 2008) since 2000. At the same time, the government's BRI (Xinhua Finance Agency, 2015), which is a development strategy and framework initiated in 2013 to increase the economic and political ties amongst the former Silk Road countries, is also encouraging Chinese firms to operate overseas. The Mekong Region includes two of the six key corridors for expanded outward investment in infrastructure, namely the China-Indochina Peninsula Economic Corridor (CICPEC) and the Bangladesh-China-India-Myanmar Economic Corridor (BCIM-EC). The BRI qualifies Cambodia, Laos, Myanmar, Thailand, and Vietnam for a number of Chinese funding initiatives associated with infrastructure needs (Motta and Matthews, 2017, forthcoming). It is being reported that Chinese leading power firms invested nearly USD 3 billion overseas (FDI China, 2015).

Many of the companies' respondents indicated that other than profits, the contributing factors for them to invest overseas include the Chinese government's Going Out Policy, stiff competition within China, sector reforms due to an increasingly saturated internal market, decreasing suitable sites for new dams in China, and a lack of international competitors and national policy directives. Low costs, access to finance (and at times, cheap loans) and a big portfolio of domestic projects also make them attractive partners for clients around the world (Tan-Mullins et al., forthcoming). This is exemplified by the following quote:

> Big dam building is an important part of the "going out" strategy, but I think it is just business, it has no strong relationship with political issues. On the one hand, there is market demand; on the other hand, China has

rich experience with dams building. The domestic capacity in China is over supplied, so that Chinese dam firms need to go global.

(Interview with ExIm Bank, 2013)

There are different Chinese ministries with varying degrees of involvement in the project cycle of an overseas Chinese dam project. They are the State Council, Ministry of Commerce (MOFCOM), Ministry of Foreign Affairs (MOFA), National Development and Reform Commission (NDRC), Ministry of Environmental Protection (MEP), and the State-owned Assets Supervision and Administration Commission (SASAC) (Urban et al., 2013b). Every project that is greater than USD 2 billion requires approval from the State Council, endorsement by NDRC, and MOFCOM approval (IR, November 2012, p. 7). Furthermore, the State Council is also the overarching agency that oversees MOFCOM and NDRC, two very important stakeholders in approving and overseeing overseas dam projects. MOFCOM is the main institute that approves and manages overseas investment of the SOEs, which includes hydropower dams. NDRC approves smaller projects (less than USD 2 billion) and regulates overseas investments. MOFA then provides advice on Chinese foreign policy, such as aid matters, while the MEP provides advice on environmental protection issues such as the use of Environmental Impact Assessment (EIA). Finally, SASAC assesses the performance of these SOEs (IR, November 2012, pp. 8–9). As indicated above, although some decisions are driven more by national policies than revenue, we should not overestimate the power of these ministries over the companies. The Chinese government can and does influence these companies if there is a strategic objective to pursue, but beyond this, the companies are not generally under the control of the national government and are governed by boards and private investors (Tan-Mullins et al., forthcoming). Beneficiaries are primarily SOEs, but also the Chinese government that receives tax incomes from the overseas operations. The following figures analyze China's overseas dam investment. As Figure 3.1 indicates, the majority of the dams (completed, under construction, and at the MOU stage) are located in Asia (57 per cent, mainly in South East Asia [38 per cent]), followed by Africa (26 per cent), Latin America (8 per cent), Europe (7 per cent, mainly Eastern Europe), and the Middle East and the Pacific (1 per cent each), according to International Rivers database (2015).

Looking at Southeast Asia in particular, the most targeted countries are Myanmar, Laos, the Philippines, Malaysia, Cambodia, and Vietnam, as Figure 3.2 indicates. Chinese dam activity in Vietnam has been reduced in the last couple of years, as the political tensions around the South China Sea and water scarcity on the downstream Mekong River in Vietnam due to China's dam-building activity upstream has worsened political ties between the two countries.

The Chinese are involved in overseas dam investments with different roles. They can act as financiers, developers, builders, as well as subcontractors only or acting as a combination of these roles. Usually they are involved in at least two of the above tasks (Urban et al., 2013b). For the majority of dam investments,

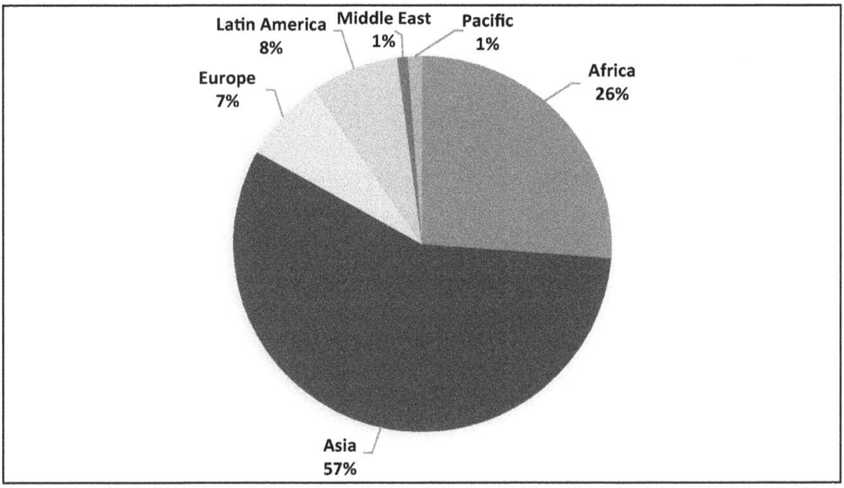

Figure 3.1 Chinese overseas dam projects by location – World regions.
Source: Amended from Urban and Siciliano, 2013.

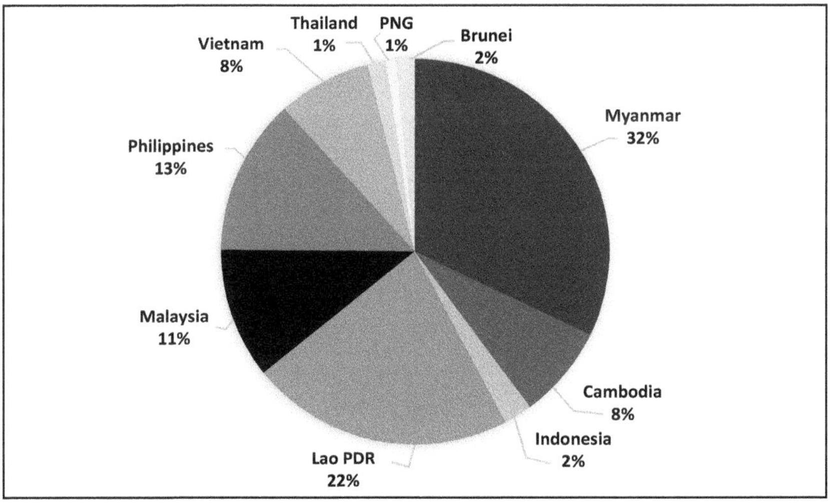

Figure 3.2 Chinese overseas dams in Southeast Asia.
Source: Amended from Urban and Siciliano, 2013.

namely for about 66 per cent, China acts as the sole financier, according to the International Rivers database (2015). In 22 per cent of the cases, host national governments participate in the investment; for the remaining 13 per cent of the cases, international investors also participate together with Chinese

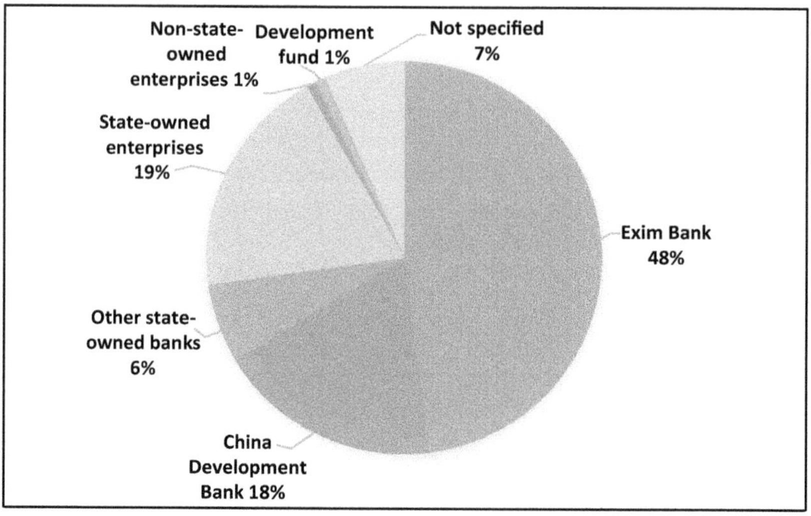

Figure 3.3 Chinese financiers involved in overseas dam investments.
Source: Amended from Urban and Siciliano, 2013.

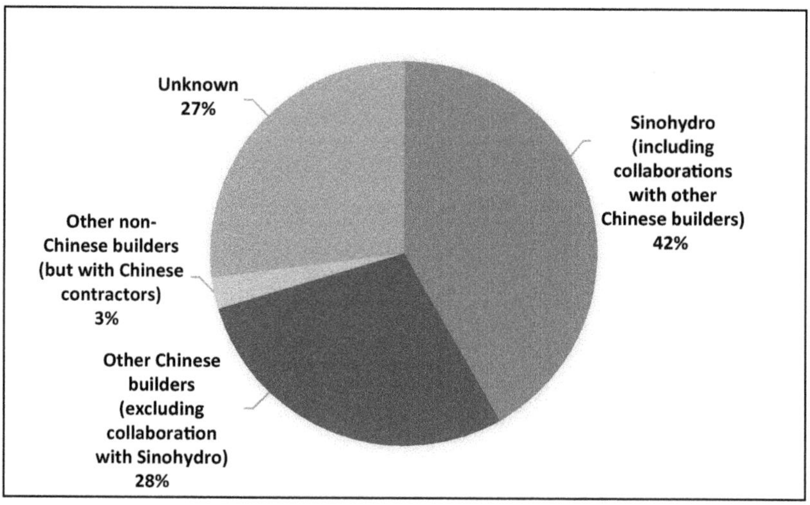

Figure 3.4 Chinese builders involved in overseas dam projects.
Source: Amended from Urban and Siciliano, 2013.

dam-builders, and in few cases, the investors are national financiers, such as the governments of host countries. This is shown in Figure 3.3.

Sinohydro is leading the global hydropower sector as the world's largest dam company in terms of number and size of dams built, investment sums, and global coverage, as Figure 3.4 shows. This is followed by China International

Water & Electric Corporation (CWE) and China Gezhouba Group Company Limited, both SOEs. In general, almost all of the Chinese companies involved in the construction of overseas dams are state-owned.

In the CMS, the Consortium of International Agricultural Research Centers (CGIAR)'s Water, Land and Ecosystems (WLE) Greater Mekong Dam Database indicates that there are currently 87 dam developments led by Chinese overseas dam-builders, of which 57 are supposed to be commissioned, 12 under construction, 16 planned or proposed, and 2 cancelled or suspended (CGIAR, 2016). The next two sections deal with Chinese-built and Chinese-financed dams in Cambodia and Vietnam.

Case study: Cambodia

Cambodia's energy setting

Cambodia had an electrification rate of only 31 per cent in 2015, which means almost 10 million people in Cambodia still lack energy access. The electrification rate in urban areas is high with about 91 per cent; however, in rural areas, the rate is considerably lower, accounting for only 19 per cent (World Bank, 2016).

Electricity production in Cambodia relies mainly on oil products such as kerosene and diesel, namely 90 per cent of the total, and for a small fraction, 4 per cent only, to hydro, followed by coal and peat at 3 per cent, biofuels at 2 per cent and solar PV at 0.3 per cent. Fossil fuel is used for both transport and electricity generation. More than 90 per cent of the electricity supply comes from decentralized generators rather than the grid. Even the batteries that rural households use for lighting are charged at diesel-powered charging stations (Clean Energy Info Portal, 2013).

Cambodia's electricity production is far below the country's needs, and imports far exceed the internal electricity production with roughly 1640 gigawatt hours (GWh) of imports and 1050 GWh of internal production (IEA, 2016). Cambodia therefore relies heavily on imported oil for the production of electricity, as well as on electricity imports, mainly from neighbouring countries, primarily Vietnam and Thailand. Overall, Cambodia has some of the highest electricity costs in the world due to the above-mentioned issues, despite being a low-income country (IEA, 2016). Electricity prices range from 0.09 to 0.25 USD per kilowatt hour (kWh) for urban areas connected to the central grid and 0.40–0.80 USD per kWh for rural areas. In comparison, the average electricity price in the US is about 0.12 USD per kWh (IEA, 2016).

This aspect creates difficulties in terms of improving energy access, especially in rural areas; imported electricity is very expensive, and the one produced by using fossil fuels depends greatly on the volatility of international fuel prices. As a consequence, the cost of electricity in Cambodia is one of the highest in the world, and the electrification rate one of the lowest in Asia. Moreover, due to system inefficiencies and poor electrification networks in rural areas, rural households usually have to pay unaffordable prices to connect to the national power grid facilities. Cambodia also suffers from an under-investment in grid infrastructure and power station infrastructure. The energy security situation in Cambodia is therefore rather unstable.

Poor energy access in rural areas is a critical aspect of Cambodia's development also in terms of poverty reduction. According to World Bank data and estimations, in 2012, about 6 per cent of the total population of Cambodia was below the poverty headcount of USD 1.9 a day (PPP) and about 37 per cent of the total population of Cambodia was below the poverty headcount of 3.1 $ a day (PPP) (corresponding to just below 5 million poor people) (World Bank, 2014).

Chinese investments in Cambodia's hydropower sector

According to the National Strategic Development Plan 2009–2013 and 2014–2018 (NSDP), energy, including from large hydropower, is central to sustainable growth and poverty-reduction in Cambodia. Improving the power sector is one of the government's key priorities to ensure a reliable, secure electricity supply at affordable prices (Government of Cambodia, 2010).

Hydropower development represents the first energy priority in Cambodia; hydropower is expected to substantially replace fossil fuel consumption for electricity generation in the country. To increase the supply of electricity, Cambodia plans to build and operate several new hydropower dams by 2019, supplying the country with 1942 megawatt electric (MWe) (Clean Energy Info Portal, 2016) and including the dams already granted to Chinese companies by the Ministry of Industry, Mines and Energy (MIME) of Cambodia, such as:

- Kamchay dam, with a capacity of 193 MW (completed and operating);
- Stung Russey Chrum Krom dam, with a capacity of 338 MW (completed and operating);
- Stung Atai dam, with a capacity of 120 MW (completed and operating);
- Kirirom 1 dam, with a capacity of 12 MW (completed and operating);
- Kirirom 3 dam, with a capacity of 18 MW (completed and operating);
- Lower Sesan II dam, with a capacity of 400 MW (under construction);
- Lower Sesam 3, with a capacity of 375 MW (under construction);
- Stung Tatai dam, with a capacity of 246 MW (under construction);
- Sambor dam, with a capacity of 7,110 MW (proposed);
- Srepok 3 dam, with a capacity of 300 MW (proposed);
- Srepok 4 dam, with a capacity of 220 MW (proposed);
- Stung Cheay Areng dam, with a capacity of 108 MW (proposed).

In Cambodia, no dams have been built directly on the mainstream Mekong River, but are underway on some tributaries. The Chinese dam-builders and financiers involved in these dams include both large and small players: financiers such as ExIm Bank, lead firms such as Sinohydro/Power China and China Guodian, as well as smaller and less well-known firms such as Hydrolancang International, China Electric Power Technology Import and Export Corporation, and Guangxi Guiguan Electric Power (International Rivers, 2016).

Overall, the exploitable mid to long-term hydropower potential of Cambodia is estimated at 8,600 MW by Chinese sources (Chinese National Bureau of Statistics, 2011). The Director of Kampot Provincial Department of Environment, which is responsible for the environmental management of the Kamchay dam, reported that the Kamcahy dam alone could meet up to 60% of the country's electricity demand in the wet season. However, in the dry season the capacity of the Kamchay Dam is down to only a third, and this will only be exacerbated further due to climate change. In the long-term, Cambodia hopes to export its electricity to neighbouring countries to gain revenue. Cambodia's Minister of Public Works and Transport, Khy Tainglim, sees the country's future as follows: "Water is our oil [...] and we should use our water to export and get foreign currency to develop the country" (cited in Goh, 2004, p. 7). The Cambodian commerce minister, Sun Chanthol, said, "Without infrastructure, you can't revive.... We have been blamed for always going to China, but it is because we need infrastructure fast and quick, nothing more than that" (SCMP, 2015, p. 1).

Cambodia's view on transboundary river management by China

Cambodia is likely to be impacted by Chinese-built dams in two different ways: one impact is likely to occur downstream as dams are being built upstream on the Mekong River in neighbouring countries, particularly in Laos, such as the Xayabouri dam. Orr, Pittock, Chapagain and Dumaresq (2012) suggest that building dams along the transboundary Mekong River is likely to lead to reduced water flow, declines in food security, and lower nutritional intake for millions of people in the GMS. Cambodia is also affected by dams built within its own borders, such as the Lower Sesan II built on the Mekong River, and dams built elsewhere, such as the Chinese-built and Chinese-financed Kamchay dam in Kampot province, which was Cambodia's first large-scale dam.

One could argue that China attempts to move from the unilateral use of shared waters to joint developments and transboundary water cooperation. Yet this view was not actively promoted by the interviewees, neither on the Chinese side nor the Cambodian side. While Chinese dam-builders and financiers invest heavily in Cambodia, their influence on Cambodia's approach to transboundary water issues is not entirely clear. Many Cambodian interviewees did not raise major concerns that Chinese dam-builders may control water issues in Cambodia disproportionally.

However, with regard to specific dams and their influence, a lot depends on the type of contracts between the dam-builders and the local government. Engineering, Procurement and Construction (EPC) contracts are usually turn-key contracts, which mean that the dam-builders act merely as contractors, but hand over the ownership of the dam to local authorities after the construction is completed, so usually after a few years. Build, Operate, Transfer (BOT) contracts, however, mean that the ownership of the dam rests with the dam-building company for several decades, usually between 20 and 40 years, before the dam is handed over to local authorities.

To give an example, the Kamchay dam is operating under a BOT contract with Sinohydro/PowerChina, which means the Chinese SOE is in charge of the dam for 44 years (until 2050) before the ownership will be passed on to the Cambodian authorities. The revenues from selling the electricity also accrue to Sinohydro/Power China during this time, while the management of the dams remains firmly in Chinese hands for four decades. This means that Cambodian authorities have limited opportunities to operate the dam and control its impacts, even though the dam is located within national boundaries. This speaks against the argument of moving from the unilateral use of shared waters to joint developments and transboundary water cooperation and reinforces the view that Chinese firms would be able to control water issues in the GMS for several decades if more dams with BOT contracts go ahead. Interestingly, the lengthy time scales of BOT contracts did not seem to worry many Cambodian interviewees. It did however worry international NGOs operating in Cambodia, as well as researchers.

At the same time, Cambodia has very limited negotiation power and decision-making power with regard to China's development activities at the upstream of the Mekong River basin. Having more Chinese-funded and Chinese-built dams in Cambodia does not seem to increase the leverage or power Cambodia has over upstream water issues.

The political ecology of the Asian Drivers: Cambodia

As indicated in the conceptual framework section, we focus on the following channels of interaction: trade, investment, aid, innovation, politics, environment, and society. We also analyze the motives, actors, beneficiaries, and impacts from both the Chinese side and the LMIC side.

With regard to the **motives** of Chinese dam-building in Cambodia, our research finds the following: China is one of Cambodia's largest trading partners. China is also one of Cambodia's largest investment partners and is of strategic importance, as Western countries don't invest much in Cambodia. In the dam sector, Chinese actors bundle aid, trade, and investment. This enables lucrative trade deals for Chinese firms. The Cambodian hydropower market is underdeveloped and there is limited domestic expertise, hence Chinese dam-builders can invest in and exploit a largely untapped market, making profits, providing jobs and generating tax income for China and the Chinese. With regard to aid, China is a big donor in Cambodia and mainly invests in infrastructure such as roads, bridges, and dams. China provides a "no strings attached", non-conditional aid opportunity that rivals Western donors. The "no strings attached" policy is a term used in development studies and international relations that explains the approach China employs to aid, trade, and investment projects in the global South. Rather than attaching conditionality to its projects, as Western donors such as the World Bank do, Chinese actors do not attach any conditionality and do not get involved in the internal politics of a country. They therefore also invest in countries where Western donors seldom invest due to political reasons, such as in Sudan, North Korea, etc. With regard to innovation, Chinese dams are state-of-the-art and enable Cambodia to access the latest hydropower technology at a reasonable cost. In return for political and economic support from China, Cambodia is supportive of China's "One China" policy. Cambodia is also siding with China regarding the South China Sea dispute in exchange for aid, trade, and investment deals. With regard to environmental motives, hydropower dams contribute to low-carbon energy generation and may deliver cost-effective electricity in the long-term. Societal motives include bringing progress, modernity, and electricity access to an underdeveloped country.

For aid, trade, and investments, **actors** include Chinese dam-builders, hence hydropower firms as well as financiers and other firms along the hydropower value chain, as well as traders securing deals for other goods and Chinese and Cambodian authorities and ministries. With regard to innovation, actors include Chinese dam-builders, with Cambodian firms and/or the state being the recipients of dam innovation in the long-run. However, ownership transferal can be delayed several decades due to BOT contracts. With regard to politics, the actors are Chinese and Cambodian authorities and ministries. With regard to the environment, the actors are Chinese dam-builders as well as Cambodian authorities that sign off EIAs and grant licences. Actors in society include local communities, mainly in rural areas and often impoverished, who are usually affected the hardest as the dam affects them and their livelihoods directly. Urban areas and industries tend to benefit from the delivery of electricity.

For aid, trade, and investment, the **beneficiaries** are dam-builders, Chinese firms and financiers, and the Cambodian state and people, as well as Cambodian firms that cooperate on trade/investment deals with China. For politics, the beneficiaries are Chinese and Cambodian authorities. For the environment, the main beneficiary is the global atmosphere, as the hydropower dams can replace fossil fuel-powered stations and thereby contribute to climate change mitigation. In terms of society, the beneficiaries are predominantly people living in urban areas, industries and services that receive electricity, dam-builders, financiers, and the political elite.

The **impacts** are both positive and negative, as well as both direct and indirect. Positive direct trade, investment, and aid impacts mean increased trade, investment, and aid relationships between China and Cambodia, mainly based on trade, imports, and aid from China to Cambodia. Indirect positive impacts are potential export opportunities from Cambodian firms to China, although at a low scale. Negative impacts are trade, investment, and aid dependencies on China. Negative indirect impacts are Cambodia potentially becoming unattractive for Western donors due to the Chinese dominance. For innovation, the positive direct impacts are access to state-of-the-art dam technology for Cambodia, while the positive indirect impacts are knowledge transfer from Chinese actors to local Cambodian firms and engineers. Direct negative impacts relate to BOT contracts, meaning innovation and knowledge will be transferred from Chinese dam-builders to Cambodian actors only after several decades rather than after a few years or immediately after construction. With regard to politics, positive direct impacts are the support for China on a domestic and regional basis and China's political support for Cambodia. Indirect positive impacts are stronger bilateral ties, and negative indirect impacts potential conflicts for Cambodia with other countries that do not support the One China Policy or China's claims in the South China Sea. In terms of the environment, the major direct positive impact is the reduction of greenhouse gas emissions from energy generation. Negative direct impacts are local and transboundary impacts, including changes in hydrology, geomorphology, impacts on fish stocks, water quality and quantity, loss of habitat for fauna and flora, erosion, etc. Negative indirect impacts are impacts on food security for millions of people along the Mekong River. With regard to society, direct positive impacts include opportunity for access to electricity. Electricity is provided mainly for urban areas, particularly Phnom Penh. Direct negative impacts are local and transboundary impacts, such as declines in or even loss of livelihoods, resettlement, sometimes inadequate compensation issues, and potential impacts on food security. Indirect negative impacts relate to transboundary impacts on people and communities downstream.

The next section will elaborate on the Vietnam case study.

Case study: Vietnam

Vietnam's energy setting

Vietnam had an electrification rate of 99 per cent in 2015, with 100 per cent in urban areas and 97 per cent in rural areas (World Bank, 2016). The country is therefore far less dependent on building dams or other new power-generation infrastructure than some of its neighbouring countries. Eight per cent of the primary energy supply and about 40 per cent of the electricity supply comes from hydropower, while the country also depends heavily on fossil fuels (coal, natural gas, and oil) (IEA, 2016).

Chinese investments in Vietnam's hydropower sector

China and Vietnam share a long and complex history of political, economic, and social ties (Rigg, 2003). According to Lamb and Dao (2015), China is Vietnam's largest trading partner today. Middleton suggests that energy trade accounts for about 20 per cent of bilateral trade between China and Vietnam. Vietnam exports coal to China, while China exports electricity to Vietnam (Middleton, 2008). China is involved in the electricity sector by supplying a small share of Vietnam's electricity supply that is being imported from China at three times the price of the local Vietnamese electricity (Lamb & Dao, 2015). Not purchasing the electricity from China would incur a penalty, hence the electricity is being imported even when there is no demand for it (Lamb & Dao, 2015).

Vietnam has between 12,000 MW (Chinese National Bureau of Statistics, 2011) and 17,000 MW (Middleton, 2008) of economically and technically exploitable hydropower resources. Chinese dam-builders and financiers have been involved in the construction of 4 dams in Vietnam, namely the Cua Dat dam, the Nam Mu dam, the Tuyen Quang dam, and the Zhan Hua dam, in addition to being involved in several others in planning or under construction (International Rivers, 2016). These hydropower projects include the involvement of Chinese firms such as China National Heavy Machinery Corporation, Dong Fang Electrical Machinery Company, Yunnan Machinery Export Import Company, Guangdong No.2 Hydropower Engineering Co Ltd., and others. The completed projects do not include the involvement of major lead firms such as Sinohydro or China Three Georges Corporation (International Rivers, 2016).

While China's involvement in the Vietnamese hydropower sector may appear minor in comparison to other countries in the GMS such as Cambodia, Laos, and Myanmar, China also supplies hydropower equipment and workers, and is involved as a business partner in larger dam contracts led by Vietnam (Lamb & Dao, 2015). Vietnam is itself a leader in dam-building, hence its hydropower firms are competing for contracts with Chinese firms. Many of its hydropower projects are constructed and/or owned by the Electricity of Vietnam (EVN), a large utility SOE. Yet, Chinese dam-builders are often involved in project design, construction, and/or equipment provision. Lamb and Dao (2015) argue that up to 90 per cent of Vietnamese dams are supplied with equipment by Chinese dam-builders. At the same time, Chinese workers are often used for dam projects in Vietnam. Many of the dams in which Chinese actors are involved are small-scale, below 30 MW, and hence reliable data is more difficult to obtain. An example is the small-scale Coc San hydropower project, for which China Southern Power Grid Company (CSG) partnered with EVN to develop the 21.4 MW hydropower station in Lao Cai province, which has an estimated value of USD 28 million (Middleton, 2008). When it comes to water management and security, Vietnamese authorities generally tend to have a rather negative perception and limited trust in Chinese infrastructure operations, especially in relation to dam safety and security systems. According to an engineer in charge of the operation of the Chinese-built Coc San Hydropower dam located in Lao Cai province interviewed in October 2016, while responsibility of construction and installation of hydropower dams in Vietnam can be given to Chinese companies, the safety and security systems usually come from European or American companies, which are perceived as being more serious in terms of monitoring the state of the dam and their vulnerability to external physical threats and risks, such as landslides.

Vietnam's view on transboundary river management by China

Governance for transboundary river management

Cross-border cooperation on hydropower and water management between China, Cambodia, Vietnam, and the other countries located upstream, such as Myanmar, Laos, and Thailand is essential to avoid severe impacts on food security and the environment of the Mekong delta region. Orr et al. (2012) suggest that building dams along the transboundary Mekong River is likely to lead to reduced water flow, reduced fish stocks, and, hence, reduced fish catch, which may result in reduced food security and lower nutritional intake for millions of people in the GMS. With regard to transboundary river management, the Mekong River Commission (MRC) is overseeing the management of the Mekong River, however it does not have enforcing power. Before dams are built on the river, the consultation of the MRC and member states needs to happen; however, the concerns of neighbouring countries, scientists, and environmentalists are often neglected. Sometimes, such as for the Xayaburi Dam in Laos, the construction started before the consultation process was completed (Zaffos, 2014). The MRC has even less power when dams are being built on tributaries of the Mekong River. The MRC works directly with the governments of Cambodia, Laos, Thailand, and Vietnam on transboundary river management. However, there is no legal requirement to inform or consult other countries along the Mekong River before building dams, and China, as a non-member of the MRC, may be even less inclined to inform or consult other countries along the Mekong River. However, the new established Lancang-Mekong Cooperation Mechanism (LMC established in November 2015), which includes cooperation on water resources, can play a fundamental role in increasing transparency and communication between China and the other Mekong countries. The new mechanism covers five different priority areas: interconnectivity, production capacity, cross-border economic cooperation, water resources, and cooperation on agriculture and poverty reduction. Through the establishment of the LMC China may be aiming to engage in a more active and positive role in water resources management in the Mekong region by increasing its cooperation and transparency of operations. This could in turn build trust between Chinese investors with the other Mekong countries in relation to hydropower development and water management (Biba, 2016).

Domestic views from Vietnam on transboundary river management

While Cambodia depends on and welcomes Chinese investments in the hydropower sector to enable economic growth and modernization, the situation is different in Vietnam. Unlike Cambodia, Vietnam is located downstream at the very end of the Mekong River where it pours into the sea. Any dams built upstream on the Mekong River in China, Cambodia, Laos, Myanmar, and Thailand have the potential to significantly reduce water levels in Vietnam and cause water scarcity and a threat to food security. Due to Vietnam's location downstream, it is very vulnerable to declines in water levels and fish stock and is disproportionally affected by the dam-building upstream. Zaffos (2014, p. 1) writes that

> Seven dams built upstream in China and the blasting of rapids to improve navigation have already altered flows, reduced fish populations, and affected communities along portions of the Lower Mekong, which flows through Thailand, Laos, Cambodia, and Vietnam. But the impacts may soon get

> much worse as a new era of hydroelectric dam-building begins in the Lower Mekong Basin. Eleven major hydroelectric dams—mostly within Laos—and dozens of dams on tributary streams that feed into the Mekong have been proposed or are under construction.

About 50 million people depend on the Mekong – the "rice bowl of Asia" – for their livelihoods and food security (Urban et al., 2013). Orr et al. (2012) suggest that food security is at a high risk when more dams are being built in the Lower Mekong River Basin as fish catch is likely to be reduced due to declining fish stocks.

The Vietnamese government is also concerned about the impacts of new hydropower dams on the upper reaches of the Mekong River in Cambodia, which could have impacts on the water quantity in Cambodia's Tonle Sap Lake. The Deputy Minister of Agriculture and Rural Development of Vietnam is particularly concerned with the fact that if water flow decreases due to hydropower development in Cambodia, the Cambodian government may divert the water from the Tonle Sap's lake for agricultural production. This can have negative impacts on water availability in Vietnam, since the Mekong River reaches the Vietnamese Mekong Delta region through the Tonle Sap Lake (VietNamNet Bridge, 2016). Scientific studies have also demonstrated that upstream water infrastructure on the Mekong River in Cambodia and other neighbour countries, such as Laos, has resulted in an alteration of the water flood and water levels of the Tonle Sap Lake (Cochrane, Arias, & Piman, 2014). Moreover, Vietnamese authorities are concerned that the construction of hydropower dams upstream in the Mekong River Delta in Vietnam can result in an increased risk of floods due to the sudden and uncontrolled release of water from upstream dams, or an increased risk of drought due to the use of water for hydropower or irrigation purposes from upstream countries (Soksreinith, 2016; VietNamNet Bridge, 2016).

In 2015/2016, Vietnam was very badly affected by climatic changes manifested particularly in a record drought exacerbated by El Niño. Government officials are arguing the drought is being further exacerbated by Chinese dams on the Upper Mekong River, and they are concerned of the impacts of the current dam-building on the Lower Mekong River (Interview with Vietnamese government official, 2016). A recent study by Vietnam for the MRC indicates that further dam construction could have devastating impacts on Vietnam and also Cambodia.

The dam-building and its severe downstream impacts have caused concern amongst government officials, experts, and scholars, some arguing that the Mekong River could soon be considered a diplomatic challenge akin to the South China Sea, which could potentially threaten Sino-ASEAN relations. Bilateral relations between China and Vietnam have certainly turned sour. A senior Vietnamese government official put it this way:

> The relationship between Vietnam and China has always been difficult. However, several years ago, we were positive about Chinese engagement

> with Vietnam, including about bilateral trade and Chinese investments in Vietnam. This has changed dramatically. The problems in the South China Sea and the dams that China has built and is building on the Mekong River are serious challenges for us. Also, Vietnam is experiencing a terrible drought this year. In the Mekong Delta, the water is scarce due to the dams upstream. In other areas of the country, farmers are advised to dig wells to find water, but there is no ground water, not even after 150 meters of digging boreholes.
>
> (Interview with Vietnamese government official, 2016)

Upstream dam-building and the exacerbated impacts of climate change are likely to put additional strain on already tense bilateral relations between China and Vietnam. Similar to Cambodia, Vietnam has very limited negotiation and decision-making power with regard to China's development activities at the upstream of the Mekong River basin. Having a few Chinese-funded and Chinese-built dams in Vietnam does not seem to increase the leverage or power the country has over upstream water issues. Yet, an improved way for both countries to negotiate transboundary water management issues with China is through the Lancang-Mekong Cooperation Mechanism.

The political ecology of the Asian Drivers: Vietnam

As indicated in the conceptual framework section, we focus on the following channels of interaction: trade, investment, aid, innovation, politics, environment, and society. We also analyze the motives, actors, beneficiaries, and impacts from both the Chinese side and the LMIC side.

With regard to the **motives** of Chinese dam-building in Vietnam, our research finds the following: China is Vietnam's largest trading partner and one of Vietnam's largest investment partners. There is less evidence of the bundling of aid, trade, and investment in the dam sector by Chinese actors in Vietnam. The Vietnamese hydropower market is well-developed with experienced domestic firms and domestic expertise; hence Chinese dam-builders only play a minor role alongside Vietnamese dam-builders, often along the value chain in terms of planning and contracting. With regard to aid, as Vietnam is a middle-income country, it is receiving a smaller amount of aid from China compared to other Asian countries. With regard to innovation, Chinese dams are state-of-the-art; yet often Vietnamese dams are built by Vietnamese dam-builders and Chinese dam-builders play a minor role as contractors for specific parts of the dam-building. There is less evidence for transfer of innovation. Political motives are complex. Vietnam is supportive of China's One China policy in return for political and economic support from China. Yet, Vietnam's political ties with China have historically been difficult and are now being strained due to extensive dam-building upstream on the Mekong River, which could harm Vietnam's food security and water availability. Vietnam is also claiming parts of the South China Sea for itself, hence opposing China on this matter. With regard to environmental motives, hydropower dams contribute to low-carbon energy generation, contribute to climate change mitigation, and may deliver cost-effective electricity in the long-term. Societal motives include bringing progress, modernity, and electricity access to Vietnam.

For aid, trade, and investments, **actors** include Chinese dam-builders, hence hydropower firms as well as financiers, often operating alongside Vietnamese firms, other firms along the hydropower value chain, as well as traders securing deals for other goods, Chinese authorities and ministries. With regard to innovation, actors include Vietnamese and Chinese dam-builders. With regard to politics, the actors are Chinese and Vietnamese authorities and ministries. Vietnamese authorities are concerned regarding upstream dam-building by China on the Mekong River. With regard to the environment, the actors are Chinese dam-builders, as well as Vietnamese authorities that sign off EIAs and grant licences. With regard to society, the actors are local communities downstream, particularly in the Vietnamese Mekong Delta. These are mainly rural areas and sometimes impoverished livelihoods are directly affected. Some benefit from electricity access.

For aid, trade, and investment, the **beneficiaries** are dam-builders, Chinese firms, and Vietnamese firms. For politics, the beneficiaries are Chinese and Vietnamese authorities. For the environment, the main beneficiary is the global atmosphere, as the hydropower dams can replace fossil fuel-powered stations. In terms of society, the beneficiaries are predominantly people living in urban areas, industries and services receiving electricity, dam-builders, financiers, and the political elite.

The **impacts** are both positive and negative, as well as both direct and indirect. Positive direct trade, investment, and aid impacts mean increased trade, investment, and, to a small extent, aid relationships between China and Vietnam. There are opportunities along the dam value chain for Chinese firms in Vietnam. Indirect positive impacts are potential export opportunities from Vietnamese firms to China. Negative impacts are trade and investment dependencies on China. For innovation, the positive direct impacts are know-how and expertise for state-of-the-art dam technology for Vietnam, although direct knowledge transfer to local firms and engineers seems limited. With regard to politics, positive direct impacts are the partial political support for China on a domestic and regional basis. Negative direct impacts include the political tension due to a series of dams built upstream on the Mekong River. Negative indirect impacts include the potential for conflict with other countries that support China unconditionally. In terms of the environment, the major direct positive impact is the reduction of greenhouse gas emissions from energy generation. Negative direct impacts are changes in hydrology, geomorphology, impacts on fish stocks, water quality and quantity, loss of habitat for fauna and flora, erosion, etc. Local and transboundary impacts are most important for upstream dams in China, Laos, and Cambodia that impact the Mekong Delta downstream in Vietnam. The major negative indirect impact includes the impact on food security for millions of people along the Mekong River and especially in the Mekong Delta. With regard to society, the major direct positive impact is the opportunity for access to electricity. Direct negative impacts are decline in or even loss of livelihoods, resettlement, sometimes inadequate compensation issues, sometimes impacts on food security, etc. There is a range of local and transboundary impacts, where the most severe impacts are expected in the Mekong Delta due to dams built upstream by Chinese dam-builders. The major indirect negative impact relates to food security threats for areas that depend on Vietnam's food production, particularly rice production, and this may even affect countries that import rice and other agricultural produce from Vietnam.

Discussion and conclusion

The analysis presented above finds that China's dam-building activities are perceived very differently by the interviewees in different countries of Southeast Asia, depending on whether they can be helpful for economic growth and development in a poor country such as Cambodia, or whether they threated growth and development, as well as national security, in a downstream-located, better-off country such as Vietnam.

Transboundary water management along the Mekong River has become a main challenge in recent years. China's building of large dams upstream within its own borders at the Lancang-Upper Mekong and in Cambodia and Laos on the Mekong River means that bilateral relations between downstream Vietnam and China are strained. Across the ASEAN region, there is concern that the excessive damming of the Mekong and its tributaries by Chinese dam-builders and others may lead to water scarcity and food insecurity across the region.

As China is not a part of ASEAN, it is difficult to hold the country accountable and to bring it to the negotiating table to discuss transboundary river management and international water governance. However, the newly established Lancang-Mekong Cooperation Mechanism (LMC), which includes cooperation on water resources, can play a fundamental role in increasing transparency and communication between China and the other Mekong countries. Yet, the media and some critics accuse China of dealing with the Upper Mekong River/Lancang as if it was only a domestic river and largely ignoring the downstream impacts. At the same time, the country's dam-builders do not seem to be very concerned about potential transboundary and regional problems caused by the dams, such as water scarcity and threats to food security. There is also a lack of data, meaning that few transboundary studies exist yet to quantify the potential impacts of these large dams on fish stocks, food security, and water security (Orr et al., 2012 is an outstanding exception). More research in this area is needed.

Some scholars (e.g. Guo, 2015; Zhang, 2014; Zhang & Lu, 2015) argue that China attempts to move from the unilateral use of shared waters to joint developments and transboundary water cooperation. Yet, this view was not actively promoted by the interviewees, neither on the Chinese side nor the Cambodian side nor the Vietnamese side. While Chinese dam-builders and financiers invest in Cambodia and Vietnam, the influence they have on transboundary water management depends partly on the types of contracts being used. EPC contracts mean that Chinese firms and financiers have very limited influence over a particular dam (or a series of dams) over time. BOT contracts, however, mean that the ownership of the dam rests with the dam-building company for several decades, up to 40 years, before the dam is handed over to local authorities. This reduces the power local authorities have to operate the dam and control its impacts, even though the dam is located within national boundaries. This speaks against the argument of moving towards joint developments and transboundary water cooperation, and reinforces the view that Chinese firms would be able to control water issues in the GMS for several decades if more dams with BOT contracts went ahead. Yet, it does not seem that this is the motivation of the Chinese government. Instead, the main reasons for China's dam industry to go global are of an economic nature and are only partly politically motivated (Matthews & Motta, 2013; Urban et al., 2013).

At the same time, Cambodia and Vietnam have very limited negotiation and decision-making power with regard to China's development activities at the upstream of the Mekong River basin. Having more Chinese-funded and Chinese-built dams in these countries does not seem to increase the leverage these countries have over upstream water issues, despite having closer economic and political ties with China.

Using the conceptual framework of the Political Ecology of the Asian Drivers, the chapter finds that different channels of interaction are used in the dam sector to engage between Chinese dam-builders and financiers and host countries. In Cambodia, the bundling of aid, trade, and investments is far more common in the dam sector than in Vietnam. In comparison to Cambodia, Vietnam has relatively little investment from China in the dam sector, and bilateral hostilities around the South China Sea have not improved this situation. With regard to political ecology considerations, the following assumptions have been confirmed: first, costs and benefits associated with environmental change are distributed unequally. Second, this unequal distribution inevitably reinforces or reduces existing social and economic inequalities. Third, the unequal distribution of costs and benefits and the reinforcing or reducing of preexisting inequalities holds political implications in terms of the altered power relationships that result. The costs and benefits of large dam-building are indeed unequally distributed. Poor people are disproportionally affected by large dams, such as people dependent on fisheries and 'the rice bowl of Asia' irrigated by the Mekong River. The winners are Chinese firms, mostly SOEs, as well as local elites such as in the Cambodian government. This exacerbates already existing inequalities and affects the poor disproportionally. Finally, the costs and benefits of large dam-building in Southeast Asia has political implications, as Chinese investors are welcome alternatives to OECD donors, at least upstream, who have been preaching conditionality and structural reforms for decades.

This project finds that Chinese dam-builders and financiers open up opportunities for low- and middle-income countries in Asia to attract large investments and to build up energy and water management infrastructure which in turn can contribute to national development goals. Accessibility of finance and technical expertise from China, without the conditionality that might be uncomfortable for the local political economy, facilitates transformational and high-risk environmental and social projects that are otherwise limited by the conditionality and practice of agencies such as the World Bank and by the higher opportunity cost for other sources of finance. The no strings attached policy of Chinese dam-builders is a welcome offer to many low- and middle-income countries. Hydropower dams also contribute to low-carbon energy generation and thereby create viable alternatives to fossil fuel energy generation, such as coal, oil, and natural gas, thereby mitigating climate change. However, dam planning and building needs to be done in a more sustainable way that takes into account national development priorities, the needs of local people, and the impacts on natural habitats and cross-border impacts. To be more specific in outlining the implications for global hydropower development, this will require more cooperation across various countries to enable valuable negotiations for transboundary river management and international water governance. As rivers know no boundaries, countries need to work more closely together to deal with the impacts of planned dams on transboundary rivers such as the Mekong to raise concerns beyond their own borders and, if possible, to get a mandate to veto controversial dam projects that could be detrimental to them or neighbouring countries.

With regard to the role of Chinese dam-builders, our research finds that indeed the corporate behaviour of Chinese dam-builders is to a large extent influenced by the national legislations, policies, and practices set by the national governments in Asia, but international institutions and industry bodies, such as the World Bank and the International Hydropower Association (IHA), do further provide international standards and monitoring for responsible corporate behaviour in the Chinese hydropower sector. In terms of policy recommendations, this means that Chinese dam-builders need to be willing to take on the recommendations of the World Bank and the IHA, which is a rather limited practice today. Countries located downstream of transboundary rivers, such as Cambodia and Vietnam, need to get a much stronger opportunity to voice their concerns and raise suggestions for how to work with Chinese dam-builders and financiers. By working together and showing more willingness to improve the hydropower sector and showing more consideration for transboundary water problems, Chinese dam-builders and financiers, national host governments, and international public institutions and regulatory bodies, such as the MRC and the LMC could help to make the hydropower sector more sustainable and reduce the impacts on local people and the environment. It also needs to be reflected on whether large dams are appropriate for certain settings, or whether several smaller hydropower schemes or other forms of renewable energy would be more suitable to cater to the development needs of LMICs.

Acknowledgements

The authors would like to thank the UK Economic and Social Research Council (ESRC) (reference ES/J01320X/1) for funding this research in China and Cambodia, as well as the Volkswagen Foundation, the Wellcome Trust, and the Svenska Riksbankens Jubileumsfond for funding parts of this research in Vietnam. Special thanks go to all the research partners, project participants, and respondents involved in this study.

References

Adams, W. (2000). *The social impact of large dams: Equity and distribution issues.* Thematic Review I.1 prepared as an input to the World Commission on Dams, Cape Town. Retrieved from http://services.iriskf.org/data/articles/Document1115200600.5004389.pdf.

Alden, C., Large, D., & Soares de Oliveira, R. (2008). *China returns to Africa: A rising power and a continent embrace.* London, UK: Hurst.

Biba, S. (2016). *China drives water cooperation with Mekong countries, the thirdpole.net: Understanding Asia's water crisis.* Retrieved from www.thethirdpole.net/2016/02/01/china-drives-water-cooperation-with-mekong-countries/.

Biswas, A. K. (1982). Impacts of hydroelectric development on the environment. *Energy Policy, 10*(4), 349–354.

Blaikie, P. (1985). *The political economy of soil erosion in developing countries.* London, UK: Longman.

Bosshard, P. (2009). China dams the world. *World Policy Journal, 26*(4), 43–51.

Brautigam, D. (2009). *The dragon's gift: The real story of China in Africa.* Oxford, UK: Oxford University Press.

Bryant, R. (1996). The politics of forestry in Burma. In P. Hirsch & C. Warren (Eds.), *Politics and environment in Southeast Asia: Resources and resistance* (pp. 107–121). London, UK: Routledge.

Bryant, R. (1997). Beyond the impasse: The power of political ecology in Third World environment research. *Area, 29*, 5–19.

Bryant, R., & Bailey, S. (1997). *Third world political ecology.* London, UK: Routledge.

Carmody, P., & Kragelund, P. (2016). Who is in charge? State power and agency in Sino-African relations. *Yale International Law Journal, 49*(1), 1–23.

Carmody, P., Hampwaye, G., & Sakala, E. (2012). Globalisation and the rise of the State? Chinese geogovernance in Zambia. *New Political Economy, 17*, 209–229.

Chang, X. L., Liu, X., & Zhou, W. (2009). Hydropower in China at present and its further development. *Energy, 35*(11), 4400–4406.

Chen, Y., & Landry D. G. (2016). *Capturing the rains: A comparative study of Chinese involvement in Cameroon's hydropower sector.* SAIS China Africa Research Initiative – Working Paper 5. Retrieved from https://static1.squarespace.com/static/5652847de4b033f56d2bdc29/t/57ff9ca8e3df28f75af06913/1476369580891/cameroon+final+draft+6.pdf.

Chinese Statistical Yearbooks, National Bureau of Statistics. (2011). *Estimated hydropower potential in the Greater Mekong Sub-Region.* Beijing, People's Republic of China: NBS.

CGIAR. (2016). WLE Greater Mekong dam database. Retrieved from https://wle-mekong.cgiar.org/maps/.

Clean Energy Info Portal – reegle. (2013). Cambodia (2012) – Policy and regulatory overviews. Retrieved from www.reegle.info/policy-and-regulatory-overviews/KH.

Cochrane, T. A., Arias, M. E., & Piman, T. (2014). Historical impact of water infrastructure on water levels of the Mekong River and the Tonle Sap system. *Hydrology and Earth System Sciences, 18*, 4529–4541.

Dauvergne, P. (1994). The politics of deforestation in Indonesia. *Pacific Affairs, 66*, 497–518.

Dittgen, R. (2015). Of other spaces? Hybrid forms of Chinese engagement in Sub-Saharan Africa. *Journal of Current Chinese Affairs, 44*, 43–73.

Dore, J., & Yu, X. (2004). *Yunnan hydropower expansion: Update on China's energy industry reforms and the Nu, Lancang and Jinsha hydropower dams.* Working Paper from Chiang Mai University's Unit for Social and Environmental Research and Green Watershed. Retrieved from www.mpowernet.org/download_pubdoc.php?doc=2586.

FDI China. (2015). *Invest in China.* Retrieved from www.fdi.gov.cn/1800000121_21_79306_0_7.html.

Goh, E. (2004). *China in the Mekong River Basin: The regional security implications of resource development on the Lancang Jiang.* Nanyang Technological University. Retrieved from http://dr.ntu.edu.sg/bitstream/handle/10220/4469/RSIS-WORKPAPER_73.pdf?sequence=1.

Government of Cambodia. (2010). National strategic development plan 2009–2013 (NSDP). Phnom Penh, Cambodia: GoC.

Greenberg, J. B., & Park, T. K. (1994). Political ecology. *Journal of Political Ecology, 1*, 1–12.

Guo, H. (2015). China's participation in the water governance of the Lancang-Mekong River: Policy evaluation and future trends. *Journal of China's Neighboring Diplomac, 2015*(1), 10–22.

Hayashi, S., Murakami, S., Xu, K.-Q., & Watanabe, M. (2008). Effect of the Three Gorges Dam Project on flood control in the Dongting Lake area, China, in a 1998-type flood. *Journal of Hydro-Environment Research, 2*(3), 148–163.

Hensengerth, O. (2013). Chinese hydropower companies and environmental norms in countries of the global South: The involvement of Sinohydro in Ghana's Bui dam. *Environment, Development and Sustainability, 15*(2), 285–300.

Hensengerth, O. (2016). Water governance in the Mekong Basin: Scalar tradeoffs, transnational norms and Chinese hydropower investment. In P. Nyiri & D. Tan (Eds.), *How Chinese engagements are changing Southeast Asia: People, money, ideas and their effects.* Seattle, WA: University of Washington Press.

Humphrey, J., & Messner, D. (2006). China and India as emerging global governance actors: Challenges for developing and developed countries. *IDS Bulletin, 37*(1), 107–114.

Hwang, S. S., Xi, J., Cao, Y., Feng, X., & Qiao, X. (2007). Anticipation of migration and psychological stress and the Three Gorges Dam project, China. *Social Science & Medicine, 65*(5), 1012–1024.

IEA International Energy Agency. (2016). *IEA Statistics.* Retrieved from www.iea.org/statistics.

International Rivers. (2012). The new great wall: A guide to China's overseas dams industry. Retrieved from www.internationalrivers.org/sites/default/files/attached-files/intlrivers_newgreatwalls_2012_2.pdf

International Rivers. (2016). *Chinese overseas dams database.* INR, Berkeley, USA.

IPCC Intergovernmental Panel on Climate Change. (2011). *Special report on renewable energy sources and climate change mitigation.* Summary for Policy-Makers. Retrieved from www.uncclearn.org/sites/www.uncclearn.org/files/inventory/ipcc_summary_for_pm.pdf.

Jacques, M. (2009). *When China rules the world: The rise of the Middle Kingdom and the end of the western world.* London, UK: Allen Lane.

Kaplinsky, R., & Messner, D. (2008). Introduction: The impact of Asian drivers on the developing world. *World Development, 36*, 197–209.

Kirchherr, J., Charles, K. J., & Walton, M. W. (2016a). The interplay of activists and dam developers: The case of Myanmar's mega-dams. *International Journal of Water Resources Development, 33*(1), 111–131. doi:10.1080/07900627.2016.1179176.

Kirchherr, J., Disselhoff, T., & Charles, K. (2016b). Safeguards, financing and employment in Chinese infrastructure projects in Africa: The case of Ghana's Bui Dam. *Waterlines, 35*(1), 37–58.

Lamb, V., & Dao, N. (2015). *Perceptions and practices of investment: China's hydropower investments in mainland Southeast Asia*. Working Paper 11. BRICS Initiatives in Critical Agrarian Studies (BICAS).

Lee, C. K. (2014). The spectre of global China. *New Left Review, 89*, 29–65.

Magee, D. (2006). Powershed politics: Yunnan hydropower under Great Western Development. *China Quarterly, 185*, 23–41.

Matthews, N., & Motta, S. (2013). *China's influence on hydropower development in the Lancang River and Lower Mekong River Basin*. CGIAR, SOK 4. Retrieved from https://cgspace.cgiar.org/handle/10568/35102.

McDonald, K., Bosshard, P., & Brewer, N. (2009). Exporting dams: China's hydropower industry goes global. *Journal of Environmental Management, 90*, 294–S302.

Middleton, C. (2008). The sleeping dragon awakes: China's growing role in the business and politics of hydropower development in the Mekong Region. *Watershed Journal, 12*, 51–62.

Mohan, G., & Lampert, B. (2013). Negotiating China: Reinserting African agency into China-Africa relations. *African Affairs, 112*, 92–110.

Mohan, G., & Power, M. (2008). New African choices? The politics of Chinese engagement. *Review of African Political Economy, 115*, 23–42.

Motta, S., & Matthews, N. (2017). Rewards and risks of Chinese hydropower in the greater Mekong Subregion (GMS). In G. Siciliano & F. Urban (Eds.), *Chinese hydropower development in Africa: Challenges and opportunities for sustainable global dam-building*. Abingdon, UK: Routledge.

Orr, S., Pittock, J., Chapagain, A., & Dumaresq, D. (2012). Dams on the Mekong River: Lost fish protein and the implications for land and water resources. *Global Environmental Change: Part A – Human and Policy Dimensions, 22*(4), 925–932.

Peet, R., & Watts, M. (2004). Liberating political ecology. In R. Peet & M. Watts (Eds.), *Liberation ecologies: Environment, development and social movements* (pp. 3–47). London, UK: Routledge.

Peluso, N. L. (1992). *Rich forest, poor people: Resources control and resistance in Java*. Berkeley: CAL University of California Press.

Perreault, T., Bridge, G., & McCarthy, J. (2015). *The Routledge handbook of political ecology*. Abingdon, UK: Routledge.

Rigg, J. (2003). Exclusion and embeddedness: The Chinese in Thailand and Vietnam. In L. J. C. Ma & C. L. Cartier (Eds.), *The Chinese Diaspora: Space, place, mobility, and identity* (pp. 97–115). Lanham, MD: Rowman & Littlefield.

Schmitz, H. (2006). Asian drivers: Typologies and questions. *IDS Bulletin, 37*(1), 54–61.

SCMP. (2015). *China-built dam in Cambodia set to destroy livelihoods of 45,000*. www.scmp.com/magazines/post-magazine/article/1858974/china-built-dam-cambodia-set-destroy-livelihoods-45000.

Schiffer, E., & Hauck, J. (2010). Net-map: Collecting social network data and facilitating network learning through participatory influence network mapping. *Field Methods, 22*, 231.

Shinn, D. (2016). The environmental impact of China's investment in Africa. *Yale International Law Journal, 49*, 25–67.

Scudder, T. (2012). *The future of large dams: Dealing with social, environmental, institutional and political costs* (2nd ed.). London, UK: Earthscan.

Siciliano, G., & Urban, F. (2017). Equity-based natural resource allocation for infrastructure development: Evidence from large hydropower dams in Africa and Asia. *Ecological Economics, 134*, 130–139.

Siciliano, G., Urban, F., Kim, S., & Lonn, D. P. (2015). Hydropower, social priorities and the rural-urban development divide: The case of large dams in Cambodia. *Energy Policy, 86*(11), 273–285.

Siciliano, G., Urban, F., Tan-Mullins, M., Lonn, P. D., & Kim, S. (2016). The political ecology of Chinese large dams in Cambodia: Implications, challenges and lessons learnt from the Kamchay Dam. *Water, 8*(45), 1–18.

Soksreinith, T. (2016). River of change: Hydropower dams and the Mekong River's uncertain future, VOA Khmer. www.voacambodia.com/a/river-of-change-hydropower-dams-and-the-mekong-river-uncertain-future/3436827.html.

Tan-Mullins, M. (2007). The state and its agencies in coastal resources management: The political ecology of fisheries management in Pattani, Southern Thailand. *Singapore Journal of Tropical Geography, 28*, 348–361.

Tan-Mullins, M., Mang, G., & Urban, F. (2017). Evaluating the behavior of Chinese stakeholders engaged in large hydropower projects in Asia and Africa. *China Quarterly, 230*, 464–488. doi: 10.1017/S0305741016001041.

Tilt, B., Braun, Y., & He, D. (2009). Social impacts of large dam projects: A comparison of international case: Studies and implications for best practice. *Journal of Environmental Management, 90*, 249–257.

Tortajada, C., Altinbilek, D., & Biswas, A. K. (Eds.). (2012). *Impacts of large dams: A global assessment.* New York, NY: Springer.

Urban, F., Mohan, G., & Cook, S. (2013a). China as a new shaper of international development: The environmental implications. *Environment, Development and Sustainability, 15*(2), 257–263.

Urban, F., Nordensvärd, J., Khatri, D., & Wang, Y. (2013b). An analysis of China's investment in the hydropower sector in the Greater Mekong Sub-Region. *Environment, Development and Sustainability, 15*(2), 301–324.

Urban, F., Siciliano, G., Sour, K., Lonn, P. D., Tan-Mullins, M., & Mang, G. (2015a). South-south technology transfer of low carbon innovation: Chinese large hydropower dams in Cambodia. *Sustainable Development, 23*(7–8), 232–244.

Urban, F., Nordensvard, J., Siciliano, G., & Li, B. (2015b). Chinese overseas hydropower dams and social sustainability: The Bui Dam in Ghana and the Kamchay Dam in Cambodia. *Asia & the Pacific Policy Studies, 2*(3), 573–589.

Urban, F., Nordensvärd, J., Wang, Y., Khatri, D., & Mohan, G. (2011) China and the African oil sector: Channels of engagement, motives, actors and impacts. *IDS Rising Powers Working Paper 2.* IDS, Brighton, UK.

VietNamNet Bridge. (2016). *Government urged to work with Cambodia on solutions to water resources.* http://english.vietnamnet.vn/fms/environment/165357/government-urged-to-work-with-cambodia-on-solutions-to-water-resources.html.

WCD World Commission on Dams (2000). *Dams and development: A new framework for decision-making.* London, UK: Earthscan.

Wolcott, H. (1990). *Writing up qualitative research.* London, UK: Sage.

Wolf, E. (1972). Ownership and political ecology. *Anthropological Quarterly, 45*, 201–205.

World Bank. (2014). World Bank open data. Retrieved from http://data.worldbank.org/.

World Bank. (2016). *Data.* http://data.worldbank.org/.

Xinhua Finance Agency. (2015). *The belt and road.* www.xinhuanet.com/silkroad/english/index.htm.

Yu, X. (2003). Regional cooperation and energy development in the GreaterMekong Sub-Region. *Energy Policy, 31*(12), 1221–1234.

Zaffos, J. (2014). *Life on Mekong faces threats as major dams begin to rise.* Yale Environment 360. http://e360.yale.edu/feature/life_on_mekong_faces_threats_as_major_dams_begin_to_rise/2741/.

Zhang, L. (2014). Water diplomacy: Transboundary water cooperation and strategic arrangements between China and the Mekong countries. *Journal of International Relations, 4*, 82–94.

Zhang, L., & Lu, G. S. (2015). Transboundary water cooperation between China and the lower Mekong countries from the perspective of water diplomacy. *Southeast Asian Studies, 1*, 51–68.

4 The evolution of China's water diplomacy in the Lancang-Mekong River Basin

Motivation and policy choices

Yanjun Guo

Introduction

The mainstream view in the international community is that Asia and many parts of the world undergoing economic development, demographic pressure, and climate change will face the risk of regional conflicts caused by water scarcity (Chellaney, 2013, p. xii). As the origin of several important international rivers, including the Lancang-Mekong River, China takes the lead both in the number of international rivers and the volume of shared transboundary water resources.

Since the 1980s, China has planned a cascade of eight dams on the lower Lancang River, which is rich in hydropower resources. After more than 30 years of construction, these dams have been completed and put into operation (China voluntarily stopped the construction of Mengsong Dam when considering the environmental protection in the lower reaches). In recent years, as Lancang-Mekong water issues have become more and more heated, the ecological impact brought by upstream dams has caught the attention of governments, the scientific community, international relations scholars, and the media. Their discussions focus on whether dams on the Lancang River will significantly affect the volume of the lower Mekong River – damaging the ecological foundations of downstream fisheries and agricultural production, jeopardizing the ecological and economic security, and the residents' livelihoods, in the basin. The new trend in the debate is that the Lancang-Mekong water problems have transcended the water issue itself and have become an overall concern over sustainable development in the basin.

With the whole ecosystem of the river in mind, we should admit that building upstream dams (especially large dams) would inevitably create some actual or potential impact on the downstream ecosystem, or even the ecology of the whole basin. The effects only vary in intensity. As early as 2006, Chinese scholars released reports on the influences of dam construction on the Lancang River's downstream water levels. Observed data show that in nearly 18 years (1986–2004), under normal operations, the constructed cascade dams on the Lancang River did not cause large fluctuations in downstream water levels at the inter-year or intra-year timescales but had significant effects on water levels at ten-day, daily, and hourly timescales in particular (Li, He, & Fu, 2006). A report by the United

Nations also pointed out that as the Lancang River dams "can store more water than all the Southeast Asian dam reservoirs combined", the impact of construction includes "changes in river flow volume, water quality deterioration, and loss of biodiversity" ("Fresh Water," 2008, p. 44). If one country wants to keep the natural ecosystem intact, it must choose not to develop the river. However, hydropower is recognized worldwide as renewable and clean energy, and its development has become a global trend. According to the International Law Association, "each basin state is entitled, within its territory, to a reasonable and equitable share in the beneficial uses of the waters of an international drainage system" ("The Helsinki Rules," 1967). China follows the trend of global economic development and the international practice in its development of hydropower resources on the Lancang River at a time when downstream countries are also vigorously promoting the Mekong hydropower development. Thus, the key question is not whether but how to develop the hydropower in the Mekong River. This involves the coordination of the relationships between hydropower development, sustainable development, water allocation, ecological protection, improvement of people's livelihoods, integration of basin management, and minimization of the negative impact of hydropower development.

In general, the big countries at the upstream tend to keep a low level of cooperation with small countries at the downstream, as evidenced by China's policy towards the Lancang-Mekong River in the past. With the establishment of the Lancang-Mekong Cooperation mechanism (LMC) in 2015, there has been paradigm shift in China's transboundary water policy towards the Lancang-Mekong River Basin. This chapter explores the key factors behind this paradigm shift, and the challenges ahead for China to implement its new transboundary water policy.

Review of China's participation in Lancang-Mekong River management

China has two goals for hydropower development. The first goal is to uphold its rights to free development and utilization of waters within its own territory. The second goal is to maintain stable relations with downstream countries and minimize any negative impact on the overall relations with them in the development process.

To achieve the two goals, China upholds the principle of "development and protection at the same time" and "active but limited participation in regional cooperation" on the condition that its development rights are guaranteed. At the same time, China strives to reduce tensions with downstream countries.

Being "active"

China has maintained self-restraint in the development process and taken proactive measures to protect the ecological environment, even at the expense of some economic benefits. China has taken multiple measures to protect the ecological environment, and even offered to give up substantial development gains to reduce the detrimental impact on downstream regions. First, it has sought to strengthen the legal system through amending a series of environment-related laws, including the Law on Environmental Impact Assessment in 2016 for regulating the project planning, facilitating the information sharing, and monitoring the project construction, aiming to improve the environmental protection. Second, it has also increased efforts at the technical level. For example, it optimized dam designs to ensure water levels, water temperature, and water quality of the Lancang River in China. Third, its investment in building migration routes for migratory fish and protecting fish resources increased. Implementing these measures can enhance downstream ecological protection and fishery (Gao, Zhao, & Dong, 2012). Furthermore, as the dialogue partner of the Mekong River Commission (MRC), China has actively uses this platform to conduct exchanges and cooperation with downstream countries.

Being "limited"

Being limited refers to restricted sharing of information and technical expertise with MRC member states (Lu, 2012, p. 32). The critics argue that by keeping the conversation contained during the primary construction period of the lower Lancang cascade, China, via Lancang Hydro, has been able to push forward dam construction, basically ignoring concerns of downstream countries and river-dependent communities. Overall, although China has maintained good relations with MRC in water resources management, their cooperation mainly focuses on the technical level, which is a low level and limited cooperation.

This policy has much success in "upholding rights". However, it falls short of the target for "maintaining stability". For example, when a severe drought hit the lower Mekong River countries in 2010, many media hyped the "Chinese Dam Threat" and blamed upstream dams for holding back the water needed to alleviate the downstream drought. This situation led to lasting negative impact and increasing diplomatic pressure on China.

Furthermore, China's rapidly growing regional influence has raised misgivings about China's policy choice in water resources. Downstream countries fear that China will jeopardize their economic development, ecological environment, and even national security. Although China has made significant efforts in hydropower development on the Lancang River to minimize adverse impacts on downstream countries, it fails to eliminate criticisms and doubts, which may intensify under certain conditions. Some critics pointed out China's poor water governance because China had neither joined the MRC nor communicated or negotiated over its hydropower development planning and project implementation with downstream countries ("Strategic Environmental Assessment", 2010). Some scholars even refer to China's upstream advantages and unilateral action as "water hegemony" (Blake, 2001, pp. 4–5; Robins & Blake, 2016). These statements have not only created pressure on China's hydropower development but also affected its relations with downstream countries, damaged China's image in the region, and denied its efforts in ecological protection – adding variables to interstate relations in the basin. Besides, as countries outside the basin such as the United States have become involved in water resources issues of the Mekong River, the problem of this basin has become increasingly internationalized.

The "active but limited cooperation" policy pursued by China in Lancang-Mekong water resources management in the past may seem to reflect its lack of motivation to promote deeper cooperation, which will face increasing difficulties and resistance as the new trends and situations emerge in the development and management of Lancang-Mekong water resources. China needs to do more than handle the potential risks in water resources management. In future, China should adjust the existing policy to focus on "maintaining stability" (Guo, 2015, p. 160). In particular, China should explore effective means of participating in basin management and innovating the concept and practice of water diplomacy. Besides, China should strengthen its initiative and participation over Lancang-Mekong water management, and avoid falling into a passive position when an emergency occurs.

Over the past years, the cooperation in water resources between China and lower Mekong River countries has not been treated as a priority on the foreign policy agenda. Institutionalized cooperation with downstream countries is mainly led by the China Ministry of Water Resources (MWR) that concentrates on limited information-sharing of hydrological data and technical cooperation. As the water issue has attracted growing attention from the basin countries, it has evolved into a comprehensive geopolitical matter that affects strategy, economy, security, and other factors (Guo, 2014). As it develops stronger diplomatic overtones, its relevance with China's neighbourhood diplomacy increases. Therefore, this author has introduced the concept of "water diplomacy", and believes that China should conduct an overall plan concerning its cooperation on water resources with the Mekong Basin countries from both strategic and diplomatic perspectives so that China can be well-prepared for future challenges.

There is no complete and authoritative definition of the "water diplomacy" concept in a strict sense. Some Western scholars pointed out that water diplomacy mainly focuses on solutions to water issues in a broad way based on science and within the scope of sensitive social constraint including environmental policies, water management strategy, engineering, and so forth. Some Chinese scholars defined the term as "the behavior of a government to solve the problems of transboundary water cooperation projects by diplomacy (which covers social and technical measures) to ensure its interests in the development and cooperation on transboundary water resources" (Islam, 2010).

The author believes that water diplomacy can be understood from both narrow and broad dimensions. Its broad meaning refers to activities of states or relevant actors around water resources issues. Its narrow meaning refers to activities of states or relevant actors around issues related to transboundary or international river water resources. Accordingly, water diplomacy can be divided into two categories: the first category being diplomatic activities aimed to achieve goals related to water itself; and the second category being water-related diplomatic activities designed to achieve other diplomatic objectives (including political, economic, and military goals). The water diplomacy carried out by China combines the two objectives.

The application of the concept of water diplomacy means that water problems have assumed greater importance on the diplomatic agenda with both subjects and objects in water policy being adjusted. As to the subjects, the most significant change is that foreign affairs departments, as the executive agencies of foreign policies, will play a leading role in the formulation and implementation of water policy. As to the objects, water diplomacy will not only spill over to water-related environmental protection, agriculture, and fisheries, but also become an effective tool to serve other diplomatic objectives.

The motivation for China to adjust its Lancang-Mekong water diplomacy

There are many factors affecting the extent of cooperation (or conflict) on transboundary water resources development between upper and lower basin countries. Some scholars have established an index system that reflects the policy orientation of basin countries. The indices include countries' economic volume and population, overall relations and relative strength vis-à-vis counterparts, infrastructure development, institution-building, geographical proximity, climate, rainfall, water availability, agriculture and energy dependence, government types, and so on (Yoffe, Wolf, & Giordano, 2003). The author argues that besides these indices, the geographical location of basin countries (upstream/downstream) is also an important factor influencing their water policy orientation.

Accordingly, the author considers national scale (relative strength) and geographical location as two important variables for analyzing Lancang-Mekong Basin countries' policy orientations. We can clearly see the correlation between the two variables with countries' policy orientations through the investigation of transboundary rivers in South Asia. India, as the largest and most powerful country in South Asia, has signed differentiated bilateral agreements with upstream and downstream countries instead of adopting the basin-wide institutional framework to protect its rights and interests. For instance, it signed the Mahakali Treaty with upstream Nepal on the Mahakali River to promote integrated water resources management. India also signed the Ganges Treaty with downstream Bangladesh, but the scope of this treaty is limited to water-sharing (Mirumachi, Zeitoun, & Warner, 2013). Both are in favor of India's content and provisions respectively.

The case is undoubtedly useful in supporting the association between national power/geographical location and policy orientation. That different policy orientations are accompanied by different policy tools, benefits, and risks, and the interaction of these variables, help determine whether a country needs to adjust its policies.

Depending on the intensity of cooperation, there are generally three types of policy orientation in transboundary water resources management: non-cooperation, low cooperation, and medium/high cooperation (Zeitoun & Mirumachi, 2008).

1 Non-cooperation: Larger upstream countries that adopt a non-cooperation policy will face relatively huge risks and even conflicts with downstream

countries even though such a policy can maximize development rights. Therefore, a non-cooperation policy is generally not an optimal option for larger upstream countries.

2 Low cooperation: This refers to limited information-sharing, technical exchange, and cooperation. For larger upstream countries, this policy may minimize conflicts with downstream countries by conducting information and technical cooperation, and by guaranteeing their development rights. However, it can also raise the suspension of downstream countries and may affect the overall relations between upstream and downstream countries.

3 Medium/high cooperation: When larger upstream countries are willing to improve upstream-downstream relations damaged by water problems, they are likely to adopt this type of cooperation. This means considerable increases in the level of cooperation by means of adequate information-sharing, signed treaties, basin-wide cooperation mechanism, integrated management, and the employment of other policy tools. Larger upstream countries tend to focus on benefits that are of non-material interest, such as rebuilding trust with downstream countries and improving their reputation. However, the risk is that their rights to independently develop water resources will be directly affected, and their economic development and even national sovereignty will be undermined. Then why would larger upstream countries promote medium/high cooperation? There are many factors driving them to enhance further cooperation. For example, these countries need to adapt to new trends in international river management, respond to the downstream coalition, reduce the pressure caused by the internationalization of water problems, achieve more ambitious diplomatic goals, and so on. Certainly, it is not easy to coax larger upstream countries to carry out a higher level of cooperation with their downstream counterparts. Any higher level of cooperation is the result of a tough game between upstream and downstream countries.

For smaller downstream countries, non-cooperation policies or low cooperation policies obviously do not serve their interests. It is always their goal to carry out substantial cooperation with upstream countries. Although medium/high cooperation will, to some extent, limit their water exploitation efforts, and an established cooperative mechanism (or organization) is very likely to be dominated by larger upstream countries, it is not enough to weaken their determination to promote closer cooperation compared with the realistic economic, ecological, and security concerns. The smaller downstream countries often gain support from extra-regional countries, environmental non-governmental organizations (NGOs), and international organizations (IOs). Such support gives them a greater incentive to urge larger upstream countries to carry out a higher level of cooperation. If downstream countries can establish a basin management agency or organization, they will be more likely to speak with "one voice" to the outside world to overcome the resistence of larger upstream countries. With "one voice", they can coax upstream countries to accept the idea of integrated management and even join the basin organization, although downstream countries often show resistance to integrated basin management, which has greatly affected the effectiveness of water governance. In addition, with the involvement of extra-regional countries, smaller downstream countries can employ integrated management to contain the growing influence of larger upstream countries. China is motivated to carry out closer cooperation on water resources with downstream countries for the following benefits:

Better adaptation to new trends in the management of international rivers

Many new approaches to transboundary water management have emerged in recent years. The author believes that water management should pay attention to the following new trends:

a *Networking.* It emphasizes the construction of an open and flexible framework for water diplomacy and an inclusive water diplomatic partnership that includes a networked research and practice mode with experts from all relevant sectors. Thus, more professional guidance and recommendations can be provided for water diplomacy. For instance, in 2012, the US announced a new cooperative partnership to confront global water challenges by employing experts on water problems (Hillary Clinton, 2012). An immediate result of the network is that the research and practice of water diplomacy becomes more open, professional, and scientific. The main players and subjects in water diplomacy will also change continuously, while the rapidly growing influences of NGOs in water diplomacy are worthy of attention.

b *Sharing.* When one country has no right to pick the larger interest, it will select equally shared interest (or at least shared interest) as its optimal strategy (Zhao, 2010). In transboundary water resources management, the concept of "benefit-sharing" is gradually accepted by all parties and has become an important guiding idea in the practice of water diplomacy (World Commission on Dams, 2005). It has also been enriched in both theoretical and practical levels over time (Daoudy, 2007; Tafesse, 2009). In 2009, the World Bank announced a new hydropower policy in which benefit-sharing becomes the core concept in this wave of hydropower development and investment ("Directions in Hydropower", 2009). In 2011, a guidance document released by the MRC pointed out that benefit-sharing has been widely recognized as a powerful and practical tool to enhance cooperation in basin management and in the development of sustainable river infrastructures ("Knowledge Base on Benefit Sharing," 2011).

c *Securitization.* The United Nations World Water Development Report 2009 pointed out that water problems will severely constrain global economic and social development in the 21st century and may cause interstate conflicts (WWAP, 2009). In February 2012, the US National Intelligence Council released its "Global Water Assessment", which came to a "critical conclusion": The danger of war will increase in the following decade due to competition for water ("Global Water Security," 2012). Former US Secretary of State Hillary Clinton also noted that water is "an essential ingredient of global peace, stability, and security" (US Department of State's Bureau of International Information Programs, 2015). The trend to securitize water diplomacy is bound to further enhance the importance of water issues on the national security agenda.

d *Legalization*. There are mainly two Conventions guiding the management of transboundary rivers in the international community: one is the Convention of the Law of Non-Navigable Uses of International Watercourses ratified by the International Law Commission of the United Nations in 1997; the other is the Convention on the Protection and Use of Transboundary Watercourses and International Lakes signed by the United Nations Economic Commission for Europe in 1992. In May 2014, Vietnam signed the Convention of the Law of Non-Navigable Uses of International Watercourses and became its 35th signatory, which means that the convention came into effect in September 2014. In future, the possibility cannot be ruled out that some countries will introduce legal means into Lancang-Mekong water management.

e *Integration*. More and more countries believe that the best way to solve water disputes in the basin is to gradually conclude a just and reasonable basin-wide treaty accommodating the interests of all countries through cooperation and consultation, and ultimately establish a basin-wide water management agency (He, 2013, p. 40).

Meeting new requirements for building the 21st Century Maritime Silk Road

The building of the 21st-Century Maritime Silk Road has been met with a mixed response from the international community. This is evident among the Association of Southeast Asian Nations (ASEAN) countries along the Maritime Silk Road, where high hopes for the project have been dampened by some scruples (Pillalamarri, 2014; Zeng, 2015). The smooth roll-out of the Maritime Silk Road is, in large part, contingent upon the political mutual trust between China and the countries alongside the Maritime Silk Road. And such political mutual trust hinges upon easing and finally resolving the security disputes or conflicts between China and other Maritime Silk Road countries. However, as we can see, besides the sovereignty disputes over the South China Sea, China is also at odds with some Mekong countries insofar as the conservation and use of the water resources is concerned. These disputes are most likely to pose a major obstacle to the building of the 21st-Century Maritime Silk Road.

As an important node of the 21st-Century Maritime Silk Road, the Mekong region has already become a testing ground for China to promote the new concepts of its neighbourhood diplomacy and to build the China-ASEAN Community of Shared Destiny (Liu, 2014). Addressing water issues are at the heart of the cooperation and positive steps will help China to promote its neighbourhood diplomacy and shape its surroundings.

China's vigour in promoting its neighbourhood diplomacy is of great significance to the building of the 21st-Century Maritime Silk Road. First, it reduces the tension and differences between China and its neighbouring countries over the management of transboundary rivers and enhances political mutual trust, thus consolidating China's relations with the river-basin countries and fostering a sound political and social environment for the building of the 21st-Century Maritime Silk Road. Second, it is conducive to the formation of sound "River-Sea" interactions and the settlement of territorial and maritime disputes in the South China Sea and other disputed areas. The "dual-track" approach has accentuated ASEAN's important role in maintaining the stability in the South China Sea. Therefore, China and ASEAN will speed up their "Code of Conduct" (COC) consultation process. Building political mutual trust with the countries through cooperation on water resources will undoubtedly help China gain more support from the ASEAN countries for its diplomacy in the South China Sea. Third, during the process of water resources cooperation, the identification of new growth drivers will also contribute to the interconnectivity in the region. China, which enjoys great geopolitical, economic, and technological advantages, is able to provide more public goods on water resources for its neighbours (Li, 2013). Not only will this move shift the focus of the river-basin countries from the differences in hydropower development to regional common development, it will also create new economic growth drivers that facilitate the outbound transfer of the related industries from China.

Easing new pressure on the internationalization of water issues

Quantitative research suggests that extra-regional intervention has very limited influence on China's transboundary river issues (Li, 2015). However, the degree of the internationalization of water issues on the Lancang-Mekong River is much higher than that of China's other transboundary rivers because the extra-regional involvement is far greater.

Ever since 2009, when the US launched the Lower Mekong Initiative, it has frequently attacked China over water issues. After years of effort, a US-led long-term strategic deployment has taken shape – institutionalized, networked, and multilayered. In 2013, the US announced a new aid package of USD 50 million (2013–2015) to the Lower-Mekong countries to strengthen its cooperation with countries there. As a result, the cooperation, which originally only covered environment, education, health, and interconnectivity, was extended to "the six pillars": agriculture and food security, interconnectivity, education, energy security, environment and water, and health. At the same time, the US also increased its financial commitments to the MRC. It has plans to launch the Lower Mekong Initiative 2020 to continue to provide long-term aid to develop the Lower-Mekong countries.

Japan, as one close ally of the US, has been vigorously cooperative in the US-led Mekong River Initiative. In 2009, Japan, together with five Mekong River countries, set up the mechanism of Japan-Mekong Summit, bringing their cooperation all the way up to the very top level. Under this mechanism, Japan's aid to this part of the world is increasing by the year (Nishizawa, 2011; Pan, 2014), and Japan has become the biggest aid donor and investor in the region. The aid programs include everything from infrastructure, trade and investment facilitation, social development, and environmental protection. In addition, countries such as South Korea, Australia, and India have all revved up their cooperation with Mekong River countries as well.

Apparently, with the US' unprecedented intensification of the extra-regional involvement in the Mekong River affairs, the Mekong River has all but turned into a testing ground for the US rebalancing strategy in the Asia-Pacific as well as an arena for the "Great Game" among major powers (Liu & Lu, 2013). On the one hand, the US has repeatedly attacked and pressured China over water issues that have become increasingly politicized, securitized, and internationalized. On the other hand, the US is taking advantage of the issues surrounding water resources to strengthen its presence by institutionalization in the Mekong region and hedging against China's influence. If left unchecked, this trend is likely to have an adverse impact on China's neighbourhood diplomacy.

Recommendations on implementing the water diplomacy

To counter the trend mentioned above and better cooperate with Mekong countries, China needs to upgrade its limited technical participation in the management of water resources to full participation to improve water resources management of the Lancang-Mekong River. China's full participation should be cooperation that starts with but goes beyond water issues, so as to strategically explore and blaze a path for China's cooperation with the Mekong countries.

In November 2015, China's substantial progress in its Lancang-Mekong diplomacy was marked by the First Foreign Ministers' Meeting on Lancang-Mekong Cooperation. Foreign ministers from China, Thailand, Cambodia, the Laos, Myanmar, and Vietnam agreed to formally launch the Lancang-Mekong Cooperation mechanism (LMC). The Joint Statement released at the meeting identified three key cooperation areas, namely political security, economy and sustainable development, as well as social and cultural affairs, fully "docking" with the three pillar areas in ASEAN's community-building.

The Chinese foreign minister Wang Yi (Wang, 2015) highlighted the following points:

a The LMC should systematically move from the easy areas to the more difficult ones.
b All parties should stay in line with the current conditions and development needs of the Mekong Countries and give priority to the cooperation in

interconnectivity, production capacity, transboundary economic affairs, water resources, agriculture, and poverty reduction.

c All parties should provide policy, financing, and intellectual support, and focus on concrete projects to ensure their smooth implementation.

d Water resource cooperation should be developed into the flagship area of the LMC.

The first LMC Leaders' Meeting held in China in March 2016 marked a step towards maturity for the LMC. And the 45 "early harvest" projects are also entering the stage of implementation. Compared to other cooperation mechanisms in the region, though the LMC had a late start, it is higher-levelled, more extensive, comprehensive, and down-to-earth (Guo, 2016). The biggest advantage of the LMC is that it is the first cooperation platform composed purely of the Lancang-Mekong countries; thus, the interests of these countries could be well-represented. This explains why its development prospects are generally considered promising. The launch of the LMC marks China's start to full participation in the Lancang-Mekong water resources cooperation. It also indicates that water diplomacy will be in the limelight, and the focus will be on China's participation in the Lancang-Mekong cooperation. To make water resources cooperation a true paragon for the cooperation between China and the Mekong countries, China should make a comprehensive and systematic blueprint to set the direction and priorities for its Lancang-Mekong water diplomacy.

Popularize and put into practice new ideas and ways

As China's assertion of its right to develop hydropower in the Lancang River has almost come to a conclusion, its focus on Lancang-Mekong water resources cooperation should be shifted to the maintenance of stability. In other words, China is pursuing a more positive water diplomacy. It aims to fully participate in regional cooperation, seriously consider and respect the interests of all Mekong River countries, and conduct water resources cooperation with the Lower-Mekong countries. China's aim is to consolidate and improve relations with Lower-Mekong countries and lay a solid foundation for advancing its neighbourhood diplomacy. To fully participate in the water diplomatic policy calls for innovation in philosophy and practice, and the LMC provides an effective platform for such diplomatic innovation.

Both traditional Chinese and Western philosophies advocate for the practice of "Do unto others as you would have them do unto you", encouraging people not to impose upon others what they themselves do not like. This idea demonstrates a philosophical tendency towards high self-discipline. It also reflects a value judgment standard with the self at the centre and thus has its own limitations. Zhao Tingyang, a renowned Chinese philosopher, improved this idea by putting forward the concept of "do not do to others what others do not like". The part "what others do not like" focuses more on others' value judgment and represents a philosophical concept that transcends egocentrism (Zhao, 2010, p. 26). The "by all, for all and of all" concept guiding the Belt and Road Initiative

(BRI) shows that China is by no means imposing its own strategy on other countries. Rather, this initiative is an ideal cooperation model based on mutual respect, ideal for all countries to explore and pursue common development. All these principles are demonstrating that China will never impose its strategies upon others. Rather, it commits itself to common development by working with others to explore the best cooperation mechanism on the basis of mutual respect. These principles of the Initiative, by putting such philosophical thinking into practice, is a further improvement that China should adhere to while pushing forward with the LMC. There was a good beginning, for example, the 45 "early harvest" programs adopted by the LMC leaders, among which 25 were initiated by the Mekong countries.

When designing and carrying out water resources programs, it is important for relevant parties to fully respect and appreciate the practical demands, cooperation intentions, and traditional cultures of the countries and regions involved. This is important for various reasons: (i) formulating policies in line with the different economic and social development levels and structural features of different countries, (ii) improving the livelihood of the people in the region, and (iii) facilitating the sustainable development and capacity-building in the region. For instance, China should refrain from thinking big at every turn. Building a large-scale hydropower station often involves higher political and economic risks and usually comes at an ecological price as well. At present, the Laos, Vietnam, and other Mekong River countries have ridden on a new wave of hydropower development. Contrary to the old trend of constructing of high-gorge and level-lake kinds of dams, these countries are increasingly gravitating towards low-dam or dam-free hydropower stations. Although not as profitable, the latter is in reality an effective alternative towards more environment-friendly hydropower development. For a river like the Mekong River that has so many branches and water resources, such an alternative has broad prospects, and therefore should be made an important direction in China's future participation in hydropower development in the Mekong River.

Seek new balance

As a new regional mechanism, LMC should not only seek balance with the existing mechanisms but also keep balance between bilateral and multilateral cooperation within the LMC.

Regarding the interactions among existing mechanisms, besides the LMC, the Greater Mekong Subregional Economic Cooperation (GMS) and the MRC are the major mechanisms dedicated to Mekong cooperation. The GMS, a regional economic cooperation platform led by the Asian Development Bank (ADB), has been devoted to promoting the Greater Mekong Subregion's economic development since 1992. Its broad cooperation range covers nine major areas (such as trade and investment, agriculture, and connectivity through which ADB has accumulated rich experience in promoting the GMS' development) with China playing a positive role. The MRC is the only regional intergovernmental international organization dedicated to the water resources management in this basin. Despite being criticized for its insufficient capacity and weak influence, it still plays a unique and indispensable role in water resources management in the Lancang-Mekong region (Boer & Hirsch, 2016). In this sense, the MRC has a strong authority, especially in knowledge-generation and information-collection regarding water resources management. Although China is not a member of the MRC, it has maintained long-term friendly relations with it. It is inevitable that the establishment of LMC may overlap with the existing mechanisms in some areas of cooperation. This may result in competition among the mechanisms and waste. Hence, it is particularly important to conduct dialogue and coordination within the existing mechanisms.

In terms of bilateral and multilateral cooperation within the LMC, it is equally important to seek balance for maintaining the dynamics of LMC. The LMC, in fact, is a multilateral mechanism. But some individual countries doubt this China-led mechanism. This may have a direct impact on the overall cooperation advancement. At the same time, their specific interests and concerns differ from each other. Therefore, while promoting the "1+5" multilateral cooperation, attention should be paid to bilateral cooperation. This will not only make it easier to promote the projects, but can also push the multilateral cooperation to play a model role. For instance, many of the "early harvest" projects are bilateral projects for which we can adopt flexible and differentiated policies to implement some of them at an earlier time to benefit relevant countries.

Take Vietnam as an example. Vietnam has been concerned about the agricultural production in Mekong River Delta. However, over the years, the seawater intrusion phenomenon led by the decrease of the water volume of the Mekong River in dry seasons is becoming more and more serious and has brought huge losses to the agricultural production in Vietnam. In March 2016, Vietnam suffered a severe drought which caused 9 of 13 provinces and municipalities in the Delta to suffer from seawater intrusion. Seawater intrusion affected nearly 40 per cent of the Mekong Delta area. Nearly 200,000 hectares of orchards and rice fields suffered different degrees of loss, and more than 15,000 households suffered from the lack of domestic water. To tackle this situation, the Vietnamese government issued an emergency response to minimize losses in the Mekong River Delta. To alleviate the drought in Vietnam and Cambodia, China decided to open the Jinghong Hydropower Station Gate in Yunnan Province. Its emergency water replenishment in the lower Mekong countries was embraced by Vietnam and Cambodia. At the same time, China proposed the establishment of Lancang-Mekong Cooperation Center on Water Resources to share river information, protect ecological resources along the river together, and enable the residents in Lancang-Mekong coastal area to better "live off the water" ("Five 'whats'," 2016). This initiative has increased the transparency of water resources management of all countries in this basin and provided an institutional guarantee for future cooperation. Moreover, it will gradually resolve other countries' concerns about China's desire to seek "water hegemony".

Build preventive diplomacy measures for water resources

Cross-border water resources management, as an economic problem and a non-traditional security issue, needs to be tackled with joint efforts of the riparian countries. In the process of promoting water diplomacy, China has experienced both success and failure. Take the settlement of the problems in voyage safety at Mekong River as an example. After the Mekong "10.5" attack on a Chinese cargo ship, China, Laos, Myanmar, and Thailand launched the Mekong River joint patrol and law enforcement mechanism to combat the illegal activities, respond to emergencies, and safeguard voyage security in Mekong River Basin together. By June 2015, the four countries have launched 35 rounds of joint patrol and law enforcement. This mechanism has become a new model of joint law enforcement for China and its neighbouring countries to enhance stability in the Mekong basin and establish connectivity between China and the downstream countries on the Mekong River. However, the local government and residents opposed the construction of Myitsone Dam because the Chinese side did not adequately address compensation for local residents and ecological protection in the dam design and construction (Qin, 2012). The suspension of Myitsone Dam project has become a watershed in terms of Chinese enterprises' investment in Myanmar. Statistics show that China's investment in Myanmar decreased from USD 8.3 billion in 2010 to USD 20 million in 2013. What makes it worse is that the Myitsone Dam issue has gradually evolved into a sensitive political topic and became a landmark in the history of the bilateral relations.

Both contrasting cases show that preventive diplomacy in the field of water resources should be well-established. Although China and the countries in the basin have pursued preventive diplomacy in water resources and gained positive outcomes, their attempts are mainly limited to the construction of single-problem preventive measures. Besides, the successful experience gained from solving one problem does not necessarily apply to other problems because of the lack of theoretical guidance. Against the background of "full participation" in Lancang-Mekong water diplomacy, the connectivity between water resources and the relevant issues has been strengthened. The preventive diplomacy measures targeting at one problem is inadequate for handling the possible comprehensive risks. Therefore, it is necessary for the countries along the basin to discuss and promote the construction of institution-oriented water resources preventive diplomacy and build regional consensus on theories and practices. The preventive diplomacy should cover the concepts, goals, applied fields/problems, behaviour standards, operating procedures, and other relevant aspects by harnessing their successful local experience in water resources governance. It is helpful for developing the preventive diplomacy theories and practices suitable for Lancang-Mekong water resources management, enhancing the effectiveness of the cooperation, and accumulating experience for the preventive diplomacy in the Asia-Pacific region.

Conclusion

From "limited cooperation" to "full participation", the LMC is a major platform for China to participate in the water resources management along the Mekong River. The important manifestation of China's full participation should be that cooperation starts with and also goes beyond water issues, so as to strategically explore and blaze a path for China's cooperation with the Mekong countries. Among the many more problems and challenges ahead, China must strengthen the mutual political trust with the lower countries, shape the cooperation norms and culture to achieve good governance of water resources in the basin, avoid the marginalization of water issue, and increase the effectiveness of water management by adopting the integrated water resources management (IWRM) approach (Islam & Susskind, 2012). For the downstream countries involved, because of the long-existing obvious divergences in economic/technical development, social/environmental grievances, and structural constraints stemming from different political systems, the task of getting state and non-state actors to effectively participate in cross-border water resources management will be a long, drawn-out challenge (Everard, 2013). In this process, both the decision-making organs and policymakers need to keep learning and adapting to changing conditions to reduce the negative impact on water resources management brought about by these differences and emerge with a solution that is acceptable to all parties.

Acknowledgement

This chapter is funded jointly by "the research projects of China-ASEAN Collaborative Innovation Center for Regional Development and Program for Changjiang Scholars and Innovative Research Team in University (PCSIRT), Ministry of Education" (contract number: CWZ201505).

References

Blake, D. (2001). Proposed Mekong Dam scheme in China threatens millions in downstream countries. *World Rivers Review, 16*, 4–5.

Boer, B., & Hirsch, P. (2016). *The Mekong: A social-legal approach to river basin development.* London, UK: Routledge.

Chellaney, B. (2013).Water, peace and war: Confronting the global water crisis. *Foreign Affairs, 92*(6), 172–173.

Clinton, H. (2012). *Secretary Clinton's remarks on world water day.* Retrieved from http://iipdigital.usembassy.gov/st/english/texttrans/2012/03/201203222611.html#axzz40Osv8tOO.

Daoudy, M. (2007). Benefit-sharing as a tool of conflict transformation: Applying the inter-SEDE model to the Euphrates and Tigris River Basins. *The Economics of Peace and Security Journal, 2*, 26–32.

Everard, Mark. (2013). *The hydro-politics of dams: Engineering or ecosystem.* London, UK: Zed Books.

Five "whats" for Lancang-Mekong Cooperation. (2016). *Foreign Ministry of the PRC.* Retrieved from www.fmprc.gov.cn/web/zyxw/t1348356.shtml.

Freshwater Under Threat: Vulnerability Assessment of Freshwater Resources to Environmental Change: A Joint Africa-Asia Report Summary. (2008). *United Nations environment programme*. Retrieved from https://wedocs.unep.org/rest/bitstreams/15169/retrieve.

Gao, Z., Zhao, H., & Dong, S. (2012). Study on stoplog gate in multi-level intake of Nuozhadu Hydropower Station. *Water Power, 9*, 35–37.

Global Water Security: The Intelligence Community Assessment. (2012, May 9). *US department of state*. Retrieved from https://2009-2017.state.gov/j/189598.htm.

Guo, Y. (2014). A new trend in Mekong water governance and China's response. *Oriental Morning Post*, January 17.

Guo, Y. (2015). China's participation in the water governance of the Lancang-Mekong River: Policy evaluation and future trends. *Journal of China's Neighborhood Diplomacy*. Beijing, People's Republic of China: Social Sciences Academic Press.

Guo, Y. (2015). The role of water diplomacy in the implementation of China's "One Belt One Road" Strategy. *Asia-Pacific Security and Maritime Affairs, 2*, 81–93.

Guo, Y. (2016). The Lancang-Mekong cooperation leaders' meeting brings China-ASEAN cooperation to a new high. *China Daily Online*. Retrieved from www.chinadaily.com.cn/hqgj/2016-03/24/content_24075609.htm.

He, Y. (2013). *Study on legal issues concerning China's utilization and protection of transboundary water resources*. Shanghai. People's Republic of China: Fudan University Press.

International Law Association. (1967). *The Helsinki rules on the uses of the waters of international rivers*. Retrieved from www.internationalwaterlaw.org/documents/intldocs/helsinki_rules.html.

Islam, S., (2010). *Water diplomacy welcome*. Retrieved from http://sites.tufts.edu/waterdiplomacy.

Islam, S. & Susskind, L. E. (2012). *Water diplomacy: A negotiated approach to managing complex water network*. New York, NY: Routledge.

Knowledge Base on Benefit Sharing. Initiative on Sustainable Hydropower. (2011). *Mekong river commission*. Retrieved from www.mrcmekong.org/assets/Publications/Manuals-and-Toolkits/knowledge-base-benefit-sharing-vol1-of-5-Jan-2012.pdf.

Li, S., He, D., & Fu, K. (2006). An analysis of the correlation between the Lancang River and the water levels of the Lower Mekong River. *Chinese Science Bulletin, 51*(s2), 100–105.

Li, Z. (2013). Water issues and international relations: From the perspective of regional public goods. *Foreign Affairs Review, 2*, 108–118.

Li, Z. (2015). An analysis of the factors affecting China's cross-border river issues. *Quarterly Journal of International Politics, 2*. Beijing, People's Republic of China: Social Sciences Academic Press, 90.

Liu, Z. (2014). *Report on the development of the Greater Mekong Sub-region cooperation*. Beijing, People's Republic of China: Social Sciences Academic Press.

Liu, Z., & Lu, G. (2013). *Blueprint for the development of the Greater Mekong Sub-Region (GMS): Report on the development of the GMS cooperation (2012–2013)*. Beijing, People's Republic of China: Social Sciences Academic Press.

Lu, G. (2012). The pros and cons for China to join the Mekong River Commission. *World Affairs, 8*, 30–32.

Mirumachi, N., Zeitoun, M., & Warner, J. (2013). *Transboundary water interactions and the UN watercourses convention: Allocating water and implementing principles*. Environment, Politics and Development Working Paper Series. London, UK: Department of Geography, King's College.

Nishizawa, N. (2011). The development of the Mekong River Region and Japanese government's ODA. *A Quarterly Journal of Translations, 1*, 10.

Pan, N. (2014). *Japanese ODA to Asian countries: An empirical study of Myanmar compared with Cambodia, Laos, and Vietnam.* Retrieved from www.mof.go.jp/pri/international_exchange/visiting_scholar_program/ws2014d.pdf.

Pillalamarri, A. (2014, September 18). India's answer to China's Maritime Silk Road. *The Diplomat.* Retrieved from http://thediplomat.com/2014/09/project-mausam-indias-answer-to-chinas-maritime-silk-road/.

Qin, H. (2012). The puzzlementin Myitsone Dam. *Economic Observer,* February 13.

Robins, L., & Blake, D. (Eds.). (2016). *Water governance dynamics in the Mekong region.* SIRD, 148.

Strategic Environmental Assessment of Hydropower on the Mekong Mainstream. (2010). *International Centre for Environmental Management.* Retrieved from http://icem.com.au/portfolio-items/strategic-environmental-assessment-of-hydropower-on-the-mekong-mainstream/.

Tafesse, T. (2009). *Benefit-sharing framework in transboundary river basins: The case of the Eastern Nile Subbasin.* Conference Papers no.1. International Water Management Institute. Retrieved from http://publications.iwmi.org/pdf/H042519.pdf.

US Department of State. (2013). *2013 US engagement in the lower Mekong initiative.* Retrieved from www.scoop.co.nz/stories/WO1307/S00047/2013-us-engagement-in-the-lower-mekong-initiative.htm.

US Department of State's Bureau of International Information Programs. (2015). *Clinton boosts U.S. commitment to world water challenges.* Retrieved from https://site.douban.com/119254/widget/notes/3502751/note/206863072/. [In Chinese.]

Wang, Y. (2015). *Remarks at the first LMC foreign ministers' meeting.* Retrieved from www.fmprc.gov.cn/web/wjdt_674879/wjbxw_674885/t1314376.shtml.

World Commission on Dams. (2005). *Dams and development: A new framework for decision-making.* Beijing, People's Republic of China: China Environmental Science Press.

World Bank Group. (2009). *Directions in hydropower.* Working Paper No. 54727. Retrieved from http://documents.worldbank.org/curated/en/164581468336679451/pdf/547270WP0Direc10Box349424B01PUBLIC1.pdf.

WWAP. (2009). *UN world water development report 3. Water in a changing world.* Paris, France and London, UK: UNESCO.

Yoffe, S., Wolf, A. T., & Giordano, M. (2003). Conflict and cooperation over international freshwater resources: Indicators of basin at risk. *Journal of the American Water Resources Association, 39*(5), 1109–1126.

Zeitoun, M., & Mirumachi, N. (2008). Transboundary water interaction I: Reconsidering conflict and cooperation. *International Environment Agreements, 8*, 297–316.

Zeng, X. (2015). The central Asian countries's understanding and expectations of the silk road economic belt. *People's Daily Online.* Retrieved from http://world.people.com.cn/n/2014/0409/c1002-24857680.html. [In Chinese.]

Zhao, T. (2010). *Politics in everybody.* Beijing, People's Republic of China: Social Sciences Academic Press.

Part II

Major transboundary rivers

5 Transboundary cooperation on the Amur River Basin in recent decades

Eugene Simonov and Eugene Egidarev

The evolving policy context

Many policies and patterns in transboundary cooperation between China and its neighbours are now influenced by the new Belt and Road Initiative (BRI), proposed by China, that promotes trade, international investment in infrastructure and sharing of China's industrial capacity with more than 60 countries and is viewed by some as a blueprint for continental economic integration (Preston, Bailey, Bradley, Jigang, & Changwen, 2016; Tracy, Shvarts, Simonov, & Babenko, 2017; Xin, 2016). The BRI is expected to have profound influence on natural resource management and environmental protection in Eurasia (Suocheng et al., 2015). In particular, it is expected that major changes may happen in the management of transboundary rivers basins. While previously China was interested in ensuring water security within its national borders, nowadays it has to pay attention to water-related problems in whole transboundary basins to ensure that water is at least available for planned investment schemes. On the other hand, the environmental health of shared river basins should also receive much greater priority due to more environmentally responsible domestic development polices in China, illuminated by "Ecological Civilization" Policy, that prescribes a comprehensive set of reforms driving the whole of China's governance system towards sustainable resource use and nature conservation (State Council, 2015a; UNEP, 2016). All of these policies are very new and immature and, if they persist, their influence on transboundary water management will be fully revealed only in a decade or more distant future.

In a given transboundary basin, the impact of those policies would be further complicated by specific relationships between China and particular neighbours, and the policies of countries that share the basin. In the case of China-Russia strategic relationships, we see a growing subordination in the bilateral relationship to Chinese regional policies (Blank, 2016), so raising concerns about existing problems (including those in environmental field) could be constrained in this partnership (Wishnick, 2016). Because of that, many real problems in bilateral water management may be no longer reflected in official negotiations and communication issued by Russian authorities in order to not harm some "higher-priority policy objectives". Besides, according to Korolev (2016), as

Russia failed its post-Soviet project of becoming a full-fledged member of the West (or legitimate part of the European integration process), it launched a new geopolitical project of becoming a transcontinental Eurasian power by means of reorientation to Asia. Prospects of success of this reorientation are still uncertain due to the low effectiveness of Moscow's policies, which is illustrated by the fact that several planned cooperative megaprojects listed in a fresh paper by Korolev (2016), according to our data, have already failed by the end of 2016. The new wave of Sino-Russian economic cooperation may repeat the fate of the "Programme of Cooperation between the Regions of the Far East and East Siberia of Russia and Northeast China for the Period 2009–2018" (2009, September 23), most objectives of which have not been fulfilled (Shvarts, Simonov, & Progunova, 2011). However, "turn to the East" still grants greater attention of the State to all things "Asian" including management of transboundary rivers. As Wishnick (2016) has argued, Russia's integration in Asia has been devised as a meta-project, destined to reaffirm the country's global status, rather than a development project. Therefore in official high level Sino-Russian cooperation discourse ideology and political mythology prevails over accurate monitoring and reporting of actual progress in achieving practical objectives of joint projects on the ground. For the expert community, this complicates the observation and analysis of current transboundary water management due to a lack of reliable data and an abundance of propaganda constructs.

So far, the new heights of political trust and cooperation between China and Russia have not yet significantly changed water management problems and tendencies that have been formed during the previous several decades. Therefore, in this chapter, we seek to establish a "baseline" account of transboundary water management in the Amur River Basin in the wake of major changes dictated by wider transboundary and domestic policies.

Mongolia, being sandwiched between two "superpowers" since the fall of its mighty ally, the Soviet Union, has been struggling to preserve its cultural and national identity through counterbalancing Russian influences by Chinese influences and vice-versa. It also seeks active political and economic cooperation with remote "third neighbours" such as US, Japan, India, etc. However, by 2012, China's influence became so predominant in the region and Mongolia's national economy, that a new development paradigm was set forward by Mongolian leadership known as the "Steppe Road". This envisioned Mongolia acquiring a role on the map of the BRI as the shortest transportation corridor via highways, rail, oil and gas pipelines, and electricity transmission from eastern China to western Russia and European countries. Russia and China approved this approach, and the three countries declared development of the China-Mongolia-Russia economic corridor of the BRI. (Tracy et al., 2017). Water supply to new industries along the economic corridor in Mongolia is an important limiting factor due to dry climate and natural water scarcity in the southern part of the country. It is noteworthy that river basin management and efficient water use has not been listed as explicit part of trilateral agreement on the "Programme for Development of China-Mongolia-Russia Economic Corridor signed" in June 2016.

(NDRC, 2016b). This, probably, shows that neighboring countries were shy to include cooperation on this topic due to growing controversies in shared river basins. At the same time the Programme includes commitments to joint work to combat desertification and wildfires, protect wetlands, conserve biodiversity and develop protected areas and general cooperation in the field of environmental protection.

Since China and Mongolia share a limited number of relatively small river basins, their water management relationships have much less prominent political status than those between China and Russia. However, recently, Sino-Mongolian transboundary water management has also witnessed a transboundary dispute on water allocation in the same Amur River Basin.

Amur River Basin at a glance

The Amur River (Heilongjiang in Chinese) is formed by the confluence of Shilka and Argun Rivers; it flows into the Sakhalin Bay of the Sea of Okhotsk. The length of the river from the confluence is 2.8 thousand km and the catchment area is 2.1 million km^2 (counting the periodically closed basin of Lake Hulun/Dalai). The Amur River Basin is shared by four countries: Russia (49% of the total basin area), China (42%), Mongolia (9%) and North Korea (0.00025% -less than 5 sq. km). The Amur River Basin is a classic example of a transboundary river network: the Russian-Chinese border goes along the rivers Argun, Amur, Ussuri, Tur, Turga and Sungacha for more than 3,500 km.

The Amur River's normal annual discharge near Khabarovsk-Fuyuan is 267 km^3 and the river mouth – 368 km^3. Most rivers of the basin are usually frozen from October to April/May, many of tributaries may freeze to the bottom. The Amur River Basin is located in the area affected by East Asian monsoons. Pronounced summer floods are typical for the Far Eastern regime, accounting for 75–80% of the annual flow. The total area of riverine floodplains of large rivers is more than 80,000 km^2 (Egidarev, 2012). In 2013, the region experienced severe flooding, that, while devastating to the local human population, resulted in an improvement in water quality and river habitat conditions.

The natural climate cycle in the Amur River Basin, with alternating dry and wet periods, which typically spans 25–40 years, is a major force in shaping regional ecosystems and local people's lifestyles. In addition, climate rapidly changes in the Amur River Basin, and continuing warming could cause habitat alteration and even habitat disappearance (Kirilyuk, 2012).

The Amur River Basin has tremendous biodiversity and is a freshwater ecosystem; according to international classifications, it has six different freshwater ecoregions, whereas another nearby system its size, the Yangtze River Basin, only has two. There are at least 6,000 species of vascular plants, 130 fish species, 600 bird species and 200 mammal species. Among fish, there are at least 10 salmonids, including the rare Siberian Taimen, as well as three species of sturgeon. Endangered Kaluga and Amur sturgeon are endemics of this river basin (Simonov, Egidarev, Nikitina, Osipov, & Shalikovsky, 2016). The Amur River

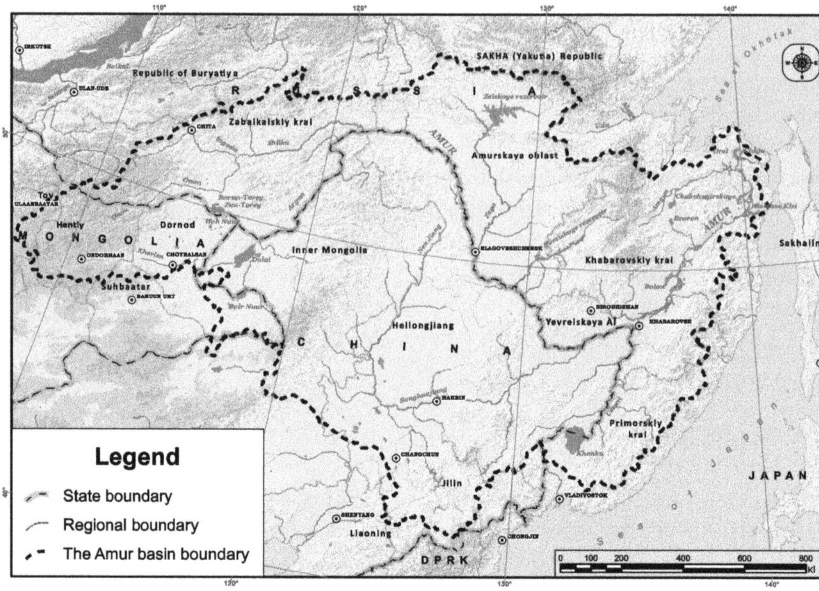

Figure 5.1 Map of the Amur River basin.
Source: WWF-Russia.

Basin has been identified as one of the world's 200 most valuable wilderness places (Olson & Dinerstein, 2002).

The basin's global significance is also due to its large areas of wetlands, which serve as habitat for the diverse bird species, including several critically endangered cranes. Major bird migration flyways cross the region with stopover sites in wetlands.

Amur River Basin hosts about 75 million people. The population ratio of Chinese, Russian and Mongolian is 400:25:1. Average population density is 35 people/km^2 in the basin, which translates into more than 90 people/km^2 in China, 3.5 people/km^2 in Russian Far East and 0.83 people/km^2 in Mongolia. This creates a very uneven pattern in the distribution of economic activities, in nature resource use and in human pressure on natural environment.

In Northeast China, the prevalence of heavy industry, state-owned enterprises and large scale agriculture slow economic development and makes it excessively dependent on large government investments. From 2003 to 2013, an aggressive new policy to revitalize the "Old Industrial Bases" promoted the restructuring and growth of those very traditional sectors, which, in previous waves of industrialization, have already significantly contributed to the degradation of natural river ecosystems. By 2014, as China's economic growth slowed down, the Northeast economy faced extreme difficulties and even social unrest due to layoffs in the coal industry. A renewed plan to revitalize the "Old Industrial Bases" was approved recently, which shifts priorities from state-owned enterprises to promoting private businesses and from extensive extraction of natural resources to development of hi-tech manufacturing (NDRC, 2016a).

Trade and international economic cooperation between basin countries has been almost solely based on natural resource extraction. Mongolia and Russia are major sources of raw materials processed in Northeast China and, with time, more Chinese capital is invested in neighbouring countries to secure resource bases for processing industries. Both Russian and Mongolian portions of the basin increasingly rely on China as a source of investment, technological innovation, and major market. As China's demand for raw natural resources is slowing down, adjacent countries experience serious economic difficulties. At the same time, outdated and conservative administrations with poor enforcement capability leave Mongolia and Russia with little hope for adequate environmental oversight of resource extraction processes, or pursue other "green" development alternatives. Serious human impacts on the region's biodiversity are already very evident (Shvarts et al., 2011).

New problems may be added by China's "Ecological Civilization" Policy that imposes land-use restrictions to secure ecosystem services delivery and promotes higher environmental standards for companies operating inside China (MEP, 2015; State Council, 2015a). Coupled with domestic economic and social stability problems, these policies facilitate the migration of inefficient resource intensive, and often dirty industries and technologies, into adjacent countries relieving China from "excessive industrial capacity". The BRI that facilitates the "export" of services by giant construction SOEs may have similar consequences and exacerbate environmental situations in countries adjacent to China (Preston et al., 2016).

Bilateral river management discourse

Drastically different cultures, population density, mode of economic development, and water use in Russia, China, and Mongolia, make it very difficult to build trilateral or even bilateral mechanisms to manage and protect river ecosystems. Many agreements related to water and environment have been signed between the basin's countries, but the holistic field of integrated river basin management is fragmented and there is little or no coordination between bodies managing different treaties (Table 5.1) (Agreement..., 1994; MFARF, 2017; MNRERF, 2005; Simonov, 2008).

Mongolia and China signed the Agreement of Transboundary Water in 1994, long before a similar Sino-Russian agreement was drafted. The Agreement covers transboundary waters of Kherlen, Khalkh, and Bulgan Rivers and Buir Lake (TFDD, 1994).The key issue of transboundary water cooperation between Mongolia and China China is joint monitoring and data exchange on transboundary rivers and lakes.

In contrast to the Sino-Russian Agreement, the scope of Mongolian-Chinese cooperation in addition to water resource management includes a focus on aquatic biota and fisheries management. Thus, two sides carried out, in 2013, the first joint fish survey of Buir Lake, which identified two exotic species.

Table 5.1 Intergovernmental agreements between China, Russia, and Mongolia related to water management and nature conservation

Year	*Title*	*Description*
1956	Sino-Soviet Agreement on development of "Grand Amur Scheme"	Agreement between the USSR and China on joint research operations on planning and survey operations to prepare a scheme for the multi-purpose exploitation of the Argun River and the Upper Amur River.
1986	Sino-Russian Agreement on development of "Joint Comprehensive Scheme for Water Management on Amur and Argun Rivers"	Bilateral overview of developments planned by the water and energy authorities of China and Russia led by the Song-Liao Water Resource Commission of China and Sovintervod Hydro-engineering Institute of USSR Water Resources Ministry.
1994	Mongolia-China – Agreement on Use and Protection of Transboundary Waters	Agreement on the protection and utilization of transboundary waters including aquatic biota
1994	Russia-China Agreement on protection of aquatic bio-resources in transboundary Amur and Ussuri Rivers	Protects 25 fishes, two crustaceans, one turtle, one mollusk, three aquatic plants. Regulates size limits for fish, net mesh sizes and lengths, seasonal fishing bans, closure of waters to fishing, and permitted fishing gear. Does not cover Argun River and Khanka Lake.
1994	Agreement on Dauria International Protected Area	Trilateral agreement was signed by China, Mongolia, and Russia to establish Dauria International Protected Area (DIPA) to protect globally important grasslands in the headwaters of the Amur River Basin. Includes three biosphere reserves with Ramsar wetlands.
1994	Russia-China Cooperation in Protection of the Natural Environment	Governed by Task Force on Environmental Protection should have met annually, but was stalled. This non-effective mechanism was succeeded by Environmental Sub-commission under the Commission on Regular Meetings of Heads of State in 2006.
1995	Russia-Mongolia - Agreement on Use and Protection of Transboundary Waters	Agreement between the government of Mongolia and the government of the Russian Federation on the protection and use of transboundary waters. Replaced much more detailed and binding agreement "On Selenge river Basin water resources management"
1996	Russia-China Agreement on Khanka/Xingkai Lake International Nature Reserve	The agreement envisioned a broad range of cooperative activities and established a "Mixed Chinese-Russian Commission on Lake Khanka/Xingkai International Nature Reserve". Commission was formed only in March 2009, but cooperation between nature reserves started from 2003.

2002	Russia-China Treaty on good neighbour relations, friendship and cooperation	Has chapter on cooperative development of the border region with a clause on protection and improvement of the natural environment and just and equitable management of transboundary rivers.
2006	Sino-Russian Environmental Sub-commission under the Commission on Regular Meetings of Heads of State	Highest level commission coordinated by MNR in Russia and Effectively replaced mechanisms set under 1994 environmental agreement. Meets annually. Has three task forces on: pollution prevention and cooperation in case of environmental emergencies; protection of transboundary waters and monitoring of water quality, and "green issues": biodiversity, protected areas, ecosystem conservation, etc.
2006	Sino-Russian protocol on "common approaches to monitoring of transboundary waters"	2006 a special protocol on "common approaches to monitoring of transboundary waters" was signed between SEPA and MNR. It calls for the establishment of two working groups for planning and coordinating water quality monitoring in transboundary rivers: Amur-Heilong, Ussuri-Wusuli, Argun and Razdolnaya (Suifen).
2008	Sino-Russian Agreement on Use and Protection of Transboundary Waters	Framework agreement that sets mechanism for consultations and information exchange. Joint Commission is governed by Ministry of Foreign Relations, MEP and Ministry of Water resources from China side and MNR from Russia side. In January 2014, the 6th meeting of China-Russia Transboundary Water Joint Commission tasked its Working Group on Water Resources Management to conduct research and produce a Joint Report on 2013 flood on Amur River.
2011	Sino-Russian strategy for development of transboundary protected area network in Amur River Basin	Rationale for cooperation: "as economic cooperation in border areas increase, the pressures and threats to biodiversity may also increase and therefore more active and comprehensive cooperation in nature conservation is needed." The Strategy envisions cooperation on 12 aspects of transboundary ecosystem conservation, including: biodiversity inventories, ecological monitoring, evaluation of management performance, protected areas planning, information sharing, enforcement measures, joint research, mutual training and public education efforts.
2014	Intergovernmental memorandum of intent on flood management cooperation	Signed by Russian Ministry of Emergencies and PRC Ministry of Water Resources. Joint Sino-Russian Group for Flood Fighting was formed and since held annual meetings.

Source: Compiled by the authors based on various official documents.

Several recent high-profile events strongly facilitated the evolution of water management and related environmental priorities of Sino-Russian cooperation in the Amur River Basin:

- catastrophic floods of 1997–1998 affecting three provinces in the Songhua River Basin triggered development of comprehensive river basin management beyond mere engineering in China;
- joint development and then shelving of the "Joint Comprehensive Scheme for Water Management on Amur and Argun Rivers" (1986–2000) has shown a difference in national approaches and limits to cooperation;
- the toxic spill into the Second Songhua River in November 2005, that triggered in China both a "fight on industrial pollution" and "environmental information disclosure", also became the first incident of very close bilateral cooperation in environmental crisis management;
- in 2009, the Hailaer-Dalai water transfer canal was built by China in dry steppes of Amur River headwaters despite Russian protests and without joint environmental impact assessment and/or establishing environmental flow norms for the transboundary Argun River. This triggered regular annual mutual inspections of "problematic water infrastructure" on each other's territory as a measure to improve mutual trust and understanding;
- catastrophic 2013 flood of the Amur River led to much closer cooperation on flood management which in future may have both good and bad consequences for the environmental protection.

Several Sino-Russian agreements have been signed since the mid-1990s, and formation of the Environmental Sub-commission under Mechanism for Sino-Russian Meetings of Heads of State enabled regular communication environmental issues (Table 5.1). Most agreements signed between 1994 and 2004 are non-binding and do not provide tools for joint control over common resources, but rather provide communication venues to talk about arising environmental issues.

Some agreements on "national borders", "navigation", and "mining and exploration" (not listed in Table 5.1) also have a profound influence on water management, because their implementation triggers changes in the natural character of riverbeds and riverbanks. Historically throughout the 19th and 20th centuries, the main influence factors in intergovernmental cooperation that affected the Amur River Basin riverine policies have been:

- border demarcation rules and related engineering practices;
- navigation rights and sustaining navigable channels;
- military security issues;
- energy policies, primarily hydropower;
- joint use of disputed islands and wider issues of joint use of natural resources.

An Agreement on Transboundary Waters was originally proposed by Russia around 1997 as a general framework agreement opening communication channels between the water management agencies of two countries.

The resulting agreement signed only in 2008 is very narrowly focused on "water" and does not use terms "environmental", "ecology", or "ecosystem", neither does it define "transboundary waters" as basins. It even does not use terms "basin", "watershed", "catchment", or equivalents thereof. Finally, it does not speak of environmental flows and water use limits or other mechanisms of regulating water flow alteration. The agreement omitted the larger issues of sustaining ecosystem processes, conserving biodiversity and habitats, wetland management, and strategic environmental assessments. Lacking these components, such agreement is not a promising tool for achieving integrated river basin management or for safeguarding ecosystem health. It does not have any binding requirements beyond mutual information and consultations, neither does it propose any specific path for conflict resolution. Up to date there have been two permanent working groups established, one – on water quality and emergencies and the other – on the water resources management.

Environmental issues only recently gained prominence in the Sino-Russian Amur River discourse. Pollution is the most commonly recognized environmental issue central to Sino-Russian dialogue in the basin. Rapid economic growth of the Northeastern provinces in China (the construction of chemical and pulp plants, widespread use of agricultural fertilizers and pesticides, etc.) has a significant impact on water quality in rivers both inside China, and in rivers bordering Russia such as the Argun, the Amur, and the Ussuri Rivers. This is especially noticeable downstream from the confluence of the Songhua River in the Amur River. After an accidental spill of toxic substances into the Songhua River in 2005, the governments of China and Russia, with the support of local research institutions, organized a joint monitoring of water quality in transboundary water ways. Ever since, specialists continue to carry out an annual assessment of the quality and condition of transboundary waters as part of the joint monitoring.

It should be noted that from 1996 to 2010, the researchers from the Institute of Water and Ecological Problems, Far Eastern Branch of the Russian Academy of Sciences in Khabarovsk, annually recorded increases in the statistical indicators in phenol and other toxic substances, as well as the exceeding permissible concentrations for polyaromatic hydrocarbons, pesticides, and heavy metals (Nagao et al., 2015; Shesterkin, 2010).

Recent monitoring records show that, according to 2016 measurements, the ecological condition of the Amur River has become more stable with a tendency to improve. Over the past three years, the level of water pollution in the Amur River has changed from fourth to third class. This often attributed to the success of clean-up efforts and many authors praise cooperation between Russia and China in the Amur River Basin (Bolgov, Demin, & Shatalova, 2016; Oleinikova, 2016). This improvement has primarily happened for the Amur and Ussuri Rivers, while transboundary Argun River remained heavily polluted. Although we cannot deny positive developments in transboundary water quality monitoring and can confirm that China dramatically improved its environmental control system, there are also natural factors that obviously contribute to water quality improvement such as an increase in annual discharge of the Amur River in recent years that improved capacity to dilute chemical substances.

The Amur River Basin ecosystem generates and brings nutrients to the Sea of Okhotsk, boosting the sea's biological productivity and thus supporting major sea fishery industries of Japan, Russia, and other nations (Makhinov, 2014). Therefore, problems of water quality in the Amur River extend beyond the Russian-Chinese relationships.

As noted before, Sino-Russian discourse on pollution is widely known and well-studied by other scholars (Kondratieva,Fisher & Bardyuk, 2012; Makhinov, 2014; Nagao et al., 2015; Vinogradov & Wouters, 2013). Further on, these chapter describes lesser known aspects of transboundary water management in the basin, focusing on the interaction between governments.

Case of hydropower: legacy of old agreements

In 1956, China and the Soviet Union signed an agreement for cooperative research on development of an Amur River Basin natural resource base, known as the "Grand Amur Scheme", which suggested development of a cascade of 4–9 reservoirs in the Upper and Middle Amur River with total storage volume of more than 250 km^3 and surface area of 6,000 km^2 (Gotvansky, 2007). In the 1960s, relationships between the two countries deteriorated and this plan was never implemented. Meanwhile, both countries proceeded with an uncoordinated development of water resources within their national territories. Russia created the giant Zeya Reservoir and started construction of Bureya River Hydro, while China added several new hydropower plants (HPP) to already existing Xiao Fengman HPP on the Second Songhua River.

Bilateral relationships improved by 1986, and a new agreement was signed to develop "USSR-China Joint Comprehensive Scheme for Water Resource Management in Transboundary Stretches of the Argun and Amur Rivers". The initial intent was to review development opportunities in hydropower, flood prevention, fisheries, and clean water supply. However, while China clearly prioritized hydropower and dismissed any modifications that threatened electricity outputs, Russia was eager to explore trade-offs between all sectors of the economy and sought compromise (Gotvansky, 2005).

The "Joint Comprehensive Scheme" proposed up to six dams on the Amur River, while the Argun River also was to be developed in a three-dam cascade. However, by 1999, the sides failed to agree on many specific issues including dam height, exact location, reservoir volume and regime, mitigation of impact on fish stocks, and many other environmental issues. Finally, in 2000, country delegations declined to approve the full voluminous Joint Scheme document, agreeing only on its 100-page synopsis with many points of disagreement listed in the text and all resulting materials were shelved. On the positive side, these two joint planning efforts yielded an extensive and diverse volume of research materials on the Amur River Basin (Joint Comprehensive Scheme, 1993, 1999).

The "Joint Comprehensive Scheme" evoked considerable public debate in Russia because it did not carefully review alternatives in river basin management and socio-economic development. According to Russian data, implementation of the Joint Scheme would result in radical alteration of hydrological and ecosystem processes throughout the basin. Beyond obvious generic impacts from inundation by reservoirs, most notable effects include radical changes in sedimentation patterns in the Lower Amur River, creation of an impenetrable barrier for migrating fish, and significant alteration of the wetland hydrological regime of the Amur River valley downstream (IWEP, 2003; Podolsky, Darman, & Simonov, 2006).

In Russia the focus of hydropower planning in Amur River Basin shifted from the idea to dam main stem to planning hydropower cascade development on tributaries. RusHydro State Company that holds all hydropower assets in the basin does not mention Amur River main stem sites in any of publicly available plans. RusHydro completed in 2014 construction of 2000 MW Bureya HPP on Bureya tributary and is presently competing 420MW Lower Bureya HPP downstream. Trial launch of the Lower Bureya HPP in August 2017 was attended by President Vladimir Putin, and coincided with the largest blackout in Far-Eastern electricity system, allegedly caused by sudden addition to the grid of new generating capacity , and serious failure of one of its brand-new flood gates.

Russian Far East already has a significant surplus of electricity, which makes justification for construction of new HPPs problematic. As early as 2005, a plan emerged to build new power plants to deliver up to 60 billion KWh annually to China by 2020. In light of those ambitions, construction of HPPs in the main stem of the Amur River seems to be the less desirable option for Russia in comparison with exports from inner regions (Simonov & Dahmer, 2008).

The most recent Russian Water Management Scheme for Amur Basin (WMSAB, 2015), among its priorities, does not list hydropower, but prevention of riverbank erosion and flood mitigation measures on transboundary watercourses, as well as curbing transboundary water pollution that threatens water supply, fisheries, and river ecosystem integrity.

By 2005, existing hydropower plants in China's part of the Amur River Basin exceeded 100 instalments, the majority of them being small hydro well below 50 MW. Most prominent reservoirs built in recent years in China are multipurpose power generation, sometimes supplementing more important functions such as irrigation and water transfers to agricultural and industrial areas, like the Nierji reservoir on the Nen River, which has flood control, water supply, and power generation functions.

Nevertheless, from 2000 to 2013, China's Ministry of Water Resources (CMWR) had consistently supported implementation of the "Joint Comprehensive Scheme" and damming of the Amur River main channel. All dams proposed by the "Joint Comprehensive Scheme" on the Amur River mainstream are still found in the lists of future hydropower construction sites and related research papers compiled by water engineering entities (CAE, 2007). Since 2007, China's side even proposed to cover the full costs of dam construction. Environmental issues and damage to migratory fish stock was presented in the Chinese press as the main impediment to agreement with Russia. Russia's side did not support this proposal either, at the provincial or national level.

Recently, an initiative to promote dams in the Amur River's main stem has shifted from China's national government agencies to companies and local authorities. In early 2016, Chinese solar power giant Hanergy Holdings approached the Russian Ministry of Eastern Region Development with an "innovative proposal" to build a transboundary dam on the Amur River at Taipinggou. This company has been facing major financial difficulties due to a suspended trade in stocks at HK Stock Exchange that also led to prohibition for its owners to hold management positions in Hong Kong business companies (Hanergy Thin Film Power Group Limited, 2017). With help of this proposal the Hanergy Holdings, likely, was trying to take advantage of the BRI and raise its own profile after failure at the HK Exchange. In conjunction, the Hegang City of Heilongjiang Province, plagued by crisis in its major coal enterprises, proposed to the adjacent Jewish Autonomous Province in Russia to promote jointly construction of the Khingansky-Taipinggou Dam.

This Khingansky-Taipinggou Dam has been recently assessed as having potentially the highest negative environmental impacts from among 46 possible hydropower projects in the Amur River Basin (Simonov, Egidarev, & Nikitina, 2015). After extensive consultations held in Russia, several resource-management agencies and the Government of the Jewish Autonomous Province responded with a polite refusal to consider this project any further. At the same time, environmental experts and NGOs started public discussions in the Russian press on potential detrimental impacts of Amur River main stem dams. In sharp contrast to Russian NGOs, environmental movement in China, which carries out active campaigns to preserve transboundary Nu (Salween) River in Yunnan Province, has not been perceiving the Amur River as the "last large free-flowing river of China" and so far expressed little concern about possible dam construction on its main stem.

The present unfavourable economic situation and existence of active opposition to the plan among a wide spectrum of Russian stakeholders will likely prevent the re-emergence of such damming projects in the next several years. The long-term future of the free-flowing Amur River, to a great extent, depends on values and opinions held by the government and society in China. So far, the 13th Five-Year Plan for Hydropower Development in China includes twice less hydropower facilities than the previous plan and does not include any hydropower dams on the Amur River. The Plan for Northeast China incudes only the development of pumped-storage facilities (Ministry of Energy, 2016).

Case of water transfers: competition for water

It has been predicted by experts, that eventually, the Amur River Basin would become an arena for competition for water resources (Lassere, 2003; Simonov, Podolsky, & Darman, 2006). The first well-known episode was the construction of the Hailaer-Dalai canal in China, which resulted in significant Sino-Russian controversies that have not yet been resolved (Bolgov & Frolova, 2016).

Now acute competition for water resources is likely to emerge between China and Mongolia. Early in the 21st century, when the Mongolian economy started to be driven primarily by the Chinese market, mineral licenses were given to various companies to develop ore and coal deposits: Oyu Tolgoi, Tsagaan Suvarga, Tavan Tolgoi, Shivee-Ovoo, etc. However, their development was slowed by the absence of readily available water sources in Gobi regions. Even more water is required for coal-fired power plants and coal-gasification complexes planned with China's assistance. Converting coal to electricity or gas makes it easier to export products to China. Many localities in the adjacent Inner Mongolia Region in China have already experienced a significant shortage in water resources and the administration of the border town of Erenhot expressed a desire to build a pipeline to import water from Mongolia.

The transboundary Kherlen River draining into the Hulun/Dalai Lake in China is the closest river in the East Gobi, and is eyed as the primary water source for development plans. Therefore, in 2007, some old Soviet engineering designs for long-distance water transmission were dusted off and presented to the government of Mongolia. The pipeline was initially proposed to supply water to Chinese-funded export-oriented 8–10 GW coal-energy base planned in Shivee-Ovoo east of Ulaan Baatar, as well as to growing settlements near recently developed industrial mining sites and to support large-scale planting of a "green shelterbelt" along the edge of the desert. Water transfer is expected to have major negative social and environmental impacts both in Mongolia and in China.

Kherlen-Gobi water transfer has been discussed by the China-Mongolia Water Commission and joint field surveys were conducted along the Kherlen River. China claimed that the Kherlen River and Dalai Lake could be negatively impacted by planned water transfer. The worst consequences of such a scheme are expected both from reduced floods and reduced water flow during the dry phase of the climate cycle. Finally, in early 2013, China's side was assured by Mongolia counterparts that the Kherlen-Gobi project was shelved (Songliaowei Basin Commission Engineers, pers. communication 2014).

However, during the 2013 election campaign, the Mongolian president openly announced a plan for water transfer from the transboundary Kherlen River to the Gobi. No construction has started yet, likely because Chinese investors doubt they can afford using a water supply scheme that through its effects on the Kherlen River can directly damage environmental and social conditions in their own country. The draft Kherlen River Basin Management Plan, issued in 2016 in Mongolia, calls for comprehensive strategic environmental assessment of proposed water transfer, but it does not even mention associated transboundary disputes and likely consequences for Dalai Lake (Simonov & Wickel, 2016). At a meeting of the Mongolian-Chinese Resource, Energy, and Infrastructure Cooperation Commission in Beijing on April 26, 2017, the Government of Mongolia asked again for assistance in "implementing the Kherlen Gol Project to supply water for the construction of the Tavan Tolgoi coal washing plant, the Tavan

Tolgoi power plant, and the copper concentrate processing factory"[1]. Chinese sources do not confirm that this item was discussed then or later. Nevertheless in September 2017 the Mongolia Cabinet of Ministers decided "to take urgent measures to conduct technical and economic feasibility study and environment impact evaluation on *Flow Adjustment in Kherlen River Project*". The MONTSAME Information Agency reported :"If the study concludes that the flow adjustment project is feasible, water supply issues for infrastructure development project in South Gobi and other projects will be solved, and furthermore, it will create conditions to maintain stability of flow in the river".[2]

This issue should be viewed in the context of Mongolia's recent negotiations with Russia and World Heritage Committee regarding very similar Orkhon River-Gobi Desert Water Transfer Project in Selenge River -Lake Baikal Basin which was stalled due to request for comprehensive and transparent assessments of transboundary impacts made by Russia and international bodies (WBIP, 2017, World Heritage Committee 2017). Since Dalai/Hulun Lake fed primarily by the Kherlen River is listed as wetland of international importance under the Ramsar Convention, we expect that similar assessments of transboundary impacts may be requested by international organizations and\or China side.

In the downstream areas of the Amur River Basin, the prevailing trend in China so far is bringing water-thirsty industries to the water-abundant Amur River Basin, rather than transferring its waters to the South. Wishnick (2016) argues that water scarcity represents an important source of resource vulnerability for China's Northeast, that could be partially solved with using Russia's resources. However, some water infrastructure initiatives of China are viewed by Russia's side with growing concern and may evoke frictions in medium term. For example, the China MWR since 2013 is developing a "Three River Connection Scheme" for Heilongjiang Province to use up to 5 km^3 of water from the transboundary Ussuri and Amur Rivers to support irrigation and other needs in the Sanjiang Plain (Three River.., 2015; Wang, Changlei, Xishan, & Yang, 2015). The scheme potentially posess a huge risk for fragile wetlands of the Ussuri River but is less likely to affect the Amur River main stem. For the Amur RiverBasin as a whole, one of the greatest environmental impacts should be expected if China decides to transfer its waters in large volumes to the south (North-South Water Transfer).

Case of flood management: 2013 Amur flood and beyond

The largest flood during the whole period of observation (more than 110 years in Khabarovsk city, Russia) took place on the Amur River in July–September 2013, lasting for about two months (Dugina, 2013). The flood affected almost the whole basin including the Russian Far East and Northeastern China. Peak water levels in the Middle and Lower Amur River exceeded previous all-time highs by 0.4–2.1 m. The 2013 flood has demonstrated deficiencies in overall flood management policies and practices in Russia. Since the 1990s, the government has been declaring necessity to undertake zoning of flood-prone areas, issue appropriate regulations for land-use in floodplains, and support flood-related insurance schemes. None of those promises have been fulfilled.

According to official data in the Russian section of the Amur River Basin, the flood negatively affected: 366 settlements where 13,000 residential buildings were waterlogged and 2,400 of those were damaged beyond repair (Russian Emergency Situations Ministry, 2013).

As a follow-up in July 2014, the Russian Minister of Natural Resources presented the "Integrated system of measures on reducing risks of floods in the Far Eastern Federal District" (Decisions…, 2014a) that consists predominantly of "structural" measures:

- increasing flood-prevention capacities of water storage reservoirs' (including construction of new "flood-control" hydropower dams);
- reducing risk of floods by increasing river conveyance (by dredging) at specific sections;
- protecting settlements and infrastructure with engineering structures (mostly by dykes);
- increasing accuracy of forecasting meteorological and hydrological phenomena;
- preparing protective hydraulic facilities, communal and transport infrastructure for accident-free passage of flood waters;
- preparing local and functional subsystems of the Russian emergency management system for taking adequate action during emergencies.

This list shows that Russian authorities are still more in favour of building infrastructure than taking any other types of risk prevention measures as envisioned by Integrated Flood Management concepts (APFM, 2009).

Russian President issued a call to develop the flow regulation system in the Amur River Basin, which by the beginning of 2014 triggered production of a list comprising 8–10 potential "flood-control hydropower plants" (Table 5.2; Figure 5.2).

In order to regulate flows in the Amur River Basin during flood periods, in the middle of 2014 the Russian Government instructed the Ministry of Natural Resources, Ministry of Energy, and Ministry of Foreign Affairs "to hold consultations with the PRC on planning and construction of hydraulic facilities on the Amur and its tributaries, including funding of relevant projects" (Decisions…, 2014b). Thus, Chinese entities were welcomed to invest into hydropower in Russia.

In 2013–2015, the China Three Gorges Corporation (CTGC) signed a number of broad agreements with the RusHydro to consider building four hydropower plants with flood-control function on Amur tributaries, and to become a shareholder in the half-built Lower Bureya hydropower plant. In exchange, the CTGC had to arrange for energy exports to China (Centre for Political Information, 2015; RusHydro, 2014). The Chinese company announced its eagerness to help reduce flood risks in the Amur River Basin, but soon discontinued

Table 5.2 Main characteristics of proposed new flood-control hydropower plants compared to existing reservoirs

Hydropower plant	*River*	*Reservoir live volume, cubic km*	*Average annual power generation, mill. kWh/year*
Proposed flood-management plants			
Shilkinskaya (Trans-Siberian), and counter regulator Utesnaya	Shilka	8,8	3000
Giluyskaya	Giluy	3,3	1150
Gramatukhinskaya (Lower Zeya)	Zeya	1,0	1970
Dagmarskaya	Selemdzha	5,2	980
Rusinovskaya	Selemdzha	4,2	1370
Nizhne-Nimanskaya	Niman	8,3	2230
Nizhne-Bureyskaya	Bureya	0,1	1650
Dalnerechenskaya-1, Dalnerechenskaya-2	Bolshaya Ussurka	0,7	1000
Total values for the proposed plants		31,6	13350
Existing plants			
Zeyskaya	Zeya	31,6	4900
Bureyskaya	Bureya	10,7	7100
Large hydropower plants in the Chinese section of the basin	Songhuajiang basin	27,0	5715
Total for major hydropower plants in 2013, China included		69,6	19715

Source: Simonov et al., 2016.

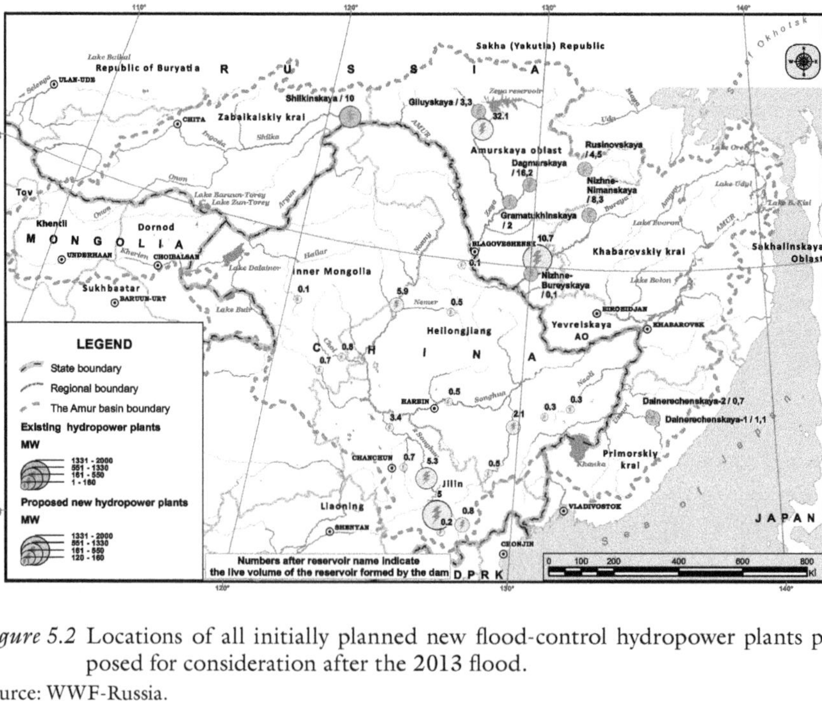

Figure 5.2 Locations of all initially planned new flood-control hydropower plants proposed for consideration after the 2013 flood.

Source: WWF-Russia.

negotiations on the topic. In late 2017, the Lower Bureya Hydro is being completed with the help of Russian taxpayers' money, while exports of electricity to China stagnate for the third year in a row barely reaching 3 billion KWh per annum. Plans for all new flood-control dams have been postponed indefinitely by RusHydro in 2015 and in fall 2017 it announced liquidation of its subsidiary JSC Nizhne-Zeyskaya HPP, which was the last remaining project from among new hydropower plants proposed after the flood.(Rushydro, 2017). This is partly due to Russia's austerity program amidst economic sanctions and partly because any new water storage reservoir would have a much lower water accumulation potential than existing ones, which have not been very effective in 2013 flood control despite their enormous live volume.

When designing flood-control hydropower plants, their feasibility should be assessed and compared with alternative risk-reduction measures, as well as their environmental impacts. But first of all planners have to compare the efficiency of regulating flows by building new hydropower reservoirs with that of the preservation of flood retention capacities of the natural flood plains, which during 2013, floods accumulated more than 130 km^3 of flood waters – much more than what was retained in all hydropower reservoirs. Therefore, preserving natural floodplains is likely a priority of any modern integrated flood management programme in the Amur River Basin. Providing legal protection for natural floodplain ecosystems could contribute both to bilateral objectives on reducing flood risks and to the implementation of the "Sino-Russian Strategy for Transboundary Network of Protected Areas in Amur River Basin" (Egidarev, Simonov, & Darman, 2016).

In China, the Integrated Flood Risk Management Plan designed for the Songhuajiang basin worked well enough on the whole, with all key objectives met in 2013 (State Council…, 2008). However, flood damages in the Chinese portion of the Amur River Basin, both in terms of financial losses and loss of human life, had been much higher than those in Russia due to 10 times greater population density and therefore much greater exposure of humans and assets to flood hazards.

Comparison shows that in China's flood management efforts in the Songhuajiang basin, in 2013, was much more efficient than along the Amur River's main channel. An obvious reason is that designing a joint integrated flood risk management plan with the Russian side was considered impossible (and/or hopelessly difficult) in the past. Another clear reason is that territories along the Amur River's main channel is currently less economically important to the PRC compared with the densely populated banks of the Songhuajiang.

Flood management measures taken in 1993–2013 by China along the Amur River itself included many environmentally or economically unjustified steps taken not so much because of the need to protect the economy from floods, but to minimize the loss of national territory due to natural riverbed dynamic processes. The construction of dykes cutting off natural floodplains created risks of increased water levels and emergence of dangerous floods under discharges which previously resulted only in non-catastrophic floods.

Disastrous dyke failures occurred along the Amur River in Jiayin, Luobei, and Tongjiang counties of Heilongjiang Province in 2013, which resulted in the flooding of large populated areas. If the Russian bank had been protected by a similar unbroken line of giant dykes too the water level would have risen much higher and damages would likely quadruple.

Still, multiple dyke failures along the Amur River have prompted new engineering protection projects. During three years (2014–2016) 25 billion yuan (4 billion USD) has been invested by China in construction and reinforcement of dykes on the rivers Heilongjiang (Amur), Songhuajiang, and Nenjiang with a total planned length of 2.7 thousand km (Three Rivers in Heilongjiang, June 2015).

Planning of the large scale water infrastructure along the borders of China (and abroad) should be viewed not only in the light of China's water and national border policies, but also considering current economic situation. Pace of development is slowing down in China and populated southern and eastern regions have serious industrial overcapacity responsible for extremely degraded environment. New Ecological Civilization Policy imposes limitations on large scale development of infrastructure in those regions (e.g. such limits explicitly prescribed for Yangtze Basin in the 13th five-year plan) (NPC, 2007). Therefore, development of huge water infrastructures in less populated boundary regions not only allows to employ otherwise idle state construction companies as well as local workforce, but also to support cement, steel, and machinery-making factories. As recent analysis of China's infrastructure development shows these short-term economic benefits in a long run could translate into significant bad debts of provincial and local governments (Ansar, Flyvbjerg, Budzier, & Lunn, 2016).

If this dyke construction programme is implemented in full along the Amur and Ussury rivers, these transboundary river valleys will be deprived of up to 20 km^3 natural flood retention volume of floodplain ecosystems. Therefore, during future floods the same volumes of river discharge will result in higher maximum water levels increasing hazard to unprotected settlements on opposite riverbanks.

The Sino-Russian Working group on Water Resources Management conducts joint inspections and assessments of hydraulic facilities – potential sources of transboundary impact, including increased risks during floods. For example, the Chinese side since 2010 has certain reservations about the new embankment in the Russian city of Blagoveshchensk which is being extended at the expense of the Amur River's main channel and allegedly affects the City of Heihe on China's bank. Therefore, since 2012, the sides have repeatedly exchanged modelling results trying to prove to each other the effect on the opposite bank's erosion and passage of flood between Blagoveshchensk and Heihe cities, or lack thereof. Finally, in summer 2015, they came to an official conclusion that Russia's embankment may affect water level and with high probability may cause erosion on the other riverbanks. In 2017 the China side opposed Russian proposal to extend this assessment to explore similar impacts arising from freshly-built embankements in the Heihe City. Keeping in mind that China is building thousand kilometres of grandiose dykes along the transboundary rivers, it's crucial that they become a subject for similar scrutiny (Simonov et al., 2016).

In January 2014, at the 6th meeting of China-Russia Transboundary Water Joint Commission created a temporary working group to conduct research and produce a "Joint Report on 2013 flood on Amur River" which was approved by the Joint Commission in 2015 (Sino-Russian Working group, 2015).

The Report calls to establish basin-scale coordination mechanism, and optimize regulation of existing large reservoirs. It suggests to carry out the following cooperating work in flood control step by step:

1 strengthen the establishment of hydrological monitoring network;
2 information sharing enhancement;
3 share methodologies and enhance cooperation on hydrological forecasting in Amur River Basin, including cooperation on development of the Amur River Basin hydrological model and flood forecasting operating system;
4 conduct joint research on fluvial processes, impacts of human activity or large hydraulic engineering structures, impacts on floodplain and ecological environment caused by changes in flooding and fluvial processes.

The Joint Report represents a serious achievement in bi-lateral information sharing. But, as of September 2017, the "Joint Report on 2013 flood on Amur River" still has not been published, in sharp contrast to prompt disclosure of the "Joint Observation and Evaluation of the Emergency Water Supplement" produced by the Mekong River Commission and China Ministry of Water Resources (MRC & MWR. 2016)). Unfortunately, this cooperative work had no systemic continuation, and in 2016 during the typhoon "Lionrock" two countries faced the same persistent problems as before. In 2017 at the meeting of the Sino-Russian Working group on Water Resources Management Chinese delegation came up with comprehensive proposal to increase data exchange and joint analysis, but we are yet to learn whether Russian side has capacity and willingness to follow-up on that.

Concluding remarks

The Amur River Basin, divided between three countries, provides ecological services important for all of them and other nations. China shares with Russia greater transboundary water resources than with any other country, and for both countries transboundary water management is among the highest matters of national security. However, despite the Amur River Basin's importance in biodiversity, fisheries, and food production (wetlands conservation, climate change adaptation, etc.), no international treaties have been signed that could provide a solid basis for holistic river basin management. Health of river ecosystem is yet to become a real practical priority in bilateral water management agreements and management efforts. The Sino-Mongolian water agreement is slightly more holistic and this may lead to more comprehensive joint environmental assessments.

Cooperation between countries is seriously complicated by the re-emergence of old megaprojects such as Kherlen-Gobi Water Transfer or Khingansky-Taipinggou Hydropower Dam, that effectively prevents them from concentrating on mutually beneficial environmental objectives in river management.

Major water engineering projects are pursued unilaterally in the transboundary Amur River Basin, not because they have been assessed as the best available options in river management, but due to the perceived benefit of state subsidies, boosting local economy during crisis, protection of national territories from natural riverbed processes, and other motifs that override water management and environmental considerations. Parties that invest in and benefit from unsustainable unilateral engineering projects become natural opponents of any joint strategic environmental assessment of transboundary river management, therefore reducing scope of jointly conducted analyses and concealing its results from the public. Probably, that is why the "Joint Report on 2013 flood on Amur River" was produced in Chinese and English, but not in Russian, and was not made available to the public in any language. Serious contradictions in water management, at least in part fueled by repeated promotion of highly risky megaprojects, slow down progress in developing a bilateral platform on wider cooperation in environmental protection and regional development. For example, once China fully cancels its stated objective to dam the main stem of the transboundary Amur River Basin, it may open space for a meaningful dialogue with Russia about comprehensive transboundary river management, including recovery of fisheries, ecosystem-based flood management, more nature-friendly border delineation measures, common environmental flow and water quality norms based on ecosystem-health indicators. Such a programme may be part of joint regional development plans striving to ensure proper climate adaptation and favourable environmental conditions in all settlements along the transboundary rivers of the basin. Honest discussion of such objectives is hardly attainable while one side still strives to fragment the free-flowing river by damming (Shvarts et al., 2011). As another example, lack of recognition of the transboundary nature of the Kherlen River exposed in the new river management plan issued by Mongolia makes joint efforts in climate adaptation and sustainable development in shared basins highly problematic (Simonov & Wickel, 2016). Since many bilateral issues are unresolved and only a small portion of the basin and water resources belong to Mongolia, trilateral cooperation between governments on the whole Amur River Basin management can hardly emerge any time soon. Current environmental priorities under the trilateral "Program for Development of the China-Mongolia-Russia Economic Corridor of the Silk Road Economic Belt" do not explicitly include water management, but name protected areas, wetland conservation, management of natural disasters, and preventing of desertification as priorities for joint activities (NDRC, 2016b).

Cooperation during and after the 2013 flood has shown that China and Russia have a need for cooperation on "soft" non-infrastructure measures to reduce flood risks. There is also a good opportunity for joint work on the conservation of wetlands along the border to sustain enormous natural flood retention capacity and implement the "Sino-Russian Strategy for Transboundary Network of Protected Areas in Amur River Basin (2011)". However, in practice, both countries opt to implement unilaterally structural measures that are of questionable value for flood-control and have profound negative impact on river ecosystems.

Unfortunately, the 2013 cooperation has not yet resulted in development of joint integrated flood management system as was suggested in the Joint Report produced after the flood.

There is urgent need for a common definition for environmental flow norms on transboundary watercourses, which became particularly evident during debates on water transfers in the Argun (Hailaer) and Kherlen (Kelulun) river basins. But this need is equally evident when considering the cumulative impact of reservoirs altering flow regimes of the Zeya, Bureya, and Songhua rivers and the transboundary channel of the Amur River. Given that the provision of environmental flow for protected floodplain wetlands has already become management practice in the PRC (Wang, Zhang, & James, 2009), there is hope for finding of a common language on these issues. Since the new five-year plan for Northeast China (NDRC, 2016a) attaches high priority to wetland and biodiversity conservation along transboundary rivers and lakes, this may positively influence the formulation of environmental water needs in transboundary water management.

Recently, China started the "Silk Road Economic Belt" Initiative that promotes integration between countries of Eurasia and shifts some of domestic industrial overcapacity to other resource-rich countries of the region (NDRC, 2015; State Council, 2015b). This change may necessitate adjustment in transboundary water policies, because now it is also important for China to ensure that the water resources of its neighbours are managed well and are sufficient to support jointly pursued economic development plans. At the same time, in the light of "Ecological Civilization" Policy (State Council, 2015a), preservation of environmental health and ecosystem services of transboundary basins is also a matter of growing priority. However, the cases we analysed so far do not show positive influence from either of these new policies on transboundary basin management and even indicate that they may bear some environmental risks.

In April 2017 China came up with new policy "Guidance on Promoting Greening of Belt and Road Initiative" which proposes development of many tools to improve environmental safeguards in overseas investment, jointly develop environmentally sound spatial planning schemes with neighboring countries, promote green economy, boost green finance shemes, reduce cross-border pollution, etc. (NDRC,MFA,MEP, MoFCom, 2017). A glaring gap in that new policy is absence of any environmental safeguards and green development mechanisms in the sphere of transboundary river basin management, provision of environmental flows, protection of aquatic biodiversity and ecosystems. Only partly this omission could be explained by the fact that the new policy was prepared primarily by the Ministry of Environmental Protection without explicit participation of Ministry of Water Resources. An additional possible explanation is that transboundary water management is such a conflict-laden field, that China is hesitant to promote it as a generic part of high-profile Belt and Road Initiative. The third possible explanation mirroring the second one is that by omitting those issues China acknowledges the fact that neighboring countries are often hesitant to widen transboundary water cooperation, because it may be dominated by China, which possesses greater technical, financial and organizational capacity to deal with water management and related environmental issues. At this point we would abstain from any decisive conclusions because both Ecological Civilization and BRI policies are very new and may later be equipped with better -defined provisions on the water management and mitigation of environmental impacts in transboundary river basins.

The future tendency of the Sino-Russian water resources cooperative management is difficult to predict, but any scenario will likely result in greater information sharing and interconnection between national monitoring systems. Due to continued economic crises and inefficient governance, Russia will also likely see a decrease in the government's capacity to match or respond constructively to China's initiatives in water resources monitoring and management, therefore we may see increasing reliance of joint river management committees on capabilities of the China side in monitoring, modelling, and data analysis. Management decisions resulting from such cooperation will likely reflect primarily the Chinese point of view, as it was already exemplified by the dispute about Blagoveshensk andHeihe city embankments.

Mongolia-China water related relationships will likely also see greater dominance of interests of China, as it tightens its overall economic and political influence on Mongolia, which is fully dependent on the Chinese market. However, it is unknown now whether sustainable water management in shared basins will be a priority in future Sino-Mongolian discourse. If it happens, it is not unlikely that some trilateral arrangement for joint adaptation to climate change focused on environmentally responsible wetland and grassland management, as well as biodiversity conservation in the Argun River-Dalai Lake basin may emerge in conjunction with the China-Mongolia-Russia Economic Corridor of the Silk Road Economic Belt.

Notes

1 2017-04-27 http://montsame.mn/en/read/9770.
2 2017-08-18 http://montsame.mn/en/read/11168.

References

Agreement between the Government of the People's Republic of China and the Government Mongolia on the Protection and Utilization of Transboundary Waters. (1994, April 29). Retrieved from http://extwprlegs1.fao.org/docs/pdf/bi-17921.pdf.

Ansar, A., Flyvbjerg, B., Budzier, A., & Lunn, D. (2016). Does infrastructure investment lead to economic growth or economic fragility? Evidence from China. *Oxford Review of Economic Policy, 32*(3), 360–390. Retrieved from https://arxiv.org/ftp/arxiv/papers/1609/1609.00415.pdf.

APFM (Associated Programme on Flood Management). (2009). *Integrated Flood management.* Concept paper. Geneva, Switzerland: World Meteorological Organization, 27p. Retrieved from www.apfm.info/publications/concept_paper_e.pdf.

Blank, S. (2016, September 13). *Russian writers on the decline of Russia in the far east and the rise of China.* Jamestown Foundation. Retrieved from jamestown.org/program/stephen-blank-russian-writers-on-the-decline-of-russia-in-the-far-east-and-the-rise-of-china/.

Bolgov, M., & Frolova, N. (2016). *Assessment from the consequences from the implementation of the development of the water-economy compiles on the Argun river.* Proceedings of the Baikal International Ecological Forum: *Clean Planet.* Irkutsk, Russia: V. Sochava Institute of Geography, 64–80.

Bolgov, M. V., Demin, A. P., & Shatalova, K. Y. (2016). The Russian-Chinese cooperation in the field of use and protection of transboundary water objects: Experience and problems. *Use and Protection of Natural Resources in Russia, 2*(146), 89–95.

CAE (Chinese Academy of Engineering). (2007). *On some strategic questions in water and land resource allocation, environment and sustainable development in North East China.* Summary Report, Shen Guo Fang, et al. (Ed.). Beijing, People's Republic of China: Chinese Science Publishing.

Centre for Political Information. (2015). *The development of Russian-Chinese relations on the example of global projects.* Moscow, Russia: CPI, 22p. Retrieved from http://polit-info.ru/images/data/gallery/0_8803__muhin_na_pechat_.pdf.

Decisions of the Russian Government. (2014a, July 10). *Meeting of the government of the Russian Federation.* Retrieved from http://government.ru/meetings/13674/decisions/.

Decisions of the Russian Government. (2014b, July 16). *Meeting of the government of the Russian Federation.* Retrieved from http://m.government.ru/news/13782/.

Dugina, I. O. (2013). *Outstanding on the Amur River flood in 2013 and its features* [Vy`daiushcheesia navodnenie na reke Amur 2013 goda i ego osobennosti]. Khabarovsk: Dal`-gidromet, 24p. Retrieved from http://dalgidromet.ru/uploads/navodnenie2013.docx.

Egidarev, E., Simonov, E., & Darman, Yu. (2016) Amur-Heilong River Basin: Overview of wetland resources. *The Wetland Book.* The Netherlands: Springer Publishers, 2, 1–15. doi:10.1007/978–94–007–6173–5_7-2. Retrieved from https://link.springer.com/referenceworkentry/10.1007/978-94-007-6173-5_7-2.

Egidarev, E. G. (2012). Mapping and assessment of floodplain complexes in the Amur River valley [Kartografirovanie i ocenka poi`menny`kh kompleksov v doline reki Amur]. *Vestnik DVO – FEB RAS Bulletin, 2*, 9–16.

Gotvansky, V. I. (2005). Preliminary study of the plans of dam building on Amur River. *Science and Nature in Russian Far East, 1*, 34–45.

Gotvansky, V. I. (2007). *Amur Basin - preservation through development* [Bassei`n Amura - osvaivaia -sokhranit`]. Khabarovsk, Russia: Arkhipelago fine print, 200p.

Hanergy Thin Film Power Group Limited. (2017). *Discussion with the securities and futures commission on resumption of trading (Announcement).* Retrieved from www.hanergythinfilmpower.com/images/e-announcement-on-s214-proceedings-and-resumption-plan—final.pdf.

IWEP (Institute of Water and Ecology Problems). (2003). *Water-ecological problems of the Amur River Basin* [Vodno-e`kologicheskie problemy` bassei`na reki Amur]. In A. N. Makhinov (Ed.), Vladivostok: Far East Branch of Russian Academy of Sciences, 56–70.

Joint Comprehensive Scheme. (1993). *Joint Russian-Chinese comprehensive scheme for water development in transboundary waters of Argun and Amur rivers.* Detailed project documentation. Moscow, Russia and Changchun, People's Republic of China: Sovintervod, Songliaowei, Volumes I–XIV.

Joint Comprehensive Scheme. (1999). *Joint Russian-Chinese comprehensive scheme for water development in transboundary waters of Argun and Amur Rivers (Synopsis).* Moscow, Russia and Changchun, People's Republic of China: Sovintervod, Songliaowei, 98p.

Kirilyuk, O. K. (Ed.). (2012). *Adaptation to climate change in river basins of Dauria: Ecology and water management* [Problemyi adaptatsii k izmeneniyu klimata v basseynah rek Daurii: ekologicheskie i vodohozyaystvennyie aspektyi]. Chita, Russia: Express Publishing House, 180p. Retrieved from www.wwf.ru/resources/publ/book/713.

Kondratieva, L., Fisher, N., & Bardyuk, V. (2012). Bioindication of transboundary pollution of the Amur River with aromatic hydrocarbons anfter technologic accident in China. *Siberian Environmental Journal, #2*, 245–252.

Korolev, A. (2016). Russia's reorientation to the east: Causes and strategic implications for East Asia and the world. *Pacific Affairs, 89*(1), 53–73.

Lassere, F. (2003). *The Amur River border. Once a symbol of conflict, could it turn into a water resource stake?* [Le fleuve Amour: Symbole de conflit passe, futur enjeu de ressource hydraulique?]. Cybergeo: *European Journal of Geography, 242*, 37p.

Makhinov, A. N. (2014). *Outline of the Amur River.* Proceedings of the 3rd International Meeting of the Amur-Okhotsk Consortium in collaboration with the Conference on "Sustainable Nature Management in Coastal Areas". Institute of Low Temperature Science, Hokkaido University, Research Institute for Humanity and Nature, Mitsui & Co., Ltd. Environmental Fund, 43–48.

MRC & MWR (Mekong River Commission and Ministry of Water Resources of the People's Republic of China). (2016). Technical Report – Joint Observation and Evaluation of the Emergency Water Supplement from China to the Mekong River. Mekong River Commission, Vientiane, Lao PDR, www.mrcmekong.org/assets/Publications/Final-Report-of-JOE.pdf.

MEP (Minstry of Environmental Protection). (2015). The National Ecological Function Division [全国生态功能区划(修编版)]. Retrieved from www.mep.gov.cn/gkml/hbb/bgg/201511/t20151126_317777.htm.

MFARF (Ministry of foreign Affairs of Russian Federation). (2017). *List of bilateral treaties.* Retrieved from www.mid.ru/foreign_policy/international_contracts/2_contract.

Ministry of Energy. (2016). *13th 5-year plan for hydropower development in China.* Retrieved from www.nea.gov.cn/2016-11/29/c_135867663.htm.

MNRERF (Ministry of Natural Resources and Ecology of the Russian Federation). (2005). *International treaties and agreements with the participation of Russian ministry of natural resources.* Retrieved from www.mnr.gov.ru/activities/list.php?part=146.

Nagao, S., Yan, B., Kim, V. I., Shesterkin, V. P., Levshina, S. I., Yoh, M., … Makhinov, A. N. (2015). *Water chemistry of the middle Amur River.* Digest of Environmental Change and the Social Response in the Amur River Basin International Perspectives in Geography. Japan, Copyright holder Springer Japan: "AJG Library", 105–128.

NDRC (National Development and Reform Committee of the PRC). (2015). *Vision and actions on jointly Building Silk Road Economic Belt and 21st-Century Maritime Silk Road.* Retrieved from http://en.ndrc.gov.cn/newsrelease/201503/t20150330_669367.html.

NDRC. (2016a). *Plan to revive the old industrial base in Northeast China during the 13th Five-Year Plan period.* Retrieved from www.gov.cn/xinwen/2016-12/20/5150168/files/7779d2ddc7d24744ac036acaf6a89037.pdf.

NDRC. (2016b). *Program for development of the China-Mongolia-Russia economic corridor of the Silk Road Economic Belt.* Retrieved from www.sdpc.gov.cn/gzdt/201609/t20160912_818237.html.

NDRC, MFA, MEP & MoFCom. (2017). Guidance on Promoting Green Belt and Road-(GPGBR) (关于推进绿色"一带一路"的指导意见) Issued by the Ministry of Environmental Protection, Ministry of Foreign Affairs, National Development and Reform Commission & Ministry of Commerce (2017, April 24) October 12, 2017. Retrieved from www.yidaiyilu.gov.cn/wcm.files/upload/CMSydylgw/201705/201705161104041.pdf.

NPC (National People's Congress) of the People's Republic of China. (2007). *National economic and social development of the PRC in the twelfth five-year plan* [中华人民共和国国民经济和社会发展 第十三个五年规划纲要]. Retrieved from www.npc.gov.cn/wxzl/gongbao/2011-08/16/content_1665636.htm.

Oleinikova, A. Ya. (2016). Russia – China: Problems of economic use in river Amur [Rossia – Kitai: Problemy hozyaistvennogo ispolzovania reki Amur]. *Rule of Law in Modern Society, 33*, 174–183.

Olson, D. M., & Dinerstein, E. (2002). The Global 200: Priority ecoregions for global conservation, *Annals of the Missouri Botanical Garden, 89*(2), 199–224. Retrieved from www.worldwildlife.org/publications/the-global-200-priority-ecoregions-for-global-conservation.

Podolsky, S. A., Darman, Yu. A., & Simonov, E. A. (2006). *Where does Amur flow?* [Kuda techet Amur?]. Vladivostok, Russia, WWF Russia, 72p.

Preston, F., Bailey, R., Bradley, S., Jigang, W., & Changwen, Zh. (2016). *Navigating the new normal.* The Development Research Center of the State Council (DRC). Beijing, People's Republic of China: The Royal Institute of International Affairs, Chatham House, 97p. Retrieved from www.chathamhouse.org/sites/files/chathamhouse/publications/research/2016-01-27-china-global-resource-governance-preston-bailey-bradley-wei-zhao-final.pdf.

Programme of Cooperation between the Regions of the Far East and East Siberia of Russia and Northeast China for the Period 2009—2018. (2009, September 23). Approved by the Russian President Dmitry Medvedev and the Chinese President Hu Jintao Retrieved from www.vedomosti.ru/politics/articles/2009/10/12/rossiya-stanet-syrevym-pridatkom-kitaya.

RusHydro. (2014, November 9). *RusHydro to cooperate with China Three Gorges Corporation in development of hydropower projects in the Russian Far East.* Retrieved from www.eng.rushydro.ru/press/news/95544.html.

RusHydro JSC. (2015, December 14). *Investment plan 2016–2021.* Retrieved from www.rushydro.ru/upload/iblock/484/Prilozhenie_3_IP_2016-2020.pdf.

Rushydro JSC. (2017, September 1). *Results of the Board of Directors* on August 29, 2017 www.eng.rushydro.ru/investors/IR_news/104201.html.

Russian Emergency Situations Ministry. (2013). *A catastrophic flood in 2013 in the far eastern federal district.* Lessons and conclusions: Scientific and methodical work. Moscow, Russia: FGBU VNII GOChS (FC), 1, 156p. Retrieved from http://elibrary.ru/item.asp?id=21134265.

Shesterkin, V. P. (2010). Centennial variation in the chemical composition of river water in the Khabarovsk water node. *Russian Journal of Pacific Geology, 4*(2), 187–193.

Shvarts, E., Simonov E., & Progunova, L. (2011). *Environmental risks to Sino-Russian transboundary cooperation: From brown plans to a green strategy.* WWF's Trade and Investment Programme report. Moscow, Russia, WWF-Russia, 200p. Retrieved from www.wwf.ru/resources/publ/book/eng/440.

Simonov, E., & Wickel, B. (2016). *Kherlen river – The lifeline of Eastern Steppe.* Report prepared with support of UNECE Water Convention. Executive summary of the report published in Mongolian and English by RwB-Mongolia, Ulaan Baatar, Mongolia, 40p. Retrieved from www.transrivers.org/2015/1515/.

Simonov, E. A. (2008). *China-Mongolia environmental agreements.* [List of official documents]. Retrieved from www.amur-heilong.net/aic/en/1/09_int_argeements/0902chinamongolianagreements/.

Simonov, E. A., & Dahmer, T. (2008). *Amur-Heilong River Basin reader.* Hongkong, People's Republic of China: Ecosystems Ltd., 426p. Retrieved from www.wwf.ru/resources/publ/book/299.

Simonov, E. A. Egidarev, E. G., & Nikitina, O. I. (2015). *Comprehensive environmental and socio-economic assessment of hydropower development in the Amur River Basin.* Environmental part of the report. Moscow, Russia: WWF-Russia, Evrosibenergo, EN+Group, 279p. Retrieved from www.wwf.ru/resources/publ/book/1002.

Simonov, E. A., Egidarev, E. G., Nikitina, O. I., Osipov, P. E., & Shalikovsky, A. V. (2016). *Amur floods and we: Unlearned lesson?* [My` i amurskie navodneniia: nevy`uchenny`i` urok?]. Moscow, Russia. WWF-Russia, 216p. Retrieved from www.wwf.ru/resources/publ/book/1094.

Simonov, E. A., Podolsky, S. A., & Darman, Y. A. (2006). *Water resource utilization in Amur River basin and possible environmental consequences: An early warning.* Problems of sustainable use of transboundary territories. Proceedings of the international conference: *Problems of Sustainable Use of Transboundary Territories* (pp. 133–138). Vladivostok, Russia: PGI FEBRAS.

Sino-Russian Strategy for Transboundary System of Protected Areas in Amur River Basin. (2011). 中俄黑龙江流域自然保护区网络建设战略. Annex 4 to the Protocol of the sixth session of the Sub-Commission on cooperation in the field of environmental protection of the Russian-Chinese Commission on preparation of regular meetings of Heads of Government. Harbin, China, 24p. Retrieved from http://news.xinhuanet.com/world/2011-06/02/c_13908170_2.htm.

Sino-Russian Working group. (2015). *Chinese-Russian joint report on the analysis of the extreme flood in Amur River in 2013.* Bureau of Hydrology, Ministry of Water Resources, China; Water Problems Institute, Russian Academy of Sciences. Beijing, People's Republic of China: Sino-Russian Working group under Agreement on Transboundary Waters.

State Council. (2015a). Integrated reform plan for promoting ecological progress. Retrieved from www.china.org.cn/china/Off_the_Wire/2015-09/21/content_36644574.htm.

State Council of China. (2015b). *Guiding opinions on promoting the cooperation in international capacity and equipment manufacturing* [国务院关于推进国际产能和装备制造合作的指导意见]. Retrieved on October 17 from www.gov.cn/zhengce/content/2015-05/16/content_9771.htm.

State Council on the Songhua River Flood Control Plan. (2008, March 28). *Integrated flood risk management plan for the Songhuajiang Basin* [国务院正式批准实施《松花 江流域防洪规划]. Retrieved from www.gov.cn/zhengce/content/2008-03/28/content_2911.htm.

Suocheng, D., Zehong, L., Yu, L., Guangyi, S., Huilu, Y., Juanle, W., … Yongbin, H. (2015). Resources, environment and economic patterns and sustainable development modes of the Silk Road Economic Belt. *Journal of Resources and Ecology, 6*(2), 65–72. Retrieved from www.jorae.cn/article/2015/1674-764x-6-2-65.html.

TFDD (Transboundary Freshwater Dispute Database). (1994). *Agreement between the government of the People's Republic of China and the government of Mongolia on the protection and utilization of transboundary waters.* Oregon State University. Retrieved from http://ocid.nacse.org/tfdd/treaties.php?page=full&origin=river&tn=528.

Three River Connection Project Implementation will Bring Important Results [黑龙江省三江干流治理和三江连通工程建设成果颇丰]. (2015, January 5). *Heilongjiang daily.* Retrieved from http://hlj.people.com.cn/n/2015/0105/c220027-23442519.html.

Three Rivers in Heilongjiang Province are harnessed by a project improving flood-defence. (2015, June 17) [В провинции Хэйлунцзян запущен проект по упорядочению трех крупных рек для улучшения противопаводковой защиты] Xinhua News Agency (in Russian). Retrieved from http://russian.people.com.cn/n/2014/0617/c31516-8742538.html.

Tracy, E. F., Shvarts, E., Simonov, E., & Babenko, M. (2017). China's new Eurasian ambitions: The environmental risks of the Silk Road Economic Belt. *Eurasian Geography and Economics, 58*(1), 56–88. doi:10.1080/15387216.2017.1295876.

UNEP (United Nations Environment Programme). (2016). *Green is Gold - the strategy and actions of China's ecological civilization.* Retrieved from http://web.unep.org/greeneconomy/research-reports/green-gold-strategy-and-actions-chinas-ecological-civilization.

Vinogradov, S., & Wouters, P. (2013). *Sino-Russian transboundary waters: A legal perspective on cooperation.* Stockholm and Nacka, Sweden: Institute for Security and Development Policy, 95p. Retrieved from http://isdp.eu/content/uploads/images/stories/isdp-main-pdf/2013-vinogradov-wouters-sino-russian-transboundary-waters-legal-perspective.pdf.

Wang, S., Changlei, D., Xishan, Z., & Yang, L. (2015). Influence factor analysis of China and Russia's hydrological communication under the background of Heilongjiang main stream flood. *Journal of Water Resources Research, 4*, 55–61 (In Chinese).

Wang, X., Zhang, Y., & James, C. (2009). Approaches to providing and managing environmental flows in China. *International Journal of Water Resources Development, 25* (2), 283–300.

WBIP (World Bank Inspection Panel). (2017). Report No. 117391-MN. Third and Final Report and Recommendation on a Request for Inspection Mongolia: Mining Infrastructure Investment Support Project (P118109). Washington DC, July 13, 2017. http://ewebapps.worldbank.org/apps/ip/Pages/ViewCase.aspx?CaseId=107.

Wishnick, E. (2016). In Search of the "other" in Asia: Russia-China relations revisited. *The Pacific Review, 30*, 114–132. doi:10.1080/09512748.2016.1201129.

WMSAB (Water Management Scheme for Amur Basin). (2015). *Scheme of complex use and protection of water resources of the Amur River Basin.* Ekaterinburg, Russia: FG-PUP RosNIIVH, 367p.

World Heritage Committee. (2017). Decision: 41 COM 7B.6 (Lake Baikal. Russian Federation) adopted by the 41st Session of the Committee, Kracow, Poland, July 2017. http://whc.unesco.org/en/soc/3618.

Xin, L. (2016). *Chinese perspective on the creation of a Eurasian economic space.* Valdai Discussion Club Report, 20. Retrieved from http://valdaiclub.com/files/12585/.

6 Analysis on China-DPRK joint development in the Yalu River and Tumen River

From the perspective of China

Zhifei Li

Introduction

Boundary rivers constitute the majority of transboundary rivers in northeastern China, including approximately ten boundary rivers and three boundary lakes of a total length of 5000 km. Among these, Yalu River and Tumen River, the two major transboundary rivers in this region, are the boundary rivers between China and North Korea, officially the Democratic People's Republic of Korea (DPRK), where residents in the border area of both countries have settled down along the river from long ago. After the Cold War, in the context of fundamental changes in the geopolitical environment, the central government and local authorities of China took the initiative to collaborate with DPRK. Their aim was to jointly develop the Tumen River and Yalu River to enhance the overall national security and development strategy as well as economic transformation and development on a local level. Tremendous efforts to explore the geoeconomic value and potential of the two rivers forged strong bonds that were conducive to the joint development of China and DPRK.

This chapter consists of three parts. Part one introduces the historical background of the Tumen River and Yalu River. Part two covers the Chinese perspective on both the central and local levels in an attempt to explain why China and DPRK have facilitated and taken actions in joint development of the Yalu River and Tumen River. The author analyses the motives behind these efforts in detail, while pointing out the internal relationship between geopolitics and the safeguarding of China's rights and interests in river development. Part three focuses on the analysis of the cooperation contexts of both countries on the Tumen River and Yalu River, and then predicts the cooperation tendency of China and DPRK.

Historical background: geopolitics and game between countries

Since the founding of the People's Republic of China (PRC), the Yalu River and Tumen River have witnessed changes in ownership rights, agenda and approach of China-DPRK cooperation, given the context of their unique geographical location and continuous strategic game between countries in the river basin and their neighbouring countries. Therefore, the first step in understanding China-DPRK cooperation in transboundary rivers would be a systematic review of the historical changes of the Yalu River and Tumen River.

Yalu River: from China's inland river to co-ownership by China and DPRK

Yalu River got its name from its colour, resembling that of a duck's head, and is pronounced as Yalu Ula in the Manchu language, where yalu means border of the land or boundary; hence Yalu Ula means "boundary river". Located in the eastern part of Jilin and Liaoning Provinces, with its source located on the south of Changbai Mountain, the Yalu River flows through Changbai Korean Autonomous County, Linjiang, Ji'an in Jilin and Dandong in Liaoning southeastwards along the China-DPRK border, until it reaches the West Korean Bay in the north of the Yellow Sea near Donggang in Dandong, Liaoning as it flows southwards. With a total length of 795 km and watershed area of 61,500 km^2, including 32,500 km^2 within China's territory, the Yalu River has an annual runoff of 32.76 billion m^3 ("Yalu River," 2014).

The Yalu River was originally China's inland river. In 735 AD, during the Tang Dynasty, Emperor Xuanzong set the boundaries along the Datong River, the south belonged to Shilla while the north was the territory of Tang. However, in 993 AD, Emperor Shengzong of Liao Dynasty granted Korea (then under the rule of Wang) the land stretching hundreds of *li* (known as the Chinese mile, is a traditional Chinese unit of distance, 500 metres) to the east of the river (which used to belong to Jurchen). Since then, Korea started to build castles and moats in the Jurchen community, pushing the frontiers to the upper and middle stretches of the Qingchuan River (Ch'ongch'ongang) and the lower stretches of the Yalu River. During the Ming Dynasty, Yi Seong-gye (first emperor of the Lee Dynasty of Korea) seized the throne and expelled the Jurchen tribes from the south bank of the Tumen River and the east bank of the Yalu River, expanding his kingdom northwards along the river from the estuary (which was traditionally regarded as the boundary between the two countries) and set "the Four Prefectures of the Northwest" along the upper and middle stretches of the Yalu River (where many migrants were forced to settle down), hence taking effective control over the northern regions. Up to 1443, Korea incorporated the south bank of the Yalu River into its territory as well. The Yalu River, formerly China's inland river, has become a boundary river on the west border between China and Korea.

In 1962, the government of the PRC signed the Sino-Korean Border Treaty in Pyongyang with the DPRK, defining the Yalu River and Tumen River as boundary rivers. Based on the first China-Korea joint survey of borders from 1972 to 1975, the treaty stipulated that 13 out of the identified 61 islands and sandbanks belonged to China. Major islands in the Yalu River (including Hwanggumpyong Island, Huangjinxia Island, Chouduan Island, and Xin Island) were identified as

Korean territory (Zheng, 2013). Currently, the estuary of lower reaches of the Yalu River is completely within the territory of DPRK.

Loss of estuary of the Tumen River in China and the access rights to the sea

With its source on the east side of the main peak of Changbai Mountain on China-DPRK border, the Tumen River (Dooman-gang) flows northwards through four cities in China, namely Helong, Longjing, Tumen, and Huichun, to the Ryanggang Province and the North Hamgyong Province in DPRK, to Khasansky, Primorsky Krai (Maritime Territory) of Russia, until it reaches its estuary on the Russia-DPRK border into the Sea of Japan. The main stream is 537 km in length; while the boundary river is 505 km between China and DPRK (Zhu, 2007) and 15 km between Russia and DPRK (Committee for the Compilation of Local Chronicles, 2006), with a total basin area of 33,168 km^2. The upper and middle reaches of the Tumen River constitute the boundary river between China and DPRK, with 70 per cent of the basin area (i.e. 23,000 km^2) within the territory of China. On 3 November 1998, the Agreement on the Demarcation Line of National Water Boundaries was signed by China, DPRK, and Russia, defining the Tumen River as the demarcation line between the boundary water area shared by the PRC and the DPRK, the water area of the DPRK and the water area of the Russian Federation ("The Agreement," 2001).

Before the 15th century, both banks of the Tumen River were under the dominion of Jurchen, an ethnic minority in China. During the Tang and Liao Dynasties, Emperor Xuanzong of Tang and Emperor Shengzong of Liao gave the land south of the Datong River as well as the territory stretching hundreds of *li* along the east bank of the Yalu River to the Kingdom of Korea at the time. Since the beginning of Lee's Dynasty of Korea, the Jurchens were treated with a combination of placation and persecution, and the borders of Korea continually expanded northwards. By the first half of the 15th century, the northeastern border of Korea gradually extended to the south bank of the middle and lower reaches of the Tumen River today.

In June 1885, Korea ceded the Tumen and Douman Rivers to the Qing government, with the statement that the south of the Hailan River (originally Yanbian in China) was part of Korean territory, and demanded for boundary surveys by both countries. Two boundary surveys were conducted respectively in 1885 and 1887 by China and Korea (Shen & Dong, 2011). Both countries reached agreement on the name of the rivers, acknowledging that Tŭmén, Dòumǎn and Túmén referred to the same river, and that the Tumen River was the boundary river between China and Korea (with China on the north shore and DPRK on the south shore).

The First Sino-Japanese War broke out in 1894. China ended in defeat and was forced to sign the Treaty of Shimonoseki, a mark of humiliation to the country and a forfeit of its sovereignty. The Treaty acknowledged the independence of Korea and abolished the suzerainty-feudatory relationship between

China and Korea. Relying on the close relationship with Czarist Russia, Emperor Gojong of Korea made a claim for the borders, insisting on the border by the Hongtu Mountain and River as the authentic source of the Tumen River, and denying the consensus and results of the second joint boundary survey by China and Korea in 1887, claiming that Tǔmén, Dòumǎn and Túmén referred to two different rivers instead of one river. In 1906, with Japan as a conspirator, Korea forced the Qing government, deeply troubled by external threats and internal unrest at the time, to make a major compromise by signing the treaty on boundary issues between China and Korea along the Tumen River in September 1909, stating that the "Tumen River shall be the border between China and Korea" (Shen & Dong, 2011); its source region shall extend from the boundary marker to Shiyi River (Shen & Dong, 2011). Since the founding of the PRC, the two countries have successively signed the China-Korea Boundary Treaty and China-Korea Boundary Protocol, marking a complete settlement of the boundary issue between China and Korea (Shen & Dong, 2011). According to the treaty, the rivers, from the upper stretches of the Yalu River and Tumen River, shall be the boundary line between China and Korea.

Like the estuary of the Yalu River, the estuary of the Tumen River (the only estuary in northern China with accessibility to the Sea of Japan) was forfeited by the Qing government. From the end of the First Opium War, China started to be reduced to a semi-colonized country, into which Czarist Russia accelerated its invasive moves, forcing the Qing government to sign the Treaty of Aigun in May 1858. According to the treaty, over 600,000 km^2 of Chinese territory from the north of the Amur River and the south of the Stanovoy Range was allotted to Russia, while the Chinese territory on the east of the Ussuri River was "under co-domination by China and Russia" ("Treaty of Aigun," 2003). By the Treaty of Aigun, Russia gained considerable territory interests from China, seizing navigation rights of the Amur River and the Ussuri River as well as the estuary to the Pacific Ocean.

In November 1860, the Qing government was again forced to sign the Sino-Russia Treaty of Peking. By this treaty, the Amur River and Ussuri River would be the east section of China-Russia boundary, while the territory north of the Amur River and east of the Ussuri River would be classified as Russian territory. Based on Article 3 of the Sino-Russia Treaty of Peking, the Qing government and Czarist Russia started to conduct surveys on the eastern border and marked the boundaries. On 26 June 1861, they signed the Sino-Russia Agreement on Survey and Determination of the Eastern Boundary, followed by the determination of eight boundary marks by China and Russia. A boundary tablet was built on the west of the Ussuri River estuary, with the Russian letter E and "Boundary Mark" in Chinese written on the tablet. From the north to the south, another six tablets were built and respectively marked with I, K, J, I, H, O and II, with the last tablet set "20 *li* to the estuary of Tumen River" with the letter T ("Tu" Tablet, 2015).

The Qing government forfeited the rights to set the tablet with T to Czarist Russia, which did not only refuse to include the estuary into Chinese territory but also arbitrarily set the boundary mark with "T" 46 *li* from the estuary of the Tumen River rather than 20 *li* as stipulated in the treaty ("Tu" Tablet, 2015), hence occupying even more Chinese territory. By this time, China has not only lost the estuary of the Tumen River but also the sea access from the Tumen River.

In 1886, the military minister Wu Dacheng was appointed by the Qing government as the imperial envoy for the joint survey of the east boundary from the Ussuri River to the estuary of the Tumen River, to sign the Sino-Russian Treaty of East Boundary of Hunchun and seven protocols on boundary surveys with representatives of Czarist Russia. Wu forcefully argued for the settlement of boundary marks on the China-Russian border, placing the tablet with "T" 20 *li* from the estuary of the Tumen River. He obtained the rights to sea access from the Tumen River. But China's legitimate sea navigation through the Tumen River ended when the Battle of Zhanggufeng broke out in 1938. At that time, the invading Japanese army blocked the sea access from the Tumen River to guard against the Soviet Union's army (Shi, 2014).

Motive of joint development: national strategy versus local development

China's attempts to facilitate cooperation on the Yalu River and Tumen River is a result of fundamental adjustments in China's national and regional development strategies in the context of substantial geopolitics changes. The Chinese central government conducted the overall strategic planning for transboundary rivers and actively facilitated its implementation. To develop the local economy, the local government also acted in line with the strategic arrangements from the central government, facilitating the river basin cooperation and regional cooperation with the rivers as a vehicle.

The strategy of developing the coastal regions, encouraging and facilitating provinces on China's eastern coast to pioneer the development was first implemented in China in the late 1970s (i.e. the opening and reform policy featuring "internal reform and opening up to the outside world"). Up to the 1980s, the centre of gravity in the global economy started to move eastwards to the Asia-Pacific region where the economy of Northeast Asia flourished. Therefore, leveraging external opportunities for boosting the regional economy in Northeast China and for building a stable regional environment in Northeast Asia has become an important issue on the agenda of the central government of China. Therefore, the local government is seeking ways to leverage its geographical location, exploring matching points between international and national strategies and breaking through the bottleneck to boost the development of traditional industrial bases in Northeast China.

According to several researchers and experts in Northeast Normal University and Jilin Academy of Social Sciences, study on the feasibility of regional trade between the USSR and Jilin Province in 1984 shows that China had the legitimate rights for sea access and navigation from the Tumen River. After an in-depth analysis of the political and economic situation in Northeast Asia, the sea access and navigation history of the Tumen River and its hydrology, and another meticulous study on the restoration of its sea access and navigation rights as well as the plan and measures for the development along the Tumen River, a proposal was submitted to the government in 1985 for the restoration of China's sea access rights through the Tumen River. By the end of 1986, this proposal attracted the attention of Huan Xiang, renowned expert in international affairs and chairman of Pacific Economic Cooperation Council (PECC-China) at the time. It was he who brought up the suggestion to the central government.

In March and May 1987, Song Jian commissioned the senior leaders of the State Oceanic Administration and experts in ocean policies to conduct a survey in Jilin for the restoration of sea access and navigation rights on the Tumen River, hence arousing keen interest of the Provincial Government of Jilin in the restoration of sea access rights. On 14 and 20 May 1987, the People's Government of Jilin Province and the State Oceanic Administration respectively sought suggestions from the State Council and proposed the restoration of China's sea access rights on the Tumen River. The navigation route development of the Tumen River has therefore been put on the top of the agenda of local economic development and national strategies implementation at both central and local levels.

From the central level, with the geographical advantage and strategic importance becoming visible, the restoration of sea access rights and marine navigation on the Tumen River, the restoration and construction of the Hunchun deepwater port, and the struggle for China's legitimate rights and interests in the Sea of Japan have become increasingly significant. These moves will soon enable a convenient and efficient passageway to be built between Northeast China and Russia, DPRK, South Korea, and Japan as well as north, central, and south regions of China. The passageway will significantly reduce transportation costs, facilitate internal and domestic trade, as well as attract domestic and overseas investment. These benefits play an important role in re-energizing the traditional industrial base in Northeast China. This will foster regional development in Northeast Asia and support substantial implementation of the Greater Tumen Development Zone, reducing the distance between China and Russia, South Korea, Japan, and DPRK as well as the distances between Russia and DPRK, between Russia and Japan, and between North and South Korea (Shi, 2014).

According to the Provincial Government of Jilin, the restoration of sea access and navigation rights through the Tumen River is linked with the implementation and development of the Changchun-Jilin-Tumen River Open Cooperation Zone, and is of significant political and economic importance in boosting the economic and social development of traditional industrial bases in Jilin and in competing for centrality of Northeast Asia. On the other hand, water transportation is an environmentally friendly and energy-efficient method of transportation. Therefore, the relaunching of sea access and navigation on the Tumen River will revitalize the overall transportation system of Jilin Province.

As stated in the *Outline of Comprehensive Development Research of Tumen River Estuary* which was introduced in 1990, the initial development plan focused on ensuring sea access through the Tumen River by building river ports along the Tumen River within Chinese territory (i.e. Hunchun would be a strategic point on the shores of the Sea of Japan). At the same time, it involved the restoration of the sea access rights through the Tumen River, clearing out the navigation route along the river and building ports to ensure the passageway to the Sea of Japan, building social infrastructure, attracting investment and importing advanced technologies, and strengthening economic exchange and cooperation with neighbouring countries, hence facilitating the opening up and economic development of Yanbian Korean Autonomous Prefecture and the entire Jilin Province.

Besides the development of the transboundary river, the Chinese government is also taking the initiative to promote development and cooperation in the entire river basin with the river as a vehicle, making the transboundary river a common interest that deepens regional cooperation. Former chairman Jiang Zemin has paid two visits to Hunchun. He wrote "Develop Hunchun, develop Tumen River and develop the friendship and cooperation with Northeast Asian countries" when he visited the region of the Tumen River for the second time in June 1995 ("Common interest," 2009).

Since 1992, in an attempt to push for international cooperation in the development of the Tumen River region, the Coordination Group for the Tumen River Development Project (consisting of over 20 ministries and ministerial commissions) compiled the *Outline for Comprehensive Development Plan of Hunchun Region in Lower Tumen River* and *Plan for the Development of Tumen River Region of China* in 1992 and 1999 respectively.

In November 2009, the State Council officially responded to the *Outline of Joint Development Plan for China Tumen River* with *Changchun-Jilin-Tumen as Pilot Zone of Development and Opening up*. According to the State Council, the construction of the Changchun-Jilin-Tumen Pilot Zone of Development and Opening up is the only development and opening up zone on the border approved by the central government up to now and has already been incorporated into national strategy. The State Council pointed out that Jilin and Tumen would play a pioneering role in the development and opening up of Changchun. Joint regional development along the Tumen River would be expected to be implemented in a comprehensive manner, with the Tumen River as the foothold, oriented towards Northeast Asia and serving the entire Northeast China. The Tumen River region, comprising mainly Jilin Province, occupies an important strategic position in the opening up structure of border regions in China.

Currently, as a pioneer in opening up of border regions, Changchun-Jilin-Tumen Pilot Zone of Development and Opening up has reached a mature stage of strategic implementation. In the implementation of the Belt and Road Initiative (BRI), both central and local governments are dedicated to the transformation of the Changchun-Jilin-Tumen Pilot Zone into a new corridor, new platform and new gateway along the north line of BRI. Through development and opening up of the region, as well as regional cooperation along the Tumen River, the pilot zone would span across the east and the west, covering the sea and the land while connecting domestic markets with overseas potential ("An overview," 2010). Therefore, it is predicted that China will continue to facilitate regional cooperation in the drainage basin with the Tumen River at the centre, both at national and local levels.

Regrettably, however, the DPRK withdrew from the Greater Tumen Initiative (GTI) Cooperation Mechanism in 2005. With a slowdown in China-DPRK cooperation along the transboundary river, Jilin Province subsequently identified "cooperation with Russia to open up a multimodal transport corridor eastwards combining land and sea" as key in the implementation of the Changchun-Jilin-Tumen strategy and the core task in regional cooperation and development along the Tumen River.

Local governments on the municipal level also maximize the Yalu River's resources, alongside with the development strategy of the central government and local provincial government: "bridging domestic and international markets". Ji'an, a city along the river, has made hydropower a key industry. The construction of hydropower stations on the boundary river is important for infrastructure development, maximizing potential for economic and social development of the country, increasing the aggregate economic volume and improving overall competitiveness. During this period, many attempts were made to obtain approval and funding from relevant ministries and commissions while multiple talks were held with DPRK counterparts for the construction of one or two hydropower stations on the Ji'an section of the Yalu River for the benefit of local governments.

On 25 May 1995, the Ministry of Power Industries approved the Letter Concerning the Construction of Power Stations on the Upper and Mid Stretches of Yalu River. The letter included demands for power stations with installation capacity under 100,000 kW to be financed by local governments. In the context of the adjustment of international policies of the DPRK and the power demand for national construction, the two parties finally identified their common interest. It has been confirmed that both countries have begun the construction of the Wangjianglou (Lintu) Hydropower Station and Wenyue (Changchuan) Hydropower Station on the Yalu River since December 1995.

Agenda of cooperation: water conservancy and waterway development versus river basin and regional cooperation

The agenda of China-DPRK cooperation along the Yalu River and Tumen River is considerably diversified. It mainly covers four areas: (1) hydropower development, (2) waterway development, (3) river island joint development, and (4) river basin and regional cooperation driven by the two rivers as a vehicle.

Hydropower development

China-DPRK cooperation has a long history in hydropower development. On 17 April 1955, Li Fuchun, influential representative of the Chinese government, and his DPRK counterpart Park Chang-ok signed the Agreement on Yalu River Hydropower Station. According to the agreement, all assets of the Yalu River Shuifeng Hydropower Station shall be co-owned by China and the DPRK, and both governments agree to the establishment of China-DPRK Yalu River Shuifeng Hydropower Corporation for the joint management of the Yalu River Shuifeng Hydropower Station. Besides, power generated by the Shuifeng Hydropower Corporation would be, in principle, shared by both countries on an equal basis. Moreover, the corporation's business activities are exempted from all taxes in both countries. On 7 May 1955, the two governments signed the Protocol on China-DPRK Yalu River Shuifeng Hydropower Corporation, reaching agreement on assets auditing, assessment and other issues concerning finance and accounting of Yalu River Shuifeng Hydropower Corporation as well as the restoration of engineering projects of Shuifeng Hydropower Station. The China-DPRK Yalu River Shuifeng Hydropower Corporation was thus officially established (Zhang, n.d.).

In December 1958, the China-DPRK Yalu River Shuifeng Hydropower Corporation was renamed the China-DPRK Yalu River Hydropower Corporation for the planning of the Yunfeng Power Station. In May 1985, the 38th board meeting of the China-DPRK Hydropower Corporation was held as the company was celebrating their 30th anniversary. At the meeting, it was decided that the hydropower resources of the Tumen River would be surveyed and developed. Besides, the company's name would be changed from the China-DPRK Yalu River Hydropower Corporation to China-DPRK Hydropower Corporation.

Up to now, four hydropower stations on the Yalu River, namely Shuifeng, Yunfeng, Weiyuan, and Taiping Bay, have been co-established by China and the DPRK. According to statistics, a total of 162.443 billion kilowatt-hour have been generated from 1955 to 1990, of which 80.258 billion kW-hours were supplied for China and 81.790 billion kW-hours were supplied to DPRK. Among the total volume, 34.247 billion kW-hours were generated by the Shuifeng Hydropower Station, 2.205 billion kW-hours by the Weiyuan Hydropower Station, and 2.926 billion kW-hours by the Taiping Bay Hydropower Station. During the 38th meeting of the board of directors of the China-DPRK Hydropower Corporation held in 1985, it was decided that the fifth and the sixth cascade power stations (Linjiang Hydropower Station with an installation capacity of 400,000 kW and Uiju Hydropower Station with an installation capacity of 100,000 kW) would be built on the Yalu River, constituting a step forward in the overall development of the drainage basin of the Yalu River (Zhang, n.d.).

On 1 December 1995, the minutes of the China-DPRK meeting on hydropower resources development on the upper and middle stretches of the Yalu River were approved during the 48th board meeting of the China-DPRK Hydropower Corporation. Both sides confirmed that China would invest in the construction of the Wangjianglou (Lintu) Hydropower Station while the DPRK would invest in the Wenyue (Changchuan) Hydropower Station. In July 2004, the initial designs of both construction projects were examined and approved by China and the DPRK. On 27 June 2006, China and the DPRK signed the agreement on the construction of the Wenyue Hydropower Station in Pyongyang (Gao, 2006). In August 2006, the Ministry of Foreign Affairs, the Ministry of Public Security, and the Headquarters of People's Liberation Army General Staff approved the commencement of the construction of the Wangjianglou Hydropower Station and Wenyue Hydropower Station.

In January 2010, China and the DPRK jointly approved the launch of the two construction projects by signing the Minutes of the 9th Meeting on the Construction of Wangjianglou (Lintu) and Wenyue (Changchuan) Hydropower Stations by China and DPRK in Manpo, DPRK ("An overview," 2010). On 30 August 2012, China and the DPRK jointly implemented the Shuifeng Hydropower Station's flood control facilities renovation project. Funds were provided by China while the concrete implementation programme was decided by both countries ("PowerChina fined the biggest," 2012). Given the abundance of water resources of the transboundary rivers and the significance of hydroelectric development for the people's livelihoods and social development of China and the DPRK, both countries will continue to enhance bilateral cooperation in hydropower development.

Waterway development

Since the 1980s, China started to negotiate with the USSR and DPRK concerning the development of the Tumen River navigation route and its estuary. During the third round of China-USSR boundary negotiation in October 1988, both governmental delegations jointly made notes on the navigation rights into the sea through the estuary of the Tumen River in China. Based on the provisions of Sino-Russian boundary agreements, China stated that Chinese vessels were entitled to navigate into the sea through the estuary of the Tumen River (Tumannaya in Russian) while the USSR delegation agreed that there would be no opposition against Chinese vessels navigating in the sea through its estuary.

After four years of negotiations, China and USSR signed the Agreement between the People's Republic of China and the Union of Soviet Socialist Republics on the East Section of China-USSR Boundary on 16 May 1991 in Moscow. Both signing parties redefined the direction of the eastern section of boundary between the two countries. According to Article 9 of the Agreement,

> USSR, in the areas that may concern, agree that Chinese vessels (with the national flag of China) may navigate to and from the sea along Tumen River (Tumannaya River) below the boundary point No. 33 as described in Article 2 of this Agreement. Specific issues concerning such navigation shall be settled through consultations among parties concerned.

The Agreement between the People's Republic of China and the Union of Soviet Socialist Republics on the East Section of China-USSR Boundary was passed by the Russian Parliament and the Standing Committee of the National People's Congress of China respectively on 13 February 1992 and 28 February 1992, hence taking effect officially. After the collapse of the USSR at the end of 1991, Russia, a former Soviet Union country that inherited most of the USSR acknowledged that it respected all valid agreements signed between the USSR and China. It announced that the USSR standpoint on its boundary with China will not be revoked. Therefore, China's access to the Sea of Japan through the Tumen River remains legally valid.

Based on the progress in negotiations with the USSR, China intensified consultations with the DPRK. In November 1988, foreign minister of the DPRK Kim Yong-nam visited China and was confronted by his Chinese counterpart Qian Qichen with the question of sea access through the Tumen River, as Qian expressed the hope that the DPRK may confirm the possibility of China's sea access rights. An official reply made by the Ministry of Foreign Affairs, DPRK in January 1989 made it clear that the DPRK government approved the navigation of Chinese ships on the Tumen River between the DPRK and USSR. However, the DPRK and China have not signed any legally binding agreements concerning this issue, and there are no formal reports on the formal high-level talk between Beijing and Pyongyang regarding China's sea access rights in recent years. China has adopted the strategy of leasing ports for sea access to sail eastwards from the Tumen River by signing long-term agreements with Russia and the DPRK in leasing Zarubino Port and Khaypudyr Port in Russia, and Port of Rason and Port of Senbong in DPRK, and acquired access to the sea by "integration of expressway, port and port area" or "integration of expressway, port and customs".

In 2005, the DPRK transferred the first 50 years of exclusive management rights of the pier of Rajin Port to Hunchun, as a condition for obtaining aid in building the road from Hamgyongbuk to Rajin Port in the business area in Rason. Besides, the DPRK allowed Hunchun to build an industrial park on 5–10 km^2 of land. In 2008, a private company in Yanbian, Jilin Province acquired 10 years of lease rights of the No. 1 Dock of Rajin Port, of which dock equipment would be upgraded with some investment in infrastructure. Yanbian wishes to build an international corridor towards the Sea of Japan based on this navigation route, transporting coal from Hunchun, Yanbian to the economically developed Yangtze River Delta in China via Rajin Port, DPRK.

An ice-free port of a total acreage of 380,000 square metres, Rajin Port has three docks and ten berths, with a handling capacity of 3 million tons and a maximum tonnage of 50,000 tons. The port, directly linking the hinterland of Northeast China, allows for abundant resources and manufactured products to be transported to southern coastal regions in China. Products and materials from the coastal regions can also be shipped to the area surrounding the port. As the port becomes a hub for logistics and trade between the north and the south, it will not only open up a domestic shipping route for marine transportation of goods circulating on domestic markets, but it will also enable imports and exports to be shipped by sea. This measure will counter the shortage of customs clearance and railway transport capacity in meeting the demand of Northeast China and southeastern coastal regions, hence reducing the pressure on domestic ports. Moreover, this will also significantly reduce the mileage and time needed for freight transport, increase the capacity and effectively cut costs. It can be safely stated that the Rajin Port is the most ideal option for "sea access via the port" for goods and materials shipped from Northeast China.

Currently, China has gained access to the Sea of Japan by leasing Rajin Port, which has become an important passageway for China's access to the Sea of Japan. According to media reports, "for the first time after over a hundred years, China got a direct foothold in the Sea of Japan", and "China has opened up a passageway through the Sea of Japan". But some Japanese and South Korean researchers and government officials are worried about China's action, and argued that the DPRK port city is considered a hub that will facilitate forays into the Pacific region from China's northeast. Besides, the DPRK-China agreement will have a big impact on geopolitics in the region. China also has a very strong navy. The DPRK port remains ice-free during the winter. With China's direct access to the Sea of Japan, Japan feels pinched in the region (Lee, 2010).

River island joint development

On the Yalu River, China-DPRK joint development of the Yalu River is focused on river island development for the promotion of regional cooperation. In 2010, DPRK opened up the two biggest islands in the Yalu River along the border: Hwanggumpyong Island and Wihwa Island. Both islands are identified as free trade areas where foreigners, including Chinese citizens, pass freely without visas.

In May 2010, Kim Jong-il, supreme leader of DPRK visited China and reached consensus with Chinese president Hu Jintao on joint development and management of the Rason Economic and Trade Zone, Hwanggumpyong and Wihwado Economic Zones. In November 2010, a Chinese delegation led by the minister of commerce Chen Deming visited DPRK and officially signed the agreements for joint development and management of Rason Economic Zone as well as the Hwanggumpyong and Wihwado Economic Zones with the Korean counterparts, constructing the most fundamental and legally binding guidelines for joint development by China and DPRK.

On 3 December 2011, the law on Hwanggumpyong and Wihwado Economic Zones of the DPRK was passed by the Standing Committee of Supreme People's Congress of DPRK as No. 2006 decree. This law, comprising 7 chapters and 74 articles, covers the following: basics of the Law on Hwanggumpyong and Wihwado Economic Zones; development and management of the economic zones; establishment, registration, and business activities of enterprises; conditions guaranteeing economic activities; promotional and preferential policies; and claim procedures and dispute settlement, among others. It provides details concerning investment in the economic zones.

As the second largest island in the Yalu River, the Hwanggumpyong Island is located in Sindo County, North Pyongan Province of DPRK and is divided only by the Yalu River from the country's main territory. The island is approximately 11.94 km^2 in acreage and is one of the major grain-producing areas in Sinuiju,

DPRK. When the tide is in, Hwanggumpyong Island is only a waterway away from Anmin Town, Zhenxing District, Dandong in China. At low tide, the island is connected by land with Wenbin Village, Anmin Town and Hailong Village, Qianyang Town of Donggang City, and is separated only by a wired fence.

According to the agreements and relevant documents between the two governments, the Ministry of Commerce of China commissioned CIECC to complete the Outline for 2011–2015 and 2025 Long-Term Plan for China-DPRK Joint Development of Rason Economic and Trade Zone and Hwanggumpyong and Wihwado Economic Zones as supplementary to the agreements. In December 2010, the Public-Private Investment Commission of DPRK and the Ministry of Commerce of China signed the MOU on Joint Development of Hwanggumpyong, confirming that Hwanggumpyong Island will be leased to China with its development rights transferred over a period of 50 years, extendable for another 50 years. All development plans, provided that non-military or non-political projects are involved and that they constitute no threat to the security of the DPRK, will be authorized. To facilitate the development of Hwanggumpyong Island, the DPRK government is also planning to build a bridge over the Yalu River to strengthen connection with China.

Most islands on the Yalu River were classified as territories of the DPRK when the boundaries were defined. However, with the rapid economic development in Dandong, the city is experiencing a worsening shortage of land in the "golden belt" along the river. On the other hand, even though the islands of DPRK are not part of Chinese territory, yet geographically speaking, they are closer to Dandong than DPRK. The Hwanggumpyong Island is a case in point. Therefore, these islands are very suitable to be leased for development. Owing to sedimentation, these islands, almost connected to the continent, are only divided by wire fences from Dandong and have actually become DPRK's apanage on the west bank of the Yalu River. As a result, the old Dandong Port was deserted as outgoing vessels have to pass the territory of DPRK, and a new port has to be built elsewhere to solve this issue.

Considering the geographical conditions and actual needs, the municipal government of Dandong presented its proposal of a 50-year lease of Hwanggumpyong Island to the central government. This island is comparatively large on the Yalu River and it has fertile land and favourable conditions for building roads that link to the downtown area of Dandong. However, it is used by DPRK merely as cultivated land with much of it left in waste, hence wasting the potential for development. Currently, a series of construction plans have been drafted by Dandong (including zones for tourism, leisure, business, and agri-industrial development), promising many possibilities for development.

On 6 June 2011, the Standing Committee of Supreme People's Assembly of DPRK stated that "for the strengthening of the traditional friendship between DPRK and China and further development of international economic exchange, the decision has been made to approve the development plan of Hwanggumpyong and Wihwado Economic Zones" in the decree On the Democratic People's Republic of Korea Assigning Hwanggumpyong Island and Wihwa Island as

Economic Zones. According to the plan, Hwanggumpyong Island will be developed into a centre for logistics, tourism, and industrial manufacturing.

The Second Meeting of China-DPRK Joint Steering Committee of the Development and Cooperation of Rason Economic and Trade Zone and Hwanggumpyong and Wihwado Economic Zones was held from 7 June to 9 June 2011. During the meeting, the principle of "government guidance, enterprises playing major role, market-based operations, mutually beneficial and win-win cooperation" became clear to both parties, who expressed willingness to build the two economic zones into a demonstration zone for China-DPRK economic and trade cooperation as well as a platform for economic and trade cooperation with the rest of the world. Senior leaders of both countries, including Chinese minister of commerce Chen Deming and Jang Song-thaek from the DPRK side attended the launching ceremony of Hwanggumpyong Economic Zone (China and DPRK 2011). As previously agreed, a joint development model will be adopted for the Hwanggumpyong project: DPRK would provide land and labour force while China would provide capital and technology. Information technology, tourism, light industry, and modern agriculture would be the four pillar industries.

On 14 August 2012, the 3rd Meeting of China-DPRK Joint Steering Committee of the Development and Cooperation of Rason Economic and Trade Zone and Hwanggumpyong and Wihwado Economic Zones was held in Beijing. Both countries announced the establishment of the Administration Commission of Rason Economic and Trade Zone and Administration Commission of Hwanggumpyong and Wihwado Economic Zones, and signed agreements on the establishment and operation of the administration commissions and protocols on economic and technological cooperation. On 17 August, Jang Song-thaek, chief of the central administrative department of the Workers' Party of Korea, visited Liaoning Province and held comprehensive talks on the joint development and administration of the Hwanggumpyong Economic Zone. Both sides reached a series of consensuses and signed the relevant MOUs. On 15 September, the Groundbreaking Ceremony for the Office Building of the Administration Commission of Hwanggumpyong Economic Zone of Joint Development and Administration by China and DPRK was held in Hwanggumpyong Island, DPRK, marking the official kick-off of Hwanggumpyong Economic Zone development among the "Two Islands Economic Zones" under joint administration of China and DPRK. The joint development of the two islands is fully managed by Dandong Lingang Industrial Port, with a "Two Islands" Development Office separately set for specific and substantial issues in joint development. Approximately USD 500 million and USD 300 million would be invested in Hwanggumpyong Island and Wihwa Island, respectively, by Chinese enterprises.

China's lease of Hwanggumpyong Island is no less than a win-win solution for China and DPRK. After the nuclear crisis in DPRK, the country has been under severe economic sanctions and blockade from the international community. After a Republic of Korea (ROK)'s vessel was sunk by DPRK forces, the international sanction against DPRK tightened while the economic aid by ROK was terminated. This aggravated food shortage in DPRK due to poor harvest, making it necessary for the country to import large quantities of grains, including wheat, to meet the demand. Currently, most of the bilateral trades between China and DPRK are facilitated by the railway across the Yalu River Bridge linking Dandong in China and Sinuiju in DPRK. With growing trade volume, the two islands – Hwanggumpyong Island and Wihwa Island – leased by China will be transformed into warehousing and trans-shipment hubs to enhance trade ties between the countries.

The joint development of the Hwanggumpyong Economic Zone has strategic significance for both countries as well. For China, leasing the island is strongly conducive to further economic development of Dandong and stronger economic and trade ties with DPRK across the river. For DPRK, on the other hand, the joint project would intensify cooperation with China, hence politically and economically binding itself with China. In the case of isolation by the international community, it can undermine ("blackmail") China's diplomatic policies and therefore circumvent grave consequences of sanction.

Another consideration is that Hwanggumpyong Island used to be a very small island formed by sediment owned by DPRK but continued to expand with the deposit of sediment. Therefore, DPRK invited China to carry out development plans to safeguard this island, as Chinese investors would have to build foundations lest the island is completely or partially washed away by flooding river. Once such foundation is built, Hwanggumpyong Island would become a well-secured part of DPRK territory, which is considered a good deal in the long run.

River basin and regional development

As early as in the 1990s, the UNDP has proposed the establishment of a regional economic organization in the Tumen River Basin. According to the Report by Tumen River Region Development Survey Group published in 1991, due to the important strategic position of the Tumen River estuary, this region's development would bring tremendous potential to global economy, trade, and development. Therefore, the proposal to build a transportation hub integrating port, airport, and railway stations as well as business and financial hubs of Northeast Asia reaching the 21st century level is warmly embraced by China and DPRK.

In December 1995, during the 6th Meeting of Tumen River Region Development Project Steering Group held by the UNDP in New York, the Chinese, DPRK and Russian governments signed the Agreement on the Establishment of Coordination Committee of Tumen River Region Development. Chinese, Russian, DPRK, South Korean, and Mongolian governments signed three documents: (1) the Agreement on the Establishment of Tumen River Economic Development Zone, (2) the Consultative Committee of Northeast Asia Development, and (3) the Memorandum of Understanding Concerning Environmental Principles of Tumen River Economic Development Zone and Northeast Asia. This move laid the legal foundation and framework for the joint development of the drainage basin of the Tumen River. The first free economic and trade zone was created in the Rajin-Senbong region in the lower stretches of the Tumen River. However, due to the re-emphasis on the "Military First" strategy of DPRK and the UN sanctions since the beginning of the century, in November 2009, DPRK announced its withdrawal from the Greater Tumen Initiative (GTI) cooperation mechanism not long after its second nuclear test. This resulted in a slowdown in cooperation in the drainage basin of the Tumen River.

Nevertheless, in the same month, after the official reply to the Outline of Joint Development Plan for China Tumen River—with Changchun-Jilin-Tumen as Pilot Zone of Development and Opening-up by the State Council of China, Kim Jong-il, supreme leader of DPRK, personally visited Rason city in December. The visit sent a positive signal from the DPRK side for the development of Rason. Rason was elevated to special city in the following year, followed by the revision of Law on Rason Economic and Trade Zone and the creation of Taepung International Investment Group and National Development Bank to facilitate international economic cooperation. This shows that the enthusiasm of DPRK in developing Rason was far from fading away.

Conclusion

Comparing with other transboundary rivers, China-DPRK cooperation on the Yalu River and Tumen River reflects more geopolitical considerations. From the Yalu River's experience of the shift from an inland river in China to a jointly owned boundary river between China and DPRK to the loss of the estuary of the Tumen River and the rights to sea access, chapters of history were marked by China's failure in the game between nations. Amid changes in the geopolitical environment in Northeast Asia, with China rising as a nation and its growing comprehensive strength, the task of safeguarding the country's political, economic, and security rights and interest while expanding its interests in development dominate China's agenda for cooperation on these two transboundary rivers. And the implementation of overall national development strategy while aligning regional development to national strategy has driven joint efforts at central and local levels in facilitating transboundary river cooperation with DPRK. Therefore, such integration of geopolitics and national rights and interests means that China and DPRK's cooperation of the Yalu River and Tumen River extends beyond water resources development to cover comprehensive cooperation in river island development, navigation route development and regional development.

Another indication is that during the cooperation process, the progress and achievement of these joint efforts will unavoidably be subject to significant influence of changes in geopolitics. As a result of repeated nuclear tests launched by DPRK, international sanctions and oppositions from neighbouring countries have hindered the progress of cooperation on these two transboundary rivers to the point of setbacks and even prolonged suspension. However, it is predicted that China-DPRK cooperation on the Yalu River and Tumen River will continue, especially in the context of BRI implemented by China. The government at both central and local levels will seek to maximize the contribution of transboundary rivers and take initiative to drive the bilateral cooperation forward. Nevertheless, the tensions in Northeast Asia triggered by DPRK's nuclear tests will unavoidably lead to swings and slow progress in bilateral cooperation.

References

Agreement between the People's Republic of China and the Union of Soviet Socialist Republics on the east section of China-USSR Boundary (Zhonghua renmin gonghe guo he Suwei aishehui zhuyi gongheguo lianmeng guanyu Zhong Su guojie dongduan de xieding), (1991/05/16). (2006, March 17). *China Net.* Retrieved from www.china.com.cn/zhuanti2005/txt/2006-03/17/content_6157570.htm.

An overview of the groundbreaking and project construction of Wangjianglou and Wenyue hydropower stations in Ji'an (Dangchun naifa sheng—Ji an Wangjianglou he Wenyue dianzhan dian jiji qi xiangmu jianshe xunli). (2010, April 13). *Jilin Daily.* Retrieved from http://jlrbszb.chinajilin.com.cn/html/2010-04/13/content_609285.htm.

China and DPRK held second meeting of Joint Steering Committee of Development and Cooperation in Economic Zones (Zhong Chao jingji qu kaifa hezuo lianhe zhidao weiyuanhui dierci huiyi zhaokai). (2011, June 9). *Xinhua Net.* Retrieved from http://news.xinhuanet.com/world/2011-06/09/c_121514139.htm.

China-DPRK joint development project of Hwanggumpyong Island is officially launched (Zhong Chao hezuo gongguan "Huangjin ping" dao kaifa gongzuo zhengshi qidong. (2012, September 17). *Embassy of PRC in DPRK.* Retrieved from http://kp.china-embassy.org/chn/zcgx/t970156.htm.

China and DPRK plan for joint development of Hwanggumpyong Island, of which China obtains 100-year right of lessee (Zhong Chao nigong tong kaifa Huangjin ping dao, Zhongguo huo 100 nian chengzuquan). (2011, May 11). *Business Sohu.* Retrieved from http://business.sohu.com/20110511/n307252329.shtml.

China and DPRK start to build "Bridge of Gold" for north-to-south coal transportation Borrow the Hatbour (Jiegang Chuhai Zhong Chao kaixiu beimei nanyun "Huangjin zhiqiao"). (2010, March.). *Sina Net.* Retrieved from http://news.sina.com.cn/o/2010-03-16/063317222676s.shtml?from=wap.

Chinese enterprises to develop Hwanggumpyong and Wihwa Islands, attracting attention from ROK media (Han meiti guanzhu Zhong qi jiang kaifa Weihua dao he Huangjiping er dao). (2010, March 1). *Radio Free Asia.* Retrieved from www.rfa.org/mandarin/yataibaodao/han-03012010101425.html.

China's lease of DPRK port arouses concerns, ROK media calls it "an accelerated move into the Sea of Japan" (Zujie Chaoxian gangkou zaocai ji, Hanmei cheng Zhongguo zhengjiia sujin ru Ribenhai). (2010, March 10). *Global Times.*

Committee for the Compilation of Local Chronicles. (2006). *Tumen City, Jilin Province: Chorography of Tumen City (Tumen Shi Zhi)* (p. 61). Changchun, People's Republic of China: Jilin Literature and History Press.

Common interest of China, Russia and DPRK shall be sought in regional development along Tumen River (Tumenjiang kaifa yingxun zhao Zhong Er Chao sanguo liyi qi hedian). (2009, December 2). *China Economic Times.*

DPRK transfers development and management right of Rajin Port to Hunchun of Jilin Province, China (Chaoxian xiang Zhongguo Jilin Huichun shi churang Luojingang kaifa jingyingquan). (2005, September 18). *Wangyi News*. Retrieved from http://news.163.com/05/0918/13/1TUGOPPR0001124T.html.

Gao, H. (2006, June 28). China and DPRK will co-build a hydropower station on the middle reaches of Yalu River (Zhong Chao shuangfang jiangzai Yalujiang zhongyou hezuo xiujian yizuo shuidianzhan). *Revitalization of the Northeast*. Retrieved from http://chinaneast.xinhuanet.com/2006-06/28/content_7377479.htm.

Lee, S. (2010, March 14). China's acquisition of Sea of Japan port rattles its neighbors. *The National World*. Retrieved from www.thenational.ae/news/world/asia-pacific/chinas-acquisition-of-sea-of-japan-port-rattles-its-neighbours#full.

Liu, Y. (2012, November 26). Unveiling the mysteries of China-DPRK Hwanggumpyong Economic Zone (Zhongchao Huangjin ping jingji qu tanmi). *People's Daily*. Retrieved from http://paper.people.com.cn/zgjjzk/html/2012-11/26/content_1152472.htm.

DPRK approves China-DPRK joint development of Hwanggumpyong and Wihwado Economic Zones (Chaoxian pizhun Zhongchao hezuo kaifa Huangjinping he Weihua dao jingji qu). (2011, June 7). *Global Times*.

Power China fined the biggest hydropower station flood control facilities renovation project (Zhongguo dianjian wancheng Zhong Chao jiehe zuida shuidianzhan fanghong sheshi gaizao gongcheng). (2012, September 4). *State-owned Assets Supervision and Administration Commission of the State Council*. Retrieved from www.sasac.gov.cn/n1180/n1226/n2410/n314274/14812243.html.

Rajin Port (Luojing gang). (n.d.). *Baidu Encyclopedia*. Retrieved from http://baike.baidu.com/view/1852930.htm.

Shen, Z., & Dong, J. (2011, April). The solution of China-DPRK boundary disputes (1950–1964) (Zhong Chao bianjie zhengyi de jiejue). *The Chinese University of Hong Kong*. Retrieved from www.cuhk.edu.hk/ics/21c/media/articles/c124-201103001.pdf.

Shi, Y. (2014). Past and present of sea access from Tumen River (Tumen jiang ru Haitong dao de qian shi jin sheng). *World Affairs, 21*. Retrieved from www.faobserver.com/Newsinfo.aspx?id=10783.

The agreement on the demarcation line of national water boundaries among China, DPRK and Russia (Zhonghua renmin gonghe guo zhengfu, Chaoxian minzhu zhuyi renmin gonghe guo zhengfu he Eluosi lianbang zhengfu guanyu queding Tumen jiang sanguo guojie shuiyu fenjie xian de xieding). (2001, January 3). *The National People's Congress of the PRC*. Retrieved from www.npc.gov.cn/wxzl/gongbao/2001-01/03/content_5007106.htm.

The State Council officially approves Outline of Regional Joint Development in China's Tumen River Region (Guowu yuan jiang zhengshi pifu Zhongguo Tumen jiang quyu hezuo kaifa guihua gangyao). (2009, November 16). *The Central People's Government of the PRC*. Retrieved from www.gov.cn/jrzg/2009-11/16/content_1465540.htm.

Third Meeting of China-DPRK Joint Steering Committee of Development and Cooperation in the two Economic Zones held in Beijing (Zhong Chao liangge jinjj qu kaifa hezuo lianhe zhidao weiyuan hui di sanci huiyi zai Beijing zhaokai). (2012, August 14). *Ministry of Commerce, PRC*. Retrieved from www.mofcom.gov.cn/article/ae/ai/201208/20120808284471.shtml.

Treaty of Aigun was signed on 28 May 1858 (1858 nian 5 yue 28 ri "Aigun tiaoyue" qianding) (2003, August 1). *People's Daily*. Retrieved from www.people.com.cn/GB/historic/0528/1746.html.

Treaty on boundary issues between China and Korea along Tumen River (Tumen jiang Zhonghan jie wu tiaoyue). (2016). *Baidu Baike*. Retrieved from http://baike.baidu.com/view/10076097.htm.

"Tu" Tablet. (2015, June 26). *Xinhua Net.* Retrieved from www.jl.xinhuanet.com/2015-06-26/c_1115735057.htm.

Wang, X. (2015, April 14). Embracing blossoming flowers on the journey towards Belt and Road—On Jilin Province's involvement in the OBOR initiatives (Benxiang Silu kan huayu—Wosheng jiji rongru "Yidai yilu" gongzuo jishi). *Jilin Daily.* Retrieved from www.cnjiwang.com/2015zhuanti/content/2015-04/14/content_3598546.htm.

"Yalu River". (2014). World Rivers Database. *China Water.* Retrieved from www.chinawater.net.cn/riverdata/Search.asp?CWSNewsID=17868.

Zhang, B. (n.d.). Study on China and DPRK's history of power supply (Zhong Chao gongdian shi yanjiu). *Korean Peninsula Economic and Cultural Research Center.* Retrieved from http://cxbd.thnu.edu.cn/Article/ShowArticle.asp?ArticleID=2031.

Zhang, H., & Jin, X. (2015). History, present and future of DPRK's involvement in regional cooperation along Tumen River (Chaoxian canyu Tumen jiang quyu hezuo de lishi, xianshi yuwei lai). In T. Li (Ed.), *20 Years of Tumen River Cooperation* (pp. 223–224). Beijing: the Social Science Academic Press.

Zheng, J. (2013, January 4). Origins and issues of China-DPRK border disputes (Zhongchao bianjie zhengduan de youlai he zhuyao neirong). *Baidu Library.* Retrieved from http://wenku.baidu.com/view/4c1d450af12d2af90242e6ed.html.

Zhu, D. (2007). *Chinese Dictionary of River System (Zhongguo shuixi cidian)* (p. 48). Qingdao, People's Republic of China: Qingdao Publishing House.

7 Linking environmental security to transboundary water governance to manage the Mekong River

R. Edward Grumbine

Introduction

Since the 1990s, as global economic development has become increasingly integrated and environmental problems have worsened, perspectives on resource management that link social and ecological problems have become more influential (Ostrom, 1990). Over this same period, understanding of security has also evolved. Driven by environmental and economic change in an interdependent world, state security considerations are expanding from the traditional focus on maintaining borders through military means to begin to include non-traditional elements of security such as ecological degradation, resource scarcity, and human well-being (Floyd & Matthew, 2013). As this broadening evolves, scholars and experts have used the phrase "environmental security studies" to capture some of these developments. Floyd and Matthew (2013, p. 2) point out that environmental security encompasses "a wide range of analytical and normative meanings and positions". For the purposes of this chapter, environmental security represents efforts to inject interdisciplinary understanding of ecological and social concerns into international deliberations with the goal of influencing states toward more adaptive, transboundary behaviour. A major goal would be the creation and implementation of policies to reduce risk and maintain critical ecological functions while supporting human capacity to adapt to change.

Over roughly the same period, there has been much work done on defining standards of transboundary water governance. Water governance comprises: "all social, political, economic, and administrative organizations and institutions..." and "their relationships to water resources development and management" (Tortajada, 2010, p. 299). Instead of assuming that only sovereign nations control decision-making around water, adaptive water governance focuses on clarification of the roles of governments and other actors; design and implementation of water policies, laws, and institutions; equity and efficiency in resource allocation and distribution; peoples' cultural perceptions regarding ownership and management of water resources; stakeholder participation and conflict resolution; and more (Grumbine et al., 2015; see Pahl-Wostl, 2009). Adaptive water governance behaviours highlighted repeatedly in international expert (Blake & Robins, 2016; Bogardi et al., 2012; Earle & Neal, 2017) and policy literatures (UN & ADB, 2012) portray a strong consensus around: open information exchange; government transparency; institutional coordination; iterative decision-making; and multi-stakeholder participation and conflict resolution. Yet, many nations' governance behaviour is in conflict with growing quantitative and qualitative evidence that countries that can best practice adaptive transboundary management will likely be more successful at building increased state and system resilience to future change (ADB, 2014; Pahl-Wostl, Lebel, Knieper, & Nitikina, 2012).

The Mekong River Basin, where transboundary cooperation between countries has been debated for over two decades, provides an insightful example of challenges to the current influence and future evolution of environmental security and adaptive water governance in a major river basin in Asia. The Mekong is uniquely important among transboundary rivers with headwaters emanating from China for several reasons. First, the Mekong is home to some 60 million river resource-dependent people, more than any other human population among China's transboundary rivers (MRC, 2016). Second, current and planned hydropower development is far greater in scope and projected environmental and social impacts than other rivers in the region. Third, the Mekong has a decades-long history of attempts to understand, manage, and mitigate development impacts under the auspices of the Mekong River Commission (MRC); no other Asian transboundary river has such a long-running river basin organization with members from multiple nations. As a result of these three factors, more is known about the Mekong's environmental and governance drivers of change than any other river in Asia (MRC, 2016).

In this chapter, six security stressors are identified – ecosystem degradation, food, energy, and water issues, human development, and climate change – that will need to be managed cooperatively in the Mekong region. In addressing these stressors, a qualitative meta-review is provided that: (1) assembles current data from a wide range of sources to spotlight specific stressors and their linkages that most influence environmental security and management in the Mekong; (2) identifies critical gaps in Mekong governance and institutional capacity; and (3) recommends actions that may assist the region's governments to plan for and implement adaptive, security-based strategies. China's potential role as a leader in the management of the Mekong River is highlighted since, as the regional powerhouse, the country will play an important role in maintaining or reducing barriers to the spread of environmental security ideas and improved water governance behaviours.

Methods

To gauge the current state of environmental security and transboundary management in the Mekong River Basin, a comprehensive literature review was performed with documents published through early 2017. The Science Direct and Google Scholar databases were used to search for published, peer-reviewed work using the general keywords: "Mekong River environmental security" and "transboundary water governance". "Ecosystem degradation", "food", "water", "energy", "human development", and "climate change" were then added to the keyword template. In general, for each search, the first 50–75 results were reviewed after which increasing repetition of citations and/or decreasing topic relevance was detected. Some 417 abstracts were scrutinized; 190 papers and documents were selected for in-depth analyses. To capture non-academic publications from governments, development agencies, and NGOs, such references from the papers chosen above were reviewed. To find general news stories online, internet searches were also performed using keywords linked to specific topics, for example, "Lancang-Mekong Cooperation" and "Mekong River Commission".

Results

Environmental security in the Mekong River Basin

The Mekong is one of the most contested rivers in the world as six countries with geopolitical power asymmetries and differing levels of social, scientific, and institutional capacity, continue to develop economically (Middleton & Dore, 2015). Upstream, China has served as both an engine for regional economic growth as well as a role model for unilateral hydropower development (Grumbine, Dore, & Xu, 2012; Tullos, Brown, Kibler, Magee, Tilt & Wolf, 2010). Food insecurity is increasing for millions of rural poor in the Lower Mekong Basin (LMB) since many people living there depend on wild-capture fisheries which are under threat from current and proposed hydropower development (Orr, Pittock, Chapagain, & Dumaresque, 2012). Widespread and ongoing land-use changes contribute to reduced rates of biodiversity and ecosystem functioning (Fox, Castella, & Ziegler, 2013). Growing cross-border flows of goods, people, and information are stimulating regional economic growth but also challenging the capacity of states to manage these flows (Lebel, Naruchaikusol, & Juntopas, 2014). And virtually all models project regional climate impacts to grow over the coming decades; in 2016, the Mekong region experienced the worst drought in some 90 years and this event may portend a glimpse of the scale of future climate impacts (see Hoang et al., 2016).

Transboundary water governance in the Mekong River Basin

A rich literature on the need for transboundary river basin management in the Mekong has developed across twenty years of research. Badenoch (2002), Osborne (2004), Hirsch and Jensen (2006), and Goh (2007) were among the first to assess Mekong transboundary water governance and its security implications. In producing their work, these authors did not overtly consider environmental security as a framework as it was undergoing development during this period. More recently, Grumbine (2014) has written about environmental security and adaptive governance in China (with reference to the Mekong), and Allouche, Middleton, and Gywali (2014) and Contreras (2017) have discussed security in the region and its links to human development and environmental issues.

Until recently, the 1995 Mekong River Agreement, created to promote cooperation and coordinate development in the basin, was seen as relatively successful at guiding member states (Laos, Viet Nam, Cambodia, Thailand; China and Myanmar are only 'dialogue partners') toward common goals (Suhardiman, Giordano, & Molle, 2015). But now, weaknesses in the Agreement are being exposed as cumulative hydropower and other developments reach a critical stage. Laos is constructing the first three of multiple planned dams on the mainstream Mekong despite protests from Vietnam and Cambodia. Upstream, China continues to develop more mainstream hydropower capacity. Despite projections of significant loss to downstream fisheries, Cambodia is moving ahead with construction of several dams on a major tributary of the Mekong (Sithirith, Evers, & Gupta, 2016). In spring 2016, Thailand began to withdraw water from the Mekong to alleviate drought conditions; this was done without the required prior consultation with signatory countries under the rules of the Mekong River Agreement (Yee, 2016). And the MRC is under structural and fiscal reform due to controversies over its capacity to manage Mekong issues (Hunt, 2016). While the Mekong Agreement was never designed as a full international treaty to guide the sharing of transboundary resources, it is clear that tipping points around the Mekong's hydrological and social systems are closer at hand.

Both environmental security and transboundary water governance offer frameworks for inclusive, and, therefore, more realistic consideration of multiple ecological and social drivers of change, not just one (i.e., hydropower development) (for an example, see Dore, Lebel, & Molle, 2012). Another advantage of both frameworks is geopolitical – that is, if Mekong countries could somehow come to understand that a state-centric transboundary management calculus increasingly will lead away from regime stability, then looming crises that appear to be leading toward widespread ecological and social instability in the river basin might be averted.

Six social–ecological stressors

An important contribution of environmental security to transboundary management in the Mekong is evaluation of stressors that are driving regional change.

Ecological degradation

Biodiversity and ecosystem functions in both terrestrial and riverine Mekong ecosystems "have degraded considerably" (MRC, 2016, p. 39) and are under growing pressure. From 1973 to 2009, forest cover in the Mekong region was reduced by about 30 per cent and, though the rate of loss is slowing, all studies project ongoing losses (WWF, 2013). Data from China show afforestation is increasing, but this result is difficult to interpret due to definitions of 'forest' that include monocultural plantations of non-native species (i.e. rubber, eucalyptus) (Ahrends et al., 2017). A primary driver of loss is the broad regional land-use transition away from smallholder, swidden-based agriculture to commercial-scale cash crops (often grown in monocultures). For freshwater ecosystems, hydropower development, overfishing, and introduction of non-native species are the main drivers of degradation, and plans to build many more dams on both the mainstream and tributaries of the river yield a poor prognosis for aquatic and floodplain ecosystem integrity (Dudgeon, 2011).

Food security

Current and projected land-use, agricultural, and hydropower transformations in the Mekong are creating uncertainties in local and regional food systems. Given that the Mekong accounts for about 13 per cent of the world's wild-capture fisheries with tens of millions of people dependent to some degree on this resource (Nam et al., 2015), the key driver of food insecurity is dam development. Lower basin countries' dependency on protein from wild-capture fisheries from the Mekong River ranges from 47 per cent (Thailand) to 80 per cent (Cambodia) (Hortle, 2007). Yet if all mainstream dams are constructed, the Mekong fisheries catch is projected to decrease by 27–44 per cent (Baran, Guerin, & Nasielski, 2015), with impacts especially challenging for the LMB's rural poor.

Energy security

Energy demand and provision are evolving rapidly in all Mekong River Basin countries. For every country, energy demand is projected to increase dramatically over the next several decades (IEA, 2015). By 2030, demand in Thailand is projected to double; demand in Vietnam may triple (Middleton & Dore, 2015). Energy sources are also shifting. Today, Thailand uses natural gas for some 70 per cent of its electricity, but domestic supplies of this fuel may be exhausted as early as 2020 (Reuters, 2014). China is often blamed for downstream impacts due to its many mainstream dams, yet every Mekong country is building or planning to build dams (Grumbine, Dore, & Xu, 2012). To sum, there are multiple, complex energy export and hydropower investment links between most Mekong states.

Water security

There are three major issues around Mekong water security: the scale of hydropower development with projected changes to the river's hydrology; effects of such development on local peoples' livelihoods; and lack of river basin cooperative mechanisms and integrated analysis of cost/benefit trade-offs within and between countries. The cumulative impacts of constructing all planned dams (mainstream and tributaries) have never been fully assessed (see Tullos, Tilt, & Reidy-Leirmann, 2009). But planned dam construction would likely result in dramatic changes in the Mekong's hydrograph with wet season flows decreasing 17–22 per cent, and dry season flows increasing 60–90 per cent, with associated changes in flow timing, amplitude, and duration (Rasenen, Koponen, Lauri, & Kummu, 2012). So, many dams built on the mainstream could lead to a projected 96% loss in sediment load reaching the Mekong Delta (Kondolf, Rubin, & Minear, 2014) with serious impacts on downstream fisheries and food production and, therefore, local livelihoods. By 2050, agricultural demand for water may reach 32–50 per cent of the Mekong's total flow with this demand competing with local livelihoods, environmental flows, hydropower operations, and a projected 250 per cent increase in LMB-wide urban water use (ADB, 2013b).

Human development

As some of the least developed countries in the world, while also being part of rapidly rising Asia, Mekong River Basin countries are experiencing a complex mix of social forces that influence environmental security. Chief among these are population growth/shifts and poor management of rapid infrastructure development. Though growth rates are falling, human population in the five Mekong River Basin countries (excluding China) from 2010 to 2025 is projected to increase by 23.6 million (UNESCAP, 2013). Urban areas are projected to grow to accommodate from 29.6 per cent to 49 per cent of the total regional population (UNDESA, 2014). However, excluding Thailand and China, Mekong River Basin countries rank low on measures of human development and this limits their capacity to manage change. For example, much of the growth in the Mekong region goes largely unregulated as it is happening outside official municipal boundaries; by 2030, 40 per cent of projected urban population growth in Asia (200 million people) may be in these peri-urban areas (Kontgis et al., 2014). Since 1992, the Asian Development Bank has funded regional roads, railways, and pipelines across the Greater Mekong Subregion in an effort to stimulate and coordinate growth. These efforts have been successful at stimulating economic infrastructure development but they have not been well-coordinated with environmental or social planning (Glassman, 2010).

Climate change

Under scenarios representative of current global emission trends, climate projections show mean temperature increases over 2 C by 2050 for the Mekong River Basin region (Zomer, Trabucco, Wang, & Xu, 2016). Precipitation projections are more variable and, though this leads to considerable uncertainty in projecting Asian river discharges, there will likely be increases in runoff at least to the mid-century (Lutz, Imerzeel, Shrestha, & Bierkens, 2014). However, more runoff is not all positive; runoff may interact with greater likelihood of extreme events (including flooding) that are projected for the Mekong River Basin (CDKN, 2012). There will also be impacts on agricultural productivity throughout the region as crop species respond differentially to climatic change. Maize yields in selected areas in the LMB, for example, may decline 3–12 per cent by 2050 (USAID, 2013). The Mekong Delta is of particular concern as it is so important for global rice production and Vietnam's economy. Climate change impacts will not only impact agriculture; some 16–18 million people live in the Mekong Delta and this subregion, along with most large urban areas of the LMB, is at high risk for sea-level rise and salinization (Hanson et al., 2011).

Links between environmental security stressors

In their framing of environmental security, Loring, Gerlach, and Huntington (2013) emphasize links between social and ecological stressors. While a full accounting of these links is beyond the scope of this chapter, one thing is clear. Forest loss and land-use changes, the historical drivers of ecosystem degradation in the Mekong, are now being joined by hydropower development.

Constructing 112 dams (in addition to the current 58) will dramatically alter Mekong waterscapes (WLE Greater Mekong, 2015) (Figure 7.1).

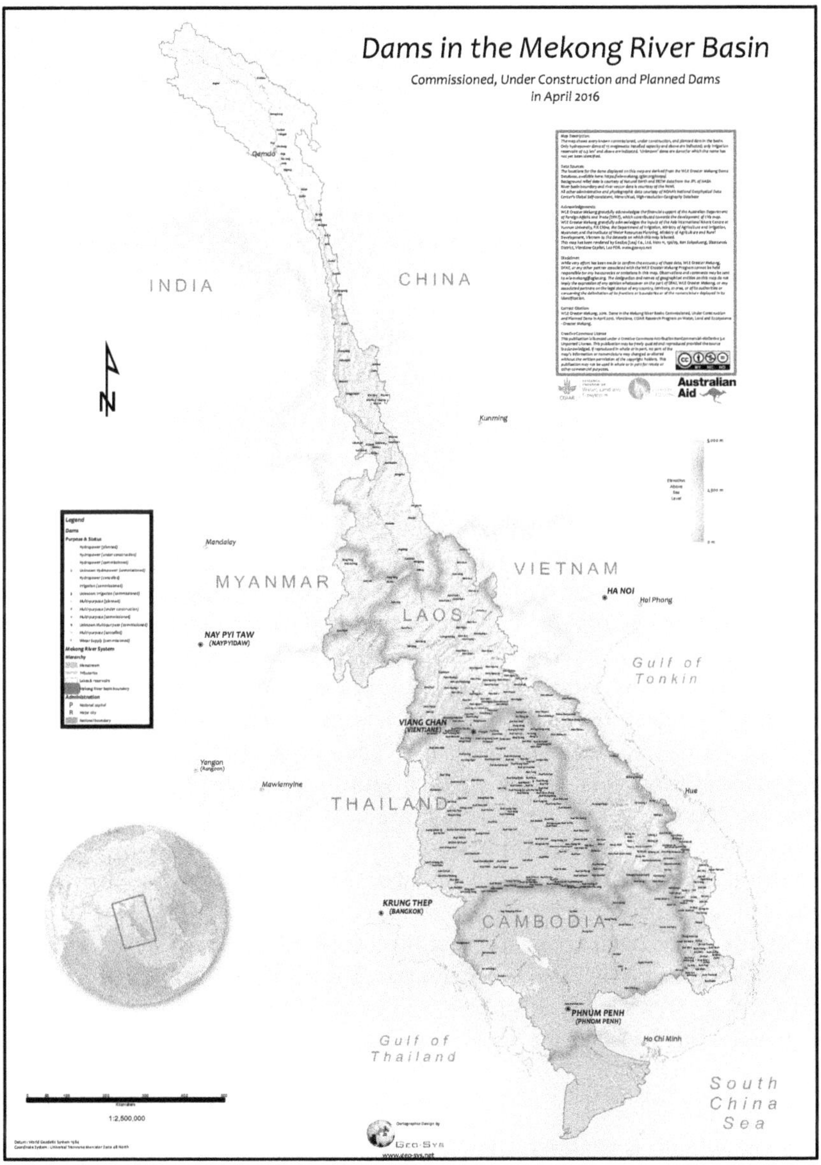

Figure 7.1

Over the next decades and beyond, these changes, combined with large-scale, climate-driven shifts in species ranges and ecosystem boundaries (see Zomer, Xu, Wang, Trabucco, & Li, 2015), are likely to result in dramatic alterations to the ecosystem structure, function, and provisioning services – clean air and water, hydrological and nutrients, and more – that people living in the Mekong River Basin depend upon.

Mekong River food, energy, water, and social issues are linked in numerous other ways. While a major concern is how dam development will alter the Mekong's transboundary hydrology with impacts on food security for downstream nations, conflicts are also brewing over allocating water between natural ecosystems, irrigated agriculture, energy production, and urban uses. But a simple focus on any one stressor or sector is likely to miss important trends. For example, there is speculation that loss of wild-capture Mekong fisheries can be offset by greater productivity from aquaculture in combination with enrichment of riverine nutrients due to increased cropping intensity, more crop irrigation and discharges of human and animal wastes from expanding urbanization. But production from reservoir fisheries is projected to replace only some 10 per cent of fish lost due to dams, let alone the entire wild-capture Mekong fishery that is expected to be impacted by hydropower development (Baran et al., 2015). Overall, these data on stressors and their linkages indicate a trajectory of general decline in ecological and social system resiliency leading toward increasing security risks and a growing need for better water governance.

Discussion

Managing the Mekong for transboundary environmental security

If the goal is to reduce threats from the six stressors described above so that Mekong River Basin governments can make informed decisions about economic development *and* environmental protection and move toward adaptive, transboundary water governance, China and its Mekong neighbours face several interrelated problems. First, Mekong countries are only now beginning to experience the full range of the environmental costs and benefits of development within and between nations. Evidence for this is seen most clearly in projected cumulative impacts from the continuing expansion in construction and operation of China's upstream hydropower cascade, the near-completion of Laos' first mainstream dams and ongoing dam building on Mekong tributaries by many countries throughout the basin. Up to today, transboundary water governance cost accounting has focused narrowly on impacts from dams on Mekong hydrology and food security, just as benefits accounting has focused on what (i.e. electricity) can be delivered to individual sovereign states (see Sadoff & Grey, 2002). Second, most Mekong states are guided by relatively closed governance systems that do not prepare them well to navigate adaptive governance problem-solving under growing resource limits. For example, four of the six Mekong countries fall into the bottom 25 per cent of nations with capacity to protect environmental and human health (Yale University, 2014) and three of six are in the bottom 25 per cent of corrupt states (Transparency International, 2013). There are problematic disconnects within and between states' institutional capacity (Suhardiman, Giordano, & Molle, 2012) to manage resource decision-making. And the wide political power imbalances among Mekong countries continue to constrain adaptive transboundary decision-making (Verbiest, 2013).

This leads to critical questions: Will China and other Mekong states be willing and able to reframe and reform their governance systems to meet the challenges arising from the six environmental security stressors within and across political boundaries? If so, who will provide leadership to accomplish these things, and what manner of leadership – hegemonic or collaborative – will be employed? What can adaptive water governance contribute to reducing impacts from these stressors?

Opportunities for mitigating security stressors

Much can be done by the countries in the Mekong to move toward transboundary environment security. What follows are brief descriptions of promising first steps keyed to each stressor mentioned above.

Ecosystem degradation

Though Mekong states' environmental laws are implemented poorly due to inadequate funding and institutional capacity challenges, MRC member countries have already committed to broadscale environmental assessments (Ke & Gao, 2013), and new research demonstrates how a transboundary scaling up of environmental impact assessment could serve as the basis to improve regional ecosystem conditions (Carew-Reid, 2017). The MRC is in the process of completing its Council Study, the first interdisciplinary assessment of the ecological-social state of the basin in seven years (MRC, 2017), and this effort could spur more adaptive decision-making among Mekong nations. Given the regional commitment to economic development, various payments for ecosystem services schemes are obvious candidates for reducing loss of ecosystem functioning. However, evidence from Vietnam (Suhardiman, Wichelns, Lestrelin, & Hoanh, 2013) and China (Tilt & Gerkey, 2016) shows that state control can undercut the effectiveness of such programmes.

Food

With demand growing and many farmers shifting from subsistence farming to cash crops, food security in the Mekong requires improvements in production efficiencies to use less water to produce more food (Fukai & Ouk, 2012). Given recent projections of dam impacts leading to the possibility of 34 per cent reductions in net primary productivity in Cambodia's Tonle Sap wild fisheries-dependent ecosystem (Arias et al., 2014), already-existing analyses (see Orr et al., 2012) that link aquatic and terrestrial food capacities could be further refined and employed before policy decisions are made. There also must be more emphasis placed on local, low-cost water storage, not just large-scale plans to divert Mekong water for new irrigation schemes.

Energy

The dynamism in demand forecasts, supply options, and their transboundary security implications create great uncertainty here. Some scenarios show that by 2025, 25 per cent of Mekong energy could come from renewables, but not without more targeted state support (ICEM, 2010). Meanwhile, under the Greater Mekong Subregion infrastructure programme, there are bids to build an "energy highway" with electricity grids spanning the region and other plans to create regulated markets that deliver energy across multiple state borders. In a best-case scenario, new energy from hydropower development would lead to coordinated dam operations among and between countries. To be clear – the current scale of hydropower development is now moving from one country (China) operating multiple dams to multiple countries operating multiple dams, and this could spur more commitment to transboundary governance coordination.

Water

Transboundary water resources are key to environmental security and adaptive water governance in the Mekong, and there are abundant ideas about more efficient and collaborative ways to manage waters. Virtually all observers accent better governance, cooperation, and benefit sharing (see Dore, Lebel & Molle, 2012; Earle & Neal, 2017). Experts emphasize more information sharing on dam building/operations and flow data (Hennig, Wang, Magee & He, 2016; Tullos et al., 2010). In fact, to help alleviate the dry season drought of 2016, China released water from its Jinghong mainstream dam for use in the LMB. While this act shows that China is ready to lead in addressing short-term water management problems, it does not address long-term sediment capture or projected loss of fisheries (partially) resulting from Chinese dams. New efforts are exploring how to manage sediments behind dams in the Mekong so that they can pass through infrastructure and move downstream (Kondolf, Annandale, & Rubin, 2015). There is a collaborative Hydropower by Design planning framework being tested in Myanmar that holds promise (TNC, WWF, University of Manchester, 2016). With increasing private sector involvement in hydropower delivery, voluntary agreements such as the Hydropower Sustainability Assessment Protocol could play important roles in planning, forecasting, and dam operations, though the value of these assessments remains unclear (Tahseen & Karney, 2017). Evidence from water governance research does suggest, however, that such agreements are not substitutes for water treaties and stronger government regulation (Giordano et al., 2013).

Development

In the Mekong River Basin, the combination of low development levels and closed systems of governance makes progress difficult in strengthening environmental security and adaptive water governance. The key is acknowledging that all Mekong countries are in stages of economic development that will continue to dramatically alter livelihoods and landscapes; adaptation is about managing, not eliminating change. Studies show how China can better manage investment in hydropower to support human livelihoods in the LMB (Urban, Nordensvard, Khatri, & Wang, 2013). China can also learn from governance research that elucidates the costs of displacing local people due to dam projects in the Upper Mekong (Tilt & Gerkey, 2016). Chinese experts have suggested ways to better manage rivers within China that can provide lessons in transboundary river basins like the Mekong (He et al., 2014; Yang, Lu, & Ran, 2016). Links between improved land–use planning leading to decreasing human livelihood vulnerability have been mapped in China (Yi et al., 2014), Laos (Castella, Lestrelin, & Hett, 2013), and Myanmar (Webb et al., 2014). To manage urban human security, recent research has established methods to couple city planning with flood control measures (Marchand, Pham, & Le, 2014). Throughout the Mekong River Basin, there is a developing focus on peri-urban places where human populations are concentrating (Sajor, 2017). Even in Vietnam, where many peri-urban areas are being appropriated by cities (van Leeuwen, Dan, & Dieperink, 2016) or managed as if they were still rural (Webster, Cai, & Muller, 2014), plans have been offered for increasing human livelihoods resilience to change through more coordination between public and private sector actors. To sum, there are a host of practices to manage the social elements of environmental security using basic principles from adaptive governance, but they are only now beginning to be tested in the Mekong.

Climate

Recommendations for reducing risk and building resilience to climate change echo those offered to reduce pressures from other stressors – Mekong states need to increase their focus on integrated planning across ecosystem, food, water, energy, and livelihoods sectors. China's advanced capacity in the technical aspects of modelling and assessing climate change in relation to other Mekong countries could be a great benefit here. But more policy coordination between different levels of government in China is needed (Zhang, Mol, & He, 2016). Right now, this lack inhibits China's capacity to lead at broader regional scales. Data from Thailand and Vietnam show that local governments can support peoples' innovative adaptations to support climate resilience by building farmers' technical capacity, subsidizing credit for farmers' costs, linking what products farmers grow with market demand, and improving planning coordination across sectors (Bastokoti, Gupta, Babel, & van Dijik, 2014). But in the Mekong, solutions to climate issues are often less a matter of technical capacity and more an issue of policy choices, governance capacity, and political will.

Governance for environmental security

The evidence for each specific social-ecological stressor outlined above shows that environmental security in the Mekong River Basin is undermined by states that have not (yet) bought into the benefits of adaptive governance and management. At some point, environmental security for Mekong nations cannot be supported under current conditions of unilateral implementation of large-scale hydropower development, closed information, reduced transparency, inefficient institutional coordination, and limited participation from those people who are most affected by decisions.

To address constraints on transboundary behaviour that limit environmental security in the Mekong, several steps are necessary. First, one must understand how states are and are not subject to incentives for cooperation, support for local participation, and open information exchange. International donors and NGOs have not always done this, seeing institutional and legal fragmentation as rooted in a lack of "capacity" rather than as a direct consequence of state development goals and strategies (Suhardiman & Giordano, 2014). But scientific approaches that do not account for unruly politics and institutional disincentives to accommodate change are less likely to influence decision makers (see Suhardiman et al., 2015; Villamayor-Tomas, Avagyan, Firlus, Helbing, & Kabakova, 2016).

Second, scholars and practitioners who wish to solve environmental security and adaptive governance issues in the Mekong can benefit from a multidimensional, multi-actor view of state decision-making behaviour (Ptak, 2017). Too often in the past, observers assumed that countries were monolithic in their governance behaviour; today, we are aware that many actors influence decisions: governments at many levels (central, provincial, municipal), private businesses, NGOs, and local people (who continue to bear inequitable development burdens) (see Dean, 2017; Hirsch, 2016).

The potential problem-solving power of an environmental security framework represents a third strategy to push for adaptive reforms. Previous security scholarship linking resource scarcity with violence and instability showed that countries will often continue to "go it alone" until environmental conditions have deteriorated to the point of social conflict (Homer-Dixon, 1999). To reduce this likelihood, the environmental security approach accented here focuses on the benefits of collectively managing ecosystem, economic, social, and, especially, *political* risks for countries that share transboundary resources. Environmental security emphasizes that without adaptive collaboration, state stability in a rapidly changing world, will (at some point) be reduced.

One would expect that this realization would help to shift the attention of governments intent on maintaining power toward more transboundary collaborative behaviour (Cui, 2013; Grumbine, 2014). So far, this has not been the case; negative signals are not yet strong enough to change decision-making. And, of course, the risk here is that regional governments would (continue to) use their individual power to uphold their own definitions of "security". To be clear, neither environmental security nor adaptive water governance are panaceas and they remain untested in the Mekong. But given projected ecological and social instability, the ultimate fate of governments who continue to subscribe to status quo transboundary behaviour appears uncertain.

A strategic focus on China's outsized role in the region is another critical element to Mekong environmental security. While cultivating strong bilateral economic relations with all Mekong states, China never signed the Mekong Agreement. But China's use of applied ecological information in decision-making is improving (He et al., 2014) and China's "security identity" may be opening to the fact that wielding regional power requires at least some degree of regional cooperation (Bradley, 2014). The recent formation of the China-led Lancang Mekong Cooperation mechanism (LMC) as an alternative to (or replacement for) the MRC may represent a step toward reinvigorating regional cooperation in the Mekong (Ministry of Foreign Affairs, PRC, 2016). This new mechanism gives China a chance to engage in international-scale leadership dealing with critical security issues. The LMC mandate is quite broad with economic concerns primary and transboundary water management only one of many foci. No code of conduct or specific guiding rules to adjudicate claims are yet part of the LMC. The LMC may turn out to be more of an Asian Development Bank like vehicle where China funds and controls the direction of policy reforms, and less like a mutual forum for building better transboundary regional governance (Middleton & Allouche, 2016). While some observers are ready to declare success (Han, 2017), it is too soon to tell how the LMC will play out. The second meeting of LMC parties in late 2016 did little to develop the group's intent or clarify China's role (VBN, 2016). One thing is clear – without leadership from China that includes a commitment to more transparency and cooperative behaviour, there can be no environmental security in the Mekong River Basin.

Conclusion – timing and uncertainty

For China and the Mekong River Basin states, differential projected water, food, energy, and climate impacts between countries are going to make any transition toward transboundary collaborative management challenging. Right now, each Mekong country uniquely interprets projected rates and scales of ecological and social impacts, and these influences narrow assessments of geopolitical risk. When uncertainty is high, present impacts relatively low, and projected negative consequences are perceived as distant in time, momentum for change is slow.

What signals might be strong enough to support change toward environmental security and adaptive governance in the Mekong that could lead to more transboundary accord? No one knows. It could be that environmental security with its emphasis on adding explicit geopolitical analyses to the now-standard calls for more adaptive governance action presents little that would move Mekong nations forward. Certainly, the USD 340 million in foreign funding spent by the MRC over the years has yielded little relative to the price tag (Wright, 2016). But Chartres (2014) calculate that by the mid-2030s, food demand in Asia will outpace supply. The IPCC (2013) estimates that regional climate impacts will be felt increasingly after 2030. Closer to the present, dam development decisions will likely determine water/food/energy tipping points, especially when mainstream dams in Laos are completed at Xayaburi (2017), Don Sahong (2018), and Pak Lay (2020). These hydropower tipping points would be added to if these Mekong dams do in fact have their projected impacts on fisheries (Pittock, Orr, Stevens, Aheeyar, & Smith 2015; Ziv, Baran, Nam, Rodriguez-Iturbe, & Levin, 2012), and Cambodia does move toward planned large-scale irrigation of its rice paddies, diverting up to 30 per cent of total downstream flows that are now flowing to Vietnam.

Overall, these cumulative signals define a rough decision space of 5–7 years for Mekong countries to begin to act more cooperatively. This is a short timeline for moving toward transboundary resource cooperation using insights from environmental security and adaptive governance. Yet, the host of mainstream dams have not yet been built and climate projections remain just that. Change could come in the form of new agreements to share data as was recently negotiated by India and China on South Asia's transboundary Brahmaputra River (Gupta, 2014). Or deliberations under the LMC could encourage Mekong states to move away from debates over abstract "water supplies" and instead take steps toward benefit sharing (see McIntyre, 2015). And, after decades of delay in ratification, in August 2014, the UN Law on Non-Navigable Watercourses went into effect providing Mekong countries with another opportunity to cooperate. To date in the Mekong region, only Vietnam has signed on to this treaty.

If not acted upon soon, the opportunities for transboundary cooperation that abound in the Mekong River Basin today will turn into greater challenges tomorrow. To continue with a political status quo that appears ineffective at managing change or to prepare for future conditions that demand adaptive governance – the future of environmental security in the Mekong is in the hands of the regions' decision makers with China firmly in a position of leadership.

Acknowledgments

Part of this research was supported by the Canadian IDRC project "Building Effective Water Governance in the Asian Highlands" and Chinese Academy of Sciences (Grant 2010T1S2) during my 2010–2014 Visiting Professorship for senior international scientists.

References

ADB (Asian Development Bank). (2013a). *Asian development outlook 2013. Asia's energy challenge.* Mandaluyong City, Philippines: Asian Development Bank.

ADB (Asian Development Bank). (2013b). *Asian water development outlook 2013: Measuring water security in Asia and the Pacific.* Mandaluyong City, Philippines: Asian Development Bank.

ADB (Asian Development Bank). (2014). *Climate change and rural communities in the Greater Mekong Subregion: A framework for assessing vulnerability and adaptation options.* Mandaluyong City, Philippines: Asian Development Bank.

Ahrends, A., Hollingsworth, P., Beckschafer, P., Chen, H., Zomer, R., Zhang, L., ... Xu, J. (2017). China's fight to halt tree cover loss. *Proceedings of the Royal Society B, 284*, 20162559. Retrieved from http://dx.doi.org/10.1098/rspb.2016.2559.

Allouche, J., Middleton, C., & Gywali, D. (2014). *Nexus nirvana or nexus nullity? Adynamic approach to security and sustainability in the water-energy-food nexus.* Working Paper No. 63. Brighton, UK: STEPS Centre.

Arias, M. E., Cochrane, T. A., Kummu, M., Lauri, H., Koponen, J., Holtgrieve, G. W., & Piman, T. (2014). Impacts of hydropower and climate change on drivers of ecological productivity of Southeast Asia's most important wetland. *Ecological Modelling, 272*, 252–263. doi:10.1016/j.ecolmodel.2013.10.015.

Badenoch, N. (2002). *Transboundary environmental governance: Principles and practices in Mainland Southeast Asia.* Washington, DC: World Resources Institute.

Baran, E., Guerin, E., & Nasielski, J. (2015). *Fish, sediment and dams in the Mekong.* Penang, Malaysia: WorldFish, and CGIAR Research Program on Water, Land and Ecosystems.

Bastokoti, R., Gupta, J., Babel, M., & van Dijik, M. (2014). Climate issues and adaptation strategies in the Lower Mekong basin. *Regional Environmental Change, 14*, 207–219. doi:10.1007/s10113-013-0485-8.

Blake, D., & Robins, L. (Eds.). (2016). *Water governance dynamics in the Mekong Region.* Petaling Jaya, Malaysia: Strategic Information and Research Development Center.

Bogardi, J. J., Dudgeon, D., Lanford, R., Flinkerbusch, E., Meyn, A., Pahl-Wostl, C., … Vorosmarty, C. (2012). Water security for a planet under pressure: Interconnected challenges of a changing world call for sustainable solutions. *Current Opinion in Environmental Sustainability, 4*, 35–43. doi:10.1016/j.cosust.2011.12.002.

Bradley, D. (2014). A "new situation": China's evolving assessment of its security environment. *China Brief* 14(15). Retrieved from www.jamestown.org/programs/china-brief/single/?tx_ttnews%5Btt_news%5D=42690&tx_ttnews%5BbackPid%5D=25&cHash=a2e2aa7077cc6b608a3ab58390699076#.U-DP7Y1dXHQ.

Carew-Reid, J. (2017). The Mekong: Strategic environmental assessment of mainstream hydropower development in an international river basin. In P. Hirsch (Ed.), *Routledge handbook of the environment in Southeast Asia* (pp. 334–355). London, UK: Routledge.

Castella, J. C., Lestrelin, G., & Hett, C. (2013). Effects of landscape segregation on livelihood vulnerability. *Human Ecology, 41*, 63–76. doi:10.1007/s10745-012-9538-8.

CDKN. (2012). Managing climate extremes and disasters in Asia: Lessons from the SREX report. Climate and Development Knowledge Network, London. Retrieved from www.cdkn.org/srex.

Chartres, C. (2014). Is water scarcity a constraint to feeding Asia's growing population? *International Journal of Water Resources Development, 30*, 28–36. Retrieved from http://dx.doi.org/10.1080/07900627.2013.846713.

Contreras, A. (2017). Transboundary environmental politics in Southeast Asia: Issues, responses, and challenges. In P. Hirsch (Ed.), *Routledge handbook of the environment in Southeast Asia* (pp. 147–156). London, UK: Routledge.

Cui, S. (2013). Beyond history: Non-traditional security cooperation and the construction of Northeast Asian international society. *Journal of Contemporary China, 22*, 868–886.

Dean, K. (2017). Commentary. Philip Hirsch's "The shifting regional geopolitics of Mekong dams". *Political Geography, 58*, 128–130. Retrieved from https://doi.org/10.1016/j.polgeo.2016.10.007.

Dore, J., Lebel, L., & Molle, F. (2012). A framework for analysing transboundary water governance complexes, illustrated in the Mekong Region. *Journal of Hydrology, 466/467*, 23–36. doi:10.1016/j.jhydrol.2012.07.023.

Dudgeon, D. (2011). Asian river fishes in the Anthropocene: Threats and conservation challenges in an era of rapid environmental change. *Journal of Fish Biology, 79*, 1487–1524. doi:10.1111/j.1095-8649.2011.03086.

Earle, A., & Neal, M. (2017). Inclusive water governance. In E. Karan (Ed.), *Freshwater governance for the 21st century* (pp. 145–158). Berlin, Germany: Springer. doi:10.1007/978-3-319-43350-9_8.

Floyd, R., & Matthew, R. A. (Eds.). (2013). *Environmental security: Approaches and issues.* London, UK: Routledge.

Fox, J., Castella, J. C., & Ziegler, A. D. (2013). Swidden, rubber and carbon: Can REDD+ work for people and the environment in Montane Mainland Southeast Asia? *Global Environmental Change, 29,* 318–326. doi:10.1016/j.gloenvcha.2013.05.011.

Fukai, S., & Ouk, M. (2012). Increased productivity of rainfed lowland rice cropping systems of the Mekong region. *Crop and Pasture Science, 63,* 944–973. doi:10.1071/CP12294.

Giordano, M., Drieschova, A., Duncan, J. A., Sayama, Y., De Stefano, L., & Wolf, A. T. (2013). A review of the evolution and state of transboundary freshwater treaties. *International Environmental Agreements, 13,* 245–264. doi:10.1007/s10784-013-9211–8.

Glassman, J. (2010). *Bounding the Mekong: The Asian Development Bank, China, and Thailand.* Honolulu: University of Hawaii Press.

Goh, E. (2007). Developing the Mekong: Regionalism and regional security in China-Southeast Asian relations. *Adelphi Papers, 46,* 1–71.

Grumbine, R. E. (2014). Assessing environmental security in China. *Frontiers in Ecology and the Environment, 12,* 403–411. doi:10.1890/130147.

Grumbine, R. E., Dore, J., & Xu, J. (2012). Mekong hydropower: Drivers of change and governance challenges. *Frontiers in* Ecology *and the* Environment, *10,* 91–98. doi:10.1890/110146.

Grumbine, R. E., Nizami, A., Rana Tharu, B., Niraula, R., Su, Y., & Xu, J. C. (2015). *Water governance in the Asian Highlands.* ICRAF Working Paper 198. Kunming, People's Republic of China: World Agroforestry Centre East and Central Asia. doi:10.5716/WP15013.PDF.

Gupta, J. (2014). China, India formalize Brahmaputra Agreement. Retrieved from www.thethirdpole.net/china-india-formalise-brahmaputra-agreement/.

Han, H. (2017). China, an upstream hegemon: A destabilizer for the governance of the Mekong River? *Pac Focus, 32,* 30–55. doi:10.1111/pafo.12085.

Hanson, S., Nicholls, R., Ranger, N., Hallegatte, S., Corfee-Morlot, J., Herweijer, C., & Chateau, J. (2011). A global ranking of port cities with high exposure to climate extremes. *Climate Change, 104,* 89–111. doi:10.1007/s10584-010-9977-4.

He, D., Wu, R., Feng, Y., Li, Y., Ding, C., Wang, W., & Yu, D. W. (2014). Review. China's transboundary waters: New paradigms for water and ecological security through applied ecology. *Journal of Applied Ecology, 51,* 1159–1168. doi:10.1111/1365-2664.12298.

Henning, T., Wang, W., Magee, D., & He, D. (2016). Yunnan's fast-paced large hydropower development. A powershed-based approach to critically assessing generation and consumption paradigms. *Water Alternatives, 8,* 476. doi:10.3390/w8100476.

Hirsch, P. (2016). The shifting regional geopolitics of Mekong river dams. *Political* Geography, *51,* 63–74. Retrieved from https://doi.org/10.1016/j.polgeo.2016.10.007.

Hirsch, P., & Jensen, K. M. (2006). *National interests and transboundary water governance in the Mekong.* Sydney, NSW: Australian Mekong Research Centre.

Hoang, L., Lauri, H., Kummu, M., Koponen, J., van Vliet, M., Supit, I., … Ludwig, F. (2016). Mekong River flow and hydrological extremes under climate change. *Hydrology and Earth System Sciences, 20,* 3027–3041. doi:10.5194/hess-20–3027-2016.

Homer-Dixon, T. (1999). *Environment, scarcity, and violence.* Princeton, NJ: Princeton University Press.

Hortle, K. G. (2007). *Consumption and the yield of fish and other aquatic animals from the Lower Mekong Basin.* MRC Technical Paper No. 16, Vientiane, Laos. Mekong River Commission.

Hunt, L. (2016). Mekong River Commission faces radical change. Retrieved from http://thediplomat.com/2016/01/mekong-river-commission-faces-radical-change/.

ICEM. (2010). *Strategic environmental assessment of hydropower in the Mekong mainstream.* Vientiane, Laos: Mekong River Commission. www.mrcmekongrg/assets/Publications/Consultations/SEA-Hydropower/SEA-FR-summary-13oct.pdf.

IEA. (2015). *Southeast Asia energy outlook.* Paris, France: International Energy Agency.

IPCC. (2013). Summary for policymakers. In T. F. Stocker, D. Qin, G.-K. Plattner, M. Tignor, S. K. Allen, J. Boschung, A. Nauels, Y. Xia, V. Bex, & M. Pm (Eds.), *Climate change 2013: The physical science basis* (pp. 1–30). New York, NY: Cambridge University Press. doi:10.1017/CBO9781107415324.004.

Ke, J., & Gao, Q. (2013). Only one Mekong: Developing transboundary EIA procedures of Mekong River Basin. *Pace Environmental Law Review, 30*, 950–1004. Retrieved from http://digitalcommons.pace.edu/pelr/vol30/iss3/3.

Kondolf, G. M., Annandale, G., & Rubin, Z. (2015). Sediment starvation from dams in the Lower Mekong River basin: Magnitude of the effect and potential mitigation opportunities. E-proceedings of the *36th IAHR World Congress*, June 28, 2015–July 3, 2015, The Hague, The Netherlands. Retrieved from http://89.31.100.18/~iahrpapers/88661.pdf.

Kondolf, G. M., Rubin, Z. K., & Minear, J. T. (2014). Dams on the Mekong: Cumulative sediment starvation. *Water Resources Research, 50*, 5158–5169. doi:10.1002/2013WR014651/.

Kontgis, C., Schneide, A., Fox, J., Saksena, S., Spencer, J. H., & Castrence, M. (2014). Monitoring peri-urbanization in the greater Ho Chi Minh City metropolitan area. *Applied Geography, 53*, 377–388. doi:10.1016/j.apgeog.2014.06.029 0143-6228/.

Lebel, L., Naruchaikusol, S., & Juntopas, M. (2014). Transboundary flows of resources, goods, and services in the Mekong Region. In L. Lebel, C. T. Hoanh, C. Krittasudthacheewa, & R. Daniel (Eds.), *Climate risks, regional integration, and sustainability in the Mekong Region* (pp. 54–71). Petaling Jaya, Malaysia: Strategic Information and Resource Development Centre.

Loring, P. A., Gerlach, S. C., & Huntington, H. P. (2013). The new environmental security: Linking food, water, and energy for integrative and diagnostic social-ecological research. *Journal of Agriculture, Food Systems, and Community Development, 3*, 55–61. doi:10.5304/jafscd.2013.034.005.

Lutz, A. F., Imerzeel, W. W., Shrestha, A. B., & Bierkens, M. F. P. (2014). Consistent increase in High Asia's runoff due to increasing glacier melt and precipitation. *Nature Climate Change, 4*, 587–592. doi:10.1038/nclimate2237.

Marchand, M., Pham, D. Q., & Le, T. (2014). Mekong Delta: Living with water but for how long? *Built Environment, 40*, 230–243. doi:10.2148/benv.40.2.230.

McIntyre, O. (2015). Benefit-sharing and upstream/downstream cooperation for ecological protection of transboundary waters: Opportunities for China as an upstream state. *Water International, 40*, 48–70. Retrieved from http://dx.doi.org/10.1080/02508060.2014.990350.

Middleton, C., & Allouche, J. (2016). Watershed or powershed? Culture, hydropolitics, China and the 'Lancang-Mekong Cooperative Framework'. *Intl Spectator, 51*, 100–117. doi:10.1080/03932729.2016.1209385.

Middleton, C., & Dore, J. (2015). Transboundary water and electricity governance in mainland Southeast Asia. *International Journal of Water Governance, 3*, 93–120. doi:10.7564/14-IJWG54.

Ministry of Foreign Affairs, Peoples Republic of China. (2016). Sanya declaration of the first Lancang-Mekong Cooperation (LMC) leader's meeting. Retrieved from www.fmprc.gov.cn/mfa_eng/zxxx_662805/t1350039.shtml.

MRC (Mekong River Commission). (2016). *Basin development strategy*. Vientiane, Laos: Mekong River Commission.

MRC (Mekong River Commission). (2017). Regional stakeholders forum on the Pak Beng hydropower project and the Council Study. Luang Prabang, Laos PDR: Mekong River Commission. Retrieved from, www.mrcmekong.org/assets/Publications/Council-Study/Forum-report-for-website.pdf.

Nam, S., et al. (2015). Lower Mekong fisheries estimate to be worth around $17 billion a year. *Catch and Culture, 21*, 4–7.

Orr, S., Pittock, J., Chapagain, A., & Dumaresque, D. (2012). Dams on the Mekong River: Lost fish protein and the implications for land and water resources. *Global Environmental Change, 22*, 925–932. Retrieved from http://dx.doi.org/10.1016/j.gloenvcha.2012.06.002.

Osborne, M. (2004). *River at risk: The Mekong and the water politics of China and South East Asia*. Lowy Paper 02. Sydney, NSW: Lowy Institute of International Policy.

Ostrom, E. (1990). A general framework for analyzing sustainability of social–ecological systems. *Science, 325*, 419–22. doi:10.1126/science.1172133.

Pahl-Wostl, C. (2009). A conceptual framework for analyzing adaptive capacity and multi-level learning processes in resource governance regimes. *Global Environmental Change, 19*, 354–365. doi:10.1016/j.gloenvcha.2009.06.0.

Pahl-Wostl, C., Lebel, L., Knieper, C., & Nitikina, E. (2012). From applying panaceas to mastering complexity: Toward adaptive water governance in river basins. *Environmental Science & Policy, 23*, 24–34. Retrieved from http://dx.doi.org/10.1016/j.envsci.2012.07.014.

Pittock, J., Orr, S., Stevens, L., Aheeyar, M., & Smith, M. (2015). Tackling tradeoffs in the nexus of water, energy and food. *Aquatic Procedia, 5*, 58–68. Retrieved from http://dx.doi.org/10.1016/j.aqpro.2015.10.008.

Ptak, T. (2017). Considering multiple Chinas in the shifting regional geopolitics of Mekong river dams. *Political Geography, 58*, 136–138. Retrieved from https://doi.org/10.1016/j.polgeo.2016.09.007.

Rasenen, T. A., Koponen, J., Lauri, H., & Kummu, M. (2012). Downstream hydrological impacts of hydropower development in the upper Mekong Basin. *Water Resources Management, 26*, 3495–3513. doi:10.1007/s11269-012-0087-0.

Reuters. (2014). Thailand seeks LNG, new energy resources as gas reserves dwindle. Retrieved from http://uk.reuters.com/article/2014/01/09/thailand-energy-idUKL3N0KJ1L120140109.

Sadoff, C., & Grey, D. (2002). Beyond the river: The benefits of cooperation on international rivers. *Water Policy, 4*, 389–403. Retrieved from http://dx.doi.org/10.1016/S1366-7017(02)00035-1.

Sajor, E. (2017). Peri- urbanization and environmental issues in mega-urban regions. In P. Hirsch (Ed.), *Routledge handbook of the environment in Southeast Asia* (pp. 264–279). London, UK: Routledge.

Sithirith, M., Evers, J., & Gupta, J. (2016). Damming the Mekong tributaries: Water security and the 1995 MRC Agreement. *Water Policy, 18*, 1420–1435. doi:10.2166/wp.2016.003.

Suhardiman, D., & Giordano, M. (2014). Legal plurality: An analysis of power interplay in Mekong hydropower. *Annals of the Association of American Geographers, 104*, 973–988. Retrieved from http://dx.doi.org/10.1080/00045608.2014.925306.

Suhardiman, D., Giordano, M., & Molle, F. (2012). Scalar disconnect: The logic of transboundary water governance in the Mekong. *Society & Natural Resources, 25*, 572–586. Retrieved from http://dx.doi.org/10.1080/08941920.2011.604398.

Suhardiman, D., Giordano, M., & Molle, F. (2015). Between interests and worldviews: The narrow path of the Mekong River Commission. *Environment and Planning C Government and Policy, 33*, 99–217.

Suhardiman, D., Wichelns, D., Lestrelin, G., & Hoanh, C. T. (2013). Payments for ecosystem services in Vietnam: Market-based incentives or state control of resources? *Ecosystem Services, 5*, 94–101. doi:10.1016/j.ecoser.2013.06.001.

Tahseen, S., & Karney, B. (2017). Reviewing and critiquing published approaches to the sustainability assessment of hydropower. *Renewable and Sustainable Energy Reviews, 67*, 225–234. Retrieved from http://doi.org/10.1016/j.rser.2016.09.031.

TI (Transparency International). (2013). Corruption perceptions index. Transparency International, Berlin, Germany. Retrieved from www.transparency.org/cpi2013/results.

Tilt, B., & Gerkey, D. (2016). Dams and population displacement on China's Upper Mekong River: Implications for social capital and social-ecological resilience. *Global Environmental Change, 36*, 153–162. doi:10.1016/j.gloenvcha.2015.11.008.

TNC, WWF, University of Manchester. (2016). *Improving hydropower outcomes through systems-scale planning: An example from Myanmar.* Prepared for the UKs Department of International Development. Arlington, VA: TNC.

Tortajada, C. (2010). Water governance: Some critical issues. *International Journal of Water Resources Development, 26*, 297–307. Retrieved from http://dx.doi.org/10.1080/07900621003683298.

Tullos, D., Brown, P., Kibler, K., Magee, D., Tilt, B., & Wolf, A. (2010). Perspectives on the salience and magnitude of dam impacts for hydro development scenarios in China. *Water Alternatives, 3*, 71–90.

Tullos, D., Tilt, B., & Reidy-Leirmann, C. (2009). Introduction to the special issue: Understanding and linking the biophysical, socioeconomic and geopolitical effects of dams. *Journal of Environmental Management, 90*, S208–S223. doi:10.1016/j.jenvman.2008.08.018.

UN and ADB. (2012). *Green growth, resources and resilience. Environmental sustainability in Asia and the Pacific.* Bangkok, Thailand: United Nations and Asian Development Bank.

UNDESA. (2014). *World urbanization prospect, the 2014 revision.* New York, NY: Population Division, UN Department of Social and Economic Affairs.

UNESCAP. (2013). *Statistical yearbook for Asia and the Pacific.* Bangkok, Thailand: UN Economic and Social Commission for Asia and the Pacific.

Urban, F., Nordensvard, J., Khatri, D., & Wang, Y. (2013). An analysis of China's investment in the hydropower sector in the Greater Mekong Sub-Region. *Environment, Development and Sustainability, 15*, 301–324. doi:10.1007/s10668-012-9415-z.

USAID. (2013). *USAID Mekong ARCC: Climate change impact and adaptation study.* Bangkok, Thailand: USAID, Asia Regional Office.

van Leeuwen, C. J., Dan, N. P., & Dieperink, C. (2016). The challenge of water governance in Ho Chi Minh City. *Integrated Environmental Assessment and Management, 12*, 345–352. doi:10.1002/ieam.1664.

VBN (Vietnam Breaking News). (2016). DPM attends 2nd Lancang-Mekong foreign ministerial meeting. Retrieved from https://m.vietnambreakingnews.com/2016/12/dpm-attends-second-lancang-mekong-foreign-ministerial-meeting/.

Verbiest, J.-P. A. (2013). Regional cooperation and integration in the Mekong region. *Asian Economic Policy Review, 8*, 148–164. Retrieved from http://dx.doi.org/10.1111/aepr.12015.

Villamayor-Tomas, S., Avagyan, M., Firlus, M., Helbing, G., & Kabakova, M. (2016). Hydropower vs. fisheries conservation: A test of institutional design principles for common-pool resource management in the lower Mekong basin social-ecological system. *Ecology and Society, 21*(1), 3. Retrieved from http://dx.doi.org/10.5751/ES-08105-210103.

Webb, E., Jachowski, N. R. A., Phelps, J., Friess, D. A., Than, M. M., & Ziegler, A. D. (2014). Deforestation in the Ayeyarwady Delta and the conservation implications of an internationally-engaged Myanmar. *Global Environmental Change, 24*, 321–333. Retrieved from http://dx.doi.org/10.1016/j.gloenvcha.2013.10.007.

Webster, D., Cai, J., & Muller, L. (2014). The new face of peri-urbanization in East Asia. *Journal of Urban Affairs, 36*, 315–333. doi:10.1111/juaf.12104.

WLE Greater Mekong. (2015). *Dams in the Mekong Basin: Commissioned, under construction and planned dams, August, 2015*. Vientiane, Lao PDR: CGIAR Research Program on Water, Land and Ecosystems – Greater Mekong.

Wright, S. (2016). Mekong effort fails after years of lavish foreign funding. Retrieved from https://phys.org/news/2016-10-mekong-effort-years-lavish-foreign.html.

WWF. (2013). *Ecosystems in the Greater Mekong: Past trends, current status, possible futures*. Bangkok, Thailand: World Wide Fund for Nature.

Yale University. (2014). *Environmental performance index*. New Haven, CT: Yale University. Retrieved from http://epi.yale.edu/.

Yang, X., Lu, X., & Ran, L. (2016). Sustaining China's large rivers: River development policy, impacts, institutional issues and strategies for future improvement. *GeoForum, 69*, 1–4. Retrieved from http://dx.doi.org/10.1016/j.geoforum.2015.11.019.

Yee, T. H. (2016). Drought-hit Thailand taps Mekong water. Straits Times, Singapore. Retrieved from www.straitstimes.com/asia/se-asia/drought-hit-thailand-taps-mekong-water.

Yi, Z-F., Wong, G., Cannon, C. H., Xu, J., Beckshaeffer, P., & Swetnam, R. D. (2014). Can carbon-trading schemes help to protect China's most diverse forest ecosystems? A case study from Xishuangbanna, Yunnan. *Land Use Policy, 38*, 646–656. Retrieved from http://dx.doi.org/10.1016/j.landusepol.2013.12.013.

Zhang, L., Mol, A., & He, G. (2016). Transparency and information disclosure in China's environmental governance. *Current Opinion in Environmental Sustainability, 18*, 17–24. Retrieved from http://dx.doi.org/10.1016/j.cosust.2015.03.009.

Ziv, G., Baran, E., Nam, S., Rodriguez-Iturbe, I., & Levin, S. A. (2012). Trading-off fish biodiversity, food security, and hydropower in the Mekong River Basin. *PNAS*, 109, 5609–5614. doi:10.1073/pnas.1201423109.

Zomer, R., Xu, J., Wang, M., Trabucco, A., & Li, Z. (2015). Projected impacts of climate change on the effect of the existing protected area network for biodiversity conservation within Yunnan Province. *Biological Conservation, 184*, 335–345. Retrieved from http://dx.doi.org/10.1016/j.biocon.2015.01.031.

Zomer, R. J., Trabucco, A., Wang, M. C., & Xu, J. C. (2016). *Projected climate change impact on hydrology, bioclimatic conditions, and terrestrial ecosystems in the Asian Highlands*. ICRAF Working Paper 222. World Agroforestry Centre East and Central Asia.

8 Conceptualizing Chinese engagement in Myanmar

An analysis of the Mong Ton and Hat Gyi Dam projects

Julian Kirchherr

Introduction

This chapter conceptualizes Chinese engagement in Southeast Asian dam projects. Chinese dam developers allegedly dominate the global dam industry (Urban, Nordensvärd, Khatri, & Wang, 2015, p. 577 ff.; Verhoeven, 2015, p. 178 ff.). Yet, precise data on the overall engagement of Chinese dam developers overseas is lacking. Yeophantong (2013) reports that Chinese players are linked to more than 300 dam projects in 74 countries worldwide, but this number equates to only 8 per cent of the total 3,700 dam projects worldwide (planned or under construction, with a size of ≥1 MW) recently identified by Zarfl, Lumsdon, Berlekamp, Tydecks, and Tockner (2014). International Rivers (2014), an NGO mostly advocating against large dams, lists a mere 209 dam projects with Chinese engagement worldwide. Whereas Yeophantong (2013) does not critically discuss the reliability of the data presented, International Rivers (2014) acknowledges that "we [...] cannot vouch for the accuracy of the information" which was mostly collected from media reports as well as government and company websites.

Whereas data on Chinese engagement in dam projects overseas is ambiguous, scholars such as Hensengerth (2015), Matthews and Motta (2015), and Gleitsmann (2015) are largely unanimous in their analysis of Southeast Asian dam development with Chinese involvement, conceptualizing this engagement as being driven by China's political leadership as part of a package that yields various political, economic, and social benefits for China, but exploits non-Chinese contractual parties of the project (more details in the next section). This chapter aims to rebut this notion. It is argued that dam projects with Chinese involvement in Southeast Asia can also be driven by a Chinese dam developer as standalone projects that yield growth and profit for the Chinese dam developer, while bringing benefits for the remaining contractual parties involved. An analysis of the Mong Ton and Hat Gyi Dam projects, which are among seven dam projects to be built on Myanmar's Salween River, and feature the involvement of the Chinese dam developers China Three Gorges Corporation (CTGC) and Sinohydro, is presented to support this argument.

These two case studies are analysed from the Chinese, Thai, and Burmese engagement perspective (which includes the perspectives of dam developers, policy-makers, NGOs, etc.) to ensure a comprehensive view on these projects. Yet the role of lenders in these projects is not analysed in the case studies due to the lack of access to information regarding lenders. Challenges faced while seeking information for this study are discussed in the section 'Methods'.

On the organization of the remainder of this chapter: previous scholarly literature on dam projects with Chinese engagement is synthesized in the next section, followed by a discussion of methods. An overview on the dam projects pursued on the Salween River and in Myanmar is presented before the analysis of the cases of the Mong Ton and Hat Gyi Dam projects on Myanmar's Salween River. The argument is summarized in the final section.

Literature review

Academic research on Chinese dam developers overseas in English is burgeoning (Kirchherr, Pohlner, & Charles, 2016, p. 122 ff.). Relevant key analyses have been carried out by Middleton (2008), McDonald, Bosshard and Brewer (2009), Hensengerth (2012), Tan-Mullins and Mohan (2012), Matthews and Motta (2013), Urban, Nordensvärd, Khatri and Wang (2013), Chellaney (2014), Gleitsmann (2015), Hensengerth (2015), Lamb and Dao (2015), Matthews and Motta (2015), Nordensvard, Urban and Mang (2015), Kiik (2016), Kirchherr, Charles and Walton (2016) and Kirchherr, Disselhoff, and Charles (2016).

Three observations stand out when examining this body of literature. First, Southeast Asian dam projects with Chinese engagement are frequently described as projects directly driven by China's political leadership. According to Hensengerth (2015, p. 520), negotiations regarding Cambodia's Kamchay Dam were conducted "between Chinese and Cambodian government officials". Both the dam developer and the lender are state-owned enterprises (SOEs) whose stock are largely retained by the central Chinese government (McDonald et al., 2009, p. 298). SOEs are seen as an extended arm of China's political leadership at best. For instance, Matthews and Motta (2015, p. 6274) write that "the Chinese government and its SOEs have employed a number of [...] narratives [...] of hydropower", a depiction largely echoed by Gleitsmann (2015, p. 65 ff.).

Second, scholars usually point out that the projects in question would be part of a larger deal. For instance, Matthews and Motta (2013, p. 4) argue that dam projects with Chinese involvement in Southeast Asia "must be viewed as a package rather than separate initiatives". This claim is echoed by Urban et al. (2013), Nordensvard et al. (2015), as well as Hensengerth (2012) and Kirchherr, Disselhoff, and Charles (2016). However, the latter two studies primarily focus on dam projects with Chinese involvement in Africa. Political, economic, and social benefits are believed to accrue via such a package. Middleton (2008, p. 51 ff.) and Chellaney (2014) argue that these projects would help expand China's political influence in the region but both authors remain rather vague regarding the exact mechanisms that can turn a dam project in a Southeast Asian country into political influence for China (on dams and power: Moore, 1998; McCully, 2001), and that these projects would be pursued to export their electricity to

China (Matthews & Motta, 2015, p. 6279 ff.; Urban et al., 2013, p. 305 ff.) and be designed to ensure that China's own rivers remain untouched and thus dam-induced resettlement is avoided in China (Urban et al., 2013, p. 305 ff.).

Some works Tan-Mullins & Mohan, 2012; Urban et al., 2013; Kirchherr, Disselhoff, et al., 2016) note that dam projects with Chinese engagement are also pursued mainly because the Chinese dam developer involved aims to realize business growth and profit. Yet this statement is restricted to dam projects with Chinese involvement in Africa and explicitly excludes projects in Asia which would "pose a stark contrast to Chinese dams in Africa [where] motives such as business opportunities [are] key" (Urban et al., 2013, p. 313). It is imaginable that electricity exports to China are initiated primarily because the dam developer involved aims to realize a business profit assuming electricity prices in China are higher than in the country the dam is built in. However, the works of some scholars (Matthews & Motta, 2013; Urban et al., 2013) which did not suggest this argument proposed that electricity exports to China would be undertaken to supply sufficient and affordable energy for China. At least implicit in this suggestion is the allegation that these projects would exploit the resources of the country the dam is built in – which relates to the third overall observation.

Third, Southeast Asian dam projects with Chinese involvement are oftentimes believed to lead to win-lose results with China winning and the remaining contractual parties losing out. Lamb and Dao (2015, p. 2) provide an example of this viewpoint arguing that Chinese-led package dam projects would "suck resources (or is it blood?)" from Southeast Asian countries, while Kiik (2016, p. 22) writes, in an analysis of the Myitsone Dam in Myanmar, that this project package would be perceived as "Chinese exploitation and 'takeover' of Myanmar". This claim is also echoed by Kirchherr, Charles, and Walton (2016).

In sum, it can be argued that Chinese engagement in Southeast Asian dam projects is conceptualized as hegemonic by many current works – with the term 'hegemon' used with a negative connotation particularly by Chellaney (2014). The negative connotation of the term is adopted for this chapter. While it is acknowledged that the term can also carry a positive one, the negative one seems to be dominant in the social science literature on water (Furlong, 2006; Warner & Zeitoun, 2008, p. 805 ff.).

The conceptualization of Chinese engagement in Southeast Asia presented in the scholarly literature written in English is tested in this chapter, but it is acknowledged that any synthesis of mostly qualitative literature is at least partly subjective.

Methods

Two case studies on Myanmar's Salween River, the Mong Ton and the Hat Gyi Dam projects, were chosen for in-depth investigation for this chapter. This choice was driven by two criteria.

First, only dam projects on the Salween River were considered for in-depth investigation that did not seem to fit the current scholarly conceptualization of Chinese engagement overseas according to discussions with experts and a preliminary skimming of press reports. This would ensure that the case studies researched would likely further nuance scholarly writings on the topic. The Mong Ton Dam project and the Hat Gyi Dam project were identified as those two dam projects with Chinese engagement on the Salween River whose electricity would be exported to Thailand. Yet, scholarly writing on the topic suggested that electricity generated from dam projects with Chinese involvement in China's neighbouring countries would be exported to China, as outlined in the previous section.

Second, only dam projects on the Salween River which had been the subject of earlier scholarly study and significant press reporting were considered for in-depth investigation. This would ensure that interview data collected could be triangulated which is particularly essential when carrying out research under less than optimal conditions (further discussed below). Numerous press reports and scholarly studies on the Mong Ton Dam project and the Hat Gyi Dam project such as Kirchherr, Charles, et al. (2016) and Lamb and Dao (2015) were identified.

The two case studies presented in this chapter were analysed via semi-structured interviews as well as a systematic review of scholarly writings on Chinese engagement overseas and the Salween River and relevant news articles.

Semi-structured interviews

This chapter is based on 79 semi-structured interviews carried out from April to August 2015 and February to June 2016. Interviews have been conducted, inter alios, with senior government officials at the local and national levels in Myanmar, local NGOs in Myanmar, China and Thailand, international NGOs as well as with relevant Burmese and Chinese dam developers. In contrast, Hensengerth (2015), Lamb and Dao (2015) and other scholars who published on the same topic have not carried out interviews with Chinese dam developers. An overview of interviews mirroring the depiction of Siciliano, Urban, Tan-Mullins, Pichdara and Kim (2016, p. 5) is presented in Table 8.1. Given the sensitive nature of the topic, all interviewees were assured anonymity. Unique interview codes are used throughout this chapter: the first letter indicates the mode of interviews (T for telephone, F for face-to-face, O for online survey/e-mail), the second letter indicates the type (A for academia, AA for adversely affected communities, G for government, I for international donor, NI for international NGO, NL for local NGO, P for private sector), and the number indicates an interview number within a type. Most interviews were carried out face-to-face in Myanmar, Thailand, and China or via telephone/Skype, while some were conducted by e-mail/online survey. Information on interviewee recruiting and sample termination can be found in Kirchherr, Matthews, Charles and Walton (2017).

Some gaps in information exist in the interview data collected for this chapter because of the difficulties inherent in field research in Myanmar and in this topic, as described by Lamb and Dao (2015, p. 13) and Urban et al. (2013, p. 306 ff.). First, no interviews have been carried out with communities affected by the two dam projects specifically studied for this chapter. This is

Table 8.1 Overview of interviews

Interviewee group	*Number of interviews*
Academia	8
Adversely-affected communities	4
Government	5
International donor	6
NGO (international)	14
NGO (local)	15
Private sector	27
Total	*79*

Source: Author's depiction.

because the NGO representative (which the author was collaborating with) argued that it would be too dangerous even for their local staff to visit these communities during the time of field research (FNL2). Simpson (2013, p. 140) also found that ethnic conflicts continuing both in the relevant Shan and Karen State in Myanmar make it difficult for researchers to access these states, even though research conditions in Myanmar have generally improved since its opening up in 2010 (Lidauer, 2012, p. 89 ff.). Second, no interview has been carried out with a Thai dam developer because various interview requests were declined. Third, no interviews have been carried out with potential lenders such as China Exim Bank (CEB) because interview requests were also declined by these lenders. This indicates that the Southeast Asian dam industry is secretive and thus difficult for scholars to access (FP4; TA1).

Methodological triangulation, as described by Denzin (1978), was chosen as an approach to address these gaps. Data from semi-structured interviews are combined with a systematic collection and review of (a) scholarly writings on Chinese engagement overseas and the Salween River as well as (b) relevant news articles. Search results revealed at least partially the perspectives of those not directly interviewed for this chapter, for example, the viewpoints of the relevant Thai dam developer.

Systematic review of scholarly writings on Chinese engagement overseas and the Salween River

The systematic review of the scholarly literature on Chinese dam developers' engagement overseas and on the Salween dams was undertaken by carrying out keyword searches in several databases such as Thomson Reuters' Web of Science, the University of Oxford Search Oxford Libraries Online (SOLO), or Elsevier's Scopus. Searches included any scholarly journal articles, grey literature, book chapters, and books that featured (combinations of) relevant keywords, e.g. 'Salween river', 'Mong Ton Dam', 'Hat Gyi Dam', or 'Chinese dam developers'. Results of these searches were presented in the previous section of this chapter. It is noted that scholarly literature written in Chinese is not included in this study because the author of this chapter does not speak Chinese. This is not considered a major limitation because Chinese scholars working on Chinese engagement in dam projects overseas such as May Tan-Mullins and Bingqin Li publish their results in English to join the international scientific discourse on this topic.

Systematic review of relevant news articles

A Google News Archive search was conducted for this chapter with the keywords 'Mong Ton Dam' and 'Hat Gyi Dam' to ensure a holistic examination of relevant news articles. No limit was set for the time period with the search yielding 50 results. All articles found were reviewed by the author of this chapter. The list of articles found is provided in the supplementary material. While news articles are frequently used as data sources in studies comparable to this one, for example Urban et al. (2013) or Matthews and Motta (2015), it is acknowledged that news articles (which include articles from NGOs such as International Rivers or Burma Rivers Network) are less reliable than peer-reviewed sources. Hence, the author of this chapter attempted, whenever possible, to use information from semi-structured interviews or peer-reviewed sources instead of news articles. The author also exercised caution when sourcing information from news articles for this chapter.

Dam development on the Salween River and in Myanmar

This section provides the background on dam development on the Salween River and in Myanmar in order to contextualize the case studies.

The Salween River with a length of 2,800 km is the last remaining undammed major river ecosystem in mainland Southeast Asia (Mellino, 2016). The river originates in the Tibetan Plateau and flows through China as the Nu River, before becoming the Salween River in Myanmar and Thailand and emptying into the Andaman Sea (Figure 8.1) (Deetes, 2016). At least 6 million people in the Salween watershed depend on the river for their livelihoods (WWF, 2016).

Dam development proposals for the Nu River were collected from potential developers from 1999 onwards. According to formal reports, there were thirteen Nu River hydropower projects with a total capacity of 21 GW in 2003 (Magee & McDonald, 2006, p. 47; Tullos et al., 2013, p. 9). The planned projects were initially approved by China's National Reform and Development Commission (NRDC), the macroeconomic management agency under the State Council, China's chief administrative authority (Tullos et al., 2013). However, this approval "set off a furor among Chinese environmentalists" (Ramzy, 2013) and international environmental NGOs (Tullos et al., 2013, p. 11). In contrast, Tilt (2014, p. 98 ff.) notes that relatively little protest by the communities to be displaced "due largely to the lack of information about how projects are proceeding, weak capacity to mount a campaign [...] and the high political risks involved in any opposition strategy".

As a result of the environmentalists' resistance, the proposed projects were abruptly suspended by China's then Prime Minister, Wen Jiabao, in 2004 (Mertha, 2008, p. 160 ff.) in order to further study the projects' environmental and social impacts (OG1), and this led to a "rare victory" (Ramzy, 2013) for activists engaged in China.

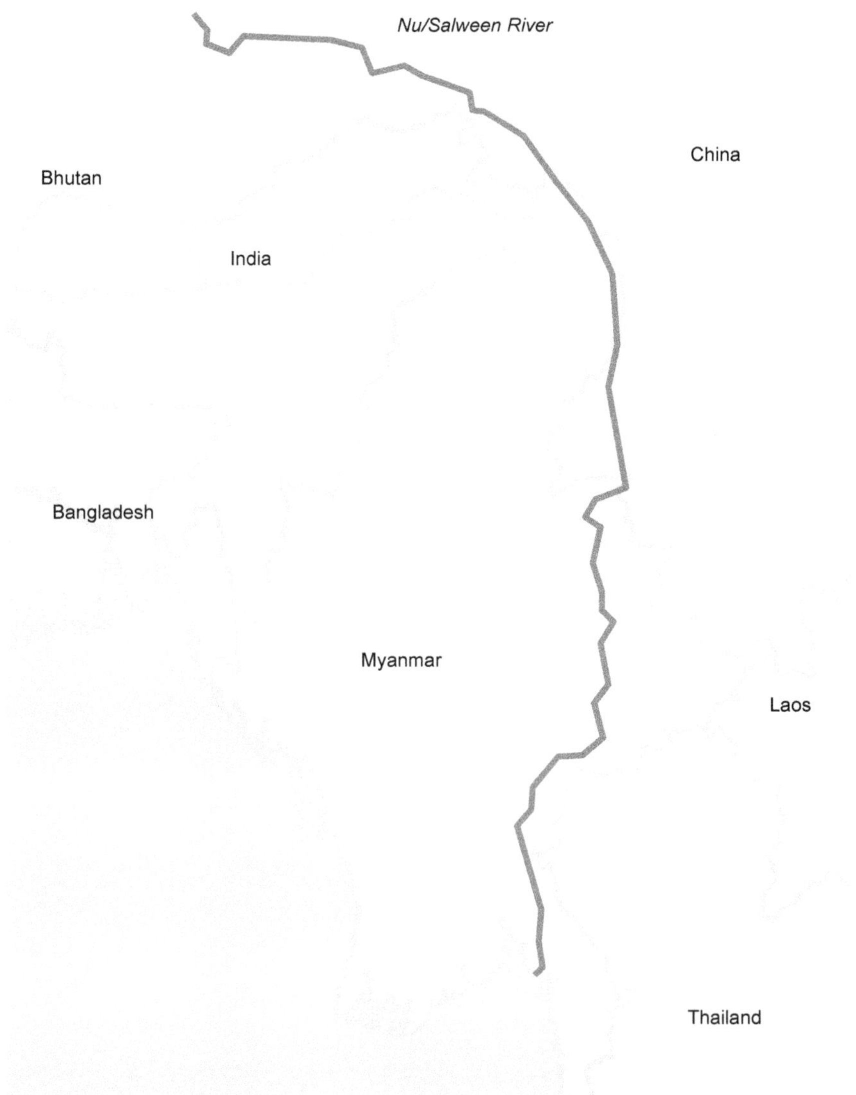

Figure 8.1 The Nu/Salween River.
Source: Author's depiction.

Nine years ago, Mertha (2008, p. 162), who has conducted the most comprehensive analysis on the protests against the Nu River hydropower projects, predicted ambiguity regarding their future because "Chinese politics is not linear". Indeed, the construction of the projects was reported to have at least partially resumed in 2011 (MacLeod, 2011). But according to a recent source, national government officials were said to be less keen to pursue the projects again (Leavenworth, 2016).

In addition, multiple projects have been planned for the Salween River since 1990 (Simpson, 2013). Currently there are seven projects waiting to be implemented featuring a total capacity of up to almost 22 GW – a capacity even 1 GW greater than that of the envisaged Nu River cascade. These projects are depicted in Table 8.2 which is mostly based on NGO information and thus caution is required regarding the information presented. Simpson (2013) notes that these projects have been also extremely controversial among civil society and project-affected communities. Myanmar's authoritarian regime attempted to suppress much of this opposition and various activists who fled to Thailand continued to oppose the projects until the 2011 regime change (FNL1; Simpson, 2013). Opposition was intensified when 122 civil society organizations in Myanmar supported the 2015 launch of the 'Save the Salween' campaign (OP3; FNL2; Naing, 2014). The current national government in Myanmar which has been in power since March 2016 has not revealed its stance on the projects yet (Aung, 2016).

Overall, a major dam development boom in Myanmar is underway because as many as 45 dams are currently included in the planning phase (Brennan & Doring, 2014). The seven projects proposed for the Salween River thus only

Table 8.2 List of dam projects to be developed on the Salween River

Project	*Capacity (MW)*	*Developer*	*Power Purchasing Agreement (PPA)*
Upper Thanlwin Dam	1400	Hanergy Holding Group (China) Asia World (Myanmar)	PPA not yet signed; power likely exported to China
Nawngpha Dam	1200	HydroChina (China)	90% to China
Mong Ton Dam	7000	China Three Gorges Corporation (CTGC) (China) Electricity Generating Authority of Thailand (EGAT) (Thailand) International Group of Entrepreneurs (IGE) (Myanmar)	90% to Thailand
Ywathit Dam	600–4500	China Datang (China) Shwe Taung Hydropower (Myanmar)	Unknown
Wei Gyi Dam	4,540–5,600	EGAT (Thailand) Myanmar Electric Power Enterprise (MEPE) (Myanmar)	PPA not yet signed; power likely to be exported to Thailand
Dagwin Dam	792	EGAT (Thailand) Electric Power Development Company (EPDC) (Japan)	PPA not yet signed; power likely to be exported to Thailand
Hat Gyi Dam	1,360	EGAT (Thailand) Sinohydro (China) MEPE (Myanmar)	90% to Thailand

Source: Burma Rivers Network (BRN) (2017); data from semi-structured interview.

equate to 15 per cent of the dams currently planned in Myanmar. Myanmar's most well-known dam project is most likely the Myitsone Dam in Kachin State. Its suspension in 2011 was widely seen as a symbol of Myanmar's transition towards democracy (Kirchherr, Charles, et al., 2016). The 6,000 MW project is pursued by the Chinese dam developer China Power Investment Corporation (CPI). With CPI as lead developer, 90 per cent of the dam's electricity would be exported to Southern China's Yunnan province and USD 17 billion would be paid to the Burmese government over a period of 50 years (Kiik, 2016; Kirchherr, Charles, et al., 2016; TP10). Since Yunnan province has repeatedly reported an electricity surplus, electricity is planned to be further exported from Yunnan province via China Southern Power Grid, an electric utility, to neighbouring provinces and even Shanghai (Xuecui, 2013).

Chinese engagement in the Mong Ton and Hat Gyi Dam projects

This chapter has presented three observations by scholars regarding Chinese engagement in Southeast Asian dam projects. This section is structured alongside the three observations arguing that these observations, and thus also the overall conceptualization of Chinese engagement in Southeast Asian dam projects are to be rebutted in the cases of the Mong Ton and Hat Gyi dam projects on Myanmar's Salween River. Key facts regarding these projects are presented in Table 8.3.

Table 8.3 Key facts regarding the Mong Ton Dam and the Hat Gyi Dam

	Mong Ton Dam	*Hat Gyi Dam*
Capacity (MW)	7,000 (largest hydroelectric power plant in mainland Southeast Asia and 6th largest worldwide if completed)	1,350 (projected to be the first of Myanmar's Salween dams to be completed)
Resettlement	12,000 people[1]	5,000 people
Lead developer	EGAT (Thailand)	EGAT (Thailand)
Project shares	EGAT (Thailand): 40% CTGC (China): 40% IGE (Myanmar): 20%	EGAT (Thailand): Minority Sinohydro (China): Majority MEPE (Myanmar): Minority
Contractual agreement	Build-operate-transfer (BOT) project Concession period of 30 years (extendable twice for 5 years each)	Engineering-procurement-construction (EPC) project
Environmental and Social Impact Assessment (ESIA)	Completed in 2015 Carried out by SMEC, Australian consultancy	Completed in 2008 Carried out by Chula Unisearch, Thai consultancy

Sources: Burma Rivers Network (2016), Kirchherr, Charles, et al. (2016), Lamb and Dao (2015), Platts (2015), Samarkand (2015) and Naing (2008); data from semi-structured interviews.

1 Samarkand (2015) notes that 300,000 people have been displaced around the dam site since 1996. These displacements are at least partly due to ethnic conflicts

Main driving actor

The first observation identified in the scholarly literature held that Chinese political leadership would directly drive Chinese dam development overseas. However, the research findings suggest that the Thai government initiated both the Mong Ton and the Hat Gyi Dam project.

The Burmese and Thai government started negotiations (initiated by the Thai government) regarding cooperation on hydropower development on the Salween River in 1997. A Memorandum of Understanding (MoU) was signed between Thailand's Minister to the Prime Minister's Office, Sompoing Amornvivat, and Myanmar's Minister of Energy, Khin Maung Thein, in July 1997. The MoU originally set out that up to 1.5 GW of electric power would be exported from Myanmar to Thailand by 2010 – a target not reached at the time of this writing (which is early 2017). Both the Mong Ton Dam project which was originally called Ta Sang project and the Hat Gyi Dam project were part of this MoU (OG1; OP5).

The original lead developer of the Mong Ton project was not EGAT, but another Thai developer MDX Group, which commenced initial construction works in 2004. Yet, the contract was terminated in 2009 because the project did not proceed as fast as the Burmese government had envisaged. Only two days upon contract termination, a new MoU was signed for the development of the Mong Ton Dam project. Its project site is only 10 km upstream of the original Ta Sang site with the EGAT as the lead developer as well as CTGC and IGE as additional developers (OG1). Contracts for the Hat Gyi Dam were signed in 2006 with EGAT also as the lead developer (Lamb & Dao, 2015, p. 13 ff.) and Sinohydro and MEPE as additional developers (Naing, 2016). Discussions between EGAT and the Burmese government had started in 2005 and EGAT was acting as a substitute for the Thai government in these discussions (OG1). EGAT has been reported to be a key implementer of the Thai government's energy policy strategy previously (Matthews, 2012) with EGAT being significantly intertwined particularly with Thailand's Ministry of Energy (MoE) and the Energy Regulatory Commission (ERC) until today (the process of liberalizing Thailand's energy sector began in 2007, but not completed [IEA, 2016]).

Both Burmese private sector players involved in the projects, IGE and MEPE, were also found to be significantly intertwined with their government. IGE is owned by the sons of the late minister U Aung Thaung, one of the wealthiest political figures in Myanmar (Moe & Ramzy, 2015; OG1) and the various businesses of U Aung Thaung's sons are reported to have particularly grown while their father was Minister for Industry from 1997 to 2011 (Kachin News, 2014). Meanwhile, MEPE is formally organized as a department within the Ministry of Electric Power (MOEP) since 1989 (MOEP is now the Ministry of Electricity and Energy [MOEE), 2017]. The Burmese government initiated the involvement of IGE and MEPE in the two case studies ex officio (by rights) with a Burmese partner being legally required for foreign companies in most business endeavours (Martov, 2012; Turnell, 2014, p. 185 ff.).

Meanwhile, the involvement of Chinese dam developers was initiated by these developers. Chinese dam developers (including CTGC and Sinohydro) approached the MOEP from 2006 onwards to discuss possibilities of hydropower development on the Salween River (OG1). One of the first Chinese dam developers reaching out to MOEP was China Huadian Group which held the development rights on the Nu River cascade (Magee & McDonald, 2006, p. 48 ff.; OG1), but lost these projects after the suspension of the cascade in 2004. Notably, China Huadian Group did not manage to secure any project involvement on Myanmar's Salween River (Table 8.2). No Chinese government officials were reported to take part in the meetings between Chinese dam developers and MOEP (OG1). It was also not suggested that the dam developer would be the extended arm (representative) of Chinese government officials (OG1).

Hence, evidence is lacking in these cases to argue that Chinese political leadership drove the Mong Ton and Hat Gyi Dam projects directly. It is acknowledged, however, that the Chinese government prepared the ground for CTGC's and Sinohydro's engagement and thus drove their involvement indirectly via its Going Out Policy adopted in 2001 to encourage Chinese SOEs to expand their operations abroad. Discussions regarding China's Going Out Policy can be found in Murphy (2008), Nordensvard et al. (2015), or Kirchherr et al. (2017). The Burmese government and Burmese dam developers did not appear to stir the course of events either, but were approached because of legal obligations. The initial approach was undertaken by the Thai government with its Minister to the Prime Minister's Office, Sompoing Amornvivat, who is thus the main driving actor. In the next section, the main benefits sought via this approach are presented.

Type of deal

The second observation identified in the scholarly literature held that single dam projects with Chinese involvement would be part of a larger deal from the Chinese perspective. Typical deal elements described by scholars are related to political, economic, and social benefits for China. While no such deal elements from the Chinese perspective were reported for both projects investigated, deal elements were found on the part of the Thai and Burmese.

While it could be hypothesized that Chinese officials encouraged CTGC and Sinohydro to take part in the projects to ensure a Chinese foothold in the country with political benefits possibly resulting from this foothold, no supporting evidence was found for this hypothesis. The electricity generated from both projects is not an economic benefit to China, as outlined previously, and thus no river in China is left untouched and no resettlement in China is avoided during these projects. It is further noted that the Upper Thanlwin Dam and Nawngpha Dam are the only projects on Myanmar's Salween River dams featuring future electricity exports to China, as shown in Table 8.2. These exports total a capacity of merely 2.3 GW with the Nu River cascade featuring a capacity of 21 GW. Thus, it can also not be argued that the multiple Salween River dams would be a substitute from the Chinese perspective for the Nu River cascade.

However, it is acknowledged that the Mong Ton and Hat Gyi Dam projects were and are part of a larger deal between the Thai and the Burmese government, as outlined previously. No political benefits were apparently sought via this deal from the Thai side, according to the research carried out. Rather, both economic as well as social benefits drove this deal. "[This] is all about energy security [for Thailand]", a consultant said (FP9). Thailand has consistently experienced rapid electricity demand growth since the early 1990s, with power consumption growing by 5 per cent a year on average (IEA, 2016). The country's hydropower potential stands at 15 GW – four times its current installed capacity (Aroonrat & Wongwises, 2015, p. 74). However, no large dams have been completed in Thailand since the Pak Mun Dam (completed in 1994) due to the fierce resistance of civil society and project-affected communities against this infrastructure (Bakker, 1999; Sneddon & Fox, 2008).

As a consequence of this resistance, Thai policy-makers started searching for sources of electricity in neighbouring countries (Hirsch, 2010). A notable result of this search is Laos' operational 1,070 MW Nam Theun 2 Dam. With 93 per cent of its electricity exported to Thailand, this dam is thus "sending more hydropower across national borders than any other project in the history of Southeast Asia" (Baird & Quastel, 2015, p. 1224). If completed, the Mong Ton Dam could break this record, even though Thailand does not intend to entirely depend upon energy imports from neighbouring countries. Thailand continues to maintain at least partial energy self-sufficiency. Its target policy is to cap the share of electricity imported at 15 per cent from 2020 onwards (IEA, 2016).

Not political, but economic and social benefits were also suggested regarding Burmese involvement. A relevant Burmese dam developer interviewed said that the firm had entered one of the two dam projects studied in order to "provide a source of income for Myanmar through [...] energy sales" (OP5). It was further told that revenues from energy sales would be used for "local job creation [and] development of local economies" (OP5) (which could be deemed social benefits), but no further details were provided by the interviewee. The developer also did not outline how profitable the dam endeavour at question would be for the company. Large dams typically take 20 years to amortize (Kirchherr, Disselhoff, et al., 2016).

Meanwhile, vague information provided supports the claim that benefits sought via these projects benefit Burmese policy-makers and businessmen rather than the people of Myanmar. The claim is also strengthened by the close intertwinement of IGE and MEPE with the Burmese government, outlined in the previous section. For instance, a former civil servant who worked in the Office of the President of the Union of Myanmar argued that one large dam project in Myanmar "creates [illegitimate] generational wealth for many public sector individuals" (TG2). No further evidence was given to support this argument though. Such a claim should be treated with great caution.

Furthermore, the research carried out suggests that the main benefit sought by CTGC and Sinohydro via the two dam projects studied are business growth and profit – benefits suggested by scholars studying Chinese engagement in Africa, as outlined previously. Chinese dam developers can only explore certain rivers because different rivers are assigned to different companies for development. For instance, CTGC is only allowed to develop the Yangtze River (TNI4). After a company is assigned to build key dams on the Chinese part of the river, overseas expansion is necessary to continue growing (TNI1; TNI2; TNI4). CTGC will have completed its final large dam project on the Yangtze River in 2020 and is thus actively looking for growth in overseas markets via standalone projects (Reuters, 2014). For instance, CTGC has set up a joint venture with Utility Energias de Portugal (EDP), a Portuguese dam developer, to pursue large dam projects in Latin America (de Clercq, 2015; TP8). Overall, the company aims to gain 25–30 per cent of its profits from overseas projects via the realization of these growth opportunities (International Rivers, 2016) and the potential Mong Ton project. Meanwhile, Sinohydro is keen to further expand its share of 50 per cent in the global hydropower construction market (CHINCOLD, 2009) and it views the Hat Gyi Dam as "a lucrative business" (Gleitsmann, 2015, p. 59) that would help in achieving this aim.

Hence, from the Chinese perspective, both the Mong Ton and Hat Gyi Dam projects appear as standalone projects pursued for growth and profit reasons. However, deal elements were found from the Thai and Burmese perspective because both sides were keen to secure both economic and social benefits. Questions were also raised over whether the Burmese side pursued these projects for personal gains. The next section is a discussion on whether these benefits can be realized.

Project results

The third observation outlined in the scholarly literature held that Southeast Asian dam projects with Chinese involvement would lead to win-lose results with China winning and the remaining contractual parties losing out. However, the research carried out suggests that both the Burmese and Thai players at least expect positive results from CTGC's and Sinohydro's involvement in the respective projects. Meanwhile, the deal between the Thai and Burmese governments is difficult to assess.

Interviewees such as TP8 and FP4 argued that CTGC was involved in this specific project because only this developer would be able to develop a project of such a scale and that the project may not be possible to complete without CTGC's engagement. CTGC may be the most experienced mega-dam developer globally, having constructed the 22.5 GW Three Gorges Dam, the largest hydroelectric power station in the world (McDonald et al., 2009; Wilmsen, Webber, & Yuefang, 2011). Meanwhile, Sinohydro's vast capabilities for constructing large dams were also repeatedly praised by interviewees including TP6 and TP8. Already, Magee and McDonald (2006, p. 49 ff.), McDonald et al. (2009, p. 297 ff.), and interviewees such as TP8 noted that Chinese companies have accumulated significant experience in constructing half of the world's 45,000 large dams. No evidence showed that CTGC or Sinohydro may be exploiting its contractual parties via unfavourable contract terms or delivery. Rather, scholars such as Nordensvard et al. (2015, p. 250 ff.) stress that Chinese dam developers tend to be particularly low priced. This was echoed by European dam developers such as TP1 and TP2. Even International Rivers (2015), an NGO which was mostly advocating against dam developers, rated CTGC 'good' for its environmental management in its projects, and 'fair' for its social safeguard policy commitments. Meanwhile, Sinohydro was rated 'good' for its environmental project management and 'good' for its social safeguard policy commitments (International Rivers, 2015). These ratings were largely echoed by TI1, FI2, TNI3, and FNL3.

An assessment of the deal between EGAT and the Burmese side would require access to the relevant contracts. This access has not yet been granted. The intransparency of the contractual details of these projects provides the ground for the claim that it would be a losing deal for the people of Myanmar. A lawyer consulting CEB noted how ill-prepared most policy-makers in Southeast Asia's poorest countries including Myanmar would usually be when negotiating such deals (FP7). This suggests that the contracts may be more favourable to the Thai than to the Burmese side. The projects may not particularly benefit those displaced by them because resettled communities are usually worse off after resettlement, as seen in Scudder's (2012) analysis of 50 resettlement cases. The social impact of the Mong Ton and the Hat Gyi Dam projects lies beyond the scope of this chapter.

Overall, while data is insufficient to assess the deal between the Thai and Burmese governments, both the Thai and Burmese players expect to benefit from the deal with the Chinese side.

Summary

None of the three observations found in the current scholarly literature regarding Chinese engagement in Southeast Asian dam projects seem to hold in the cases of the Mong Ton and Hat Gyi Dam projects. While previous literature has largely conceptualized Chinese engagement in Southeast Asian dam projects as hegemonic, these case studies suggests that it can also be – what the author of this chapter calls – contractual, which means a conceptualization that emphasizes the business lens over the political one with a decidedly more positive connotation than much of the current writing on the topic. Observations from the current literature regarding Chinese engagement in Southeast Asian dam projects are compared with the Mong Ton and Hat Gyi Dam project in Table 8.4.

While the Chinese engagement in the Mong Ton and Hat Gyi Dam projects can be conceptualized as contractual, it is noted that the Thai engagement features at least some hegemonic elements, given that in both projects, the Thai political leadership is the main driving actor seeking economic and social benefits in a package deal. Meanwhile, the conceptualization of Burmese involvement remains ambiguous.

Table 8.4 Conceptualizing Chinese engagement in Southeast Asian dam projects

	Typical dam project with Chinese engagement (according to the current scholarly literature)	Mong Ton Dam project and Hat Gyi Dam project
Main driving actor	Chinese political leadership	Chinese private sector player
Type of deal	Package	Standalone
Main benefits sought (from Chinese perspective)	Political: Expansion of political influence Economic: Electricity import Social: Avoiding resettlement in China	Business: Growth and profit
Project results (Chinese player – partners)	Win-lose	Win-win
Overall conceptualization of Chinese engagement	*Hegemonic*	*Contractual*

Source: Author's depiction.

Conclusion

A discussion with a Burmese activist carried out in the summer of 2015 may be indicative for the deeply held beliefs among Myanmar's civil society regarding Chinese engagement in the Southeast Asian dam project. The activist, FNL2, was involved in the 'Save the Salween' campaign which was supposed to focus particularly on the Mong Ton Dam project. Little was known about the project back then. But the activist hypothesized that "the Chinese government" must be behind the project that would be part of a greater effort to exploit the people of Myanmar and their political representatives (FNL2). It was outlined that these beliefs are also reflected in much of the scholarly literature on Chinese engagements in Southeast Asian dam projects.

Yet, the analysis on Mong Ton and Hat Gyi Dam projects in this chapter underscore that the main driving actor of Chinese engagement in a Southeast Asian dam project can also be the Chinese dam developer instead of Chinese political leadership, considering that the projects overall are driven by Thai players, first the Thai government, later by EGAT. Both projects are standalone deals for the respective Chinese dam developers who seek continued growth and business profit via these engagements. The Chinese dam developers' involvement led to a win-win deal for the contractual parties involved. This is because the respective Chinese developer brought in unique expertise for implementing large dam projects: CTGC constructed China Three Gorges Dam, the world's largest dam, and Sinohydro holds a 50 per cent share in the global hydropower construction market. Without such expertise, the Mong Ton Dam project, touted to be the sixth largest hydroelectric power plant in the world, could not be implemented. It could be argued that the non-implementation of both projects studied for this chapter would be in the interest of the people of Myanmar.

These case studies are not intended to undermine other scholars' earlier findings on Chinese engagement in Southeast Asian dam projects. The author of this chapter has also studied dam projects (such as the Myanmar's Myitsone Dam) that largely confirm the various observations frequently outlined by scholars regarding Chinese engagement in Southeast Asian dam projects. However, this chapter aims to nuance the generalizability of these observations. While much of the previous literature has conceptualized Chinese engagement in dam projects in Southeast Asia as hegemonic, the two case studies presented in this chapter show that it can also be contractual at times. Thus, scholars working on this topic are encouraged not to politicize Chinese engagement in Southeast Asia a priori, but to consider it on a case-by-case basis.

However, more future research is needed to further conceptualize Chinese engagement overseas. While major data collection efforts regarding dam construction on Myanmar's Salween River have been undertaken by the author of this chapter for more than two years, gaps in the interview data remain, as acknowledged in the section 'Methods'. The author of this chapter has carried out field research in Myanmar since 2012 and having gained greater ease of access to interviewees over time, the author is optimistic about obtaining additional relevant stakeholder information regarding dam construction with Chinese involvement in Myanmar. This chapter may serve as a foundation for future research on this topic.

Such future research could explore whether projects with Chinese engagement comparable to the Mong Ton and Hat Gyi Dam project also exist elsewhere in Myanmar, the remainder of Southeast Asia and possibly beyond. It can bring about a medium-N-study on the topic at hand to further generalize scholarly work on Chinese engagement in overseas dam projects. Research on Latin American dam projects with Chinese engagement would be of great interest because not much work has been carried out on such projects by the scientific community so far. Furthermore, analyses with a focus on Chinese lenders could further nuance the conceptualization of Chinese engagement in overseas dam projects. Their role in dam projects both within and outside of China also remains under-researched. Lastly, future research that conceptualizes both Thai and Burmese involvement in dam projects is also needed. This chapter has only provided a starting point for such conceptualizations.

References

Aroonrat, K., & Wongwises, S. (2015). Current status and potential of hydro energy in Thailand: A review. *Renewable and Sustainable Energy Reviews*, *46*, 70–78. doi:10.1016/j.rser.2015.02.010.

Aung, T. T. (2016). *Thanlwin dams criticised ahead of state counsellor's Thailand visit*. Retrieved from www.mmtimes.com/index.php/national-news/20794-thanlwin-dams-criticised-ahead-of-state-counsellor-s-thailand-visit.html.

Baird, I. G., & Quastel, N. (2015). Rescaling and reordering nature–society relations: The Nam Theun 2 hydropower dam and Laos–Thailand electricity networks. *Annals of the Association of American Geographers, 105*(6), 1221–1239. doi:10.1080/00045608.2015.1064511.

Bakker, K. (1999). The politics of hydropower: Developing the Mekong. *Political Geography, 18*(2), 209–232. doi: 10.1016/S0962-6298(98)00085-7.

Brennan, E., & Doring, S. (2014). *Myanmar's dams may be no show.* Retrieved from www.ocnus.net/artman2/publish/Business_1/Myanmar-s-Dams-May-Be-No-Show.shtml.

Burma Rivers Network (BRN). (2016). *Hat Gyi Dam.* Retrieved from www.burmariversnetwork.org/index.php?option=com_content&view=article&id=67&Itemid=82.

Burma Rivers Network (BRN). (2017). *Home.* Retrieved from http://burmariversnetwork.org/index.php/dam-projects/salween-dams/upper-thanlwin.

Chellaney, B. (2014). *Co-opt the water hegemon.* Retrieved from www.japantimes.co.jp/opinion/2014/09/12/commentary/world-commentary/co-opt-the-water-hegemon/.

CHINCOLD. (2009). *Sinohydro Corporation.* Retrieved from www.chincold.org.cn/chincold/zt/first/others/webinfo/2009/08/1281417028948733.htm.

de Clercq, G. (2015). *Portugal's EDP springboard for China Three Gorges investment abroad.* Retrieved from www.reuters.com/article/us-edp-china-three-gorges-idUSKBN0OY1HU20150618.

Deetes, P. (2016). *Salween/Nu River.* Retrieved from www.internationalrivers.org/campaigns/salween-nu-river.

Denzin, N. K. (1978). *The research act: A theoretical introduction to sociological methods.* New York, NY: McGraw-Hill.

Furlong, K. (2006). Hidden theories, troubled waters: International relations, the "territorial trap", and the Southern African Development Community's transboundary waters. *Political Geography, 25*(4), 438–458. doi: 10.1016/j.polgeo.2005.12.008.

Gleitsmann, D. H. (2015). *Adding fuel to the flame: The Hat Gyi Dam and ethnic conflict in Karen State, Myanmar.* Oslo, Norway: University of Oslo.

Hensengerth, O. (2012). Chinese hydropower companies and environmental norms in countries of the global south: The involvement of Sinohydro in Ghana's Bui Dam. *Environment, Development and Sustainability, 15*(2), 285–300. doi:10.1007/s10668-012-9410-4.

Hensengerth, O. (2015). Global norms in domestic politics: Environmental norm contestation in Cambodia's hydropower sector. *The Pacific Review, 28*(4), 505–528. doi:10.1080/09512748.2015.1012107.

Hirsch, P. (2010). The changing political dynamics of dam building on the Mekong. *Water Alternatives, 3*(2), 312–323.

IEA. (2016). *Thailand electricity security assessment 2016.* Retrieved from www.iea.org/publications/freepublications/publication/Partner_Country_Series_Thailand_Electricity_Security_2016_.pdf.

International Rivers. (2014). *China overseas dams list.* Retrieved from www.internationalrivers.org/resources/china-overseas-dams-list-3611.

International Rivers. (2015). *Benchmarking the policies and practices of international hydropower companies.* Retrieved from www.internationalrivers.org/resources/9065.

International Rivers. (2016). *China Three Gorges Corporation.* Retrieved from www.internationalrivers.org/campaigns/china-three-gorges-corporation.

Kachin News. (2014). Aung Thaung's family firm involved in Kachin dam deal.

Kiik, L. (2016). Nationalism and anti-ethno-politics: Why "Chinese Development" failed at Myanmar's Myitsone Dam. *Eurasian Geography and Economics, 57*(3), 374–402. doi:10.1080/15387216.2016.1198265.

Kirchherr, J., Charles, J. K., & Walton, M. J. (2016). The interplay of activists and dam developers: The case of Myanmar's mega-dams. *International Journal of Water Resources Development, 33*(1), 111–131. doi:10.1080/07900627.2016.1179176.

Kirchherr, J., Disselhoff, T., & Charles, K. (2016). Safeguards, financing, and employment in Chinese infrastructure projects in Africa: The case of Ghana's Bui Dam. *Waterlines, 35*(1), 37–58. doi:10.3362/1756-3488.2016.005.

Kirchherr, J., Pohlner, H., & Charles, K. J. (2016). Cleaning up the big muddy: A meta-synthesis of the research on the social impact of dams. *Environmental Impact Assessment Review.* doi:10.1016/j.eiar.2016.02.007.

Kirchherr, J., Matthews, N., Charles, K. J., & Walton, M. J. (2017). "Learning it the Hard Way": Social safeguards norms in Chinese-led dam projects in Myanmar, Laos and Cambodia. *Energy Policy, 102*, 529–539. doi:10.1016/j.enpol.2016.12.058.

Lamb, V., & Dao, N. (2015). Perceptions and practices of investment: China's hydropower investments in mainland Southeast Asia. In *Land grabbing, conflict and agrarian-environmental transformations: Perspectives from East and Southeast Asia.* Retrieved from www.iss.nl/fileadmin/ASSETS/iss/Research_and_projects/Research_networks/LDPI/CMCP_21-_Lamb___Dao.pdf.

Leavenworth, S. (2016). *China may shelve plans to build dams on its last wild river.* Retrieved from http://news.nationalgeographic.com/2016/05/160512-china-nu-river-dams-environment/.

Lidauer, M. (2012). Democratic dawn? Civil society and elections in Myanmar 2010–2012. *Journal of Current Southeast Asian Affairs, 31*(2), 87–114. Retrieved from https://journals.sub.uni-hamburg.de/giga/jsaa/article/view/546.

MacLeod, C. (2011). *China resumes dam projects to dismay of environmentalists.* Retrieved from http://usatoday30.usatoday.com/news/world/environment/2011-03-09-chinadams09_ST_N.htm.

Magee, D., & McDonald, K. (2006). Beyond Three Gorges: Nu River hydropower and energy decision politics in China. *Asian Geographer, 25*, 39–60.

Martov, S. (2012). *What does the future hold for Aung Thaung & Sons?* Retrieved from www.irrawaddy.com/news/burma/what-does-the-future-hold-for-aung-thaung-sons.html.

Matthews, N. (2012). Water grabbing in the Mekong Basin – An analysis of the winners and losers of Thailand's hydropower development in Lao PDR. *Water Alternatives, 5*(2), 392–411.

Matthews, N., & Motta, S. (2013). *China's influence on hydropower development in the Lancang River and lower Mekong river basin.* Retrieved from https://cgspace.cgiar.org/handle/10568/35102.

Matthews, N., & Motta, S. (2015). Chinese state-owned enterprise investment in Mekong hydropower: Political and economic drivers and their implications across the water, energy, food nexus. *Water, 7*(11), 6269–6284. doi:10.3390/w7116269.

McCully, P. (2001). *Silenced rivers: The ecology and politics of large dams.* Basingstoke, UK: Palgrave Macmillan.

McDonald, K., Bosshard, P., & Brewer, N. (2009). Exporting dams: China's hydropower industry goes global. *Journal of Environmental Management, 90*(Suppl. 3), S294–302. doi:10.1016/j.jenvman.2008.07.023.

Mellino, C. (2016). *Will China dam its last wild river?* Retrieved from www.ecowatch.com/will-china-dam-its-last-wild-river-1882167630.html.

Mertha, A. C. (2008). *China's water warriors: Citizen action and policy change.* Ithaca, NY: Cornell University Press.

Middleton, C. (2008). The sleeping dragon awakes: China's growing role in the business and politics of hydropower development in the Mekong region. *Watershed, 12*, 51–62.

Moe, W., & Ramzy, A. (2015). *U Aung Thaung, Burmese politician accused of abuses, dies at 74*. Retrieved from www.nytimes.com/2015/07/24/world/asia/u-aung-thaung-burmese-politician-accused-of-abuses-dies-at-74.html.

MOEE. (2017). *History*. Retrieved from www.moep.gov.mm/history.

Moore, M. (1998). Coalition building between native American and environmental organizations in opposition to development: The case of the new Los Padres Dam Project. *Organization & Environment, 11*(3), 287–313. doi:10.1177/0921810698113002.

Murphy, M. (2008). *China's "Going Out" investment policy*. Retrieved from https://csis-prod.s3.amazonaws.com/s3fs-public/legacy_files/files/publication/080527_freeman_briefing.pdf.

Naing, S. Y. (2008). *Karen group opposes Salween River dams*. Retrieved from http://www2.irrawaddy.com/print_article.php?art_id=14345.

Naing, S. Y. (2014). *Controversial Hat Gyi Dam blamed for Karen conflict*. Retrieved from www.irrawaddy.com/news/burma/controversial-hat-gyi-dam-blamed-karen-conflict.html.

Naing, S. Y. (2016). *Current military movement in Karen State threatens terms of NCA*. Retrieved from www.irrawaddy.com/news/burma/knla-current-military-movement-in-karen-state-threatens-terms-of-nca.html.

Nordensvard, J., Urban, F., & Mang, G. (2015). Social innovation and Chinese overseas hydropower dams: The nexus of national social policy and corporate social responsibility. *Sustainable Development, 23*(4), 245–256. doi:10.1002/sd.1591.

Platts. (2015). *The top 100- Part I - The world's largest power plants*. Retrieved from www.industcards.com/top-100-pt-1.htm.

Ramzy, A. (2013). *Chinese environmentalists lose fight to stop Nu River dams*. Retrieved from http://world.time.com/2013/02/05/chinese-environmentalists-lose-fight-to-stop-nu-river-dams/.

Reuters. (2014). *China's Three Gorges to diversify as big dam projects dry up*. Retrieved from www.reuters.com/article/us-china-power-threegorges-idUSKCN0IY0PE20141114.

Samarkand, A. (2015). *Thailand's electricity utility may be complicit in human rights violations in Myanmar's Salween dams*. Retrieved from www.mekongcommons.org/thailands-electricity-utility-may-be-complicit-in-human-rights-violations-in-myanmars-salween-dams/.

Scudder, T. (2012). Resettlement outcomes of large dams. In C. Tortajada, D. Altinbilek, & A. K. Biswas (Eds.), *Impacts of large dams: A global assessment*. Berlin, Germany: Springer.

Siciliano, G., Urban, F., Tan-Mullins, M., Pichdara, L., & Kim, S. (2016). The political ecology of chinese large dams in Cambodia: Implications, challenges and lessons learnt from the Kamchay Dam. *Water, 8*(9), 405. doi:10.3390/w8090405.

Simpson, A. (2013). Challenging hydropower development in Myanmar (Burma): Cross-border activism under a regime in transition. *The Pacific Review, 26*(2), 129–152. doi:10.1080/09512748.2012.759264.

Sneddon, C., & Fox, C. (2008). Struggles over dams as struggles for justice: The World Commission on Dams (WCD) and Anti-Dam Campaigns in Thailand and Mozambique. *Society & Natural Resources, 21*(7), 625–640. doi:10.1080/08941920701744231.

Tan-Mullins, M., & Mohan, G. (2012). The potential of corporate environmental responsibility of Chinese state-owned enterprises in Africa. *Environment, Development and Sustainability, 15*(2), 265–284. doi:10.1007/s10668-012-9409-x.

Tilt, B. (2014). *Dams and development in China: The moral economy of water and power.* New York, NY: Columbia University Press.

Tullos, D. D., Foster-Moore, E., Magee, D., Tilt, B., Wolf, A. T., Schmitt, E., … Kibler, K. (2013). Biophysical, socioeconomic, and geopolitical vulnerabilities to hydropower development on the Nu River, China. *Ecology and Society, 18*(3), 16. doi:10.5751/ES-05465-180316.

Turnell, S. (2014). Legislative foundations of Myanmar's economic reforms. In M. Crouch & T. Lindsey (Eds.), *Law, society and transition in Myanmar.* Oxford, UK: Hart Publishing Ltd.

Urban, F., Nordensvärd, J., Khatri, D., & Wang, Y. (2013). An analysis of China's investment in the hydropower sector in the Greater Mekong Sub-Region. *Environment, Development and Sustainability, 15*(2), 301–324. doi:10.1007/s10668-012-9415-z.

Urban, F., Nordensvard, J., Siciliano, G., & Li, B. (2015). Chinese overseas hydropower dams and social sustainability: The Bui Dam in Ghana and the Kamchay Dam in Cambodia. *Asia & the Pacific Policy Studies, 2*(3), 573–589. doi:10.1002/app5.103.

Verhoeven, H. (2015). *Water, civilization and power in Sudan – The political economy of Military-Islamist State Building.* Cambridge, UK: Cambridge University Press.

Warner, J. F., & Zeitoun, M. (2008). International relations theory and water do mix: A response to Furlong's troubled waters, hydro-hegemony and international water relations. *Political Geography, 27*(7), 802–810. doi:10.1016/j.polgeo.2008.08.006.

Wilmsen, B., Webber, M., & Yuefang, D. (2011). Development for whom? Rural to urban resettlement at the Three Gorges Dam, China. *Asian Studies Review, 35*(1), 21–42. doi:10.1080/10357823.2011.552707.

WWF. (2016). *Salween, Nujiang or Nu River.* Retrieved from http://wwf.panda.org/about_our_earth/about_freshwater/freshwater_problems/river_decline/10_rivers_risk/salween_river/.

Xuecui, H. (2013). *The battle over Yunnan's hydropower.* Retrieved from www.chinadialogue.net/article/show/single/en/6347-The-battle-over-Yunnan-s-hydropower.

Yeophantong, P. (2013). *China, corporate responsibility and the contentious politics of hydropower development: Transnational activism in the Mekong region?* Retrieved from www.geg.ox.ac.uk/geg-wp-201382-china-corporate-responsibility-and-politics-hydropower-development.

Zarfl, C., Lumsdon, A. E., Berlekamp, J., Tydecks, L., & Tockner, K. (2015). A global boom in hydropower dam construction. *Aquatic Sciences, 77*(1), 161–170. doi:10.1007/s00027-014-0377-0.

9 Building bridges through dialogue for the Brahmaputra River Basin

Vishaka Gulati, Arundhati Deka, Safa Fanaian, Sumit Vij, and Anamika Barua

Introduction

There are numerous definitions available for transboundary waters. The Universities Partnership for Transboundary Waters (2013) defines it as "sources of freshwater that are shared among multiple user groups, with diverse values and different needs associated with water use. In this way, water crosses boundaries – be they those of economic sectors, legal jurisdictions, or political interests". They act as a source of potential growth and development to the traditional basin communities by creating hydrological, social, and economic dependency among them. It has been estimated that at least around 90 per cent of the world's population are living in the countries with shared basins, within the nation or across the borders as riparian nations. According to the United Nations (2008) report, there are 263 transboundary lakes and river basins which covers approximately one half of the surface of the earth and nearly 60 per cent of the world's freshwater resources. Among these basins, around 30 countries have their territories entirely within them while 145 states are known to comprise territory within such transboundary basins. Apart from surface water bodies, about 2 billion people globally also rely on groundwater resources, and it has been estimated that approximately 300 transboundary aquifer systems exist worldwide (United Nations, 2008).

Management of the freshwater resources has been a global challenge, especially for transboundary river waters (TBW). Management of such communal goods or common resources becomes difficult as the interests of the diverse stakeholders involved will always vary. The assumption that the basin actors will share a common understanding and sympathy towards the issues associated with the basin, cannot be held as true. Only rarely there will be common characteristics present among the knowledge and information shared with the stakeholders regarding the crisis associated with TBW basins. In fact, the various case studies conducted on this discourse show that different regions along the boundary will have diverse level of interplay in the political dimension as well as during the stage of actual resource management (Adams, Brockington, Dyson, & Vira, 2003). The final consequence of water sharing amongst the riparian nations and the level of management success will rely on the dynamics of the level of influence that are at play at the national, regional, and international positions in the region. Therefore, the management of TBW that cut across national, political, social, economic, and sectoral boundaries is regarded as one of the supreme security challenges of the decade (Wouters & Ziganshina, 2011). This is because as rivers cross borders, their flows are diverted, dammed, or stored by national governments for multiple purposes.

South Asia has been endowed with a number of transboundary river systems in the circum-Himalayan region. But the region has also been inextricably linked to geopolitics due to the countries involved being unequal in size and power with a history of conflict and wars. The major river systems of this Hindu Kush Himalayan region consist of the Indus, the Ganges, and the Brahmaputra. These river systems traverse through the nations of China, Afghanistan, Pakistan, India, Bhutan, Nepal, and Bangladesh. India has been involved in water-related tensions with Pakistan and Bangladesh. It has been speculated that the growing scarcity of water is leading to conflicts as every person wants a large share but the availability of resources is little.

The focus of this chapter is the Yarlung Tsangpo-Brahmaputra-Jamuna Basin (henceforth will be mentioned as Brahmaputra River Basin), one of the major river basins of South Asia. Taking the initiative "Transnational Policy Dialogue for Improved Water Governance of Brahmaputra River"[1] (referred to as the Brahmaputra Dialogue henceforth) of South Asia Consortium for Interdisciplinary Water Resources Studies (SaciWATERs) as a case study, the authors advocate the role of multi-stakeholder and multilateral deliberations. Against this background, the chapter hereafter is divided into three sections after the introduction. The first section discusses the challenges associated with generating transboundary cooperation and the subsequent need for a dialogue. The second section focuses specifically on the characteristics of the Brahmaputra River Basin along with the prevailing conflicts and discusses the avenues of cooperation. The third segment takes into account the journey of the SaciWATERs' Brahmaputra Dialogue initiative, along with the challenges encountered, achievements attained so far, and the way forward.

Challenges to transboundary cooperation

Water management is a multi-objective task which should necessarily consider the heterogeneous competing interests of the stakeholders. The augmenting demand for water from environmental, domestic, and economic users is putting extra pressure on these finite resources. While nations are still struggling to manage their domestic water issues, the multinational nature of TBW adds to the complexity (Hussein & Grandi, 2017). As water is allocated to two or more sovereign states, TBW management not only cuts through the various sectoral boundaries but is also dependent on the prevailing regional, state, national, and international dynamics of the region. Owing to hydrology, TBW resources create an intricate network of interdependencies among the basin states, thereby creating the potential for discord among them (Alam, Dione, & Jeffreya, 2009).

The negotiation of the treaties and agreements for TBW management has always been a challenging task due to the existence of diverse interconnected dynamics. Furthermore, the conflicts may also evolve because of increasing demands, diverse interests, and maldistribution (Kliot, Shmueli, & Shamir, 2001). The absence of trust and confidence among the basin nations, historical contentions, prevailing power asymmetry, zero-sum game attitude, and lack of integrated frameworks have a profound effect over TBW management policies (Biswas, 2011). Apart from the prevailing water issues, the presence of other conflicting issues between the countries, be it in terms of economic or infrastructural development or their political orientation, add on to the existing complications (Wolf, 2007). The lack of political will or the focus of political parties over shorter-term goals, and the absence of integration of the water issues with other contentious issues also hinder cooperation among the riparian nations (Biswas, 2011). Non-cooperation can result in ineffective management of water resources and eventually reduce both quality and quantity of these resources (Wolf, 2007). Although the prominence of these circumstances might be different in different river basins, an interplay of these factors plays an important role in their overall governance.

The problem also lies in the way these TBW resources are viewed by each country. According to the Task force report (2010) by the Institute for Defence Studies and Analyses, New Delhi, they are neither seen as public goods nor as private goods but are viewed as collective goods. The riparian countries mostly do not exercise collective and cohesive control over these common pool resources and this leads to increasing discord among them. Interlinked by rivers, these countries' independent actions do not yield effective solutions to their problems. The creation of collective mechanisms for sustainable TBW management is required. This is a challenging task because it generally involves the establishment of regulations and institutions that encroach upon the established domestic institutions of the respective countries. Being distinctly situated – socially, economically, geographically, and politically, they have diverse interests and thus they understand the access, utilization, and management of TBW resources differently. The governments of the respective countries tend to pursue their respective national goals keeping in mind their own economic and political progress (Mostert, 2003). Addressing these diverse interests, agendas, and demands would necessitate an integrated, inclusive, and transparent basin-wide approach for sustainable water resources management (Rogers & Hall, 2003).

TBW are mostly characterized by an imbalanced power relationship between upstream and downstream countries (Zeitoun & Allan, 2008). Owing to this existing asymmetry within the basin, the negotiating power of the hegemon plays a crucial role in the riparian politics. Consequently, even though treaties and agreements have the potential to reduce conflict within the region, sometimes they are deemed as ineffectual because they become a source of tension themselves. While it is vital to address these conflicts, it should be kept in mind that official agreements between the riparian countries should not be regarded as the ultimate solution. The weaker side often signs the treaty to be a part of the game, even when the terms mainly benefit the hegemon (Warner & Zawahri, 2012). "When one social class exerts power over others beyond that accounted for by coercion or law, it may be described as hegemonic" (Zeitoun & Warner, 2006). The uneven distribution of power and the absence of a level playing field greatly affects the bargaining position of the nations and the outcome of the overall negotiations (Zeitoun & Allan, 2008). Domination can sometimes be masked as cooperation, which eventually makes the situation worse by causing more harm than good (Selby, 2003). Overall, the transnational hydro-relationships are dependent on whether the hegemon behaves as a basin leader or a basin bully.

Furthermore, a huge gap exists in the desired approach towards the governance of TBW. A common question is whether water should be managed in accordance with the administrative boundaries or their natural boundaries (Finger, Tamiotti, & Allouche, 2006). Along with the environmental characteristics, the economic aspects also need to be considered. The river water is used for many economic activities such as irrigation, energy production, and tourism (Pegram et al., 2013). The growing demand for water resources, and its usage for economic development is affecting the ecology of the basin. Hence a balance needs to be achieved between the ecological and economic approaches of governance.

While all these factors make the management of TBW a complex undertaking which is prone to discord, they have the potential for collaboration within the basin. It is important to analyse both conflict and cooperation together along with the scales within which they exist. In most of the cases, TBW management has been isolated due to conflicts and need to be brought on a middle path to be evaluated together (Zeitoun, Mirumachi, & Warner, 2011). This would help in undertaking realistic and less contentious collaborative action plans within the basin. The limited focus on either of them, would provide only a partial picture of the overall politics of TBW. To enhance the governance of the river basins, it is necessary to train the riparian nations to predict and prevent the conflicts (Wolf, 2007).

Continuous dialogues can provide opportunities for comprehending the problem, engaging in mediation, and searching for solutions (Brouwer et al., 2016; Röling & Woodhill, 2001). This approach can alleviate mistrust across the border nations and states. Dialogue and co-management of common pool resources (such as forests and fisheries) even found their way in the Rio Principles even though water management was not the point of emphasis (Warner, 2006).

Multi-stakeholder (involving the communities, local civil society organizations, non-governmental organizations, academicians, researchers, media, donor agencies, bureaucrats, and politicians) and multilateral dialogues can help to promote trust and confidence among the riparian nations. This interdisciplinary approach integrating the technical, social, economic, political, and legal perspectives is necessary for effective basin management. As defined by Röling and Woodhill (2001), a multi-stakeholder dialogue is "a contrived situation in which a set of more or less interdependent stakeholders in a resource are identified and invited to meet and interact in a forum for conflict resolution, negotiation, social learning and collective decision-making towards concerted action". It implies reaching out to groups like the local people and women who are generally not involved in the decision-making process but are affected the most by their outcomes. It involves the creation of opportunities for their effective and meaningful participation in the dialogue forum.

Such participatory dialogues help in building the capacity of the concerned stakeholders through sharing of knowledge among the participants. It enables them to partake effectively in the negotiation process. In other words, it facilitates in levelling the players both at national and regional levels. For example, at the national level, such dialogues can help policy makers to accept the views of multiple stakeholders (such as civil society organizations [CSOs] and researchers) and vice versa. It can empower the participants such as community members to discuss and articulate their concerns in a more scientific and constructive way. A huge communication gap exists between the state and the non-state actors. Common people often lack the capacity to communicate with the bureaucrats. The bureaucrats mostly use technical language, which is again not effectively communicated back to the CSOs and communities. Regular dialogues can help to reduce this gap and build trust between them.

Similarly, the existing gap between the technocrats and the policy makers can be reduced through such dialogues. Scientific research alone cannot solve the issues without their integration into the policy-making process. The technical perspective must be considered too. Bringing both scientific research and the technical perspective on one platform and maintaining consistent communication can enhance the relationship among them.

Further at the regional level, such dialogue platforms can help in challenging the power asymmetry among the riparian countries. The recognition of common areas of interests can motivate the basin hegemon to behave more like a basin leader and less like a basin bully. Identification of the points of cooperation rather than just focusing on the issues of discord and tension can help in enhancing trust and confidence within the basin. Overall, it works to enlarge the stake at hand, and moves away from positional bargaining to larger interests (Röling & Woodhill, 2001; Zeitoun & Mirumachi, 2008).

Dialogues through existing forums, workshops, conferences, celebrations, and festivals help in enhancing the informal communication among the stakeholders. Moreover, different approaches can be adopted for conducting the dialogues. Jay Rothman proposed to classify these approaches into four different types of interaction: positional dialogue, human relationship dialogue, activist dialogue, and problem-solving dialogue (Ropers, 2004). In the case of a positional dialogue, the stakeholders express their own views (which could be different and even contradictory), which only require acknowledgement. On the other hand, the focus of human relationship dialogues is on the root causes of conflicts to help build better relations among the stakeholders. Activist dialogues are one step ahead. To reach a common understanding, different parties scrutinize the problem together and delve into joint solutions. The most ideal approach is the problem-solving dialogue process whereby the participants communicate and work through their differences. These approaches represent different but complementary ways of conducting dialogues effectively and efficiently. They can represent the way in which a dialogue process for enhancing the communication among the various stakeholders could evolve over time.

Depending upon the level of disputes, bringing together the various stakeholders on one common platform can be quite challenging and might require several rounds of meetings and training programmes before the initiation of the actual dialogue process. Although the dialogue is a slow and time-consuming process which requires a great deal of perseverance from the organizers (the role which is mostly assumed by a third party), it can eventually help in dealing with the conflicts constructively and is necessary before any negotiation for cooperation can take place. It is necessary to initiate a multilateral platform for the Brahmaputra River Basin stakeholders to deliberate on the research and issues associated with the river.

About the Brahmaputra basin

The river originates in the mighty ranges of the Himalayas. Known as the Tsangpo or the Yarlung Zangbo River in southern Tibet, it starts from a massive glacier near Mansarovar Lake in the Kailash range at an elevation of 5,150 m above mean sea level (Mahanta & Saikia, 2015). The river then penetrates the Himalayas and flows through Arunachal Pradesh in India as the Siang River, winding out of the mountains. Then it flows southwest in the Assam valley as the Brahmaputra or Lohit and merges with Ganga (or Meghna in Bangladesh), and the river flows south towards Bangladesh as the Jamuna river. The drainage area of the Brahmaputra is estimated to be 580,000 km^2, covering 2,880 km before discharging into the Bay of Bengal (Mahanta & Saikia, 2015) (Figure 9.1).

Apart from possessing a rich ecology, biodiversity, and other natural resources, and influencing lives and livelihood, the river basin also holds cultural significance among the people living in the area, particularly the traditional basin communities. Although the Tsangpo river is known for its extreme conditions, its beauty, remoteness, and mystique make it one of the places considered to have inspired the concept of Shangri-La (a mystical and harmonious valley) in James Hilton's book *Lost Horizon* in 1933. In fact, the river also plays an important role in generating economic benefit in predominantly agrarian nations India and Bangladesh. The river, while flowing through the higher lands, erodes the soil and deposits them on low-lying areas, generating alluvial soils for agriculture. Bangladesh also relies heavily on the river for fishery production. While the river mostly serves as an essential inland waterway, excessive deposition of soil in the lower areas might cause frequent devastating floods. Thus, the river can act both as a creator and a destroyer.

The fact that the river originates in China makes the river strategically significant because the construction of any megastructure upstream would severely affect the downstream regions. Regional platforms encompassing basin countries are therefore essential to address vital transnational water issues.

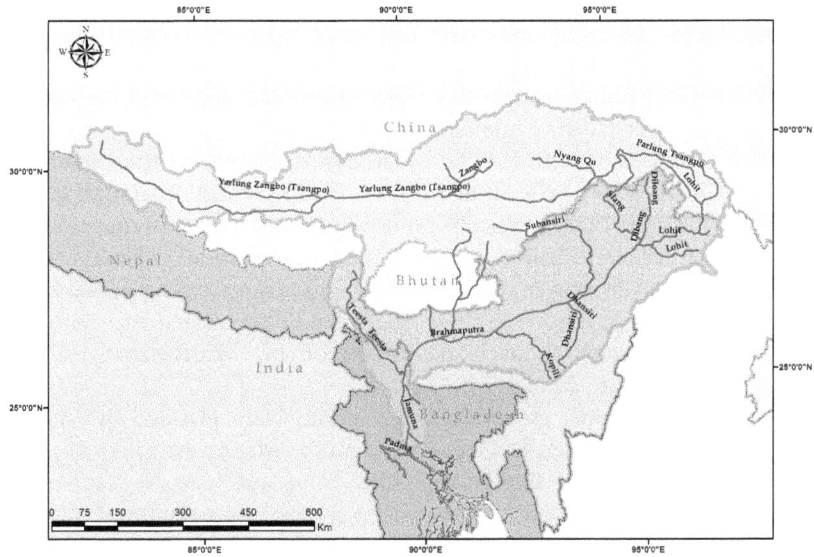

Figure 9.1 Map of Yarlung Tsangpo-Brahmaputra-Jamuna River Basin.

Source: Prepared by Suchita Jain, SaciWATERs; Data source: www.gadm.org/ & www.thethirdpole.net/).

Causes of conflicts in Brahmaputra river basin

The river has been a source of livelihood and enrichment for the basin communities. But at the same time, it has also led to the impoverishment of millions of people due to the seasonal and unseasonal disasters like floods and earthquakes.

Negotiations among the co-riparian nations in this region have been challenging. This is due to various interrelated factors such as historical stereotypical rivalries, conflict of interest on water resources development among the upstream and downstream nations, suspicion and distrust among the countries owing to previous political disagreements, lack of open communication, and asymmetric power dynamics (financially or geographically). Within the riparian nations, there are issues of augmenting nationalism and self-vested interests, tendency to pursue short-term political goals instead of investing in long-term national interests, and negotiations exclusively based on water issues which usually just reflect state-centric, technocratic, exclusionary, and nationalistic hydro-political viewpoints of elite actors with minimum public involvement (Biswas, 2011). Sometimes, the emergence of other issues of conflict between the countries might also adversely affect the negotiating atmosphere for transboundary waters, such as the escalating growth of religious extremist groups influencing the political regime, absence of proper negotiating frameworks with the capacity for an overall development spectrum, and the presence of media-savvy and single-issue NGOs that are more interested in promoting their own interests and agendas (Biswas, 2011).

Necessity of energy and development

Currently, India and China are both in a phase of rapid economic expansion leading to the increased use of water and hydropower. Apart from hydropower/dam construction, regulation of flow over time is a major water management concern in this river basin, while dam construction also plays a central role in both the issues (Huang, 2014). The hydrological reliance of the downstream nations on China as an upstream nation, is one of the most crucial geopolitical factors of this region. Technologically more advanced than any of the co-riparian nations, China desires to utilize the river water for multiple purposes (such as the generation of hydropower and electricity, agriculture, and fisheries). Specific water utilization projects such as these might have also created rifts among the basin countries due to its impact on the flow of the river towards the downstream region (Chintan, 2011).

The hydropower dams, especially the Zangmu Dam planned by China on the mainstream of the river, has caused India downstream to worry about potential significant damage. But on the other hand, the Chinese scholars have argued that its utilization of the river will not have any substantial impact on downstream countries. They claim that, considering the socioeconomic factors, China's activities would utilize only a small portion of the whole basin water resource (Huang, 2014). As an upstream nation, China does not have such concerns. But China is concerned that building dams in Arunachal Pradesh might strengthen India's hold over the disputed region and further complicate the border negotiations (Samaranayake, Limaye, & Wuthnow, 2016).

South Asian governments tend to have this intense need to control the rivers in their region because they are rich in natural resources and offer partial but concrete solutions to the most basic problems such as poverty (mostly rural and urban), industrial limitations, and urban stress (Crow & Singh, 2000). This implies conflicts will occur because as each nation wants a share of the river, the portions available might be smaller for each.

Geopolitical history of the region

According to Biswas (2011), in most South Asian transboundary rivers, water allocation treaties and agreements between the relevant co-basin countries have been very difficult to initiate or negotiate. The Indus Water Treaty has been an exception, with the negotiation being short and lasting not even a decade (Biswas, 2011). Besides, the negotiations over water in this region have been exclusively bilateral, especially on the insistence of the upper riparian nations (Crow & Singh, 2000).

Historical deliberations also influence transboundary negotiations. For example, in the case of India and Bangladesh, bilateral negotiations created obstacles to future regional cooperation. The negotiations between India and Bangladesh regarding the sharing and development of the Ganges did not go well. This affected the first multilateral deliberation between India, Bangladesh, and Nepal on regional water growth and development. The most heated and long-running river sharing argument has been between Bangladesh (and previously East Pakistan) and India over the flow of the river Ganga. On the other hand, India and Bhutan have always managed to have a cordial relationship through the development of projects in the rivers of Bhutan that will also benefit India.

Lack of policy framework

None of the co-riparian nations in this region are signatories to the UN Watercourses Convention, so there is an absence of a comprehensive multilateral treaty governing the water resources management. The ambiguity of conventional international water law may have led to misunderstandings and thus prompted the riparian nations to choose sub-optimal water utilization methods (Huang, 2014).

Despite China being more powerful economically and militarily, there are no water sharing agreements, joint river commissions, nor dispute settlement mechanisms in place between the nations. Even the existing mechanisms consist of a series of Memorandums of Understanding (MoUs) on hydrological data sharing and a body of technical experts. The MoUs are non-binding because there is no oversighting body in place to ensure its implementation (Ho, 2017).

Most of the existing agreements across the basin have been bilateral. In fact, India has constantly insisted on bilateralism, and has been a consistent prerequisite for the government for negotiations with its neighbours ever since 1947. Almost a range of key issues, from river basin development to trade and transit, have been negotiated on those terms (Crow & Singh, 2000). The negotiations and development initiatives, particularly dam-building activities, also tend to be confidential, leaving the indigenous basin communities deprived of information that they are entitled to receive; inherently, it is their land or territory.

Power asymmetry

Chintan (2011) believes that the upper riparian nations of India and China are economically and politically overshadowing their smaller neighbours downstream. Although Bangladesh has substantial interest in developing the water resources of the river, there has not been much progress in all-basin cooperation to acknowledge and protect the country's interests.

A complementary view might also contend that conflict between the rich and poor (in this case nations and stakeholders) hampers the development of local collaborative institutions for engaging water resources management effectively in the basin. "These kinds of arguments make a powerful case for river development which recognizes the political and economic forces shaping the current conflict at international and local levels" (Crow & Singh, 2000). The aforementioned differences in perceptions explain the lack of institutionalized cooperation among the basin countries in managing the Brahmaputra. Although obstructions persist, some recent agreements have opened new pathways for regional collaboration, such as shifting some negotiations from the governmental sphere to private economy; bringing third parties (other than governments) into negotiation, design, and implementation of cooperative projects; sharing of eventual benefits and costs, rather than establishing fixed payments based on expected outcomes; and making tentative and tiny steps toward limited multilateral discussion (Crow & Singh, 2000). These initiatives are anticipated to bring new ideas, activities, and parties/stakeholders to the dialogue.

Existing cooperation within the basin

Water can act as a catalyst of discord among the countries and bring the countries together. Unilateral actions mostly turn out to be ineffective and inefficient especially in the long run. As a result, establishment of mutual gains and interests among the riparian nations tend to overshadow the water conflicts among them. "Violence over water does not seem to be strategically rational, hydrographically effective, or economically viable" (Wolf, 2007). Although tensions exist between upstream and downstream nations (e.g. between India and Pakistan, between India and Bangladesh, between Ethiopia and Egypt) and among different water users (e.g. agriculturalists and industrialists), historical documentation shows that cases of cooperation over transnational water resources exceed the incidences of conflicts (Choudhury & Islam, 2015). The earliest legal instrument related to the Brahmaputra River can be traced back to the 1914 Shimla Convention, whereby Great Britain, Tibet, and China met to negotiate boundaries between India and Tibet.

India-Bangladesh

India and Bangladesh have had continuous problems since 1951, ever since India initiated its plan to build the Farakka Barrage to divert water to the Kolkata port on the Hooghly river. The diversion would affect the flow of water into the Padma, in the then East Pakistan (Chintan, 2011). In 1960, the first bilateral negotiations did take place on the Ganga, but India later announced that it would be proceeding with the Farakka project anyway. In 1972, an Indo-Bangladesh Joint Rivers Commission (JRC) had been set up by the Treaty of Friendship, Cooperation, and Peace, but the mandate excluded the sharing of river water, an aspect that must be handled at the parliamentarian or prime ministerial level. Their work has been mostly associated with the Ganges River but has spilled over to the Brahmaputra River. To substitute flows to the Farakka Barrage, it was suggested that a canal should be built to divert flows from the Brahmaputra River. The assessment for this canal, however, went beyond the purview of JRC. So far, it has been analysed that this Commission has failed to bring any permanent solution between the countries (Islam, 1987; Kliot et al., 2001).

With the acknowledgement of the lowest riparian rights in 1983, an ad-hoc agreement was signed between India and Bangladesh on sharing the water of Teesta River, which is one of the major tributaries of the Brahmaputra River. A Joint Committee of Experts was formed in 1997 to further examine the dynamics of sharing of the river water. However, by 2004, only limited progress was made by the Committee. In 2010, the prime ministers of both India and Bangladesh issued a Joint Communiqué calling for the Teesta issue to be resolved. In 2011, both governments have been willing to sign a new agreement on sharing Teesta but this did not happen due to the protest from West Bengal. In 2013, during the official visit of the president of India to Bangladesh, efforts on this front have begun again but the issues remain unresolved (Uprety & Salman, 2011).

India-Bhutan

In the area of TBW management, Bhutan has embarked upon a very different path of constructive collaboration with India, compared to either Bangladesh or Nepal, to develop its TBW bodies. Bhutan initiated a plan to work with India to develop the hydropower potential of the Wangchu Cascade at Chukha in 1980. India agreed to construct a 336 MW run-of-the-river project at the region after extensive consultations. The project was so successful that it managed to cover its costs by 1993. Owing to the support received from India for planning, construction, and management of the project, an agreement has been made between India and Bhutan to sell the excess electricity from the project to India at a mutually agreed rate (Crow & Singh, 2000). The 1949 Treaty of Friendship signed between India and Bhutan, linked to international relations, economic development, and non-interference, has provided the basis for the current joint hydropower projects on the Brahmaputra River.

India-China

China and India's first formal agreement came in 1954 when both the parties signed a MoU to share hydrological data of the river for flood protection purposes. This MoU, however, ended in 1962 due to the Sino-India war (Uprety & Salman, 2011; Wolfrum, 2013). In 2002, India and China signed an MoU towards the provision of hydrological information of the river during flood season by China to India. The MoU has been renewed again in 2005, 2008, and 2013. China has provided the hydrological data of three stations during the monsoon season of 2010 onwards.

The aforementioned existing avenues of cooperation are a few of the instances of collaboration within the basin. The treaty and agreements between India and Bangladesh rarely mention the flows of the Brahmaputra River. Most of the agreements between India and China have been made on sharing data but this association also shows a level of willingness towards moving further in dialogue on joint river management.

The issue-based cooperation and bilateral nature of the treaties act as an impediment in fostering basin-wide cooperation. Furthermore, due to the lack of participation of the stakeholders (including local communities, women, etc.) in policy-making process and the absence of guiding principles, the voices of all the stakeholders are not taken into consideration. Owing to this, the optimum level of multi-stakeholder cooperation has still not been achieved.

The Brahmaputra dialogue: journey so far[2]

Keeping the key idea of "*Dialogue before negotiation*" in mind, SaciWATERs along with its partners in 2013 initiated the Brahmaputra Dialogue. The objective of this initiative is to understand the conflicts, causal factors, and steps towards fostering cooperation to improve governance and management of the basin. This initiative is a first of its kind in the basin to clearly strategize the ways to engage various stakeholders including CSOs and bureaucrats in this process.

The first phase[3] of the project initiated collective knowledge building and bilateral dialogue processes across interdisciplinary groups of experts from India and Bangladesh in Track 3[4] mode. Mapping of current knowledge base on the Brahmaputra River was carried out through desk study which triggered discussions around the existing issues and policies documented through workshops. To encourage more prominent academicians and bureaucrats of the region, participants of the dialogue from the two nations suggested moving towards multi-track mode (Track 3+2) and including other riparian nations in the second phase.

Based on these recommendations and suggestions, the second phase[5] of the project was conceptualized. The primary focus of this was to take the dialogue process from Track 3 to Track 2 level between India and Bangladesh. The phase ended with a multilateral and multi-stakeholder dialogue with the involvement of Bhutan and China. The discussion within this phase brought out a recommendation for creation of an apex body at both national and transnational levels to bring together concerns and ideas from various nations into a mechanism for enhancing the cooperation for effective governance of the river among the riparian nations.

The project is currently in its third phase[6] and the main objective is to facilitate a multilateral and multi-stakeholder dialogue process among these nations. The structured engagements in the first two phases paved the way for meaningful knowledge-sharing exercise on a common platform. Furthermore, there has been a visible increase in the number of knowledge and implementing partners who are assisting SaciWATERs with this dialogue.[7]

This journey has come a long way, from just deliberating on conflicts and vested interest to identifying opportunities to collaborate over issues of common concerns and exploring pathways to cooperate and mutually share the benefits of resources of the river. The aim of this phase is to develop a basin-level institutional framework that is informed by the enhanced capacity of the stakeholders involved.

Brahmaputra dialogue initiative

Major initiatives that have been undertaken so far to initiate the process of dialogue among the representatives of India, China, Bhutan, and Bangladesh are as follows:

Dialogues and interviews

An informal multilateral and multi-stakeholder dialogue platform has been created to bring together the various stakeholders on one common platform. The organized yet informal nature of these platforms fosters direct and open discussions and enables the participants to share their concerns. These informed dialogues link researchers, academicians, policy makers, and social actors through a structured communication process. Both country- and regional-level dialogues have been conducted using participatory approaches to initiate the dialogue process effectively. Country-level meetings are aimed to create an enabling environment for participants of the respective countries to bring across their arguments on the table. The issues arising out of these country-level workshops that have international implications have been taken up at the regional level to facilitate the exchange of information across borders. This helped in sensitizing each riparian nation to the apprehensions of the other basin state and countries. Chinese delegates in the first multilateral dialogue mentioned the need for a platform whereby the concerns of the lower riparian countries such as India and Bangladesh can be shared with upper riparian countries such as China. This would help to increase the understanding of the concerns of the downstream nations.

The review of existing transboundary protocols and treaties to understand the processes involved in shaping institutions that manage the transboundary river basin (such as the Mekong River Commission and the Nile Basin Initiative) was also carried out. The dialogues have helped in the sharing of lessons and best practices with the stakeholders and are extended to other relevant platforms. This sharing of experience and knowledge from other river basins can help in shaping the perspectives of the stakeholders and addressing the challenges involved in the evolution and functioning of such institutions along with their relative success and failure in managing TBW resources.

The dialogue space is further being utilized to create joint collaborations for knowledge building and identification of basin-wide economic opportunities. The economic opportunities linked to the rivers are never in isolation and requires cooperation among different stakeholders. Having a common understanding of the challenges faced and the prevailing economic opportunities within the region can help in promoting cooperation among the nations. For example, a country-level dialogue in Bangladesh pointed out that investment could be made for the development of the navigation routes, among other available opportunities. Conducting joint research, sharing of information and best practices (on issues such as management of disasters – flood and erosion), will incrementally contribute to not only enabling cooperation but also fostering trust across borders.

Enabling effective participation and inclusion in dialogues is not merely dependent on bringing the women and men from local communities to be a part of the process. Therefore, a parallel process has been followed for building the capacity of the CSOs and local communities regarding their rights, the existing laws, policies, and agreements. Moreover, women's viewpoints are being collected to build discourses on the river. This exercise will eventually be helpful in enabling gender-sensitive decision making within the basin.

Apart from dialogue workshops, semi-structured interviews, and closed-door interactions, key informant meetings with the key stakeholders have also been conducted to understand the nature and causes of conflict and to build cooperation among the different stakeholders. Key informant meetings with the stakeholders include both individual and group interviews. The analysis of the collected data has helped in making these dialogue workshops more structured.

Institutional mapping

To understand the overall management process of the water resources within the basin, it is important to analyse the institutional and governance structures present within each country for river management. Hence, institutional mapping for the basin countries is being carried out to create an inventory of the relevant institutions for the identification of their geographical and functional boundaries.

Advisory committee

An advisory committee, with equal representation of bureaucrats and academicians from each of the four riparian countries, provides support for drafting the structure of the basin level institutional framework. The committee members also consider the concerns and recommendations raised during the dialogues. They also help in liaising with government officials at Track 2 and 1.5 levels by bringing them in the country- and regional-level dialogue meetings.

The combination of these initiatives will help in developing a basin-level institutional framework which incorporates the concerns of all the stakeholders. The participants of the dialogue meetings believe that this framework will eventually help in building sustainable TBW management.

Challenges and achievements of Brahmaputra dialogue

Historical conflicts and dialogues across the riparian nations of the river have played a major role in shaping constructive deliberations for river basin management. There is a need to move past these conflicts if cooperation is expected from the co-riparian nations. The national political parties of each nation in transboundary dialogues need to play the crucial role of reviewing the existing or non-existing structure of river basin management. But generating political willingness to participate in dialogues and committing to such initiatives has surfaced as a major challenge among the Track 1 delegates. Therefore, it has been decided to approach the Track 1.5 delegates to get their commitment to preempt the risk of waning individual interests due to changing political regimes.

The need for both information and policy changes within each country has emerged as one of the significant disputes during these dialogues. It is required to make the changes permanent to enhance the overall transboundary cooperation in the basin. There are different phases of policy making, from accounting for the civil society/community perception to the technical phase and the political phase to making the final decision on ground implementation. Bureaucrats and politicians make the final decisions. It is the job of the technical people, through consultation with the other stakeholders, to generate alternative solutions. It is important to facilitate communication and create a political space which would allow the policy makers to make informed and inclusive decisions.

To increase effective participation in dialogues and facilitate the subsequent decision-making process, it is important to generate awareness among the basin communities regarding the technical, social, and economic aspects of the river. But getting women from the communities to participate has been a challenge because their role has been limited to the household. Political decisions associated with the region are unknown to them. Apart from CSOs, media can also assist in disseminating knowledge regarding the existing research and news on the basin. But at this age of technology and the craving for sensational news, it is important to approach the right kind of media wisely for reaching out to the communities.

It takes a long time to learn to build upon an institutional design. Although it is time-consuming, this process is worthwhile if we want to build a sustainable and equitable framework. The institutional structure cannot be copied from other river basins so it is important to recognize the requirements and the objectives of each basin. It is also important to show the parties involved the benefits of their involvement in promoting cooperation in the basin to keep their interest alive for continuous engagement. To sustain the dialogue process, it is necessary to generate opinions from the involved stakeholders for suggestions on the issues that will receive maximum interest and investment in the near future. For example, disaster management has been a basin-wide challenge, especially for the downstream countries and would receive immediate attention from the stakeholders.

Despite the presence of the aforementioned challenges, this initiative has created an informal platform for dialogue among the different stakeholders of the riparian countries. It has also provided a neutral platform for the representatives of the riparian countries to meet regularly, share information, discuss concerns, and develop a shared vision for the Brahmaputra River Basin. This dialogue forum has brought together the Track 1.5 and 2 representatives from India and Bangladesh along with Track 3 representatives of the region to share their ideas, knowledge, and experience at both country and basin levels. To gain political support, SaciWATERs also presented the initiative to the Water Resources Department (WRD) secretary of Assam and Arunachal Pradesh. Both the states support the idea of continuing the dialogue among the riparian countries.

One of the major achievements of the dialogue was to bring on board Track 2 and 3 representatives from Bhutan and certain influential academicians from China. The value of continuing the dialogue outside the political boundaries was strongly supported by the bureaucrats and technocrats. Although the number of women representatives in the technical section is limited, the dialogue emphasized on maximizing participation.

Through this project, the stakeholders have been able to recognize the importance of a dialogue in the Brahmaputra River Basin. The stakeholders are willing to participate in the dialogues and have demanded the continuation of this process. Even the bureaucrats are willing to engage in meaningful discussions with the CSOs now; previously they were not considered strategic knowledge partners.

The continuous deliberations among the various stakeholders since 2013 have improved the way in which these dialogues are conducted. The knowledge shared through these dialogue workshops has helped the participants articulate their opinions more clearly and become more sensitive toward the concerns of others. It has built casual informal relationships among them. The stakeholders of the dialogue have been able to identify a few of the joint economic opportunities associated with the co-management of the river and have recognized the importance of conducting joint-basin research, including socio-economic and policy research.

The discussions in media revolves mostly around the topics of conflicts within the Brahmaputra River Basin. The aim of the initiative is to steer parties to work towards the identification of common areas of collaboration such as disaster management, navigation, and subsequent sharing of data (hydrological and socio-economic) for better risk assessment, recognition of economic opportunities within the basin, and conducting joint technical and social research to generate improved understanding of the entire basin. In the long run, this will enhance the riparian nations' relations.

Since 2013, the Brahmaputra Dialogue has highlighted the need to understand and acknowledge the cooperation that is already happening either in terms of sharing hydrological data or exchange of research, delegates, and professionals among the riparian countries. At present, it is essential to build consensus among the riparian countries and to generate an institutional framework or mechanism through an inclusive pathway for its acceptance and implementation that will further integrate value within these countries. Herein lies the success of this initiative and its impetus to continue the endeavour as a neutral actor.

Expectations from the dialogue

For any transboundary dialogue to move forward, it is vital to generate plurality of views within the basin through the anticipation of variable stakeholders (CSOs, community representatives, academicians, researchers, and bureaucrats) in the multilateral dialogue. It is also vital to enhance their capacity in the process so that the opinions generated are also deliberated and accepted across different levels of delegates. Generating a common knowledge base across the stakeholders and riparian nations will further enhance the quality of the dialogue with a better level of coordination and communication. Although the sharing of data and information is already happening at a certain level through formal or informal agreements, the access to scientific information, such as flow data of the river, should be enhanced, for better preparedness in time of disasters and for greater cooperation across the border. Data sharing should move beyond the hydrological data to include other socio-economic and environmental aspects of TBW management.

Riparian countries can share their expertise and knowledge on issues such as disaster management to build trust among them. Sharing of expertise can also increase the capacity of the CSOs and communities to engage with the government more adequately and effectively on various platforms. This can also help policy makers to make more informed decisions based on both the scientific information and grassroots feedback. Even within communities, it is crucial to generate opinions from both men and women in an equal ratio, regarding their association with the river and their understanding of the existing policies.

For effective management, basin-related and basin-wide planning would be required. We should try and find not only the avenues of risk identification and reduction but also the avenues for harnessing the opportunities available within the basin. There is a need to achieve a common understanding between the riparian countries and improve the knowledge base of challenges and opportunities that each country in the river basin has. The actual information does not trickle down to those who really get affected, and the information which reaches out to them is mostly biased and unscientific. Multi-stakeholder and multilateral dialogues among the representatives of the basin countries can also help in the dissemination of the right information and in building the capacity of the representatives (Track 3, 2, 1.5/1).

Having a good knowledge base will contribute in better decision making only if appropriate structures are put in place. There are various institutions available but it is imperative to focus on a suitable framework for the Brahmaputra River Basin. Institutional and power-mapping exercises can help in figuring out the kind of basin-level framework required. To uphold the trust and confidence in the basin, the dialogue needs to be sustained and brought to the attention of different existing regional platforms, such as SAARC, as the Brahmaputra has received less attention so far. This would also subsequently lead to the participation of the Track 1 delegates, bringing more attention to the cause. The dialogue should be more structured and continuous. The ultimate aim is to come up with a basin level institutional framework which continues to move ahead, evolves with time, and is a source of cooperation rather than conflicts.

Conclusion

The focus of this chapter is to emphasize upon the role of multi-stakeholder and multilateral dialogue in transboundary river water management. Taking the Brahmaputra Dialogue initiative as an example, the chapter elaborates the process, challenges and achievements of such a multi-stakeholder and multilateral dialogue. The continuous process of the dialogue and the identification of the limitations associated with it have paved the way for more structured and meaningful deliberations. The chapter concludes that although the dialogue initiative has followed a slow and rigorous process, it has been able to generate willingness among the participants (Track 3, 2 and 1.5) from the riparian nations to engage continuously with the initiative. Moreover, such dialogue platforms in the long run would serve to analyse the avenues of cooperation for generating action plans for co-management and co-utilization of the basin resources, enhancing the trust and confidence among the riparian nations. It will also help in identifying joint research themes cutting across different disciplines and filling the critical gaps within the research available for the basin. The presence of such knowledge base can validate the necessity for evidence based decision making in order to optimize the resource potential of the basin. The processes that have been incorporated within this initiative will cumulate to develop a basin level institutional framework, acknowledged by all the riparian nations, administering the activities within the basin. Such an architectural framework would assist in providing the means necessary to employ both formal and informal institutional arrangements.

Notes

1 The Brahmaputra dialogue process was initiated in 2013 with the objective of bringing together the co-riparian nations (Bangladesh, Bhutan, China, and India) for deliberating on co-management of the river basin.

2 The authors would like to acknowledge The Asia Foundation and South Asia Water Initiative for supporting the project.

3 First phase (2013–2014) of the dialogue began as a bilateral initiative between India and Bangladesh and involved mainly the representatives from Track 3 level. During this phase, SaciWATERs associated mainly with Institute of Water and Flood Management (IWFM) under Bangladesh University of Engineering and Technology (BUET) and Indian Institute of Technology-Guwahati (IITG).

4 Definitions on levels of diplomacy adapted from United States Institute of Peace, 2011
Track 3: Non-Governmental Organizations (NGOs), Academicians, Civil Society Organizations (CSOs), Grass root level community; Track 2: Influential Academics, Bureaucrats; Track 1.5: Influential Bureaucrats; Track 1: High-level politicians.

5 Second phase of the dialogue (2014–2015) involved both Track 3 and 2 representatives.

6 The third phase of the project involved Track 3, 2 and 1.5 representatives from all the four riparian countries.

7 In addition to the existing ones, new partners include Institute of Chinese Studies (ICS), Centre for North East Studies and Policy Research (C-NES) from India; Institute of Water Modelling (IWM) and Jagrata Juba Shangha (JJS) from Bangladesh; Royal Society for Protection of Nature Bhutan (RSPN) from Bhutan; Asian International Rivers Center (Yunnan University) from China; Wageningen University and The Hague Institute for Global Justice from the Netherlands.

References

Academy for International Conflict Management and Peacebuilding. (2011). *Glossary of terms for conflict management and peacebuilding*. Washington, DC: United States Institute of Peace.

Adams, W. M., Brockington, D., Dyson, J., & Vira, B. (2003). Managing tragedies: Understanding conflict over common pool resources. *Science, 302*(5652), 1915–1916.

Alam, U., Dione, O., & Jeffreya, P. (2009). The benefit-sharing principle: Implementing sovereignty bargains on water. *Political Geography, 28*(2), 90–100.

Biswas, A. (2011). Cooperation or conflict in transboundary water management: Case study of South Asia. *Hydrological Sciences Journal, 56*(4), 662–670.

Brouwer, J. H., Woodhill, J., Hemmati, M., Verhoosel, K., & Vugt, S. (2016). *The multi-stakeholder process guide*. Wageningen, The Netherlands: Practical Action Publishing Ltd.

Chintan, G. S. (2011). *Trans-boundary river basins in south Asia: Options for conflict resolution*. Berkeley, CA: International Rivers.

Choudhury, E., & Islam, S. (2015). Nature of transboundary water conflicts: Issues of complexity and the enabling conditions for negotiated cooperation. *Journal of Contemporary Water Research & Education, 155*, 43–52.

Crow, B., & Singh, N. (2000). Impediments and innovation in international rivers: The waters of South Asia. *World Development, 28*(11), 1907–1925.

Finger, M., Tamiotti, L., & Allouche, J. (2006). Introduction: Conceptual elements. In M. Finger, L. Tamiotti, & J. Allouche (Eds.), *The multi-governance of water: Four case studies* (pp. 1–42). Albany: State University of New York Press.

Ho, S. (2017, February 16). Power asymmetry in the China-India Brahmaputra river dispute. *Asia Pacific Bulletin, 371*.

Huang, Z. (2014). Case study on the water management of the Yaluzangbu/Brahmaputra river. *Georgetown Environmental Law Review, 27*, 229–250.

Hussein, H., & Grandi, M. (2017, March 21). Dynamic political contexts and power asymmetries: The cases of the Blue Nile and the Yarmouk Rivers. *International Environmental Agreements: Politics, Law and Economics, 17*(6), 795–814.

Institute for Defence Studies and Analyses. (2010). *Water security for India: The external dynamics*. New Delhi, India: Institute for Defence Studies and Analyses.

Islam, M. R. (1987). The Ganges water dispute: An appraisal of a third party settlement. *Asian Survey, 27*(8), 918–934.

Kliot, N., Shmueli, D., & Shamir, U. (2001). Development of institutional frameworks for the management of transboundary water resources. *International Journal of Global Environmental Issues, 1*(3–4), 306–328.

Mahanta, C., & Saikia, L. (2015). The Brahmaputra and other rivers of the North-East. In R. R. Iyer (Ed.), *Living rivers, dying rivers*. New Delhi, India: Oxford University Press.

Mostert, E. (2003). Conflict and co-operation in international freshwater management: A global review. *International Journal of River Basin Management, 1*(3), 1–12.

Pegram, G., Yuanyuan, L., Quesne, T. L., Speed, R., Jianqiang, L., & Fuxin, S. (2013). *River basin planning: Principles, procedures and approaches for strategic basin planning*. Paris, France: UNESCO.

Rogers, P., & Hall, A. (2003). *Effective water governance* (Vol. 7). Stockholm, Sweden: Global Water Partnership.

Röling, N., & Woodhill, J. (2001). *From paradigms to practice: Foundations, principles and elements for dialogue on water, food and environment*. Background Document for the Workshop on National and Basin Dialogue Development Workshop, Bonn.

Ropers, N. (2004). *From resolution to transformation: The role of dialogue projects*. Berlin, Germany: Berghof Research Center for Constructive Conflict Management.

Samaranayake, N., Limaye, S., & Wuthnow, J. (2016, May). *Water resources competition in the Brahmaputra river basin: China, India and Bangladesh*. Arlington, TX: CNA Analysis and Solutions.

Selby, J. (2003). Dressing up domination as 'cooperation': The case of Israeli-Palestinian water relations. *Review of International Studies, 29*(1), 121–138.

The Universities Partnership for Transboundary Waters. (2013). *Frequently asked questions*. Retrieved May 5, 2017 from http://waterpartners.geo.orst.edu/faq.html.

Trandem, A. (2008). A Vietnamese/Cambodian transboundary dialogue: Impacts of dams on the Se San River. *Development, 51*(1), 108–113.

United Nations. (2008). *Transboundary waters: Sharing benefits, sharing responsibilities.* New York, NY: United Nations.

Uprety, K., & Salman, S. (2011). Legal aspects of sharing and management of transboundary waters in South Asia: Preventing conflicts and promoting cooperation. *Hydrological Sciences Journal, 56*(4), 641–661.

Warner, J. (2006). Multi-stakeholder platforms: Integrating society in water resource management?. *Ambiente e Sociedade, 8*(2), 17–28.

Warner, J., & Zawahri, N. (2012). Hegemony and asymmetry: Multiple-chessboard games on transboundary rivers. *International Environmental Agreements: Politics, Law and Economics, 12*(3), 215–229.

Wolf, A. (2007). Shared waters: Conflict and cooperation. *Annual Review of Environment and Resources, 32*, 241–269.

Wolfrum, R. (2013). *The max Planck Encyclopedia of public international law: Index and tables* (Vol. 11). Oxford, UK: Oxford University Press.

Wouters, P., & Ziganshina, D. (2011). Tackling the global water crisis: Unlocking international law as fundamental to the peaceful management of the world's shared transboundary waters–introducing the H2o paradigm. In R. Q. Grafton & K. Hussey (Eds.), *Water resources planning and management.* Cambridge, UK: Cambridge University Press.

Wu, X., Jeuland, M., Sadoff, C., & Whittington, D. (2013). Interdependence in water resource development in the Ganges: An economic analysis. *Water Policy, 15*(S1), 89–108.

Zeitoun, M., & Allan, J. (2008). Applying hegemony and power theory to transboundary water analysis. *Water Policy, 10*(S2), 3–12.

Zeitoun, M., & Mirumachi, N. (2008). Transboundary water interaction I: Reconsidering conflict and cooperation. *International Environmental Agreements: Politics, Law and Economics, 8*(4), 297–316.

Zeitoun, M., Mirumachi, N., & Warner, J. (2011). Transboundary water interaction II: The influence of 'soft' power. *International Environmental Agreements: Politics, Law and Economics, 11*(2), 159–178.

Zeitoun, M., & Warner, J. (2006). Hydro-hegemony – A framework for analysis of trans-boundary water conflicts. *Water Policy, 8*(5), 435–460.

10 Sino-Kazakh transboundary water cooperation

History, current status, and future priorities

Zhanggui Zhou and Ruolin Wang

Introduction

The "security dilemma" is a common phenomenon facing transboundary states. Inter-state allocation and utilization of transboundary river water resources usually cause international conflicts which constitute a new hotspot in the field of non-traditional security. The relevant data released by water resource organizations shows that the number of transboundary rivers is about 263 (Li, 2015). As a country with abundant rivers, China shares over 40 major rivers with neighbouring countries. Increasingly, China and its neighbouring countries are facing disputes and conflicts over their shared rivers. Most transboundary rivers in China are concentrated in three regions: southwest, northeast, and northwest. In the southwest region, China's water development and utilization of the Brahmaputra (Yaluzangbu) River triggered serious concerns from India. Disputes over the Mekong (Lancang) River escalated between China and the downstream Southeast Asian countries (see Chapter 7). In the northeast region of China, most of the transboundary rivers are border rivers (see Chapters 5 and 6).

In the northwest region of China, China and Kazakhstan not only share a 1,700 km border, but also more than 20 rivers, among which the Irtysh and the Ili are the largest. Since the 1990s, primarily owing to China's water development and diversion, water conflicts have already been a source of tension between China and Kazakhstan. The Irtysh (Eerqisi) River originates in China's Altai Mountains, crosses into Kazakhstan, and finally flows into Russia where it joins the Ob River and spills out into the Arctic Ocean. It is the main source of fresh water for millions of people mostly living in Kazakhstan's larger northeastern cities, including the capital Astana (Biba, 2014; Zhang, 2017). It crosses four countries; its basin is shared by Russia (67 per cent), Kazakhstan (29 per cent), China (4 per cent), with a small amount flowing through Mongolia (Baizakova, 2015). It passes through 618 km of Chinese territory and 1,698 km of Kazakh territory. Its basin consists of 354,000 km (Dyusebayeva, 2012). The Ili originates at the glaciers of the Muzart in Central Tanirtau, flows into China (34 per cent), and back to Kazakhstan (60 per cent). Its overall length is 1,439 km, including 815 km through the territory of Kazakhstan with a catchment area of 77,400 km^2. The biggest source of the Ili River-Tekesi River originates from Kazakhstan. Another important tributary of the Ili River is the Khorgos

River, the 150 km border between China and Kazakhstan (Baizakova, 2015). It provides more than 50 per cent of the lake's fresh water. Both rivers are crucial sources of water for Kazakhstan (Biba, 2014; Waterpub, 2016).

Since the late 1990s, a series of canals have been built by the Chinese to transfer water from both the Ili and Irtysh rivers to several dry basins in central-north Xinjiang. Chinese water diversion projects could therefore threaten Kazakhstan's urban and industrial development (Hagt, 2003; Muzalevsky, 2013; Stone, 2012). Some environmentalists have even warned that Lake Balkhash, which receives over 50 per cent of its water from the Ili River, could become a desert. Managing the transboundary water issue has thus become a major challenge for Sino-Kazakh relations.

Despite problems that persist between China and Kazakhstan in the management of shared rivers, the two countries have engaged in a relatively high level of institutionalised cooperation since the early 2000s (Ho, 2017). In September 2001, two countries signed the agreement on "Cooperation in the Use and Protection of Transboundary Rivers". China signed such water agreement with only a few neighbouring countries (Mongolia, North Korea, and Russia). In early 2011, China finalised an agreement on water quality protection along shared rivers with Kazakhstan. In April 2011, China and Kazakhstan launched the China-Kazakhstan Friendship Joint Water Diversion Project on the Khorgos River. The Khorgos River is a 150 km long tributary of the Ili and a border river between both countries (Biba, 2014; Li & Wu, 2016). Both sides are currently negotiating a water-sharing agreement over the two rivers.

The aim of this chapter is to review the achievements and experiences of cooperation between China and Kazakhstan over the transboundary water issues, which could potentially serve as a reference for the settlement of disputes and cooperation in other areas. In addition, this chapter also discusses remaining problems and challenges of transboundary rivers issues between the two countries to shed light on how China and Kazakhstan could strengthen their cooperation on shared water resources.

Nature of Sino-Kazakh transboundary water conflict

"Conflict" refers to the "fight, battle, or struggle", or the open confrontation between the parties (Webster, 2017). However, in recent years, the definition of conflict has changed. But in any case, the highly militant words suggest a close association between conflict and security threat.

Social conflict theory argues that if conflict is defined as the divergence of perceptions of interest, two major factors must co-exist: (1) perception of the subject; (2) existence of a conflict of interests, values, or demands. Conflict can exist between individuals, groups, organizations, or countries. For Sino-Kazakh transboundary river conflicts, the two factors are: (1) the objective existence of the scarcity of resources, that is, whether the two sides are highly dependent on transboundary river resources (water resources needed for ecological balance, hydropower, and navigation); (2) subjective perception of the other party's action as a threat to one's own interests. If these two factors co-exist, a real conflict exists between two parties.

Of course, conflict is a double-edged sword with both positive and negative effects. First, on the positive side, if the conflict is put into action, it can become a fertile ground for the birth of social change. That is to say, conflict can cause a state or a society to seek innovation by applying stress to stop the system from becoming rigid (Coser, 1956, p. 197). The international system is a competitive society in which there is no forever ruling state, and the conflicts are inherent in the ever-changing global political and economic system. Second, conflict drives stakeholders to manage their divergent interests. Conflict does not necessarily mean that a party wins and the other party fails. Sometimes, a loss can produce a win-win result and promote the security state of the region as a whole. As a result, conflict is not the opposite of cooperation, but conflict breeds and is accompanied by cooperation.

Analysis of resource scarcity and benefit interdependence

Kazakhstan is severely short of water. Its surface water is about 101.2 km^3 while 44.9 km^3 (44.4 per cent) of total surface water is from international rivers, 23.6 km^3 of surface water is from China, and one third of it flows to neighbouring countries. Similar to China, Kazakhstan's surface water resources are extremely unevenly distributed within the country and are marked by significant perennial and seasonal dynamics (FAO, 2012). For instance, Central Kazakhstan has only 3 per cent of the country's total water resources while the western and south-western regions (Atyrau, Kyzylorda and in particular, the Mangystau region) have hardly any fresh water. In contrast, Kazakhstan's water resources and hydropower resources are mainly distributed in three regions: (1) eastern region (Irtysh River and its main tributaries); (2) south-eastern region (Ili River Basin); and (3) southern region (Syr Darya River, Talas River, and Chuhe River). Among these, the eastern region and the south-eastern region of the water resources are most abundant. The Balkhash-Alakol and Irtysh river basins in the south-eastern and east account for almost 75 per cent of surface water resources generated within the country (FAO, 2012; Ho, 2017; Li, 2015). Yet, the problem is that many of these rivers originate in China.

Socio-economic development of the country demands an increasing amount of water resources. Take hydropower for example, Kazakhstan Hydraulic Design Institute once completed a hydropower resources assessment report which shows projected needs of a total installed capacity of 5,631 MW, generating capacity for 234 million KWh, with the average utilization of 4,000 h, to be met by a total of 38 large hydropower stations and 540 small hydropower stations (Zhang, 2015). According to the Kazakhstan's Ministry of Energy's proposal for a large hydropower station project, many hydropower stations will be installed at various locations on the Ili and the Irtysh rivers, and other transboundary rivers. The 2012 Electric Power Industry Development Programme stipulated by Kazakhstan's Ministry of Industry and New Technologies is expected to reach a generating capacity of 1,202 million KWh by 2030, and the proportion of hydropower is expected to increase from the current 12 to 20 per cent by 2020 (Ministry of Commerce, P.R. China, 2008). Similarly, water use for agricultural and industrial needs increases at a fast rate. It is forecasted that the growth of municipal service and industrial needs will increase from 173 mln m3 in 2012 to 350 mln m3 in 2040 (Dmitriyevich & Anatoly, 2014).

Both the Irtysh River and the Ili River, which run through the region of Xinjiang, make up one-third of Xinjiang's surface water flow, and contribute to 90 per cent of Xinjiang's annual water outflow (Li, 2015, p. 69). Xinjiang is an important area for energy development that involves large projects such as gas transmission from west to east and power transmission from west to east. Xinjiang is located in the arid northwest area in China. Owing to low annual precipitation and rapid development, Xinjiang faces serious water shortage leading to desertification and decline of natural vegetation. It is a necessity to carry out large-scale utilization and development of international rivers such as the Ili River and the Irtysh River in this region.

In addition, the local agricultural development is also highly dependent on the transboundary waters (Yu & Zhou, 2009). This is particularly the case for Xinjiang's cotton production. Xinjiang, with less than 40 per cent of the country's cotton-growing area, produces more than half of China's cotton. The Xinjiang Production and Construction Corps (XPCC), which has 175 regiment farms, is the largest cotton grower in Xinjiang. In 2013, XPCC contributed 42 per cent of Xinjiang's cotton production (Chen, 2014). Cotton is a highly water-intensive crop. In recent years, substantial efforts have been made by China in improving its water irrigation efficiency by adopting the water-saving drip irrigation system and rapidly expanding Xinjiang's cotton production, in addition to other agricultural products. However, China's water resources development in its upstream region has inevitably affected water uses of Kazakhstan at the downstream.

Project 635 (Irtysh-Karamay-Urumqi Canal) is the only north–south water diversion project in China. A total of RMB 14.4 billion was devoted to the construction of 890 km of channels, five reservoirs, and three power stations. Beginning in 1997, the first stage of the project focused on water division from the Irtysh River to Karamay City, which has an important petroleum industry. This project was aimed to address China's water scarcity and enhance environmental protection. The second stage of the project involved the diversion of 850 billion m^3 of water from the Irtysh River to Urumchi City. The third stage of the project involved the west–north water diversion from the Burgin Water downstream to the Irtysh River to offset water utilization for downstream zoology and agriculture. Project 635 is scheduled to be completed in 2020. According to Sievers (2002), this billion-dollar project was anticipated to initially divert 5–10 per cent of the flow of the Irtysh to the Ulungur Lake. From the Ulungur Lake, the water will be channelled to irrigate not only the Karamay petroleum fields but also 140,000 ha of land in Xinjiang via a canal. China increased the scale of its diversion up to 50 per cent of the flow of the Irtysh River.

Awareness of threat

Water has become one of the main obstacles to the economic growth of many countries, including China and Kazakhstan. With rising global consumption of water and serious water pollution, many countries face the threat of water shortage. The UN report on global water resources estimates that in 2030, 47 per cent of the world's population will face the threat of severe water shortage. "Water is not always the only and main reason of conflicts, but it can worsen current intense situation" (Crosette, 1995).

It is self-evident whether the two parties believe that one's party's actions will threaten their own interests. Considering China's upstream dam construction, reservoir building, and water diversion projects such as Project 635, Kazakhstan is particularly concerned about the impact on its middle and lower reaches (Li, 2015; Stone, 2012). For example, the use of water from the Ili River has significant consequences on Lake Balkhash, which receives 80 per cent of its water from the Ili River. One of the largest lakes in the world, Lake Balkhash, is in a very vulnerable position (Zhang, 2017). The eastern part of Kazakhstan could suffer negative consequences such as reduction in crop yields, degradation of pastureland, degradation of the environment, deterioration of the epidemiological situation, declining fish stocks, and threatened livelihoods of local population. Any significant decrease in water supply to Kazakhstan will stall the operations of its industry.

In recent years, China has started hydro-development on some parts of its transboundary rivers by building water dams, channels, and other infrastructure for the production of water supply and for power generation. However, some neighbouring countries are concerned that such development constitutes exploitation that will damage the environment, aggravate the impact of natural water resource misdistributions, and even threaten the national security of its neighbouring states (Feng, He, & Wang, 2015). Li (2015) concluded that the transboundary river issues between China and neighbouring countries affect water quality, water allocation, water use, and river protection.

The main threat facing the Ili River and Irtysh River is caused by water allocation. In view of the potential impact of upstream water development projects, China has adopted a cooperative stance towards Kazakhstan to manage shared rivers. The various mechanisms for China-Kazakhstan transboundary water cooperation are discussed in the following section.

Existing mechanisms for China-Kazakhstan transboundary water management

Meetings between heads of states

On 7 September 2013, President Xi and President Nazarbayev signed a Sino-Kazakh Joint Declaration on Further Deepening Comprehensive Strategic Partnership in Astana. Article 3 emphasized the following:

- Both sides spoke highly of the Chinese-Kazakh Joint Committee's achievement on utilization and development of transboundary rivers. They indicated their willingness to further strengthen and expand the cooperation under the relevant mechanism by taking every possible step to complete the

Implementation Plan of Water Allocation Technical Work of Transboundary Rivers which was signed between the People's Republic of China and Republic of Kazakhstan on 13 November 2010. They agreed to start to study and consult the draft agreement on Chinese-Kazakh transboundary water allocation from 2015 onwards.

- Under the principle of mutual respect and mutual benefit, the two sides would strengthen the cooperation on utilization and development of transboundary rivers.
- The two sides spoke positively about following the schedule to implement the China-Kazakhstan Friendship Joint Water Diversion Project of Khorgos River. Both sides planned to finish all construction work for the diversion project in Sumubai River by the end of 2014, and focus on related construction and renovation work from 2015 onwards. Under the principles of mutual benefit and mutual understanding, the two sides would use transboundary water resources fairly and reasonably, and continue to consult and discuss problems related to water projects.
- Both sides would reinforce cooperation to address the Glacial Threat of Khorgos River Watershed, and will further strengthen cooperation under the Joint Committee of Chinese-Kazakh Transboundary Rivers. Both sides agreed that it would be necessary to construct a debris flow project in the upstream areas of the Friendship Joint Water Diversion Project in Khorgos River to ensure the safety of both the International Border Cooperation Centre and the residents in both countries.
- The leaders of the two countries spoke highly of the role of the Sino-Kazakh Environmental Cooperation Commission and the bilateral cooperation on water quality protection of transboundary rivers. Both sides indicated their willingness to effectively implement (a) the Agreement on Protection of Water Quality of Transboundary Rivers signed on 22 February 2011, and (b) the Cooperation Agreement on Environmental Protection signed on 13 June 2011 (The Central Government, P.R. China, 2013).
- China and Kazakhstan agreed to conduct assessment studies to effectively integrate the Sino-Kazakh Environmental Cooperation Commission into the mechanism of the Sino-Kazakh Cooperation Committee, and would make a decision on the issue as soon as possible.
- The two sides indicated their willingness to develop and strengthen cooperation on environmental protection within the framework of the Shanghai Cooperation Organization (SCO), and jointly promote sustainable regional development.

In May 2014, on a visit to China, President Nazarbayev signed the Sino-Kazakh Joint Declaration. He stressed the significance of cooperation, and spoke highly of the role of Sino-Kazakh prime ministers' regular meeting mechanism and Kazakhstan's Cooperation Committee and the sub-Commissions in coordinating and guiding bilateral cooperation. In addition, during the first Belt and Road International Cooperation Forum which was held during 14–15 May 2017 in Beijing, President Nazarbayev suggested that "it is important not to miss complex environmental issues, including the problem of rational management of water resources of intercontinental transboundary rivers, which can be transport arteries" (Orazgaliyeva, 2017).

The prime ministers' regular meeting mechanism

China-Kazakhstan's prime ministers' regular meeting mechanism, officially launched in 2012, is held once every two years. On 31 March 2012, Prime Minister Massimov and Premier Wen signed the first regular meeting joint communique. According to Article 4 of the joint communique, both sides spoke of the important role of the Sino-Kazakh Joint Committee on Utilisation and Protection of Transboundary Rivers for environmental protection. The two sides aimed to continue to improve the relevant legal basis to align with the principle of mutual benefit.

On 14 December 2014, Chinese premier Li Keqiang met with Kazakh Prime Minister Massimov and released the first regular meeting of the Joint Communique. Similarly, during the meeting, the two sides spoke of the important role of the Joint Commission for the Use and Protection of Transboundary Rivers. They agreed to reach consensus on the implementation of the work plan of the Joint Commission and to make every effort to implement the tasks according to the framework of the Joint Committee. In December 2015, Chinese premier Li Keqiang held talks with his Kazakh counterpart Karim Massimov in Beijing, vowing to step up bilateral cooperation to enhance industrial capacity, agricultural production, as well as energy and regional connectivity. In addition to issues related to logistics, customs, aviation transportation, agriculture, and localities, utilization and protection of transborder rivers were also discussed (Embassy of the Republic of Kazakhstan, 2015).

Deputy prime ministers' level cooperation

China-Kazakhstan Cooperation Committee at the deputy prime minister level was formally established in May 2004 by President Nazarbayev during his visit to China. The China-Kazakhstan Cooperation Committee, with the support of 11 sub-Committees, was tasked to oversee the cooperation and coordination between the two countries in economics and trade, energy, finance, science and technology, transportation, security, and others.

Between 2004 and 2015, the China-Kazakhstan Cooperation Committee held seven meetings:

- On 2 July 2004, during the first meeting of the China-Kazakhstan Cooperation Committee in Beijing, both sides discussed core issues related to bilateral cooperation in trade, transportation, port, science and technology, finance, energy, mining, culture, security, and other pragmatic cooperation in various fields.

- On 14 July 2005, during the second meeting of the China-Kazakhstan Cooperation Committee in Astana, the capital of Kazakhstan, both sides determined that the next stage of the core task would focus on promoting bilateral cooperation in various fields and the implementation of major projects agreed by the heads of the two states.
- On 17 November 2006, during the third meeting of the China-Kazakhstan Cooperation Committee in Beijing, the two sides achieved a lot in the relevant areas of cooperation, and reached a broad consensus on the next phase of work.
- On 8 November 2007, during the fourth meeting of the China-Kazakhstan Cooperation Committee in Astana, both sides agreed to seriously implement the agreed projects and measures, earnestly promote bilateral pragmatic cooperation, and deepen cooperation in various fields.
- On 4 December 2009, during the fifth meeting of the China-Kazakhstan Cooperation Committee held in Beijing. Transboundary water issues were discussed during the meeting.
- On 8 December 2012, after the sixth meeting of China-Kazakhstan Cooperation Committee in Astana, the two sides signed a cooperation agreement to work on the expansion of crude oil pipeline, natural gas pipeline, railway agreement protocols, and others.
- On 25 August 2015, during the seventh meeting of China-Kazakhstan Cooperation Committee in Beijing, Mr. Zhang Gaoli, vice-premier of the State Council of China met with his Kazakh counterpart Mr. SA Ginta Jef and both signed the minutes of meeting.

Expert group meeting and the Joint Committee

From 1999 to 2001, the Sino-Kazakh transboundary river experts held five rounds of consultations:

(1) In May 1999, the two sides expounded on the development and utilization of transboundary rivers, and exchanged suggestions on the development and utilization of transboundary rivers.
(2) In November 1999, experts from both countries exchanged views during the meeting and Kazakhstan submitted to China a new Kazakh government agreement on cooperation regarding the common use and protection of transboundary river water resources.
(3) In May 2000, the Kazakh transboundary river joint expert working group was formed. The Kazakhstan transboundary river joint expert working group charter was signed in November 2000 and June 2001. The working group held two meetings.
(4) In March 2001, both sides held negotiations on the transboundary river utilization and protection cooperation framework and achieved consensus.
(5) In August 2001, the government of the People's Republic of China and the government of the Republic of Kazakhstan agreed on the use and protection

of transboundary rivers. Both Chinese and Russian texts on the related documents were initiated.

On 12 September 2001, the prime ministers of China and Kazakhstan signed a cooperation agreement on joint use and protection of transboundary rivers in Kazakhstan. According to the agreement, the two countries formed the Joint Committee on the Use and Protection of Transboundary Rivers and the joint committee expert working group. The first meeting of the Joint Commission was held in Beijing in 2003. By the end of 2016, 14 meetings had been held. The meetings led to many agreements on improving water quality and negotiations on joint development and water allocation. The Chinese delegation included officials from the Ministry of Water Resources, the Ministry of Foreign Affairs, the State Environmental Protection Administration, Xinjiang Uygur Autonomous Region, XPCC, and representatives of the Chinese Embassy in Kazakhstan, normally headed by the deputy minister of the Ministry of Water Resources. From 22 to 24 November 2016, the 14th Meeting of China-Kazakhstan Transboundary Rivers Utilisation and Protection Joint Committee was held in Almaty. Mr. Zhou Xuewen, vice minister of water resources of China and head of the Chinese delegation, Mr. Ressan Baye, vice minister of agriculture of Kazakhstan and head of the Kazakhstan's delegation, and representatives from foreign affairs, environmental protection, and local authorities of both countries attended the meeting.

During the meeting, Mr. Zhou stated that water is the fundamental guarantee for the sustainable social and economic development, and water is closely linked to the basic wellbeing of the people of the two countries. Mr. Zhou stressed China's willingness to cooperate with Kazakhstan to further promote bilateral cooperation on transboundary rivers management and deepen their comprehensive strategic partnership. Mr. Ressan Baye expressed his gratitude for China's promotion of the China-Kazakhstan cooperation on transborder rivers. In particular, Mr. Ressan Baye thanked China for the increased frequency of data provision on the Irtysh and Ili rivers during the 2016 flood season. China's data provision enabled Kazakhstan to take preventive measures (Xinhuanet, 2016).

However, due to conflicts of interests and agendas between ministries and departments within both countries, implementation of the agreements made by the Joint Commission are often delayed. For instance, as pointed out by Zhulduz Baizakova (2015), owing to fragmented domestic water management systems and lack of adequate numbers of skilled specialists conducting proper water negotiations, in most cases the Kazakhstani side delays the implementation of agreements achieved by the Joint Commission. In some instances, projects as old as 20 years remain unfulfilled and lay forgotten in the drawers of Kazakh officials.

Problems related to existing cooperation mechanisms

Many successful cases of international cooperation on transboundary rivers exist. Europe's Rhine and Danube cooperation is one example (Dieperink, 2000; Gerlak, 2004; Linnerooth-Bayer & Murcott, 1996). However, developing countries in

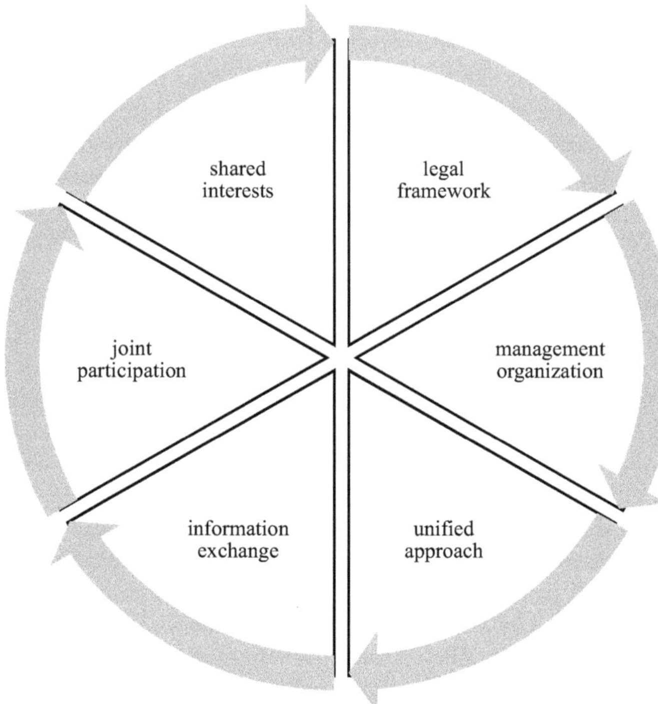

Figure 10.1 Six areas where obstacles can affect successful cooperation.
Source: The authors' own construction.

Asia, in the Middle East, and in Africa are still facing great challenges in transboundary river cooperation.

Successful collaborative cases show a common feature in success. In general, success in cooperation on transboundary rivers can be achieved by overcoming obstacles in six areas (see Figure 10.1).

Limited legal framework

As discussed, China and Kazakhstan have a multilevel communication channel on transboundary water cooperation, namely the prime ministers' regular meeting, cooperation committee at deputy prime ministers' level, China-Kazakhstan Joint Commission on the Use and Protection of Transboundary Rivers, and the expert working group meeting. Relevant cooperation agreements and legal documents on transboundary river matters were also concluded during the meetings.

The list of agreements includes:

- Agreement on the water quality data of the hydrological border station of the major transboundary rivers and agreement on the development of scientific research cooperation on transboundary rivers were signed on 29 December 2006;

- Agreement on the joint construction of the Khorgos River water diversion project and the "key implementation plan for the water distribution technology of transboundary rivers" were signed on 13 September 2010;
- Agreement on the protection of the water quality of the transboundary rivers was signed on 22 February 2011; and
- Agreement on the joint management and operation of "joint water diversion project of the Khorgos River" and its implementation details.

Currently, two countries have signed a number of bilateral agreements concerning their shared rivers, but those agreements quite often only touch on specific issues such as water information sharing and international transboundary river utilization. Agreements on international water allocation and coordinated management are few while a vital formal international management mechanism is still lacking (Li, 2015). Most agreements are not systematically incorporated into existing mechanisms. For example, the Kazakh-Chinese Joint Commission on the Use and Protection of Transboundary Rivers covered the implementation of the agreement, coordination of work, and the monitoring of stations without addressing water allocation issues and environmental issues (Baizakova, 2015).

Compared to the cooperation between China and its other neighbouring countries, China and Kazakhstan transboundary water cooperation takes the lead. The two countries have built a strong bilateral legal framework. Proper implementation of the agreements, however, has become the most urgent task for China and Kazakhstan. It is the Kazakh government's belief that international cooperation in water resources should follow four basic principles:

(1) combination of economic and ecological factors, with emphasis on the harmonious balance between economic development and ecological protection;
(2) combination of standards of water quality and water quantity, whereby water quality is critical to human health, and water quantity is needed for economic development, thereby establishing comprehensive, long-term utilization and protection measures to meet the demands of various stakeholders;
(3) combination of development and compensation (that is, whoever pollutes, whoever compensates); and
(4) combination/balancing of the interests of upstream and downstream states (including all states in the river basin; participation in cooperation should not be limited to only two states).

Inept management organization

The Sino-Kazakh Joint Commission improved overall operations, and even created a long-term stable basin management mechanism. Besides the Sino-Kazakh Joint Commission on the Common Use and Protection of Transboundary Rivers, Kazakhstan has also established joint commissions with neighbouring countries. Kazakhstan and Russia established a Joint Commission on the Common Use and Protection of Transboundary Rivers. Kazakhstan formed the Chu and Talas River Water Conservancy Facilities Committee with Kyrgyzstan. Kazakhstan and other Central Asian countries formed the Aral Sea Water Resources Multinational Coordination Committee. China-Kazakhstan Joint Commission on the transboundary river has more than 10 years of history, and its mechanism of cooperation is more advanced than the Mekong cooperation between China and the Mekong River countries, and the Brahmaputra cooperation between China and India.

Lack of a unified approach

Another obstacle is the inability of the states in the river basin to balance their respective water resources utilization goals to reach consensus. The utilization of water resources in the transboundary river water resources is not entirely consistent, and is somewhat different. However, according to the Minutes of the 2014 12th Joint Committee Meeting, the two sides have taken steps to reach their goals. According to the summary: Jiao Yong, vice minister of water resources, also the head of the Chinese delegation, pointed out that the rapid development of bilateral good neighbourly friendship and mutually beneficial cooperation led to progress in various aspects including transboundary river water quality protection, water distribution infrastructure development, border hydrological station development, hydrology and water quality data exchange, and natural disasters emergency response. Sino-Kazakh cooperation in the field of transboundary rivers has indeed been fruitful in promoting comprehensive strategic partnership between China and Kazakhstan.

Ressan Bayev, vice minister of agriculture, also the head of the Kazakhstan's delegation, expressed great appreciation for China's push for bilateral transboundary river cooperation. He highlighted China's highly responsible practices and effective measures taken in 2014 to mitigate the effects of a serious drought in the Ili River Basin. He stressed that bilateral cooperation exemplified the principles of mutual understanding, mutual accommodation, and mutual respect whereby the two sides considered each other's legitimate concerns and sought common ground while shelving differences so as to establish good working relations based on trust.

The future task is to further strengthen communication and understanding and to tap the potential for cooperation in water conservation and pollution control, among others. In addition, China-Kazakhstan cooperation should draw lessons from the experience of advanced international organizations in order to establish new modes of transboundary river development, utilization, and protection.

Inadequate information exchange

Information communication and hydrological information sharing constitute the foundation of transboundary river cooperation. Periodical updating of the hydrological database enables downstream countries to effectively improve flood control and water management. Even without a multilateral legal framework, China and neighbouring countries managed to achieve substantive cooperation whereby all riparian countries participated in a joint commission. In the past decade, China has faithfully cooperated by supplying hydrological information to the Mekong River Commission. Before and after 2008, China, India, and Pakistan signed *memorandums of understanding* (MoUs) to provide water information to three hydrological stations on the Brahmaputra River (Ho, 2017). Kazakhstan, the downstream country, hopes to strengthen information exchange with China, especially in water quality monitoring, water conservancy facilities planning, hydrological monitoring, and others to gain access to information in a more "transparent", "real-time", and "standard" way.

Limited joint participation

The success of transboundary river cooperation also depends on the degree of participation from central and local governments, the private and other stakeholders. The joint participation of stakeholders is the main driving force for promoting cooperation. It is vital to achieve a win-win situation by addressing the key concerns of the main stakeholders. It requires coordination of different factors: the upstream and downstream interests, the domestic and foreign interests, the balance between economic development and ecological protection, considerations of surface water and groundwater as a whole, etc. However, taking the case of Kazakhstan for example, there is a lack of access to information, insufficient population involvement in decision-making on transboundary water related issues. In particular, the local populations of both the Pavlodar and Eastern Kazakhstan are overwhelmingly excluded from decision-making processes on the use and protection of the Ili and Irtysh rivers (Baizakova, 2015).

In addition, Kazakhstan prefers to negotiate cross-border water issues on the multilateral platform; China prefers bilateral channels. For instance, Anatoliy Dmitriyevich Ryabtsev, chairman of the Committee for Water Resources in Kazakhstan's Ministry of Agriculture, pointed out the need for a trilateral Kazakh-Russian-Chinese cooperation in shared use and protection of transboundary water resources in the Irtysh River Basin, and the need for Russia and Kazakhstan to continue to jointly mitigate and change the position of China on this issue. He urged the two countries to make use of networking via diplomatic channels, meetings of national government officials, and consider the potential of the acting intergovernmental agreements (Ryabtsev, 2011).

Conflicting interests

Transboundary river cooperation should confront the core issues of cost investment and revenue sharing. Because of differences between the upstream and downstream on water utilization targets, it is difficult to make a complete quantitative analysis of economic benefits. However, on the whole, the economic value of hydropower development and shipping should be higher than others. Hydropower development and shipping also has important social functions such as flood control, irrigation, and ecological protection. In recent years, downstream countries have opposed upstream China's hydropower development. The new cooperative mechanism should ensure that the party that has benefited makes compensation to the disadvantaged party (i.e. the upstream state makes compensation to the downstream state). In the future, to resolve any conflict of interest, China and Kazakhstan should cooperate with each other to jointly develop water resources by building hydropower stations on the Irtysh River and its main tributaries.

Main concerns and the future priorities

Main concerns in current conflicts

In the context of transboundary water cooperation between China and Kazakhstan in the past few years, notable progress has been achieved and multilevel meeting mechanisms appear to be working well. However, some difficulties still exist:

1. Kazakhstan has high expectations of a large volume of river water diversion. This condition highlights the significance of downstream water consumption rights. The current negotiation on water quality is progressing more smoothly than the negotiation on water volume allocation.
2. Kazakhstan prefers to combine the Ili River and the Irtysh River in negotiations. Owing to the slow progress of the watershed agreement discussion, China prefers to negotiate separately. Kazakhstan has compromised to accept separate negotiation on the two rivers.
3. Kazakhstan treats energy cooperation (of oil and gas resources) as a bargaining chip and demands that China give priority to Kazakhstan's interests on transboundary waters.
4. Kazakhstan hopes to learn from the experiences of the European Union, the World Bank, and other international institutions to settle the conflicts related to transboundary rivers. Kazakhstan strives to establish a multilateral cooperation mechanism on transboundary water resources, aiming to jointly work with downstream countries to pressure China. In particular, Kazakhstan has suggested to take the water issues within the auspices of SCO so that Russia can also participate (Baizakova, 2015).
5. Kazakhstan is more concerned about the severe ecological situation in the Ili River-Balkhash Lake Basin, hoping that the international community would take action to thwart China's development plan.

Future priorities and a feasible path

It is vital to leverage existing cooperation to implement the agreements to provide a good environment for settling difficult issues. Early in the 1990s, China and Kazakhstan started communication on transboundary rivers cooperation. In 2001, the government of the People's Republic of China and the government of the Republic of Kazakhstan signed the cooperation agreement on the common use and protection of transboundary rivers. Following that, China and Kazakhstan made significant progress.

In 2010, the two countries signed the agreement on the China-Kazakhstan Friendship Joint Water Diversion Project on the Khorgos River. In April 2011, the two sides jointly funded USD 9.56 million for the project. Located in the Khorgos River alluvial, the Khorgos River Friendship Joint Water Diversion Project was the first international transboundary rivers project. To establish control over water diversion and carry out water distribution based on transparency and mutual trust, China and Kazakhstan jointly invested in the Khorgos River Friendship Water Diversion Project. After two years of construction, the project achieved a total diversion capacity of 50 m^3/s, with each side sharing 25 m^3/s. During the completion and delivery ceremony, the representative of the Republic of Kazakhstan and vice minister of environment protection, Ressan Baye J, said that the project created conditions of mutual trust and sincere cooperation for fair sharing of the water resources on transboundary rivers. The project is expected to effectively improve agricultural irrigation, ecological water guarantee rate, and reduce flood hazards in the middle and lower reaches (Xinhuanet, 2013). The project has shown the feasibility of the fair and reasonable utilization and protection of transboundary waters.

The two sides should actively consolidate existing bilateral cooperation and shelve disputes over the Ili River and the Irtysh River, among others. They can focus on expanding new channels of communication and giving priority to multilateral diplomacy platforms. The trend is to forego the bilateral communication channels of the old to make way for new multilateral channels in the future. So far, Kazakhstan has jointly led and participated in the two regional organizations and mechanisms, namely, the CICA and the SCO summit.

At the 47th General Assembly of the United Nations in 1992, President Nazarbayev proposed that the CICA serve as an Asian security cooperation platform. Between 2014 and 2016, China played the CICA presidency role. At the 4th Summit of the CICA in Shanghai, China branded the new Asian security concept as "common security, comprehensive security, cooperative security, sustainable security". The Summit provided a communication platform for China and Kazakhstan to deal with potential problems of transboundary rivers (People.cn, 2016).

Since its establishment in June 2001, the SCO has played an important platform for China-Kazakhstan cooperation. Article 3 of the SCO Charter identifies water resources cooperation as the solution for ensuring reasonable use of natural resources and joint implementation of water protection plans and programmes. But so far, cooperation among the SCO members on regional anti-terrorism and economic cooperation has overshadowed water resources cooperation.

Over the past decades, the issue of water resources or transboundary rivers was mentioned only in two SCO documents:

(1) On 17 June 2004, Article 2 of the SCO Tashkent Declaration declared that environment protection, as well as rational and efficient use of water

resources, should be included in the agenda. Relevant scientific research departments and research institutions could begin to work together to develop the organization's work strategy in the field in the same year.

(2) On 30 October 2008, after the *Meeting of the Council of Heads of Governments* (*Prime Ministers*) of the SCO Member States, a *joint communique* was issued on the outcomes. It included Article 6's statements on the role of reasonable and effective use of water resources in the sustainable development of Central Asian countries. For the first time, great significance was attached to the upcoming meeting of the SCO Member States' environmental protection department.

In the future, close attention should not only be paid to bilateral communication channels but also to multilateral communication channels, including active utilization of CICA, SCO, and other platforms. Besides official diplomacy, public diplomacy has also become an integral part of diplomacy today so it is worthy to actively explore and develop non-official diplomacy channels which attach importance to non-governmental organizations, academic institutions, media, think tanks, and other communication channels. Both countries should explore new areas of cooperation to identify more common interests. As economic and trade cooperation is the most dynamic part of the bilateral Comprehensive Strategic Partnership, both countries can make great strides in economic and trade cooperation, and further strengthen economic cooperation to ease the settlement of other problems (including transboundary rivers).

Under the existing high-level meeting mechanism, more areas should be further explored:

(1) *Border area cooperation.* In 2012, the Sino-Kazakh Joint Declaration proposed to speed up the development of adjacent areas. In recent years, the cooperation between Xinjiang, East Kazakhstan, and Almaty made great progress. Initial results were evident in programmes such as China-Kazakhstan Khorgos International Border Cooperation Centre (ICBC) and the Sub-Regional Economic Circle around the Altay Mountains. The increasing demands for local cooperation can be expected to yield bright prospects for development.
(2) *Financial cooperation.* As early as June 2011, China and Kazakhstan signed bilateral currency swaps worth RMB 7 billion. Owing to the recent rising pace of Sino-Kazakh economic and trade development, it is vital to use local currency for settlement among enterprises to avoid the loss caused by exchange rate fluctuations. And in the past two years, financial cooperation between China and Kazakhstan has deepened. In May 2014, both countries signed a series of financial cooperation agreements. For example, the Export–Import Bank of China and Development Bank of Kazakhstan signed a memorandum to provide USD 1 billion to modernize Shymkent-based oil refinery. On 26 September 2014, Kazakhstan became the first Central Asian country to conduct RMB trading on its stock exchange. This means that in

the future, RMB can be used for cross-border trade settlement in the local banks of Kazakhstan and Kazakhstan can hold RMB as reserve currency. The Sino-Kazakh Joint Declaration also mentioned expanding bilateral trade, investment, and financing in the field of local currency settlement (Xinhuanet, 2014).

(3) *Agricultural cooperation.* Efforts in promoting agricultural cooperation could help to alleviate water stress in Kazakhstan. While agriculture consumes 70 per cent of the fresh water usage in Central Asia, 50–80 per cent of that is wasted due to faulty irrigation systems. As for the Ili river, as high as 90 per cent of the water is used for irrigation and huge amounts of water goes to waste through evaporation, drainage, and leakage (Baizakova, 2015). As such, agricultural modernization will help to keep regional water conflicts under control. China has much to offer on this front. With ample foreign reserves, China could invest Kazakhstan's backward agricultural infrastructure, particularly in modernizing its irrigation systems. In addition, water-saving technologies and drought-resistant seeds from China could further reduce water demand in Kazakhstan's agricultural sector. By promoting interregional and intraregional agricultural trade across Central Asia, China could help facilitate the development of a better cropping structure in Kazakhstan as well as other Central Asian countries. There are already signs that two countries' agricultural cooperation is deepening. In November 2016, China's Asia Pacific Food Capital (APOFCO) and KAZNEX INVEST signed an agreement on the establishment of a USD 3 billion joint agricultural investment fund (Kzainform, 2016). In addition to importing a large quantity of wheat from Kazakhstan (over 280,000 tonnes in 2016), China is also facilitating Kazakhstan's wheat exports to other countries. On 5 February 2017, a shipment of 720 tonnes of wheat arrived in Lianyungang Port in Lianyungang, east China's Jiangsu Province by rail from Kazakhstan. This shipment was further transhipped to Vietnam by boat, which marked the official opening of the transit corridor though China for Kazakhstani agricultural products (USDA, 2017).

Conclusion

On the whole, the construction of dams, water diversion projects, power generation stations, and irrigation facilities on transboundary rivers could have a major impact on the water quantity, water quality, and ecological environment of the downstream country. Construction of large-scale water diversion projects, especially during the reservoir impounding period and drought period of the downstream runoff have long been criticized for drying up the river channel and escalating disputes among riparian states (Biswas, 2012; Lerera & Scudderb, 1999; Strobl & Strobl, 2011).

China and Kazakhstan have many joint transboundary organizations and agreements, but unless these are well managed and well implemented, they can disrupt the proper management of the Irtysh and Ili basins. Thus, the two countries should adopt favourable and sustainable methods to utilize the watercourses and seek to build an integrated management approach. The obstacles in the six areas discussed are in relation to an integrated approach for international transboundary rivers management. China and Kazakhstan should consolidate existing achievements and explore channels to systematically promote cooperation based on mutual trust. Cooperation on transboundary water resources should be aimed at promoting long-term sub-regional economic cooperation and bilateral comprehensive strategic cooperation.

References

Baizakova, Z. (2015). *The Irtysh and Ili transboundary rivers: The Kazakh-Chinese path to compromise*. Washington, DC: George Washington University.

Biba, S. (2014, February 24). *China cooperates with Central Asia over shared rivers.* Retrieved February 23, 2016 from Chinadialogue, www.chinadialogue.net/article/show/single/en/6741-China-cooperates-with-Central-Asia-over-shared-rivers-.

Biswas, A. K. (2012). Impacts of large dams: Issues, opportunities and constraints. In C. Tortajada, D. Altinbilek, & A. K. Biswas (Eds.), *Impacts of large dams: A global assessment* (pp. 1–18). Berlin and Heidelberg: Springer Verlag.

Coser, L. A. (1956). *The functions of social conflict.* New York, NY: Free Press.

Crosette, B. (1995). Severe water crisis ahead for poorest nations in the next two decades. *The New York Times*, 10 August, sect. 1, p. 13.

Dieperink, C. (2000). Successful international cooperation in the Rhine catchment area. *Water International, 25*(3), 347–355.

Dmitriyevich, R. A., & Anatoly, R. (2014). *Water as a source of future development of Kazakhstan.* New Delhi, India: The International Commission on Irrigation and Drainage (ICID).

Dyusebayeva, Z. S. (2012) Mnogoletneye izmeneniye vodnogo stoka r. Chernyy Irtysh i usloviy yego formirovaniya. *Vestnik nauki Sibiri*, no. 3–4.

Embassy of the Republic of Kazakhstan. (2015, December 15). *China, Kazakhstan to step up capacity cooperation.* Retrieved from Embassy of the Republic of Kazakhstan, www.kazakhstan.org.sg/content/intro.php?act=news&c_id=4530.

FAO. (2012). *Kazakhstan.* Retrieved from Food and Agriculture Organization of the United Nations, www.fao.org/nr/water/aquastat/countries_regions/KAZ/index.stm.

Feng, Y., He, D., & Wang, W. (2015). Identifying China's transboundary water risks and vulnerabilities – A multidisciplinary analysis using hydrological data and legal/institutional settings. *Water International, 40*(2), 328–341.

Gerlak, A. K. (2004). Strengthening river basin institutions: The Global Environment Facility and the Danube River Basin. *Water Resources Research, 40*(8), 1–10.

Hagt, E. (2003, July 29). *China's water policies: Implications for Xinjiang and Kazakhstan.* Retrieved from The Central Asia-Caucasus Analyst, www.cacianalyst.org/publications/analytical-articles/item/8255-analytical-articles-caci-analyst-2003-7-30-art-8255.html?tmpl=component&print=1.

Ho, S. (2017). China's transboundary river policies towards Kazakhstan: Issue-linkages and incentives for Cooperation. *Water International, 44*(2), 142–162.

Kzainform. (2016, November 28). *Kazakhstan and China set up agricultural investment fund.* Retrieved from Kzainform, www.inform.kz/en/kazakhstan-and-china-set-up-agricultural-investment-fund_a2974348.

Lerera, L. B., & Scudderb, T. (1999). Health impacts of large dams. *Environmental Impact Assessment Review, 19*(2), 113–123.

Li, Z. (2015). *Water and China's neighborhood relationship.* Beijing, People's Republic of China: Shishi She.

Li, Z., & Wu, F. (2016). China and shared water resources: Geopolitics, domestic institutions and global Governance. In F. Wu & H. Zhang (Eds.), *China's global quest for resources: Energy, food and water.* London, UK: Routledge.

Linnerooth-Bayer, J., & Murcott, S. (1996). Development, The Danube River Basin: International cooperation or sustainable. *Natural Resources Journal, 36*(3), 521–547.

Ministry of Commerce, P.R. China. (2008, May 2). 哈萨克电力工业发展情况及中哈电力合作前景 *[Status of Kazakhstan's Power Sector and the prospects of Sino-Kazakhstan cooperation in power sector].* Retrieved from Ministry of Commerce, P.R. China. www.mofcom.gov.cn/article/i/dxfw/jlyd/200805/20080505513623.html.

Muzalevsky, R. (2013). China's development plans in Xinjiang threaten Kazakhstan's water security. *Eurasia Daily Monitor, 10*(160).

Orazgaliyeva, M. (2017, May 16). *Kazakh President attends One Belt, One Road forum, meets with leaders in China.* Retrieved May 23, 2017, from The Astana Times, http://astanatimes.com/2017/05/kazakh-president-attends-one-belt-one-road-forum-meets-with-leaders-in-china/.

People.cn. (2016, April 29). 盘点：习近平关于亚信会议的三次重要讲话—国际—人民网 *[Xi Jinping at the CICA].* Retrieved from People.cn, http://world.people.com.cn/n1/2016/0429/c1002-28313020.html.

Peyrouse, S. (2007). *Flowing downstream: The Sino-Kazakh water dispute.* Washington, DC: The Jamestown Foundation.

Ryabtsev, A. D. (2011). Threats to water security in the Republic of Kazakhstan in the transboundary context and possible ways to eliminate them. In D. V. Madramootoo C. (Ed.), *Water and food security in Central Asia. NATO science for peace and security series C: Environmental security.* Dordrecht, the Netherlands: Interstate Commission for Water Coordination of Central Asia.

Sievers. E. W. (2002) Transboundary jurisdiction and watercourse. Law: China, Kazakhstan, and the Irtysh. *Texas International Law Journal, 37*(1): 1–40.

Stone, R. (2012). Transboundary rivers. For China and Kazakhstan, no meeting of the minds on water. *Science, 337,* 405–407.

Strobl, E., & Strobl, R. (2011). The distributional impact of large dams: Evidence from cropland productivity in Africa. *Journal of Development Economics, 96*(2), 432–450.

The Central Government, P.R. China. (2013, September 8). *Gov.cn.* Retrieved from 中哈关于进一步深化全面战略伙伴关系的联合宣言 [*Sino-Kazakhstan joint declaration on further deepening comprehensive strategic partnership*], www.gov.cn/ldhd/2013-09/08/content_2483546.htm.

USDA. (2017). *Kazakhstan Grain and Feed Annual Report.* Washington, DC: USDA-Waterpub. (2016). *Ili River.* Retrieved from Waterpub, www.waterpub.com.cn/jhdb/DetailRiver-1.asp?ID=32.

Webster. (2017). *Conflict.* Retrieved from www.merriam-webster.com/dictionary/conflict.

Xinhuanet. (2013, July 5). 中哈两国共同投资的联合引水枢纽工程投入使用 *[Sino-Kazakhstan jointly invested water diversion project operational].* Retrieved from Xinhuanet, http://news.xinhuanet.com/2013-07/05/c_124966145.ht.

Xinhuanet. (2014, September 26). 人民币在哈萨克斯坦开始挂牌交易 *[RMB in Kazakhstan starts trading].* Retrieved from Xinhuanet, http://news.xinhuanet.com/world/2014-09/26/c_127038983.htm.

Xinhuanet. (2016, November 30). *14th meeting of the China-Kazakhstan Joint Committee on Utilization and Protection of Trans-Border Rivers held in Almaty.* Retrieved from Xinhuanet, http://news.xinhuanet.com/politics/2016-11/30/c_129384958.htm.

Chen, Y. (2014, July 13). China's cotton base. *Global Times.* Retrieved from www.globaltimes.cn/content/870332.shtml.

Yu, X., & Zhou, Z. (2009). The use of water resources and the food security in border area of China: A case study of Xinjiang. *Journal of Yunnan Normal University, 41*(6), 25–30.

Zhang, D. (2015). Study on electricity export potential of Asian sending-ends in Asia-Europe intercontinental transmission. *Power System Technology, 39*(8), 2082–2086.

Zhang, H. (2017, February 2). *Can China solve Central Asia's impending water crisis?* Retrieved April 23, 2017, from East Asia Forum, www.eastasiaforum.org/2017/02/02/can-china-solve-central-asias-impending-water-crisis/.

Part III

China and global water governance

11 China and global water governance

New developments

Hongzhou Zhang and Mingjiang Li

Introduction

On 12 October 2015, at a study session of the Politburo of the Central Committee of the Communist Party of China, for the first time, China explicitly put forth the concept of global governance. According to President Xi, strengthening global governance and reforming the global governance system represents the general trend: "It is not simply a case of competing for the high ground of economic development, but what roles and functions nations will play in the long-term systemic arrangement of the international order" (Xinhuanet, 2015). Almost a year later on 28 September 2016, at another study session of the Politburo on global governance, Xi said that China must actively participate in global governance and play a bigger role in making rules for new areas such as the Internet, polar regions, deep seas, and outer space. China will extend greater support to cooperation mechanisms and projects on educational exchange, dialogue among civilizations, and ecological conservation. Xi added that China should defend its own interests as well as the common interests of developing countries, and focus not only on its needs as it develops, but also on the expectations of the international community (Xinhuanet, 2016). Furthermore, Xi Jinping's high profile Belt and Road Initiative (BRI) has been championed as "China's solution" to global governance (UNDP China, 2016).

The trend is clear. China has previously maintained a low-profile in global governance, but since 2013, under Xi's leadership, China has been playing an increasingly active role in many areas of global governance, not only in economic and trade where China has emerged as the leading advocate for free trade and economic integration, but also in other key global issues such as climate change. With China's ratification of the Paris Climate Agreement and the US' withdrawal from the Agreement, China is now taking the global leadership on climate change. Despite China's growing interest and increased role in global governance, Blackwill and Campbell (2016) believe that

> China will continue to limit its responsibilities in global governance … this will be particularly the case in global institutions where China does not play a rule-making role. The leadership, long hesitant to take action on such matters, may now feel less equipped to do so.

Among those matters China has long been hesitant to act, global water governance stands out because China has been particularly passive in transboundary water issues management (Wu, 2016). Internationally, China was one of three countries to vote against the adoption by the UN General Assembly of the 1997 UN Convention on the Law of the Non-Navigational Uses of International Watercourses (1997 UNWC). At the regional level, China also appears to be quite uncooperative in carrying out transboundary river management. For years, China has been criticized for being absent from the Mekong River Commission and for turning down binding water agreements with India. As discussed in Chapter 1, on these transboundary rivers, China has built, or plans to build, large dams for hydroelectricity and mega-water diversion facilities, which subsequently have triggered anxiety and complaints from downstream countries and criticism from the international society. For instance, China's hydro projects at the upper stream of the Mekong River have become one of the major sources of conflicts between China and Southeast Asian countries. Similarly, China's plans to harness the waters of the Brahmaputra River have set off ripples of unease in the two downstream states, particularly India. China's diversion of water from the Ili and Irtysh rivers to meet the rising water demands of Xinjiang's booming petroleum sectors have triggered tensions with Kazakhstan.

Then the key concern lies in whether China will remain reluctant to take on responsibilities in water governance or become more active (or even proactive) in dealing with regional and global water-related issues. This chapter is intended to shed light on China's future role in global water governance through an analysis of the potential implications of three new developments: the South China Sea Arbitration in 2016, China's BRI, and the growing US interest in global water leadership.

The spillover effects of the South China Sea arbitration

In 2016, the biggest diplomatic challenge faced by China was, arguably, the South China Sea Arbitration case brought against the country by the Philippines in 2013. In the first half of 2016, prior to the ruling, China made substantial effort to win symbolic diplomatic support from various countries to denounce the legitimacy of the case and control its potential negative impact. On 12 July 2017, the ruling released by the Tribunal in The Hague was considered "a complete and total sweeping legal victory for the Philippines on all counts – and a harsh verdict on the lawfulness of China's artificial island construction and other actions in the South China Sea" (Bergin, 2016). China's nine-dash line has been ruled inconsistent with the UN Convention on the Law of the Sea (UNCLOS) because no land features in the Spratly Islands could legally be considered islands that can generate Exclusive Economic Zones and Continental Shelf. Hence, the ruling on the South China Sea was hailed as a "game changer" and a "heavy blow" for China (Bateman, 2016). However, with the programmatic approach of the new president of the Philippines Rodrigo Duterte to engage China after the ruling and due to other Southeast Asian claimant states' low profile stances, the ruling did not create any major international waves. In fact, China seized the window of opportunity and rapidly improved relations and cooperation with the Philippines, Malaysia, Indonesia, and Vietnam on various issues. China and the Association of Southeast Asian Nations (ASEAN) countries also made good progress in the crafting of a framework for a code of conduct in the South China Sea.

Nevertheless, the validity and functionality of the Arbitration are likely to be a major source of friction between China and some parties in the years to come. China may hope to wish away the ruling and regard it as non-existent. However, judging from the various statements by key countries and what has been happening recently at various international institutions such as the G7, ASEM, ASEAN-related meetings, and a few Track 2 events, it is almost certain that much of the international community will not easily give up the Arbitration result as a policy tool in dealing with China vis-a-vis the South China Sea disputes (Li M., 2016). The South China Sea Arbitration will resound well beyond the South China Sea and even the maritime domain; one of the potential impacts of the arbitration is on China's stance towards the 1997 UNWC.

As the only treaty governing shared freshwater resources, the 1997 UNWC entered into force on 17 August 2014 when Vietnam ratified the Convention. The Convention provides a legal framework of principles that may be applied and adjusted to suit the characteristics of particular transboundary rivers. In short, the main significance of the treaty is that it helps to codify existing international law pertaining to transboundary water governance.

China did not sign the 1997 UNWC. Despite the country's active participation in the negotiation and drafting of the convention, China is one of the three states that voted against this global instrument at the UN General Assembly (alongside Turkey and Burundi). There are three key factors behind China's objection to the 1997 UNWC.

First, China felt that the 1997 UNWC overemphasized downstream states' rights at the expense of the interests of upstream states. The 1997 UNWC sought to strike a balance between upstream and downstream interests by introducing the two key principles of "equitable and reasonable utilization and participation" and "the obligation not to cause significant harm". However, there is a huge controversy over the relationship between these two fundamental principles. Apart from doubts on how to define "equitable and reasonable utilization" and "significant harm", the key question that remains unanswered is whether "equitable utilization" should prevail over the "no-harm obligation", or vice-versa (McCaffrey, 1998). From China's perspective, "no-harm obligation" favours the downstream countries because the possibility of upstream states causing harm is much higher than downstream countries (Chen, 2012). Furthermore, under the "no-harm obligation" principle, once significant harm is caused in spite of the exercise of due diligence, the countries involved must enter into consultations over two things: one is the extent to which the harmful use is equitable and reasonable, and the other is whether the state that causes harm should adjust its use to eliminate or mitigate the harm, and "where appropriate, the question of compensation" should be addressed (McCaffrey, 1998). To China, it is unfair that upstream states have to compensate downstream states for damages to the transboundary river's ecological system whereas downstream states do not need to compensate the upstream states for preserving and protecting the transboundary river's ecological system. In fact, as pointed out by Moore in Chapter 2, the eco-compensation concept has been established as one of the guideline principles in interjurisdictional water resources management in China (He et al., 2014).

Second, Part III of the 1997 UNWC on Planned Measures triggered national security and territorial sovereignty concerns from China. Three main rules of the Planned Measures include:

1 exchange of information, consultation with other parties and, if necessary, negotiations on the possible effects of planned measures;
2 notification concerning planned measures with possible adverse effects before their implementations or the granting of permits to implementation; and
3 if the implementation of the planned measures is inconsistent with the equitable and reasonable use of water and would cause harm, consultations and negotiations with the concerned countries regarding the planned measures.

However, for decades, China's data and information related to water, land, and other critical resources are treated as state secrets, and are not even available to the domestic audience, not to mention foreign countries. In the recent years, China has become slightly more willing to share hydrological data with India and other neighbouring countries. Furthermore, China maintains that each state has the inherent right to utilize the water resources within its territory, a manifestation of the principle of territorial sovereignty. Therefore, prior notification and the need to gain the consent of the notified states are deemed by China as a major restriction of its territorial sovereignty (Chen, 2012).

The third and, arguably, the most important factor is China's objection to the mandatory settlement of disputes. The 1997 UNWC states that in the event of a dispute between two or more parties, they may jointly seek the good offices of, or request mediation or conciliation by, a third party, or make use, as appropriate, of any joint watercourse institutions that may have been established by them or agree to submit the dispute to arbitration or to the International Court of Justice if parties concerned cannot reach agreement by negotiation requested by one of them. Furthermore, if after six months from the time of the request for negotiations, the parties concerned have not been able to settle their dispute through negotiation or any other means, the dispute shall be submitted, at the request of any of the parties to the dispute, to impartial fact-finding, unless the parties otherwise agree. While the peaceful resolution of disputes is also China's long-held position, the country has strong reservations towards the compulsory fact-finding dictated by the UNWC and third-party mediation or arbitration through the International Court of Justice as China believes it contradicts Article 33 of the United Nations Charter, which leaves the State the choice of the peaceful method with which to resolve disputes (Chen, 2012). China is not against fact-finding as an optional means of settlement in principle, but it does not agree to any mandatory means or procedures for the settlement of a dispute.

In the past few years, particularly since the 1997 UNWC entered into force in 2014, there has been an ongoing debate among the Chinese international law experts and transboundary water researchers on whether China should join the 1997 UNWC in China (He, 2015; Hua, 2015; Kong & Tian, 2011; Li W., 2014; Ni, 2013a, 2013b; Tan, 2011; Yu, Feng, & Wang, 2017). While many still oppose China's membership on national sovereignty grounds, some scholars and experts suggest that China should consider signing the Convention to increase the country's influences and voices in international water law fields, and enhance China's international image and relations with neighbouring countries. For instance, Wouters (2014) argues that

> As China faces pressing domestic water challenges, but also actively pursues a foreign policy based on 'win-win' cooperative solutions – it is timely for China to take on board some of the useful guidelines offered by the two UN Water Conventions ... Both conventions provide model norms and processes that China could apply in ways that demonstrate its 'good neighbour' policy in the management of its transboundary waters. This could go a long way to addressing China's upstream dilemma.

In fact, China expressed strong support for many of the norms that were eventually included in the 1997 UNWC, especially the principle of equitable and reasonable use. Moreover, a study in 2013 examining China's transboundary water treaty practice suggests that China respects the approach of the UNWC (Chen, Rieu-Clarke, & Wouters, 2013).

Unfortunately, the South China Sea Tribunal Ruling in July 2016 has effectively closed this debate as it confirms China's worst fear of signing the 1997 UNWC. Although the ruling, which came down overwhelmingly in favour of the Philippines, remains controversial, one of the more contentious aspects of the ruling, particularly from the Chinese perspective, is the legality of the ruling. China maintains that the "Arbitral Tribunal in the South China Sea arbitration established at the Philippines' unilateral request has, ab initio, no jurisdiction, and awards rendered by it are null and void and have no binding force" (State Council, P.R. China, 2016).

China argues that the ruling is illegal as the Arbitration was conducted without China's consent and the Chinese government explicitly made a declaration in 2006 to exclude itself from the compulsory arbitration procedure on maritime delimitation, historical title, and military, and law enforcement activities. However, international legal experts maintain that when a state becomes a party to UNCLOS, it agrees in advance to a system of compulsory dispute settlement that can result in a final and binding decision by an international arbitral tribunal and UNCLOS provides that if a dispute arises between two states' parties that cannot be resolved by negotiation and exchange of views, either of the parties can unilaterally institute proceedings before an international tribunal without obtaining the consent of the other party (Beckman, 2016; Graham, 2016; Ku, 2016).

Nonetheless, the South China Sea ruling has not only dramatically internationalized the South China Sea, but also marred China's international image. Prior to the release of the ruling, news reports speculated that China could even quit UNCLOS over the tribunal ruling (An & Mo, 2016; Talmon, 2016). Although China did not denounce the UNCLOS after the ruling, the Arbitration case certainly has compelled China to rethink its participation in UNCLOS and in other international legal regimes. The painful memory of the South China Sea Arbitration will not fade away quickly, and one of the potential implications is its adverse impact on China's stance towards the 1997 UNWC. Signing the 1997 UNWC anytime soon is no longer a feasible option for the country; the last thing China wants is to be brought to the International Court of Justice again by its neighbours over transboundary water issues.

Belt and Road and China's emerging water diplomacy

China's President Xi Jinping put forth the Silk Road Economic Belt and the 21st Century Maritime Silk Road proposals, also known as the "Belt and Road Initiative" (BRI), during his visits to Kazakhstan and Indonesia in September and October 2013, respectively. Since then, the BRI has become a priority in China's foreign policy drive (Li M., 2015). The BRI was included in the Resolution of the Third Plenum of the 18th Central Committee of the Chinese Communist Party, a historical document on the new leadership's push for a new round of comprehensive reforms in China. The 8th meeting of the Central Leadership Group on Financial and Economic Affairs, chaired by President Xi, specifically deliberated on the BRI in November 2014. At the annual central conference on economic affairs in December 2014, the BRI was highlighted as one of the priorities for China in 2015. China has taken follow-up actions as well. It has launched the Asian Infrastructure Investment Bank (AIIB) and set up a USD 40 billion Silk Road fund. The BRI proposal was showcased to many foreign leaders during the Beijing APEC meetings.

From all accounts, the BRI has become China's national strategy. Very likely, the initiative will be regarded by Xi as a major component of his foreign policy legacy at the end of his tenure. In May 2017, China hosted the inaugural Belt and Road Forum (BRI Forum) which saw the attendance of 28 heads of state and government, some 1,500 government officials and experts from more than 130 countries. During the two-day BRI Forum, China signed cooperation deals with 68 countries and international organizations. The deals yielded a list of 270 deliverables in areas such as policy coordination, infrastructure building, trade, investments, and finance as well as people-to-people exchanges. President Xi also announced that the next BRI Forum will be held in 2019 (Ministry of Foreign Affairs, P.R. China, 2017).

Even prior to the BRI, China had launched a "good neighbourly" policy since the mid-1990s, striving to improve its ties with the countries in its immediate neighbourhood. China has tried to resolve or set aside territorial disputes where those existed, in order to focus on developing close economic ties in its adjacent regions (Freeman, 2017). In the past decades, China has managed to settle its land border disputes with all its neighbours except India and Bhutan. Although its relations with many of its neighbours improved considerably, notable conflicts have been witnessed in China's relations with Japan, Vietnam, Myanmar, and others. In this light, a new neighbourhood foreign policy was launched in 2013 in conjunction with the BRI. In fact, right after Xi Jinping's visit to Indonesia where he unrevealed the 21st Century Maritime Silk Road, the Work Forum on Neighborhood Diplomacy was held by the Central Committee of the Communist Party of China (CPC) in October 2013. At the Forum, Xi laid down the goals of China's new neighbourhood foreign policy: to "make our neighbors more friendly in politics, economically more closely tied to us, and we must have deeper security cooperation and closer people-to-people ties". In addition to a shared geography, the natural environment was among the factors Xi stated that made the periphery "extremely strategically significant" for China (Freeman, 2017). Since then, China's neighbourhood diplomacy has focused on building friendship and partnership with its neighbours by implementing the policy of harmony, security, and common prosperity in its neighbourhood and upholding the principles of amity, sincerity, mutual benefit and inclusiveness in its neighbourhood policy, and intent on living in harmony with all its neighbours (Ruan, Chen, Lan, Song, & Guo, 2016).

With the unfolding of China's New Neighborhood foreign policy that aims to create a favourable geopolitical environment for the implementation of China's BRI, China appears to be adopting an active water diplomacy. As pointed out by Guo Yanjun in Chapter 4, and Eugene Simonov and Eugene Egidarev in Chapter 5, the BRI is expected to have profound influence on natural resource management and environmental protection along the Belt and Road countries, and major changes are happening in management of transboundary rivers basins.

This is, in part, the result of China's growing recognition of the negative impacts of transboundary water conflicts on its foreign relations with neighbouring countries and on the success of the BRI (Guo, 2015; Guo, Zhou, Xia, Huang, & Yan, 2015). Indeed, water resources risk analysts indicate that the countries along the BRI face acute water security threats as their water stress level is higher than global average. Certain regions, including Central Asia, West Asia, and North Africa suffer from severe water shortages whereas East Asia and South Asia are prone to flooding. Thus, China needs to cooperate with BRI countries to reduce the water risk and achieve sustainable development (Guo, Zhou, Xia, Huang, & Yan, 2015; Xiong & Wu, 2017; Zhang H., 2017). The water risk is particularly prominent in Central Asia and South East Asia. Given the risks posed by Central Asia's water crisis to its grand ambition, China may be forced, sooner rather than later, to embrace water diplomacy to diffuse tensions. Besides building ports and bridges, China also seriously needs to think about investing in Central Asia's crumbling and inefficient irrigational infrastructure. Agriculture in the region consumes up to 75 per cent of fresh water resources, much of which is lost to substandard irrigational systems. Better cultivation practices, higher quality seeds, and exchange of agricultural technology with China could create a new framework of cooperation across Central Asia (Chugh, 2017). Already, the wrangle over water resources alongside frequent ethnic conflicts has dampened the enthusiasm of Kyrgyzstan to participate in the construction of the railway to be linked with China. Therefore, promoting a peaceful solution to the water conflicts in Central Asia will help develop the Silk Road Economic Belt. But China must remain prudent as it also has water disputes with some Central Asian nations. What should be noted is that neighbouring countries affected by China's hydropower development activities upstream also seize the opportunity to pressure China to work on transboundary water issues. For instance, Kazakhstan's President Nursultan Nazarbayev, while attending the BRI International Cooperation Forum, suggested that "it is important not to miss complex environmental issues, including the problem of rational management of water resources of intercontinental transboundary rivers, which can be transport arteries" (Orazgaliyeva, 2017).

While many recognize that China's foreign relations with neighbouring states and the BRI implementation are vulnerable to the risks posed by challenges related to water resources, some experts and government officials discovered opportunities and potential benefits for an active water diplomacy. Central Asia, a strategically important region in the development of the Silk Road Economic Belt, has been mired in age-old rifts around water resources. Take for example, Kyrgyzstan and Tajikistan. Both states regard hydropower development as national strategy, and Uzbekistan and Turkmenistan rely on irrigation farming. The downstream countries strongly object to the large-scale hydroelectricity projects in the upstream countries. China has accumulated abundant experience and mature technology in water resources management and multipurpose utilization. Some of the techniques and ideas, such as water-conserving agriculture, small hydropower plants, and photovoltaic power generation, can be transferred to Central Asian nations to help alleviate their water shortages (Ma, Jiang, Yidelisi, Zhao, & Lei, 2017; Zhu, 2017).

Similarly, as noted by Professor Wang Hao who is an academician at the Chinese Academy of Engineering, the water issue is global and poses a common challenge that thwarts economic development of all countries along the BRI. The BRI requires the integration of economic growth, equal globalization, and interregional coordination. Professor Wang believes that BRI could help countries eradicate water-related threats. China is a typical model for the rest of the regions facing acute water challenges along the Belt and Road. China has developed its core technologies to the extent that underpins the top-down design and the strategy used in evaluation, allocation, regulation, supply, protection, and management of water resources. As evidenced in the China-Indonesia case of water cooperation, the benefits of "exporting" China's lessons and techniques to the neighbours along the Belt and Road are huge. This mastery knowledge will convert the national comparative advantage into the power driving win-win economic progress (Global Water Parntnership, 2017).

A growing number of Chinese scholars and even policy makers advocate an active water diplomacy (Guo, 2015; Xu & Sun, 2016; Zhang L., 2014; Zhang & Lu, 2015). Many scholars maintain that the conflicts on the transboundary development of water resources between China and Lower Mekong states urgently need to be solved by water diplomacy. Zhang and Lu (2015) point out that the resolution of internal and external dilemma on exploiting the Mekong River entails China's adoption of water diplomacy. Besides scholars, China's water officials have also been making similar pleas. In the paper "China's Water Diplomacy in the Era of Big Data", the lead author Yang Zechuan from China's Ministry of Water Resources calls for active water diplomacy while utilizing big data to assist China's foreign policy making (Yang, Kuang, & Yu, 2017). In February 2017, the Belt and Road Developing Countries' Water Security Research Consultation project was established in Beijing. The project is led by academician Xia Jun from China's Academy of Sciences with the support of a team of academicians and experts from diverse fields. The project addresses two primary questions: (1) how will water security challenges affect the social economic development of the developing countries along the Belt and Road and what are the potential solutions? (2) how will water security issues of the developing countries affect China's BRI and what are the potential solutions? (Wang, 2017).

China's emerging water diplomacy is clearly taking shape in the Mekong River Basin. For years, China has been criticized for not joining the Mekong River Commission (MRC) while unilaterally building dams on the upstream. However, since 2015, China has become more closely involved in cross-border cooperation in hydropower and water resources management in the Mekong River Basin. During their November 2015 meeting in Xishuangbanna, in China's southern province of Yunnan, the foreign ministers of China, Myanmar, Laos, Thailand, Cambodia, and Vietnam launched the Lancang-Mekong Cooperation mechanism (LMC), an initiative pitched at the November 2014 Summit Meeting between China and the ASEAN in Naypyidaw, Myanmar (Biba, 2016). While the new Mekong cooperation mechanism remains far from being a river basin organization (a commission set up to manage water resources across different countries that share one river), it is notable that China has now been a driver behind an initiative which explicitly includes water issues within its remit (Economist Intelligence Unit, 2017). Likewise, a strong partnership with Kazakhstan on a range of issues is critical to China's interests; particularly for the building of the Silk Road Economic Belt, China shows more willingness to cooperate on the sensitive transboundary water issues. Both countries are currently negotiating a water sharing treaty (Ho, 2017).

The involvement of the US

The growing US interest in the global water leadership could further motivate China to pay more attention to water problems, particularly the ongoing transboundary water disputes with neighbours. In January 2017, the National

Intelligence Council (NIC)'s report – "Global Trends: Paradox of Progress" – cited that at least 30 states, primarily in the Middle East, will find the demand for water at its highest by 2035 due to its diminished capacity. The political, economic, and social discord within these countries will exacerbate the chance for conflict because of water scarcity. As the instability in these regions is a direct threat to US strategic interests, the NIC report seeks to alert the US of the importance of integrating water as a key component of its national security strategy. Against this backdrop, for the first time, the US president is mandated to present a "Global Water Strategy" to the US Congress in the fall of 2017. One of the key components of the strategy is finding ways to solve the problem of water scarcity to avert conflict. It has been argued that as a world leader, the US has much to gain from crafting and implementing a global water strategy, including boosting its reputation and influence abroad (Oldfield, 2017).

While US interest in water issues might be global, its involvement or interest in regional water conflicts between China and its neighbours is of concern to China. China fears that the US could use the water disputes in the Mekong River to drive a wedge between China and its neighbours. Among the river basins shared by China and its neighbouring countries, China is very wary of US interest and involvement in the Mekong. In July 2009, the US led the establishment of the Lower Mekong Initiative (LMI) after the meeting between the then Secretary of State Hillary Clinton and four foreign ministers of the Lower Mekong states – Cambodia, Laos, Thailand, and Vietnam. One of the key LMI components is water cooperation. Apart from the development of "Forecast Mekong", a predictive modelling tool to illustrate the impact of climate change and other challenges to the sustainable development of the Mekong River Basin, the Mekong River Commission and the Mississippi River Commission of the US have signed a "sister-river" agreement to pursue a partnership to improve the management of transboundary water resources. The US has also been actively supporting projects that promote the sustainable use of forest and water resources and preserve the tremendous biodiversity of the Mekong River Basin. Under the LMI, the US provided more than USD 200 million in aid to the Lower Mekong states from 2009 to 2012. To promote cooperation in health education and environmental protection infrastructure, in 2013, the US pledged an additional fund of USD 50 million.

In 2012, the then US Secretary of State Hillary Clinton openly voiced concern about China's dam construction on the Mekong River. Many US strategists believe that US willingness to get involved in the Mekong River dispute could create an almost perfect counterweight to China's strategy among the tens of millions of people dependent on the river for sustenance:

> America's ability to keep Beijing in check over the Mekong River could remind millions of ordinary Asians that U.S. primacy in the region still matters, that American diplomatic clout and military presence has maintained the peace in Asia and kept vital sea lanes safe and open for commerce for decades.
> (Lee, 2010)

In the wake of the current president Donald Trump's "America First" policy, Borton and Nguyen (2017) suggest that the Mekong River offers the US a non-confrontational opportunity to reset Asia Pacific policy.

To a lesser extent, the US is showing an interest in other river basins as well. In 2012, the United States-China Economic and Security Review Commission, a congressional commission of the US government, held a hearing on the water issues of the Tibetan Plateau. It was suggested that the US should promote the creation of a regional framework (similar to the Lower Mekong Initiative) on water security as such a structure would facilitate cooperative agreements among all riparian states (Central Tibetan Administration, 2012). Similarly, Economy (2008) stresses that China's water disputes with neighbouring countries serves as an opening for the US to engage China directly in bilateral talk by becoming an active participant in the multilateral basin efforts and the US could play a similar role as in the Mekong River in the emergent conflicts among India, China, and Bangladesh over China's planned diversion of the Brahmaputra. In Central Asia, water issues have been one of the US' diplomatic priorities in the region (Zhao, 2017). It is suggested that the US could help Central Asia in conflict management training and technical education, water pollution reduction, and funding local or regional institutions that support the development of agreements or treaties to address water management (Kucera, 2014; The United States Senate Committee on Foreign Relations, 2011).

To many observers, China's high-profile BRI has been, to a certain extent, a response to the United States' Pivot-to-Asia Strategy and the US-led Transpacific Partnership (Grieger, 2016; Zhang F., 2016). In this light, the US unravelling of its global water strategy in general and its involvement in certain regional water issues, particularly that of the Mekong River, could certainly prompt China to react. In fact, many Chinese scholars and experts who advocate China's proactive water diplomacy for the Mekong River issues view the LMI as evidence of US growing interest in the Mekong River (Guo, 2015; Zhang & Lu, 2015). In South Asia and Central Asia, China is certainly very concerned with the US intervention in water issues as well (Lovelle, 2016; Samaranayake, Limaye, & Wuthnow, 2016).

Concluding thoughts

In the past decade, the concept of Integrated Water Resources Management (IWRM) has become the dominant approach for dealing with the problems of the world's major river basins, including transboundary rivers. However, it is increasingly recognized that the application of the IWRM's application to manage macro- and meso-scale water policies, programmes, and projects has been dismal (Biswas, 2004; Varis, Biswas, & Tortajada, 2008). As acknowledged in Asian Development Bank (ADB)'s Report on Asian Water Development Outlook 2016, despite important successes resulting from 25 years of IWRM promotion, it must also be admitted that implementation is lagging expectations (ADB, 2016). Even worse, Giordano and Shah (2014) argue that IWRM has, in some cases undermined functioning water management systems and in others set back needed water reform agendas, and yet, in others became a tool to mask other agendas. The current monopoly of IWRM in global water governance could be shutting out alternative thinking on pragmatic solutions to existing water problems (Giordano & Shah, 2014). Similar observations have been made regarding the concept of sustainable water development (Tortajada, 2005).

Borrowing the words of Asit Biswas, the founder of the Third World Centre for Water Management in Mexico: "water cooperation is not an end by itself, but only a means to an end, where the end is to improve the lifestyles of the people of the nation through a variety of complex interrelated socio-economic pathways" (Biswas, 2008). Where poverty is widespread, river basin management needs a strong developmental dimension. At the minimum, strategies for river basin management should provide details on the mechanisms for addressing imbalances in water accessibility and for establishing recognized and secure water entitlements for the poor. While much can be learned from institutional arrangements for river basin management in affluent countries, these arrangements do not operate in the same way in low-income countries that are disadvantaged by the dominance of smallholder agriculture, weak institutions, insufficient financial and human resources, marked social inequity, and extreme poverty (Molle, Philippus, & Hirsch, 2010). Cooperation is not the desired end for Third World riparian governments, as it is for China and its neighbours; rather, cooperation needs to be perceived as the basis for proceeding with the development of water resources encompassed by basins (Sneddon & Fox, 2006).

In other words, in the developing world, including China and nearly all of its neighbours, development could be the ultimate solution to the ongoing water disputes and looming water crisis. Certainly, economic development often increases the demand for water resources, which could further exacerbate the water scarcity situations in many water-stressed countries. However, as pointed out by Gleditsch, Furlong, Hegre, Lacina, and Owen (2006) and Mirumachi and Allan (2007), wealthier countries can afford to compensate for scarcities by technological substitution or innovation. They might have different priorities and challenges. A country with a high level of economic diversity and strength will have the option to combine factors of production and in turn find resource alternatives such as water desalination and waste water recycling, water saving, better irrigation efficiencies, water price reform, virtual water trade, and agricultural crop structural shifts (Beach et al., 2000). States that have a highly developed political economy will essentially have the capacity to adapt to the driving forces that shape international relations over water resources. Therefore, as it develops from a low-level political economy to a diversified and global economic power, China could move from resource capture to resource sharing and then to having alternative resources, creating the conditions for greater cooperation on transboundary water.

This development approach is exactly what China has been championing. On 15 May at the Belt and Road Forum, President Xi, in his opening speech, declared that "development holds the master key to solving all problems". Xi said that effort must be made to promote common development as peace and development are interdependent and mutually reinforcing. The causes of security threats such as war, conflict, and terrorism can all be traced back to poverty and underdevelopment, and thus relevant solutions are also to be found in development. The impacts of China on global water governance is already being felt on the water infrastructure sector, dam construction in particular. With the rise of environmental and social movements in the developed world, since the 1980s, environmental and social costs associated with the big hydropower projects have been recognized, which eventually led to the emergence of a worldwide anti-dam (especially big dams) movement. Consequently, World Bank, the Asian Development Bank and other multilateral organizations have increasingly shied away from investing in hydropower developments. For example, during the 1990s, the word bank lending for hydropower projects fell by 90%. While ensuring environmental and social issues are properly addressed in all the hydro projects has been a most welcome improvement, global debate on the benefits and costs of the hydropower projects, especially the big dams, has become emotional, dogmatic, and confrontational (Biswas, 2012). Against this backdrop, many of the studies and news reports on the impacts of the big dams were biased. For instance, for years, China's dams, especially the two big dams – Xiaowan and Nuozhadu – on the Upper Mekong Basin have been criticized for their environmental and social impacts to the downstream countries. However, a report by the Mekong River Commission in 2017 found out that these Chinese dams do affect water flows in the Lower Mekong Basin: rather than creating flood during the wet season and aggregating drought during the dry season, these Chinese dams reduce the flow during the wet season and increase it during the dry season (Mekong River Commission, 2017).

It should be recognized that water infrastructure development, or infrastructure construction in general, is critical for developing countries' social economic development. Hydroprojects, big or small, are needed by the development countries to produce food, generate energy, employment and income, provide basic services, and improve overall life quality of the people. In the past few years with the implementation of China's BRI, which has a strong focus on infrastructure development, China's hydropower companies have been rapidly expanding their presence overseas, especially in its neighbouring countries. By the end of 2016, Chinese hydropower companies have won over 200 overseas hydroprojects, accounting for over 50 per cent of the world's market share. Not only the Chinese dam builders, China's Silk Road Fund, the China-backed Asian Infrastructure Investment Bank (AIIB), as well as the country's policy banks, are actively financing the hydro projects. For instance, the Karot dam on the Jhelum river in Northern Pakistan was picked as the first investment project of the Silk Road Fund, and Pakistan's Tarbela 5th Extension Hydropower was one of the first six projects approved by the AIIB in 2016. Apart from the big hydro projects, China is actively promoting the development of small hydro projects. For instance, China Huadian Engineering, partnering with the Singaporean engineering company-ISDN, is developing mini-hydropower projects across

Indonesia. In this light, apart from shaping the current debate on the overall impacts of dams, China could push for the hydro sector's revival. As China is becoming more active in regional and global water governance, a new momentum could be injected to the development approach. Nevertheless, clearly evidenced by China's own experience, development without proper consideration of the environment results in severe resource depletion and environmental pollution, which could trigger or magnify intrastate and interstate water conflicts. For the development approach to become part of the solution rather than cause of the transboundary waters conflicts, water development strategy of each country needs to be formulated based on its specific conditions, requirements and expectations while striking a proper balance between economic, social, and environmental objectives.

References

ADB. (2016). *Asian water development outlook 2016: Strengthening water security in Asia and the pacific (AWDO 2016)*. Manila, Philippines: Asian Development Bank.

An, B., & Mo, J. (2016, July 9). *China could quit UNCLOS, expert says*. Retrieved July 23, 2016, from China Daily, http://usa.chinadaily.com.cn/china/2016-07/09/content_26023506.htm.

Bateman, S. (2016). *The South China Sea arbitration: Challenges and opportunities*. Barton: The Strategist.

Beach, H. L., Hamner, J., Hewitt, J. J., Kaufman, E., Kurki, A., Oppenheimer, J. A., & Wolf, A. T. (2000). *Transboundary freshwater dispute resolution*. Tokyo, Japan: The United Nations University.

Beckman, R. (2016). *Tribunal ruling a game changer*. Retrieved May 23, 2017 from www.straitstimes.com/opinion/tribunal-ruling-a-game-changer-south-china-sea.

Bergin, A. (2016). *A heavy defeat for Beijing: The South China Sea tribunal ruling*. Barton: The Strategist.

Biba, S. (2016, January 2). *China drives water cooperation with Mekong countries*. Retrieved July 23, 2016, from www.chinadialogue.net/article/show/single/en/8577-China-drives-water-cooperation-with-Mekong-countries.

Biswas, A. K. (2004). Integrated water resources management: A reassessment. *Water International, 29*(2), 248–256.

Biswas, A. K. (2008). 6 management of Ganges-Brahmaputra-Meghna system: Way forward. In O. Varis, C. Tortajada, & A. K. Biswas (Eds.), *Management of transboundary rivers and lakes* (pp. 143–163). Berlin and Heidelberg: Springer Verlag.

Biswas, A. K. (2012). Chapter 1 impacts of large dams: Issues, opportunities and constraints. In C. Tortajada, D. Altinbilek, & A. K. Biswas, *Impacts of large dams: A global assessment* (pp. 1–18). Berlin and Heidelberg: Springer Verlag.

Blackwill, R. D., & Campbell, K. M. (2016). *Xi Jinping on the global stage*. New York, NY: The Council on Foreign Relations.

Borton, J., & Nguyen, M. Q. (2017). *Mekong offers U.S. a non-confrontational opportunity to reset Asia pacific policy*. Retrieved March 23, 2017, from https://intpolicydigest.org/2017/02/26/mekong-offers-u-s-non-confrontational-opportunity-reset-asia-pacific-policy/.

Central Tibetan Administration. (2012). *Water security and environmental management on the Tibetan plateau*. Washington, DC: United States-China Economic and Security Review Commission.

Chen, H. (2012). The 1997 UNWC and China's treaty practice on transboundary waters. *UNWC Global Symposium*, University of Dundee, Dundee.

Chen, H., Rieu-Clarke, A., & Wouters, P. (2013). Exploring China's transboundary water treaty practice through the prism of the UN Watercourses Convention. *Water International, 38*(2), 217–230.

Chugh, N. (2017, March 24). Will Central Asia water wars derail China's silk road? *The Diplomat.*

Economist Intelligence Unit. (2017). *Water security threats demand new collaborations: Lessons from the Mekong River Basin.* London, UK: The Economist.

Economy, E. C. (2008). Asia's water security crisis: China, India, and the United States. In A. J. Tellis, M. Kuo, & A. Marble (Eds.), *Strategic Asia 2008–09: Challenges and Choices* (pp. 364–389). Seattle, WA: National Bureau of Asian Research.

Freeman, C. P. (2017). Dam diplomacy? China's new neighbourhood policy and Chinese dam-building companies. *Water International, 44*(2), 187–206.

Giordano, M., & Shah, T. (2014). From IWRM back to integrated water resources management. *International Journal of Water Resources Development, 30*(3), 1–13.

Gleditsch, N. P., Furlong, K., Hegre, H., Lacina, B., & Owen, T. (2006). Conflicts over shared rivers: Resource scarcity or fuzzy boundaries? *Political Geography, 25*, 361–382.

Global Water Parntnership. (2017). *WANG Hao on China's contribution to water and One Belt One Road.* Retrieved May 23, 2017, from www.gwp.org/en/GWP-China/WE-ACT/news-list/2017/wang-hao-on-obor/.

Graham, E. (2016). *The Hague tribunal's South China Sea ruling: Empty provocation or slow-burning influence?* Retrieved May 23, 2017, from www.cfr.org/councilofcouncils/global_memos/p38227.

Grieger, G. (2016). *One Belt, One Road (OBOR): China's regional integration initiative.* Brussels, Belgium: European Parliament Research Service.

Guo, L., Zhou, H., Xia, Z., Huang, F., & Yan, B. (2015). Water resources security and its countermeasure suggestions in building silk road economic belt. *China Population, Resources and Environment, 25*(5), 114–121.

Guo, Y. (2015). The role of water diplomacy in the implementation of China's' One Belt One Road Strategy. *Asia Pacific Security and Maritime Affairs, 2*, 81–93.

He, D., Wu, R., Feng, Y., Li, Y., Ding, C., & Wenling Wang, D. W. (2014). China's transboundary waters: New paradigms for water and ecological security through applied ecology. *Journal of Applied Ecology, 51*, 1159–1168.

He, Y. (2015). The United Nations convention on the law of the non-navigational uses of international watercourses entered into force: China's options. *Journal of Shanghai University of Political Science & Law, 30*(5), 44–57.

Ho, S. (2017). China's transboundary river policies towards Kazakhstan: Issue-linkages and incentives for Cooperation. *Water International, 44*(2), 142–162.

Hua, L. (2015). The United Nations convention on the law of the non-navigational uses of international watercourses entered into force and its implications. *Journal of Yunnan University Law Edition, 28*(2), 84–88.

Kattelus, M., Kummu, M., Keskinen, M., Salmivaara, A., & Varis, O. (2015). China's southbound transboundary river basins: A case of asymmetry. *Water International, 40*(1), 113–138.

Kong, L., & Tian, X. (2011). 国际涉水条法研究 *[Research on international water laws].* Beijing, People's Republic of China: China Hydraulic Press.

Ku, J. G. (2016, July 14). *China's legal scholars are less credible after South China Sea ruling.* Retrieved May 23, 2017, from Foreign Policy, http://foreignpolicy.com/2016/07/14/south-china-sea-lawyers-unclos-beijing-legal-tribunal/.

Kucera, J. (2014, November 19). *U.S. Congress takes on Central Asia water conflicts*. Retrieved May 23, 2017 from Eurasia Net, www.eurasianet.org/node/71016.

Lee, J. (2010). *China's water grab*. Retrieved March 23, 2017, from http://foreignpolicy.com/2010/08/23/chinas-water-grab/.

Li, M. (2015). *China's "One Belt, One Road" initiative: New round of opening up?* Singapore: RSIS Commentaries.

Li, M. (2016). *The South China Sea arbitration: Turning point in Chinese foreign policy?* Singapore: RSIS Commentaries.

Li, W. (2014, August 26). 《国际水道公约》生效中如何应对 [1997 UNWC entered into force: How should China Respond]. *Legal Daily*.

Lovelle, M. (2016). *Co-operation and the Brahmaputra: China and India Water Sharing*. Dalkeith, Scotland: Future Directions International Pty Ltd.

Ma, T., Jiang, D., Yidelisi, R., Zhao, S., & Lei, Z. (2017). Analysis of cross border resources cooperation necessity its legal countermeasure based on the concept of green and sharing under the frame of Belt and Road: Taking water resources cooperation between China's Xinjiang and Kyrgyzstan as example. *Journal of North China University of Science and Technology, 17*(2), 33–39.

McCaffrey, S. (1998). The UN convention on the law of the non-navigational uses of international watercourses: Prospects and pitfalls. In S. M. Salman & L. B. Chazournes (Eds.), *International watercourses-enhancing cooperation and managing conflict 77*, 81 (pp. 17–28). Washington, DC: World Bank.

Mekong River Commission. (2017, June 6). *The effects of Chinese dams on water flows in the lower Mekong Basin*. Retrieved from Mekong River Commission, www.mrcmekong.org/news-and-events/news/the-effects-of-chinese-dams-on-water-flows-in-the-lower-mekong-basin/.

Ministry of Foreign Affairs, P.R. China. (2017). *Joint Communique of the leaders roundtable of the Belt and Road forum for international cooperation*. Retrieved May 23, 2017 from www.fmprc.gov.cn/mfa_eng/zxxx_662805/t1462012.shtml.

Mirumachi, N., & Allan, J. (2007). Revisiting transboundary water governance: Power, conflicts, cooperation and the political economy. *International conference on adaptive and integrative water management*, Basel, pp. 1–21.

Molle, F., Philippus, W., & Hirsch, P. (2010). River Basin closure: Processes, implications and responses. *Agricultural Water Management, 97*, 569–577.

Ni, X. (2013a). UN Watercourses Convention (UNWC): The possibility of China's accession. *New West, 9*, 74–85.

Ni, X. (2013b). UN Watercourses Convention (UNWC): Analysis of the disputed articles from the Chinese perspective. *So Forum*, 160–162.

Oldfield, J. (2017, January 5). *2017 is pivotal for U.S. leadership on global water security*. Retrieved from Environmental Change and Security Program, www.newsecuritybeat.org/2017/01/2017-pivotal-u-s-leadership-global-water-security/

Orazgaliyeva, M. (2017, May 16). *Kazakh President attends One Belt, One Road forum, meets with leaders in China*. Retrieved May 23, 2017, from The Astana Times, http://astanatimes.com/2017/05/kazakh-president-attends-one-belt-one-road-forum-meets-with-leaders-in-china/.

Ruan, Z., Chen, Y., Lan, J., Song, J., & Guo, J. (2016). *China's new neighborhood diplomacy: Seeking stability through management and planning*. Beijing, People's Republic of China: China Institute of International Studies.

Samaranayake, N., Limaye, S., & Wuthnow, J. (2016). *Water resource competition in the Brahmaputra river Basin*. Washington, DC: CNA.

Sneddon, C., & Fox, C. (2006). Rethinking transboundary waters: A critical hydropolitics of the Mekong Basin. *Political Geography, 25*, 181–202.

State Council, P.R. China. (2016). *Full text: China adheres to the position of settling through negotiation the relevant disputes between China and the Philippines in the South China Sea*. Retrieved May 23, 2017, from http://english.gov.cn/state_council/ministries/2016/07/13/content_281475392503075.htm.

Talmon, S. (2016, March 3). *Denouncing UNCLOS remains option for China after tribunal ruling*. Retrieved May 23, 2017 from Global Times, www.globaltimes.cn/content/971707.shtml.

Tan, Y. (2011). 国际流域争端的若干法律问题 [International River Disputes and Several Legal Questions]. *Journal of Guang Xi University (Philosophy and Social Science), 2*(84–88), 33.

The United States Senate Committee on Foreign Relations. (2011). *Avoiding water wars: Water security and Central Asia's growing importance for stability in Afghanistan and Pakistan*. Washington, DC: Government of the United States of America.

Tortajada, C. (2005). Sustainable development: A critical assessment of past and present views. In A. K. Biswas & C. Tortajada (Eds.), *Appraising sustainable development* (pp. 1–17). New Delhi, India: Oxford University Press.

UNDP China. (2016). *The Belt and Road Initiative – A new means to transformative global governance towards sustainable development*. Beijing, People's Republic of China: UNDP.

Varis, O., Biswas, A. K., & Tortajada, C. (2008). Preface. In O. Varis, C. Tortajada, & A. K. Biswas (Eds.), *Management of transboundary river and lakes*. Berlin and Heidelberg: Springer Verlag.

Wang, H. (2017). 中国科学院地学部院士咨询项目"一带一路"发展中国家水安全战略启动 [The Belt and Road developing countries' water security research consultation project]. *China Water Resources, 5*, 76.

Wouters, P. (2014, November 3). *China's transboundary waters*. Retrieved May 23, 2016, from China Policy Institute: Analysis, https://cpianalysis.org/2014/11/03/chinas-transboundary-waters/.

Wu, F. (2016). China's ascent in global governance and the arctic. *Vestnik of Saint-Petersburg University. Ser. 6. Political science. International relations, 2*, 118–126.

Xinhuanet. (2015, October 13). *Xi stresses urgency of reforming global governance*. Retrieved May 1, 2017 from Xinhuanet, http://news.xinhuanet.com/english/2015-10/13/c_134710464.htm.

Xinhuanet. (2016, September 28). *Xi calls for reforms on global governance*. Retrieved May 1, 2017, from Xinhuanet, http://news.xinhuanet.com/english/2016-09/28/c_135720719.htm.

Xiong, Y., & Wu, X. (2017). "一带一路"沿线国家水风险分析 [Water risk analysis of countries along the Belt and Road]. *Kexue yanjiu dongtai jiance kuaibao, 10*, 8–11.

Xu, C., & Sun, Y. (2016). 基于"一带一路"战略视角的中国周边水外交 [China's water diplomacy from the perspective of Belt and Road initiative]. *Forum of World Economics & Politics, 5*, 110–121.

Yang, Z., Kuang, Y., & Yu, X. (2017). 大数据时代下的中国水外交 [China's water diplomacy in the big data era]. *Water Resources Development Research, 2*, 23–37.

Yu, S., Feng, Y., & Wang, W. (2017). Differences among the parties of "Convention on the law of the non-navigational uses of international watercourses". *Acta Geographica Sinica, 72*(2), 303–314.

Zhang, F. (2016). Challenge accepted: China's response to the US rebalance to the Asia-Pacific. *Security Challenges, 12*(3), 1–16.

Zhang, H. (2017, February 2). *Can China solve Central Asia's impending water crisis?* Retrieved April 23, 2017 from East Asia Forum, www.eastasiaforum.org/2017/02/02/can-china-solve-central-asias-impending-water-crisis/.

Zhang, L. (2014). Water diplomacy: Transboundary water cooperation and strategic arrangements between China and the Mekong countries. *Journal of International Relations, 4*, 25–36.

Zhang, L., & Lu, G. (2015). Transboundary water cooperation between China and the lower Mekong countries from the perspective of water diplomacy. *Southeast Asian Studies, 1*, 42–50.

Zhao, Y. (2017). Water resource problem in Central Asia: American cognition, intervention and evaluation. *Russia, Eastern Europe and Central Asia Studies, 3*, 79–157.

Zhu, Y. (2017, April 9). *Belt & Road must overcome water disputes in Central Asia.* Retrieved May 23, 2017, from Global Times, www.globaltimes.cn/content/1041521.shtml.

Index

For Product Safety Concerns and Information please contact our EU representative GPSR@taylorandfrancis.com
Taylor & Francis Verlag GmbH, Kaufingerstraße 24, 80331 München, Germany

www.ingramcontent.com/pod-product-compliance
Ingram Content Group UK Ltd.
Pitfield, Milton Keynes, MK11 3LW, UK
UKHW011002180926
475701UK00004B/518
* 9 7 8 0 3 6 7 3 7 5 5 9 1 *